GARRY WILLS

The

Politics

of Celebrity

JOHN
WAYNE'S
AMERICA

SIMON & SCHUSTER

SIMON & SCHUSTER
Rockefeller Center
1230 Avenue of the Americas
New York, NY 10020

Copyright © 1997 by Literary Research, Inc.
All rights reserved,
including the right of reproduction
in whole or in part in any form.
SIMON & SCHUSTER and colophon
are registered trademarks of Simon & Schuster Inc.
Designed by Edith Fowler
Manufactured in the United States of America

10 9 8 7 6 5 4 3 2 1

Library of Congress Cataloging-in-Publication Data

Wills, Garry.
   John Wayne's America : the politics of celebrity /
Garry Wills.
      p.   cm.
Includes bibliographical references and index.
      1. Wayne, John, 1907–1979.
2. Motion picture actors and actresses—
United States—Biography.   I. Title.
PN2287.W454W56   1997
791.43'028'092—dc21
[B]   96-47315   CIP
ISBN 0-684-80823-4

To Ida and Studs, no Wayne fans.
But heroes.

Contents

□ Prologue □
THE MOST DANGEROUS MAN

IN 1993, pollsters asked a representative sample of more than a thousand Americans, "Who is your favorite star?" John Wayne came in second, though he had been dead for fourteen years. He was second again in 1994. Then, in 1995, he was number one, getting more than twice the number of votes that put Mel Gibson in the third spot and nearly six times the number of Paul Newman's votes.[1] Reversing the laws of optics, Wayne seems to become larger the farther off he goes. In the 1995 list, only one other dead actor was included. Here is the list:

1. John Wayne
2. Clint Eastwood
3. Mel Gibson
4. Denzel Washington
5. Kevin Costner
6. Tom Hanks
7. Sylvester Stallone
8. Steven Seagal
9. Arnold Schwarzenegger
10. Robert De Niro
10. Robert Redford
11. Harrison Ford
11. Clark Gable
11. Paul Newman
11. Brad Pitt

The choice for number one in 1993 and 1994 was Clint Eastwood, and he is the star who has ranked second to Wayne in box-office appeal over the years. For twenty-five out of twenty-six years—from 1949 to 1974—Wayne made the top ten in distributors' lists of stars with commercial appeal, and was in the top four nineteen times. Eastwood has been in the top ten on the same lists twenty-one times, and in the top four fifteen times.[2] No other actor approaches these two. But does anyone expect Eastwood to be America's favorite star a decade and a half after his death? Wayne's durability is astonishing, though it does not impress our society's elite.

Intellectuals have other tastes in cult objects. Their pop icons are figures enlarged by special dooms. These idols tend to die young or violently—Rudolph Valentino, Jean Harlow, James Dean, John Lennon. They fascinate by their vulnerabilities (Elvis, Marilyn) or their defiance of social norms (Madonna, Michael Jackson). They are murkily erotic objects to their devotees —Marilyn Monroe to Norman Mailer, Elizabeth Taylor to Camille Paglia, Jacqueline Onassis to Wayne Koestenbaum. Cult figures who live on into old age become caricatures of their rebellious selves—the immured Garbo, Dietrich trickily lit like youth's ghost, Bette Davis imitating her imitators. Or they *become* the things that symbolized them—Charlie swallowed up in the Tramp, Groucho in perpetual ambush behind his eyebrows, Barrymore's profile lingering in the air like the grin of an alcoholic Cheshire cat.

John Wayne never won that kind of cult attention. Yet Wayne-olatry is a larger phenomenon—more consequential (for good or ill)—than any of those specialized legends. Marilyn Monroe was one of the top ten moneymakers in Hollywood only three times—and never one of the top four. Elvis started no wars. Masses of American men did not grow up imitating Valentino.

Though Wayne never served in the military, General Douglas MacArthur thought he was the model of an American soldier, the Veterans of Foreign Wars gave him their gold medal, and the Marines gave him their "Iron Mike" award.[3] The critic Eric Bentley thought he helped start the Vietnam War—which made him "the most important man in America."[4] Two boys who adored him in *Sands of Iwo Jima* grew up to become, respectively, the Speaker of the House of Representatives, and a Vietnam paraplegic. Newt Gingrich's stepfather said the young Newt always tried to walk like Wayne—his way of being a man. But Ron Kovic was unmanned by his devotion: "I gave my dead dick for John Wayne."[5]

Both friends and critics of American foreign policy in the 1960s and 1970s said it was afflicted with a "John Wayne syndrome." President Nixon thought that domestic affairs, symbolically represented for him by the Charles Manson cult-murder case, could be straightened out by taking Wayne's performance in *Chisum* as a model.[6] Ronald Reagan tried to imitate Wayne, on and off the screen.[7] Congress struck a special gold medal in his honor. The way to be an American was to be Wayne—a claim given eerie confirmation by the fact that the 1990s Chairman of the Joint Chiefs of Staff, John Shalikashvili, taught himself English, as an immigrant, by watching Wayne movies.[8] When another immigrant, Henry Kissinger, attributed his diplomatic success to Americans' admiration for cowboys who come into town alone, he was drawing on the Wayne legacy.[9]

For decades John Wayne haunted the dreams of Americans —making his face, said Joan Didion, more familiar to her than her husband's.[10] The protagonist in Walker Percy's novel *The Moviegoer* remembers Wayne's shoot-out in *Stagecoach* more vividly than the events in his own life.

Other pop icons tend to be young, rebellious, or deviant. Cult loves shadow, and theirs is a mysticism of the dark, of troubled youth and neuroses. Wayne's legend was of a rarer sort—a cult of daylight reality (or what passes for that). The legend came upon him in his maturity. He did not become a top star until he was forty; but he remained one till his death at seventy-two. He was a figure of authority, of the normative if not the normal. Yet what kind of country accepts as its norm an old man whose principal screen activity was shooting other people, or punching them out?

If one looks to other authority figures in the movies, they tend to be creaky with wisdom like Judge Hardy. Spencer Tracy stood more for integrity than authority. Robert Young had to leave the movies to become an image of stability on television (in *Father Knows Best* and *Marcus Welby, M.D.*). Most movie stars are glamorously pitted against authority—Clark Gable, Humphrey Bogart, James Cagney, Marlon Brando, Paul Newman. But Wayne, even when not playing an officer in the Seventh Cavalry, was usually on the sheriff's side.

What can explain this cult so at odds with the general run of cults? Why was Wayne's popularity mainstream and long-lived, not fleeting and marginal? Why does he still fill the channels on late-night TV? His fans remain loyal, with their own magazine *(The Big Trail)* and seasonal Western celebrations. He has more monuments than do real war heroes—an equestrian statue on a high podium in Los Angeles (before the Great Western Bank), a colossal striding statue at the airport named for him in Orange County, an eight-foot bronze statue in front of an Irish pub in San Diego. A foundry in Oregon makes a variety of statues for private devotions in the home.

Wayne's innate qualities are not enough to explain so large a social fact. He had to fill some need in his audience. He was the conduit they used to communicate with their own desired selves or their own imagined past. When he was called *the* American, it was a statement of what his fans wanted America to be. For them, Wayne always struck an elegiac note. He stood for an America people felt was disappearing or had disappeared, for a time "when men were men." Though some critics agreed with Eric Bentley that he got us into Vietnam, Wayne-olaters thought we lost in Vietnam because not enough John Waynes were left to do what was necessary for winning.

The disappearing frontier is the most powerful and persistent myth in American history. It is not a sectional myth but a national one. We do not have "Easterns" or "Southerns"—which *would* be sectional. We have Westerns—since America was, at the outset, *all* frontier.[11] America is the place where European settlers met an alien natural environment and social system. As the frontier moved from the Eastern seaboard west, Americans experienced, over and over again, the excitement of the "birth moment" when the new world was broken into, tamed, absorbed. James Fenimore Cooper created the archetypal figure for this movement when he sent his "Hawkeye," in chronologically ordered novels, from the forests of New York to the Great Lakes and then to the western prairies where he died.

After Hawkeye, other figures stood for the whole frontier experience—Daniel Boone, Kit Carson, Davy Crockett, Buffalo Bill. These men began in reality, but ended in myth. Wayne reverses the process. Beginning in myth, he entered the company of those who actually lived on the frontier. As a figure in the American imagination, he is closer to Kit Carson than to his fellow actors. He became so identified with the West that he looked out of place in other kinds of movies—even his war movies. Gary Cooper was "the Virginian" for a while, or "the

Plainsman." But he was also Sergeant York, or Mr. Deeds. Wayne was never quite at ease off the range. His large rolling walk was baffled by four walls. He was clearly on leave when doing screen duty as a modern soldier—Kit Carson holidaying with the Seabees.[12] In his own clumsy productions, the elephantine *Alamo* was at least more convincing than the hippopotamian *Green Berets*.

Some think Wayne's frequent confinement to Westerns is a sign of his narrow range as an actor. That may be true. But some very good actors have been limited by their success in one kind of role. James Cagney's stuttery urban rhythms made him a misfit in his Western *The Oklahoma Kid* (1939). Humphrey Bogart, in that same misbegotten film, had to wait for the roles that finally defined *him*. He had been out of place in most of his thirties films, with their jumpy pace and crackling dialogue. It took postwar "existentialism" to give his lassitudinous slump its mythic eloquence. A powerful image that defines a star can haunt all his or her later roles. People kept looking for Brando's blue jeans and torn T-shirt under the toga of Mark Antony or the Godfather's business suit. Other actors expressed fleeting moods in the nation—Astaire the sophistication people yearned for in the thirties, Bogart the romantic cynicism of the fifties. But Wayne was saddled up to ride across the decades.

It may be true that the greatest actors escape such restriction of their image, though even great Shakespearean players like John Gielgud, Ralph Richardson, and Alec Guinness were at times not convincing in heroic roles—just as Olivier could not equal them in comedy. The greatest screen actor, so far as range is concerned, may have been Spencer Tracy; but his very escape from any large type meant that he left few searing images on the imagination. Judith Anderson was a far greater actress than Marilyn Monroe; but she took up little psychic space in the movie audience's dreamworld. *REGEAN*

It is less useful to ask how good an actor Wayne was than to look at precisely how he did *whatever* he did that made him such a towering legend. The easiest and least truthful answer is to say that he just was what he pretended to be on-screen. That was hardly the case. Wayne hated horses, was more accustomed to suits and ties than to jeans when he went into the movies, and had to remind himself to say "ain't." He aspired, during the long courtship of his first wife, to join the Social Register set in Los Angeles. Wayne was not born Wayne. He had to be invented.

Later legend would say, as Richard Widmark does, that
"John Ford invented John Wayne."[13] Both Ford and Wayne
busily collaborated in nurturing that impression, which later
proved useful to them. But Raoul Walsh was the first director
who saw Wayne's potential as a Western star. Walsh was trying
to cast a hero for his super-epic of 1930, *The Big Trail*. Gary
Cooper was not available. George O'Brien, Ford's hero in the
1924 epic *The Iron Horse*, was not quite what Walsh wanted. He
saw Wayne working as a prop man on the Fox set, moving unwieldy things around with rhythmic ease. Wayne, though too
slow to succeed at college football, was well coordinated, surprisingly graceful for a large man. He had what Howard Hawks
would call "an 'I-own-the-world' way of walking." That was the
effect Walsh was looking for: "The sonuvabitch looked like a
man."[14]

Walsh lost no time in showing off the physical dexterity of
his discovery. In one of the earliest scenes in *The Big Trail*, Wayne
tiptoes up behind a young woman who is seated on a stool and
playing the harmonium. In one easy motion, he puts his hands
under her elbows, lifts her, turns her around in the air, and hugs
her to him. It is hard to tell how he does it, even as one watches
it over and over. He does not *throw* her, even slightly, and catch
her after turning her; he just handles her as if she were an empty
cardboard box, weightless and unresisting.

Wayne's size and strength were always important, even when
he lost the sinewy leanness of that first film with Walsh, made
when Wayne was twenty-two. This actor could not be dwarfed
by the great outdoors. He seemed more at home there than when
stooping inside a doorsill to enter the confined space of a cabin,
a cavalry barracks, or a tepee. Monument Valley itself could not
overpower him. It seemed to breathe a cognate spirit.

Yet sheer size and muscle do not carry one far. There were
always larger and more powerful men around Wayne—Victor
McLaglen, for instance, who had been a lean leading man when
Wayne was still in high school. It was not just the bulk of Wayne's
body but the way he used it that gave his motions and poses such
authority. It was another director—Howard Hawks this time
(still not John Ford)—who finally made Wayne a superstar in
1948. In *Red River*, Wayne has sworn to kill the protégé who took
his cattle herd from him. Having reached the railhead where
the herd is milling, Wayne strides toward the camera, the cattle
parting before his inexorable motion; he does not even bother to

look at them. A gunfighter calls out from behind Wayne, to stop him. But Wayne, in one fluid motion, pivots while drawing his gun, downs the challenger, and completes the circle of his turn, his regained stride undeterrable as fate. Here was Manifest Destiny on the hoof.

Most critics of *Red River* think that its flaw is the fact that the unstoppable Wayne gets stopped. So inevitable is his tread up to the climax that his collapse looks unconvincing. John Ford had the same problem with his ending to *The Searchers* (1956), where Wayne's deep fires of revenge burn so fiercely through the picture that extinguishing them in the final scene looks contrived. Few actors have had this problem, of looking so indomitable that an audience finds it hard to accept their submission. Other actors need to be built up—by camera angles, lighting, costume, blocking of crowds, suppression of others' positions— in order to command the scene. Wayne's power was such that *others* had to be built up, to give him credible opposition. As Hawks put it: "If you don't get a damn good actor with Wayne, he's going to blow him right off the screen, not just by the fact that he's good, but by his power, his strength." [15] Wayne was so sure of himself that he did not have to resort to the kinds of tricks Ronald Reagan encountered while playing opposite Errol Flynn—who shouldered him out of the best camera angles. [16] Actors talk about how generous Wayne was with them, trying to give strength to their performances. [17] He knew his own presence was so powerful that it could not fully be measured against a weak adversary. As Wayne told Roger Ebert, describing his standard Westerns: "Ordinarily they just stand me there and run everybody up against me." [18]

The Western deals with the "taming" of the West. Wayne was uniquely convincing at that task. He looked so fit for the assignment that the other problem arose—how, if necessary, do you tame the tamer? After he has broken the resistance, how do you break *him*? It is a difficulty the writers and directors had to address when Wayne's screen character died. Many people were incredulous when the real-life Wayne died. Andrew McLaglen, his friend (and the director of five of his movies), said, "Even after the cancer operations, I never *really* thought Duke could die." [19] If people resisted the mere thought in real life, how could they be made to accept it on the screen?

This air of invincibility gave Wayne his special status in Westerns. Richard Widmark, a personal and political adversary, admits, "He was the definitive Western star."[20] Howard Hawks said that he and John Ford "used to discuss how tough it was to make a good Western without Wayne."[21] One can imagine other actors replacing even very good performers in famous Westerns. Henry Fonda could have played Gary Cooper's role in *High Noon*. Jimmy Stewart could have taken Fonda's role in *The Oxbow Incident*. Several actors could have equaled Alan Ladd in *Shane*. Sergio Leone proved in *Once Upon a Time in the West* that he could make close-ups of hard eyes work as well with Fonda as with Eastwood. But no one else could be as convincingly unswerving as Wayne in *Red River, The Searchers,* or *Big Jake*. Even the jokey *True Grit* worked because, underneath all the slapstick, it was finally believable that *this* fat old drunk could face down an entire gang.

What gave Wayne his aura of slumberous power? Much of it had to do with the easy control of his large body. Hawks said that the young Wayne moved "like a big cat."[22] Harry Carey's wife, Olive Fuller Golden, a lifelong friend of Wayne, said she thought of Nureyev when she saw Wayne walking.[23] Ford's daughter, Barbara, said there was something overpoweringly sexy in the way Wayne sat and rode his horse.[24] Katharine Hepburn noticed his small feet and "the light dancer's steps he took with them."[25] Once, when he was drunk, Wayne whimsically turned Marilyn Carey (Olive's daughter-in-law) upside down while dancing with her, and didn't notice that her face was turning red until Marilyn's husband pointed it out to him. "Duke apologized," says Harry Carey, Jr. The move was so effortless for him it did not occur to Wayne in his stupor that it could be physically trying for another.[26]

Wayne's control of his body was economical, with no motions wasted. This gave a sense of *purpose* to everything he did. He worked out characteristic stances, gestures, ways of sitting his horse. He learned to choreograph his fight moves with the creative stuntman, Yakima Canutt. In stills from his early pictures, even when the face is fuzzy, one can identify Wayne by his pose or gait, the tilt of his shoulders, the contrapposto lean of his hips. Classical sculptors worked out the counterpoised position to get the maximum of both tension and relaxation, both motion and stillness, in the human body: the taut line of the body is maintained through the hip above the straight leg, while the torso relaxes, it deviates from rigid lines, on the other side, where the leg is bent. Wayne constantly strikes the pose of Michelangelo's *David* (see illustration section). Sometimes, with a wider throw of hip, he becomes Donatello's *David* (see illustration). He was very conscious of his effects. Richard Widmark used to laugh when Wayne, directing *The Alamo*, shouted at his actors: "Goddamnit, be *graceful*—like me!"[27]

When George Plimpton, playing a bit part in Hawks's *Rio Lobo*, had to enter a saloon carrying a rifle at waist level, he asked Wayne how to hold it (Plimpton was holding the gun with the trigger guard near his belt, the stock projecting out behind him). Wayne took the rifle, jammed its stock against his hip, and held it with one hand so that his whole body leaned into the gun, spoke through it, seemed to be at one with it.[28] Wayne twirled a rifle as easily as other cowboys twirl their pistols.

Western stars traditionally identified themselves with elaborate signals worked out through their costume, devices to make people conscious that this hero lived in an entirely different social system. William S. Hart wore leather and tough fabrics layered around him almost like body armor. Others added to their height with "ten-gallon hats," or to their menace with crossed bandoliers stuck with bullets. They wore two guns at the side, or a large pistol stuck in the front of their belts. They used "batwing" chaps to suggest a swooping motion even when off their horses. Metal riveted them together, from vest studs down to noisy spurs.

Wayne also had some costuming tricks—his placket-front shirt, dark and semimilitary. But his signals were sent by the body under the clothes, which was far more semantically charged than they were. His pants were folded up at the cuff, to reveal the gracefulness of his footwork. He dressed to let the body do its work—just as Fred Astaire wore form-fitting tuxedos to bring out the line of his body, the calligraphy of its tracings in the air. Wayne's silhouette was enough to identify him. When he made an uncredited appearance on the TV show of his friend Ward Bond, his face was not shown, just his horse looming up in shadow outside a camp fire—but the way his body is held reveals who he is to anyone familiar with his films.[29]

Wayne created an entire Western language of body signals. The most explicit of these were the Indian signs he often used—paradoxically dainty and slow arcs and swoops made by his large hands ("big as hams," Widmark said) and thick wrists (emphasized with a gold bracelet). His physical autonomy and self-command, the ease and authority of his carriage, made each motion a statement of individualism, a balletic Declaration of Independence.

The whole language cohered—as did the vocal aspect of his performance. Wayne's calculated and measured phrasing gave his delivery the same air of control, of inevitability, that his motions conveyed. He dealt out phrases like dooms: "Touch that gun and I'll kill ya." The stop-and-go phrasing is what all his imitators get; but few capture the melodic intervals of his cadenced speech. As a cavalry officer, he directs his troops with two notes more stirring than the trumpet's: "*Yoh*-oh" (a two-and-a-half-tone drop). Joan Didion's girlhood memory of him was an acoustical one, of the *commands* he gave.[30] His throwaway comments, quietly delivered, were just as effective: "*He'll* do" (two-tone drop). I have watched Wayne's films dubbed in Italy, and been impressed with how much of his performance depends on the timbre, the melodic and rhythmic turns, of his voice on the soundtrack.

The most obvious element in Wayne's physical performance is his walk—the manly stride Newt Gingrich tried to imitate as an adolescent. The walk became so famous that various people took credit for inventing it and drilling Wayne on how to do it. Paul Fix, the Western star who worked often with Wayne, claimed he showed Wayne how to walk in the dramatic scene of *Red River,* but Hawks scoffed at the idea: "You don't have to tell Wayne anything about walking through cattle. Wayne knew."[31] Plimpton asked him how the walk was developed, and Wayne finally told him:

> "Well, uh, the walk's been kind of a secret in our family for a long time—my Dad taught me. But I can't keep it forever. I'll tell you how he taught me . . ."
>
> "There's a trick to it, is there?"
>
> ". . . so he says, 'You pick up one foot and put it forward and set it down. Then you pick up the other foot and set *it* down—and that's walkin' forward. If you do the reverse, you're *walkin' backward.*"[32]

Wayne pooh-poohed the notion that he studied his walk, perhaps because it is "unmanly" for a male to be as conscious of his body's display as, say, Mae West was in rolling her pelvis or Marilyn Monroe in wriggling her behind. Yet Wayne *was* conscious of his effects, as he indirectly revealed in one interview: Ford, who knew how to needle people on their points of pride, would shout at Wayne things like "Damnit, Duke, you're as clumsy as Ward [Bond]." Wayne told the interviewer (Ford's grandson): "But, God knows, if I could do anything, it was move well."[33]

Any actor has to project character through his whole body, as Laurence Olivier often said. Hawks made Wayne's motions "age" in *Red River*. D. W. Griffith sent his film actresses to study movement with the dance instructor Ruth St. Denis. Actors like Richard Boone went to Martha Graham for the same reason (she told him to imitate a cat).[34] John Barrymore made his body reveal the character of Richard III in the way he limped—impeded, but gracefully *overcoming* the impediment:

> I merely turned my right foot inward, pointing it toward the instep of my left foot. I let it stay in that position and then forgot all about it. I did not try to walk badly, I walked as well as I could.[35]

How an actor moves is obviously important in what are, after all, *motion* pictures—but surprisingly little criticism has focused on this essential aspect of performance.[36] Virginia Wright Wexman applied "kinesics" to Humphrey Bogart's body language—more languorous as a Chandler hero, more nervous as a Hammett one.[37] And perceptive critics have noticed the grace of particular performers. Graham Greene said that Cagney *danced* his gangster parts "on his light hoofer's feet, with his quick nervous hands."[38] David Thomson saw signs of Burt Lancaster's acrobatic training in the way he moved.[39] Alan Ladd liked to run in little cat-crouches, turning his low stature into a slithery form of energy. Henry Fonda had a stiff storklike walk that set him against the flow of things around him—a sign of integrity in *Young Mr. Lincoln* or *The Grapes of Wrath*, of martinet irresponsiveness in *Fort Apache*, of detached inhumanity in *Once Upon a Time in the West*. What gives the dance in Ford's *My Darling Clementine* its impact is the way the rigid Fonda becomes more flexible. Cary Grant was trained as an acrobat, like Lancaster, and he can do more with less motion than any other screen actor. This is because of the way he angles his head away from what he is doing, as if it were a detached thing carried at a careful remove from what his limbs and torso are up to. (Buster Keaton has the same knack in his knockabout comedies.)

In discussing Wayne as an actor, we should take into account the *whole* of his performance. That would put him among the most expressive of those who move about in the moving pictures. Often people resist his performance not because of its quality (good or bad) but because of its content. His body spoke a highly specific language of "manliness," of self-reliant authority. It was a body impervious to outside force, expressing a mind narrow but focused, fixed on the task, impatient with complexity. This is a dangerous ideal to foster. It is "male" in a way that has rightly become suspect—one-sided, exclusive of values conventionally labeled "female."

It may seem surprising that, at a time when gender studies dominate much of film criticism, when essay after essay is devoted to masculinity on the screen, so little attention is paid to Wayne. Much of the new literature answers critic Laura Mulvey's famous claim that a male gaze makes women the sole sex objects of cinema.[40] In the responses to her, we are given counterexamples of men who have been the object of sexual "voyeurism." Wayne, wrapped against a hostile environment, does not qualify for the kind of gaze directed at the exposed bodies of men in Bible epics, boxing films, or sci-fi fantasies. This gaze is captured in Michel Mourlet's effusion, often quoted:

> Charlton Heston is an axiom. He constitutes a tragedy in himself, his presence in any film being enough to instill beauty. The pent-up violence expressed by the somber phosphorescence of his eyes, his eagle's profile, the imperious arch of his eyebrows, the hard, bitter curve of his lips, the stupendous strength of his torso—this is what he has given and what not even the worst of directors can debase. It is in this sense that one can say that Charlton Heston, by his very existence and regardless of the film he is in, provides a more accurate definition of the cinema than films like *Hiroshima mon amour* or *Citizen Kane*, films whose aesthetic either ignores or repudiates Charlton Heston. Through him, *mise en scène* can confront the most intense of conflicts and settle them with the contempt of a god imprisoned, quivering with muted rage. In this sense, Heston is more a [Fritz] Langian than a [Raoul] Walshian hero.[41]

The conservative Charlton Heston might be surprised at becoming an object of "the male gaze." When Gore Vidal wrote a homosexual infatuation with Heston's character into the script of

Ben-Hur, the director, William Wyler, said, "Don't say a word to Chuck."[42]

Wayne has largely escaped such metaphysical attention. He is neither the naked god nor the troubled adolescent. Gender criticism that defines "masculinity" has been most concerned with *conflicted* maleness, in figures like James Dean, Montgomery Clift, or Marlon Brando.[43] Maleness is acutely experienced at points where it is doubted or questioned. Wayne seems too obtuse to question his own macho swagger, which means that he can be dismissed without analysis. It is telling that Ford did not think of Wayne when casting "sensitive" roles, but chose Henry Fonda or James Stewart—and they *have* been the object of masculinity studies.[44]

By an odd turn of history, recent analyses of masculinity have less interesting things to say about Wayne than do ancient Roman critics of male performance. In the militaristic Roman society, a man's persuasiveness depended very much on his stance *(status)* and walk *(gressus, gradus).*[45] Cicero, in his book *The Orator* (17.59), describes the ideal speaker, in a culture where speaking well was an exercise in performance art. It sounds as if Cicero had just been watching Wayne films:

> He must practice an economy of movement, with no extraneous effort—the carriage of his body straight and lofty; his pacing measured and kept within bounds; lunging only to the point, and rarely; without effeminacy in turning his head; no little stage business with his hands; no "conducting himself" to a beat; but governing himself in the expression of his whole body, with a manly torsion from the waist; using powerful gestures when moved, and none at all when calm.

In Rome, military rule was the highest virtue, and the most debilitating accusation was one of effeminacy. Cicero said that orators should learn grace of movement from wrestlers, should stamp their feet in a manly (not a petulant) way, should consider the whole body (the *motus corporis*) more important even than the words of a speech.[46] Lucian drew the same picture—"a strong man, of understated power, virile stride, skin toughened by the outdoors, eyes hard and on the lookout."[47] The Roman Empire dreamed constantly of John Wayne.

Why this echo of a lost classical world? Rome trained its citizens to war. Its empire depended on a mystique of the legions intelligently led. The "Seventh Cavalry" of John Ford's Westerns had the legionary spirit—far more than do the quaintly armored "Romans" of Cecil DeMille historical epics. But even more important, the America of Ford's time had the sense of *imperial* burden that came to it with World War II and the Cold War. America submitted to a discipline of protracted struggle that made the President a full-time "Commander in Chief" even of nonmilitary citizens. Citizens were under scrutiny for their loyalty to the war effort. Classification of secrets, security clearances, lists of subversive organizations, loyalty oaths, secret funding of the CIA, internal surveillance by the FBI, the expensive buildup of an arsenal and of defenses—all these things were embraced as the price of defending the free world.

Wayne's time of maximum popularity coincided with this immense societal effort, and he internalized its demands in his own life as well as in his films. He joined the hunt for sympathizers with the foe, and helped expel them from Hollywood. He tied his own greatest financial project, the making of *The Alamo*, to the electoral struggle of 1960, in which he felt that *real* patriots should support Richard Nixon. He defended the war in Vietnam, and made *The Green Berets* as a personal statement on that conflict. Though the mystique of some Westerns has been one of freedom and individualism, of a creative anarchy, Ford's movies stressed the need for *regimentation* as necessary to survival under threat. Ironically, this reflected conditions in the real West of the 1860s–1890s more accurately than did the myth of emancipated spirits on the frontier.

Wayne-olatry grew in such a climate. It is the greatest popular expression of the tensions in that half-century of muted struggle (1945–1985). What followed, in terms of Hollywood symbols, was a reversion to radical individualism. The end of the Cold War should have been a comforting development but it was also seen as the end of empire. America *lost* Vietnam, with a corresponding breakdown in its internal imperial discipline, leading to a sense of drift, a new awareness of crime as raveling out the social fabric. It is significant that gender studies of movie masculinity have added a third item to their treatment of naked gods and troubled boys—the "hard bodies" of the Vietnam era, men engaged in revenge fantasies. Rambo goes after the abandoned relics of empire in Vietnam ("Do we get to win this time?"). "Rocky Balboa" beats the Russian giant when Rocky's government has to confine itself to nuclear standoff. Dirty Harry goes after the punks who have made the city a jungle, using tactics forbidden to the ineffective police force. Citizens must take up arms, alone or in private militias, since the government has failed its subjects, abroad and at home. Conan the Barbarian, created by John Milius (the same man who developed the Dirty Harry character), becomes an avenger after his whole village is wiped out. In Milius's *Red Dawn*, teenagers must fight for a government that adults have surrendered.[48]

The sense of opposing tremendous odds, of standing against the whole of established society, calls for a hypertrophy of the individual's musculature and weaponry. Stallone and Schwarzenegger are fitted out with bodies that are nothing but body *armor*. Stripped naked, they carry huge cannon and automatic firing systems. Dirty Harry's gun gets longer and longer, blowing away whole phantom structures of evil, not just single bad guys. The note of these films is rage. Wayne did not normally have the contempt for his opponent that Dirty Harry does. The Wayne hero could be calm, in a time of the empire's dominance. His self-discipline was counted on to awe or attract others. The mature Wayne was lightly weapa—a rifle, or one pistol, and he often did not have to use that. He faced down foes. The villain in the "shoot-out" is undone by Wayne's stride as he comes down the street.

The individualism of the Rambos is conveyed by their naked bodies. They wear no uniform, not even that of normal civil society. Bruce Willis's *Die Hard* police hero ends up shorn of civilized symbols (including shoes and shirt)—though large firing systems are magically available. The Seventh Cavalry is not going to ride to the rescue—why put on its epaulets? There is no one or nothing to turn to but one's gun. As the father tells Conan in Milius's film: "No one in this world can you trust—not men, not women, not beasts. This [steel] you can trust."

Though some critics found homoeroticism in the classic Westerns, more have explored its presence in the narcissism of the bodybuilders, Stallone and Schwarzenegger, or the phallic prolongations of Dirty Harry's gun.[49] (Anticipating such a reaction, the Dirty Harry films plant homosexuals for Harry to mock, dissociating himself from them.) The rage of these avenger movies—or the nihilism and apocalyptic violence of Sergio Leone's and Sam Peckinpah's Westerns—may make Wayne and Ford look moderate in retrospect. In Peckinpah's *The Wild Bunch*, lives previously meaningless acquire validity in the apocalyptic ending that brings down "the system." Conan tells his "sidekick" that winning is less important than the fact "that two stood against many."

Wayne helped articulate the system that could not sustain its mission of a *pax Americana*. The imperial reach led to the postimperial letdown. In that sense, we owe Rambo to Wayne, even though Rambo seems to reject what Wayne stood for. The strength of Wayne was that he embodied our deepest myth— that of the frontier. His weakness is that it was only a myth. Behind the fantasies of frontier liberation, as historian Patricia Limerick reminds us, was a reality of conquest. And conquest has a way of undoing the conquerors.

A myth does not take hold without expressing many truths —misleading truths, usually, but important ones: truth, for one thing, to the needs of those who elaborate and accept the myth; truth to the demand for some control over complex realities; truth to the recognition of shared values (however shakily grounded those values may be in themselves). Even the myths that simplify are not, in themselves, simple. It is true that Westerns work with a body of conventional situations (though a larger, more flexible body of them than most people realize). But Japanese Noh plays, ancient Greek tragedy, and the commedia dell'arte also work within strict conventions—a fact that does not deprive them of subtleties or nuance. Myth works best in such established frameworks. The Western can raise serious moral questions because it deals with the clash of entirely different social systems—not only that of Native Americans, or Mexicans, or Chinese "coolies" with European colonizers, but that of earlier colonizers with later ones. The technology that is the white man's friend becomes his enemy as waves of exploitation wash in and overlap prior waves.

Wayne was not just one type of Western hero. He is an innocently leering ladies' man in his B films of the thirties, a *naïf* in *Stagecoach*, an obsessed adolescent in *Shepherd of the Hills*, a frightened cattle capitalist in *Red River*, a crazed racist in *The Searchers*, a dutiful officer in cavalry pictures, the worldly-wise elder counselor in later movies. He is sometimes a hothead, more often the restrainer of hotheads. So it is not true that Wayne always played the same role; but it is true that all his work, especially in the Westerns, was part of one project—to build a persona full of portent, to maintain a cumulative authority in his bearing. Wayne was careful about the persona, not accepting things that would endanger it. He refused to play a coward for Howard Hawks. He refused to shoot a man in the back for Don Siegel. He would be villainous, but not weak. An early small part, in *The Life of Jimmy Dolan,* showed that he could play a coward; but later it was one of the things "John Wayne" did not do. Creating that artifact "John Wayne" was the lifelong project of the man behind the image—whatever his name was (Marion Morrison, Duke Morrison, Duke Wayne). Wayne was helped along the way by directors, writers, producers, cameramen, costumers, friends, and critics; and he was hindered by an assortment of the well-meaning, the diffident, the sycophantic. But he kept strenuously to his own program—to create a "self" so real to others that he could disappear into it, as he did.

He finally became what he had projected on the screen—a hollow triumph, for what was that but the figment of other people's imaginations? Wayne's own story is a large one—as large as the truths, the evasions, the lies of which his screen image was confected. It produced some film masterpieces (along with a large body of clinkers). It involved some of the greatest talents in film-making—John Ford, Howard Hawks, Raoul Walsh, Joe August, Archie Stout, Winton Hoch, Bert Glennon, William Clothier, Dudley Nichols, Frank Nugent, Henry Fonda, Maureen O'Hara. It also involved all Americans, whether we knew it or not. We are entangled in his story, by the dreams he shaped or inhibited, in us or in others, by the things he validated and those he scorned, by the particular definition he gave to "being American." That influenced us—whether, with Richard Nixon and Ronald Reagan, we accepted the definition; or, with Eric Bentley, we tried to renounce or discredit it. The less we advert to what he did to us, the less we can cope with it. Down the street of the twentieth-century imagination, that figure is still walking toward us—graceful, menacing, inescapable.

□ Introduction □
SCOPE OF THE BOOK

WHY *HIM?* When I began this project three years ago, that was the question most often asked when anyone learned of it. I had received no such queries when I said I was writing about Richard Nixon or Ronald Reagan. They, after all, held political office, formed political policy, and depended on a political electorate. People cast *votes* for them. They just bought *tickets* for John Wayne's movies. Yet it is a very narrow definition of politics that would deny John Wayne political importance. The proof of that is Richard Nixon's appeal to Wayne's movie *Chisum* when he wanted to explain his own views on law and order. Nixon had *policies*, but beneath those positions were the *values* Wayne exemplified.

All those values were created on the screen. There is no better demonstration of the power of movies than Wayne's impact on American life. He was not like other actors, who simply hold political views. Paul Newman was known to favor liberal positions. But his fans did not love or hate the on-screen Newman— as Hud, for instance, or Butch Cassidy—because of his politics.

Wayne did not just have political opinions. He embodied a politics; or his screen image did. It was a politics of large meanings, not of little policies—a politics of gender (masculine), ideology (patriotism), character (self-reliance), and responsibility. It was a matter of basic orientation. Its dogmas were (usually) implicit. Whatever weight attached to his "real life" was totally derived from the flickering light of his screen appearances.

29

This book asks how that embodied cluster of meanings was brought into being, developed, and altered—by creative artists of the camera, whose aim was not to create "John Wayne" but to make successful movies. By a confluence of audience demand and commercial production, the Wayne that took shape in the transaction between the two expressed deep needs and aspirations in the country. "Wayne" became the pattern of manly American virtue.

This is not the biography of a man, then. Wayne had no interesting ideas in his private life. But the complex idea conveyed on the screen in the course of his career—a compound idea of what American manhood is in the minds of the vast majority of Americans—deserves the most careful treatment, deserves a biography of that idea. Wayne's on-screen character changed over time, from the naive virtue of "the Ringo Kid" to the dark acceptance of responsibility by "Sergeant Stryker" to the grim acceptance of anachronism by "J. B. Books." But these different identities had the continuity of a myth whose contents could be sorted out in a variety of ways.

Since Wayne's importance is solely the product of his films, the studios have the importance for tracing his America that political parties had when I was studying Richard Nixon or Ronald Reagan. "Wayne" was crafted by others. That was true in a limited sense for Nixon or Reagan. They had their political "handlers," the projectors and protectors of their image—men like Murray Chotiner or Chuck Colson for Nixon, Mike Deaver or Roger Ailes for Reagan. But Wayne on the screen was nothing *but* image—lit, moved about, costumed, made up, photographed. Where the politicians had speechwriters, he had scripts. Only the superficial will think that these artistic means have a superficial impact on "real life." They are the tools for making the myths that go into our self-understanding as a people. Normally these are not directly political tools. With Wayne—and with no other actor to anything like the same degree—they *became* instruments for shaping political attitude.

Naturally, so political an art caused political resistance from those who disagreed with or feared its meaning—women, for instance, opposing the ethos of masculine supremacy. But the Wayne idea drew so deeply upon the largest myths of our past— of the frontier, of a purifying landscape, of American exceptionalism, of discipline as the condition of rule—that some had trouble resisting the idea even when they renounced its consequences.

Since I trace the history of "John Wayne" as an idea, not of John Wayne (or Marion Morrison) the man, biographical detail unrelated to the making of the movies will not be found here— except in the first chapter, which deals with the initial encounter of a pre-Wayne Wayne with his movie refashioners. Even many movies are excluded, not because they are bad (though most are) but because they had little importance in creating or maintaining the persona who had political consequences.

If this were a straight show-business biography, I would have to deal with all the important directors Wayne worked with —Jules Dassin, Cecil B. DeMille, Edward Dmytryk, John Huston, Otto Preminger, Nicholas Ray, George Stevens. But none of these men affected Wayne's political image in an important way. Only directors who helped create or advance the ideological image are considered here: Raoul Walsh, Robert N. Bradbury, Howard Hawks, Henry Hathaway, and—above all—John Ford. The complex relationship with Ford is at the heart of Wayne's political artistry, which means it is at the heart of this book.

In the same way, a straight Hollywood biography would treat Wayne's work with a number of important leading ladies —Ann-Margret, Jean Arthur, Joan Crawford, Claudette Colbert, Laraine Day, Anita Ekberg, Paulette Goddard, Susan Hayward, Patricia Neal, Donna Reed, Lana Turner. To find out what Wayne thought of Geraldine Page's atrocious hygiene or Lana Turner's sad drinking, the reader must turn to the fine biography of Wayne by Randy Roberts and James S. Olson. I deal only with actresses who played key roles in politically important films: Claire Trevor, Joanne Dru, Katharine Hepburn, Lauren Bacall, and—above all—Maureen O'Hara (five films together, though two of them were duds).

Since this is the story of a mythical figure in a make-believe industry, I must sort out the way the myth was made; and this will sometimes mean contrasting the legends with more literal fact. All Hollywood stories are dubious, given the creativity of publicity departments and the cooperative imaginings of career-oriented performers. But Wayne myths went into his political legend in ways not easily paralleled among his fellow artists. So I look at the minor myths that advanced his larger legend—the story of both his father's and his own football "stardom," of his supposed inability to serve in World War II, of his "western upbringing," of his "manly" indifference to cosmetics and all aspects of his appearance, and (above all) the many myths about his friendship with John Ford.

Ford and Wayne engaged in a continual refashioning of their joint history. The truth of Wayne's part in this is difficult to establish since Ford created false versions of almost every aspect of his life. What Samuel Johnson wrote about Alexander Pope is equally true of Ford: "In all his intercourse with mankind, he had great delight in artifice, and endeavored to attain all his purposes by indirect and unsuspected methods. He hardly drank tea without a stratagem." Wayne himself must have wondered what really happened whenever Ford told a new version of their shared exploits. One of the greatest challenges to a student of "John Wayne" is to determine how much of that confected personality the world is asked to accept on the fugitive word of John Ford.

□ Acknowledgments □

SOME OF MY RESEARCH for this book moved back over tracks I first explored for *Reagan's America*—the Hollywood of the Screen Actors Guild, of blacklistings, of an anti-Communist sub-culture, of the Motion Picture Alliance for the Preservation of American Ideals. I give somewhat less attention to this matter because of my account of Reagan's red-hunting. Wayne moved in a different circle of the screen world—his efforts went into the Alliance rather than the Guild—but the atmosphere both breathed was identical.

When I began work on this book, my first priority was to see all the important Westerns, concentrating on the growth of differ-ent cowboy ideals. I began with the silent heroes, Broncho Billy, William S. Hart, Tom Mix, Jack Holt, Harry Carey, Hoot Gibson, Buck Jones, Ken Maynard—and followed their careers (all but Broncho Billy's and Hart's) into the sound era. Madeline F. Matz, at the Library of Congress, was especially helpful in arranging for me to see the work of these Western stars; but other films were viewed at the Museum of Modern Art and UCLA.

I also set about to view all the extant movies of John Ford. Here I received extraordinarily generous and informed assis-tance from Charles Silver of the Museum of Modern Art. Besides the other film archives mentioned, I saw some rare Ford movies at the Wisconsin Historical Society. In these and other places I viewed, over time, roughly 140 of Wayne's films.

For Harry Carey's career, I drew on the Robinson Locke Collection at the Richard Rodgers branch of the New York Public

Library. Patrick Loughney at the Library of Congress unearthed the sole surviving copy of Carey's play *Montana*. The Harry Carey papers are at Brigham Young University, still uncatalogued, but James D'Arc, the university's film curator, helped me find my way through them. Carey's son and daughter-in-law, "Dobe" and Marilyn, were also helpful, showing me their own collection of Carey photographs and clippings. Since Marilyn Carey is the daughter of Western actor Paul Fix, a friend and colleague of Wayne's, and since Dobe Carey not only knew his father's career and friends but worked with Ford and Wayne himself, the Careys are a living archive of the Western film's history. Dobe is also the author of the best book on John Ford.

Ford's papers I consulted at the Lilly Library, Howard Hawks's at Brigham Young, Darryl Zanuck's at UCLA. People who worked with both Ford and Wayne, and who told me interesting things about the two men's relationship include (besides Dobe Carey) John Agar, Joanne Dru, Andrew McLaglen, Denver Pyle, and Richard Widmark. Pilar Wayne and James Bellah, Jr., offered observations of Ford from a greater distance.

For Wayne's background and life, I am grateful to the college historian at Simpson College, Iowa, to the archivist of the athletic program at the University of Southern California, and to the curators of local history collections at the public libraries of Winterset and Earlham in Iowa, of Lancaster and Glendale in California, of San Antonio in Texas, and of Tucson in Arizona. For Ford and Wayne at the Naval Academy, I am grateful to the Academy's Professor of History, David Peeler, who helped me with archival materials.

I appreciate the offer to try out my ideas on Ford with helpful lecture audiences at the Naval Academy in Annapolis, the Morgan Library in New York, the Newberry Library in Chicago, the Wisconsin Historical Society in Madison, and the nation's assembled Henry R. Luce Professors. I am grateful, as well, for the documentary research of Wayne's assiduous biographers, Randy Roberts and James S. Olson, as well as to my prompt and meticulous typist, Joan Stahl. My son John, an historian, helped me understand the American West. My son Garry, a film-maker, helped me with technical problems of cinema. Charles Silver and Randy Roberts read and improved the manuscript.

Most of all, as usual, I owe the three women *sine quibus non* —Alice and Anne and Natalie, editor, agent, and wife. Especially Natalie.

Part One

INVENTING A COWBOY

The Hollywood star system invented childhoods to fit an actor's later image, suggesting that, for instance, Starlet X was "born to play the siren." The studio publicist in Evelyn Waugh's *The Loved One* invents a Gaelic past for a woman about to star in Irish roles:

> He footled with a new name for Juanita and a new life-story: Kathleen FitzBourke the toast of the Galway Blazers; the falling light among the banks and walls of that stiff country and Kathleen FitzBourke alone with hounds. . . .

So people try to find a young "John Wayne" in the Marion Morrison of history: a football hero descended from a football hero, a westerner, an outdoorsman, a horseman—one born to be a cowboy star.

But there was nothing to indicate this would be Wayne's career until director Raoul Walsh put him in a great movie, *The Big Trail* (1930), that failed because of the Depression's impact on its wide-screen process. Wayne's non-Western bit parts in the early thirties were a dead end because the studios were too damaged by the Depression to develop young players. The only quick money Wayne could make was in B Westerns, using and improving skills he first learned for Walsh's *The Big Trail*. He labored for a dreary decade in such roles, wasting his twenties in trivial productions. He still did not think his future would be

35

defined by Westerns. He stayed out of World War II to try new roles, as in his three films with Marlene Dietrich. But the hard apprenticeship to Westerns was only apparently a trap. It laid the foundation for his best later work.

MAN FROM NOWHERE

JOHN WAYNE, like Ronald Reagan (born four years after him), was part of Iowa's great exodus to California.[1] A net of commercial and filial connections dragged people from their cornfields off to citrus groves. Wayne's family was typical: first his paternal grandfather went, then his father, then his mother with his maternal grandmother and grandfather. Reagan went, taking a whole cluster of friends from his broadcasting days, to be followed by his brother and his parents. Iowans turned like sunflowers toward the California sun.

Wayne forgot Iowa, and Iowa forgot him, while Reagan kept up ties with his Midwestern past. This is mainly, but not only, because Wayne left as a child (seven), and Reagan as a young man (twenty-five). Studio publicists highlight or invent links to a star's roots if they are useful to the star's image. It served Reagan to be a homey and down-to-earth Iowan, the unpretentious star of Des Moines radio. But Western heroes appear from nowhere. Their past is mysterious, their name a title or a mask —the Virginian, the Texan, the Kid. Is Shane a first or last name —or both, or neither? Even when not masked, this Western hero is always a lone ranger, come back from beyond the farthest ridge, not formed "back East" in settled ways. John Wayne had nothing to gain from the farmlands in his past. It is accidental but appropriate that Reagan lost his nickname (Dutch) in California, returning to his real name (Ronald), while Wayne lost his real first name (Marion) there, gaining a nickname (Duke) before trading his family name (Morrison) for a stage name. If Wayne was not quite Sergio Leone's "Man with No Name," he was at least a man from nowhere. The nowhere was Winterset, Iowa.

Later on, residents of Winterset entertained a myth that Wayne sneaked back, once, to look at his native place—as if Wayne could slip unnoticed through the rows of corn.[2] Wayne's son Michael fed this illusion by saying that he showed Wayne, toward the end of his father's life, a movie made in Winterset . *(Cold Turkey)*, without telling him where it was set. Wayne, his son averred, found something familiar about the Madison County courthouse—a remarkable achievement for a child who left Winterset at age two, moving on to other towns in Iowa.[3]

The Wayne family took few happy memories away from Iowa, and some of the happy few were false. Wayne later boasted that his father's Iowa pharmacy was a *real* drugstore, not a place for selling general products. But the store Clyde Morrison owned specialized in paint and wallpaper, and the drugs he sold were mainly patent medicine. Even more important was the memory that Clyde had been a football star, an "all-state halfback" at Simpson College.

The Simpson College yearbooks and school papers tell a different story. Clyde Morrison grew up in Indianola, the site of Simpson College, and attended its preparatory academy. In his freshman year at the college, he started on the football team's first string but was replaced as the season wore on.[4] His home-town paper made this embarrassing report: "Morrison did well [in an early game] but does not get into condition for proper work."[5] In his second and last season, Morrison was on the bench, not mentioned in a single game's newspaper report.[6] In a college with only 106 male students, one that did not have an entire second eleven (the roster was sixteen players), this is hardly an "all-state" career.[7] Yet the legend is still being passed on.[8]

The Clyde Morrison who went to Winterset in 1906 to clerk in a drugstore was no star, and there would be few memories of him or his family after they left in 1909. Two decades later, when "John Wayne" had acquired some fame, there was an attempt to connect him with the baby Marion Morrison, but local report gave different stories about things as basic as the house where he was born. The woman doctor who delivered him told her daughter that she did it in a second-story apartment.[9] A former secretary of the Madison County Historical Society, Lloyd H.

Smith, told the ghostwriter of Wayne's unfinished autobiography, Maurice Zolotow, that there were three or more contenders for the honor. Smith himself assigned it to a house now destroyed, a picture of which appears in Zolotow's *Shooting Star*.[10]

When, after Wayne's death, the Winterset Chamber of Commerce decided to honor the site of his birth, no documents (sale, rent, or phone records) revealed where the Morrisons were in 1907, and no address was given on Marion's birth certificate. Local authorities relied on one woman's testimony. The late Alice Miller, then in her eighties, said that she remembered, as a girl, watching the excitement across the street as John Wayne was born in 1907, though Marion Morrison had disappeared from Winterset in 1909.[11] Alice Miller was also a source for the biographical pamphlet, sold at the birthplace, that remembers Clyde Morrison as a football star.

Perhaps the designated birthplace, which drew fifty thousand tourists in 1994, is the actual house.[12] It has an advantage Lloyd Smith's candidate lacked. It is still standing. Or perhaps when Wayne made his rumored secret visit to Winterset, he was a phantom Iowan visiting a phantom home.

Clyde Morrison went to work in 1906 at M. E. Smith's Drug Store, whose ads ran to items like this: "Foley's Kidney Cure . . . Take it at once, Do not risk having Bright's Disease or Diabetes . . . 50¢ and $1.00 Bottle, Refuse Substitutes."[13] Clyde proved no more successful at holding a job than at staying on the first string at Simpson. By 1909, he was a drug clerk in another Iowa town (Brooklyn).[14] A year after that, Clyde used some family money to buy a Rexall store in Earlham, a store which folded in a year. This was the place that sold paint and wallpaper—the kind of thing he was selling, a year later, at a general store in Keokuk.[15] In 1913, having exhausted the possibilities of pharmacies and of Iowa, Clyde went to California where his father had preceded him. In 1914, Clyde's wife and two sons joined him there. The future Wayne was seven, and had already lived in four different Iowa towns. No wonder his recollections of the state were vague to nonexistent. In his aborted autobiography, he says that his younger brother ("Bobby") was born in Winterset, though he was actually born two towns later (in Earlham).[16]

The Morrison family had been unhappy in Iowa, and would become unhappier still in California, where Marion was now old enough to hear more of his parents' quarrelings. Clyde, with his unfailing gift for failure, made two reckless decisions—a) to become, with no experience, a farmer, and b) to do his farming in Antelope Valley. The Valley is an arid basin just over the coastal range of California mountains north of Los Angeles. Other Iowans went to lush fruit fields or seaside views. Clyde contrived to find a desert in the garden, one sealed off from verdure and the ocean.

It was a terrible place for crops, but ideal for playing cowboy, if Wayne had wanted to. In fact, he would come back, in his B Western days, to ride this arid strip of land. Newhall, in the coastal foothills overlooking the valley, was a favorite spot for film-makers like W. S. Hart (who built his home there), Harry Carey, and John Ford (who, at age nineteen, arrived in California the same year Wayne did).

But Wayne hated this first exposure to "the Old West"—to its gas lighting (electricity had not come to the Valley by 1914), its outdoor johns, its swarming jackrabbits (which ate the thin crops his father was able to coax from the soil), its rattlesnakes (they would always scare him), and the bony horse he rode from the farm to school in a nearby town (Lancaster).[17] When Wayne was asked, in 1974, to contribute to an anniversary publication in Lancaster, he did not send the usual warm reveries of childhood. He wrote:

> I had to ride to school on horseback. The horse developed a disease that kept it skinny. We finally had to destroy it but the nosey biddies of the town called the humane society and accused me, a 7 year old, of not feeding my horse and watering him. This was proven in time to be a lie. I think it was occasioned by the fact that I had allowed a boy even younger than myself to ride him the full length of the town—from one telephone pole to the next—and he fell off the horse, which did not upset him but it upset the dear ladies of Lancaster.[18]

Wayne's lasting hatred of horses seems to have begun here, along with unpleasant memories about everything connected with his father's farm. That small house without electric lights was racked by the torments his mother inflicted on his father (sometimes abetted by her visiting parents).

Luckily, Clyde could not keep at anything for long. When Wayne was nine, Clyde went to work again in a pharmacy, this time in Glendale, the largest city Wayne had yet lived in. With seven thousand inhabitants in 1916, Glendale was a booming

suburb of Los Angeles.¹⁹ Like Wayne at this point, the city had
no fondness for raw frontiers. The mansions and movie palaces
it was putting up had classical façades. At its high school, the
boys wore ties and jackets, the girls wore skirts and Navy-style
blouses with collar-sashes tied in front.²⁰ Community spirit
multiplied institutions, and Wayne was soon joining all those
available to him—the Boy Scouts, the YMCA, the Masonic youth
fraternity (DeMolay).²¹

Glendale had an airplane landing strip and a rail stop that
directors from nearby Hollywood used for things like Fatty Arbuckle comedies. Douglas Fairbanks came over to shoot a woodland scene for *Robin Hood*.²² Several small companies set up
their own studios in the town, where the Kalem company made
a very popular serial called *The Hazards of Helen,* starring Helen
Holmes, a chubby but athletic twenty-two-year-old when she
began the serial's nineteen episodes. In the tapes for his autobiography, Wayne claimed he saw the imperiled Holmes doing her
stunts and fell in love with her. But the nine-year-old Wayne
arrived in Glendale a year after she had completed the serial and
left Kalem.²³

Wayne would see many other films made on the lots and
streets of Glendale. The newspaper publicized events to be filmed
—a balloon lift, an air "dogfight," a crowd scene needing extras.²⁴
It is not surprising that Wayne became very active in the Glendale High dramatic society. Two of his friends in Glendale, Bob
and Bill Bradbury, were already starring in their father's commercial shorts, *The Adventures of Bob and Bill.* Bill played football with Wayne. Bob, who was rather small for football,
changed his name to Bob Steele when, later on, he became a
cowboy star. His father, the elder Robert Bradbury, would direct
Wayne himself in a dozen B Westerns. One early Bradbury project, *Davy Crockett at the Alamo* (1926), may have interested
Wayne in a special way, since his friend Bob had a good part in
it. This was a giddy social world for Wayne to enter, after isolation in the dark farm near Lancaster, where he had no company
but embattled elders. At last he could begin making an impression on his peers.

Though young Marion Morrison blossomed in Glendale,
Clyde shifted about with his normal fecklessness. Wayne lived in
five different Glendale houses during his nine years there. It was
in Glendale that his parents finally divorced, just after he left
Glendale High. Mary (Molly) Brown Morrison was exasperated

by failure, and kept reminding Clyde of that fact. Each boy sided
with the parent he did not resemble. Molly, the driven parent,
was lean-featured (vaguely vulpine) like her older son, who
shared her ambition and will to succeed. Clyde, round-faced, an
easygoing drifter, passed on his looks and character to Bobby.

Yet Bobby was always Molly's favorite child, and Marion
kept finding excuses for Clyde, the old "football hero." Defending
the indefensible made Wayne even less sympathetic toward his
nagging mother. It made things worse for him to know, deep
down, that she was right. Wayne did not like to speak to outsid-
ers of what went on in his family, but he put in his projected
autobiography this judgment: "I had grown up in a house of
petty bickering."[25] Wayne's estimate of his own family can be
seen in the family choices he made for himself. Wayne sought
out women (including all three of his wives) who came from the
macho Latin culture of supportive (if not downright submissive)
women. Wayne's father was a dreamy nonachiever, and Wayne
idolized John Ford ("the finest relationship in my life"), a hard
taskmaster and ruthless professional.[26] "Wayne was like a kid
around John Ford," Richard Widmark says.[27] He was not a kid
with his own father. With Clyde, he was a pal. When his parents
squabbled, Wayne got out of the house—to work or to school
activities by day, to male social groups (Scouts, YMCA, DeMolay)
by night. It set a pattern his wives criticized later on, Wayne's
urge to be "out with the boys" (on Ford's or his own boat, at
meetings of the clubs he formed with other members of the Ford
circle). Ford was another truant from his own home, and Wayne
would be glad to trail behind him.

Not that Wayne was sowing wild oats in Glendale. He later
told stories that portrayed him as a Peck's bad boy. But reminiscences and the ample record of his busy life tell a different story.
The groups he first joined were still energetically religious and
patriotic in 1916—all three professed a brand of "muscular
Christianity." Wayne worked at odd jobs and delivered newspapers. In school, he earned good grades and was salutatorian
when he graduated from junior high school. His teachers remember him as courteous and nonflamboyant, despite his striking good looks and the height to which he shot up in his teens.

Delivered from the nightmare time in Antelope Valley, where
he was the unwilling auditor of his mother's accusations and his
father's evasions, Wayne rushed out toward Glendale's opportu-
nities. At a time when other children are trying to "break out,"

he was trying to break in—to get inside some larger, if more constraining (more supportive), social order. That is obvious in the flurry of activities he undertook. He was a superachiever, a model student. His popularity redeemed the loneliness of the past, all those moves and cover stories and pretenses that things were well at home. Aristotle calls the man without society a game-piece without a game.[28] In Glendale, Wayne discovered his game board and moved happily around on it.

At Glendale High, which he attended between 1921 and 1925, Wayne was class vice president in his sophomore and junior years, and president as a senior. He was star guard on the football team, sportswriter on the school paper, actor and crew member in the dramatic society, a staffer on several social committees. He was also an honor student and the school's representative to the Southern California Shakespeare Contest.[29]

His Shakespeare performance may amuse those who think Wayne could only drawl, "Waa-al, *pilgrim.*" But Wayne had not yet learned to be "Wayne." He was still becoming a confident Marion Morrison. He delivered Cardinal Wolsey's famous speech from *Henry VIII.*[30] Back on campus, he played an English nobleman (a different kind of "Duke") in *The First Lady of the Land* and an old man in *Dulcey* (for *Dulcinea*). A yearbook picture of him in the former role shows him standing with eighteenth-century frills of lace at his wrists and neck ("Never before has a class put over such a spectacular and finished performance").[31] Already, in pictures of the stage crew, Wayne strikes the sinuous pose of later years.[32] For the annual football "fashion show" he appeared as a long-haired and bespectacled nerd in his junior year, and every player came in drag for the senior year.[33]

In football, Wayne did not play end or in the backfield because, well coordinated though he was, he was slow—slow but unstoppable against smaller high school boys ("Morrison battered great holes through the line").[34] In the movies, he would compensate for slowness by the economy of his moves, giving them energy by his focus. In his sophomore football picture, he looked like a starving refugee, so thin was he. But already by his junior year he has acquired the familiar adult face—one that would not change very much for the next two decades.[35] In appearance, anyway, he was already the Ringo Kid.

Not that he aspired to be a cowboy, to ride over dry tracts like those of Antelope Valley. His high grades made it reasonable for him to aspire toward law school. The only obstacle to that was money. Clyde had none. But a football scholarship with the prestigious University of Southern California team removed that barrier. After a miserable childhood, Wayne had been given a glorious adolescence. Good things were showering down on him. Even his parents' divorce in his first year at college seemed less a tragedy than the resolution of one.

At USC, across Los Angeles from Glendale, Wayne's luck held at first. He had to work in the fraternities to supplement his scholarship money, but he loved fraternity life and was pledged in Sigma Chi, another male club. He made his letter on the freshman team and was ready to move up onto the team coached by the legendary Howard Jones. But his one year under Jones was not successful. He lost his place on the team, and with it his scholarship. That ended his college days. He later said an injury disqualified him—in the most common but not the only version, a body-surfing blow to his shoulder.[36] But injuries (Wayne was not hurt for long) do not make a good coach drop a truly promising sophomore. By what would have been his senior year, Wayne was moving heavy properties around on the Fox set and doing risky stunt work. The real reason for Wayne's dismissal from the football team can be inferred from the football programs of 1926. Jones had moved Wayne from guard to tackle—guards had to be fast enough to "pull" and act as interference in running games like Jones's. And even at tackle Wayne stood at the bottom of a long list of talent.

The lack of speed that had kept him out of the high school backfield kept him off Jones's rapid line. At the beginning of Wayne's first and last year on the varsity, a fellow sophomore is listed as one of the two starting tackles, followed by a list of five others aspiring to the position. Wayne, placed last of these seven, is not mentioned as a player in the game accounts.[37] It is significant that on the tapes for his autobiography, Wayne falsely remembers his USC position as "running guard."[38] *Guard* is the position he played successfully at Glendale High, and *running* interference is the reason he was not really useful to Jones. In the USC program for his one season under Jones, he was actually a tackle. Wayne's football legend came to resemble his father's. Clyde was remembered as "all-state" tackle (though he played halfback). Alumni from Wayne's time would spread the tale that he was on his way to becoming an All-American until he was injured.[39]

In 1927, when he left USC, Wayne was no star, though football players mingled with the movie stars who came to their games and offered them bit parts in their movies. Wayne claimed that he was part of this celebrity world, telling a dubious story that cowboy star Tom Mix offered him a job as his personal trainer.[40] The truth is that Wayne spent two years doing physical tasks at Fox Studios, moving property equipment, appearing as an extra when one was needed. He had two small speaking parts in Ford films—*Salute* (1929), which had Ward Bond in a bigger (though still small) role, and *Men Without Women* (1930)—but there was no sign that Ford was getting ready to use Wayne (who was still Morrison, of course) in a serious way.

It was Raoul Walsh who looked at Wayne's graceful body, when Wayne was doing property work in 1929, and decided, on the spot, to make him a star. Walsh was the one who changed his name, erasing a whole history that belonged to Marion Morrison. The man who hated horses would finally be taught to ride. (Walsh, a fine rider himself, gave Wayne an Indian slouch in the saddle he would later have to get rid of.) The reciter of Shakespeare was taught to make graceful signs to communicate with Indians. Suit and tie were shed, for buckskins and moccasins. A classic Hollywood makeover was being done on Morrison/ Wayne. "Let your hair grow long," Walsh told him.

Wayne was ready for this break in 1929. He had, now, no more reason to return to Glendale than to Winterset. Glendale residents would later wonder why he never came back, from next-door Los Angeles, to see his old school, his last "hometown."[41] But the hopes of Glendale had been shattered at USC. He was truly without a past, a man from nowhere. That was the proper background for the persona being forged by Walsh. Walsh liked to think of himself as blending a fictive world of the old frontier (where he had been a cowboy) with the male world of Hollywood playboys (including Walsh's playmates, "Jack" Barrymore and Errol Flynn). He saw that Wayne could be processed to fit this fictive world. Marion Morrison had come out of nowhere and, as John Wayne, was riding into Never-Never Land.

□ 2 □
RAOUL WALSH

By the 1950s, John Ford was saying that he "discovered" John Wayne. It is not the only achievement of Raoul Walsh, his fellow director at Fox, that Ford tried to appropriate. Ford claimed to have been a cowboy on his way out West before he reached Hollywood; but Walsh had in fact ridden herds in Mexico. Ford, who idolized D. W. Griffith, claimed to have acted (behind a Klan mask) in *The Birth of a Nation;* Walsh played John Wilkes Booth in that movie, with his face fully exposed. Ford boasted that he knew authentic heroes and bad men from the Old West (he, like many, had talked with Wyatt Earp in the latter's Hollywood days). But Walsh, for a Griffith production, had gone to negotiate with and film Pancho Villa during the Mexican Revolution.[1]

Harry Carey, Jr., thinks "Walsh was the kind of guy Ford admired"—a "man's man," a wit and practical joker, a heterosexual swashbuckler. "He showed up on the set every day with a gorgeous blonde," says Carey, who acted in Walsh's *Pursued* (1947).[2] "While the scene was being filmed, Walsh would casually roll his own little cigarettes from a Bull Durham bag." After he lost one eye in 1929, Walsh made even his eye patch a mark of distinction. Ford, who never lost an eye but whose eyes had a great sensitivity to light, wore dark glasses early in his career, but later adopted an eye patch, which he used to great dramatic effect—flipping it up to look at things close at hand, flipping it down when he wanted to see no more of someone. Carey says he was "mysterious with the patch—he loved that patch."[3]

46

Walsh was eight years Ford's senior, old enough to join Griffith at his peak. But by the twenties both men were making films at the same studio—Ford often did "homey" subjects as well as Westerns, while Walsh tended more to big action features (war films, Westerns, exotic tales like the Doug Fairbanks [Senior] *Thief of Bagdad* in 1924). Ford filmed some second-unit scenes for Walsh's 1926 war hit, *What Price Glory?*[4]

Both men paid more attention to their actors than to their actresses, but they had different ideals of male beauty. Ford, especially in the 1920s, favored brawny types, like George O'Brien, a weightlifter who posed for muscular nude shots. Ford often stripped O'Brien's shirt away at the climax of the action. The fight that ends *The Iron Horse* is a good example. He also took off the young Victor McLaglen's shirt *(The Black Watch, The Lost Patrol)*. When Ford used some USC football players for the 1929 movie *Salute,* he focused on the beefy Ward Bond, not the still-willowy Marion Morrison. Harry Carey (Senior) and Joe Harris, who had worked with Ford in his silent days, speculated about the "crushes" he formed for various beefcakes.[5] Ford even took George O'Brien with him on a South Sea island cruise, giving him the ticket he had bought for his wife—much to that wife's disgust.[6] This sudden decision—it was made the day before the scheduled departure—reflected Ford's panic whenever he had to leave an enclave of male control (his own set, his own boat, his club, the Navy, the veterans' retreat house he founded). Those were the times when he drank heavily.

Walsh, by contrast, liked the "Latin" male sometimes ridiculed in the twenties as a "lounge lizard," the Valentino type. He wrote the first "Cisco Kid" movie in 1929, and cast himself as the hero—he thought of himself as "Latin" because his mother had some Spanish blood.[7] He redeemed the denigrative term for a Mexican in his movie *Greaser* (1915). When he directed Douglas Fairbanks in *The Thief of Bagdad,* he made the leading man's performance one long ballet of lifted arms and slow turns, though Fairbanks in other films (e.g., *The Mark of Zorro*) went bounding around like an India-Rubber Man. Walsh cast his brother George in a number of films meant to give him a "Doug Fairbanks image."[8]

Walsh's most popular film of the late twenties, *What Price Glory?,* was built on the contrast of two male types in the Marines—the toughie against the smoothie, "Flagg" against "Quirt."[9] This was typical of Walsh's films.[10]

The male-female relationship was less interesting than the contrast in styles of the male wooers. That is why Flagg and Quirt go from woman to woman in their competitive relationship, maintaining the contest while its objects shift and disappear. The male contrast Walsh worked with was not always of brawn against brains. Sometimes it was a clash of the "natural" man with "the sophisticate." That is what Walsh had in mind for his Wayne character in *The Big Trail*. Wayne plays a scout, a person attuned to nature, who competes for the woman (Marguerite Churchill) with a slick but crooked gambler (Ian Keith). But in this saga of a wagon train going to Oregon, a larger social scene had to be suggested. As in his war films, Walsh created a *range* of contrasting male types (earthy sidekick, henpecked husband, stoical father, etc.) but with the emphasis on three towering figures—the scout, the gambler, and a huge villainous "bull whacker" (leader of the bull-drawn wagons).

In this trio, the brains-vs.-brawn contrast lies in the nefarious alliance of the smart gambler and the rough bull whacker. The latter is played by Tyrone Power (Senior) hunched inside a shabby buffalo coat, from which his basso profundo grunts come like the roars of a bear from its cave. Ian Keith, as the gambler, is a deft suitor of Marguerite Churchill, and a keen plotter against Wayne. But Wayne, slim in his light buckskins, eludes the wily Keith as easily as he foils the hirsute Power. Keith stalks Wayne cautiously; Power gropes and lumbers; Wayne glides. The *pictorial* interplay of the three is at the heart of the film. That explains why Walsh was so quick to promote an untried furniture mover to the starring role. Wayne looked right; he moved right; he offered just the visual contrast with the other characters that Walsh desired. Sound had just come to Hollywood in 1929; but Walsh was trained in the silent era, and still thought more in pictures than in words.

When Wayne shows his strength, in the early scene, by lifting a girl by her elbows and turning her around in midair, the point is not that he is strong—Power looks even stronger in a loutish way—but that he is *gracefully* strong. Power blocks the flow of things. He is a predator on man and nature, one who stole the trapped skins of Wayne's friend. Wayne works with the rhythms of nature. Power is buttressed with a hedge of dead fur; Wayne wears Indian garb as if it were his own skin. Wayne has no boots or gun belt or hat—just a knife tucked into his waistband. Moccasined, bareheaded even in the snow, he is a nearly naked Adam of the new Western Eden.

The gambler is graceful, but not strong; and his grace is perverted to sneakiness (he tries to shoot Wayne from ambush). Wayne, natural, open, has no need for artifice or subterfuge. He combines the best qualities of his two rivals, and defeats the worst qualities. Outnumbered by them, he slithers through their grasp. It is a dance of combat where the weaker but nimbler wins: David against *two* Goliaths.

Walsh imposed this version of differing masculine styles on a huge and unwieldy epic. The studio had bought a *Saturday Evening Post* story, by Hal Evarts, about a buffalo hunt ("The Shaggy Legion"). Walsh had something quite different in mind —the first "trek westward" movie to repeat in sound the silent triumphs of *Covered Wagon* (1923) and *The Iron Horse* (1924). Though he took the hard-drinking Evarts along with him to re-write dialogue, that author's main product was a "log" of the production written for publicity purposes.[11] Walsh made his script up as he went along, modeling himself on the silent epics, which had told the story of the Mormons' westward migration (James Cruze's *Covered Wagon*) or the railroads' surge across the continent (John Ford's *The Iron Horse*). This kind of migration movie, done on a large scale against authentic landscapes, had by 1929 attained a canonical form, one that includes eight elements.

1. *Social diversity*. Since the aim is to show a whole people on the move, not just a few trappers, scouts, cavalrymen, or gunfighters, the film gives a prominent place to women and children. Since the myth of the frontier forbids division by *class*, social diversity is achieved by including different ethnic types (which become stereotypes). In *Covered Wagon*, there is a Jewish tailor treated with a condescension typical of the time. In *The Iron Horse*, Irishman John Ford lets his Irish workers mock lazy and gluttonous Italians. In *The Big Trail*, a Swede (Ed Brendel) does endless vaudeville routines about his bossy mother-in-law.

2. *Temporal extension*. The vertical layering of social types is balanced with a horizontal expansion through time, signaled by changing seasons, altered human relations, births along the way, deaths and burials. This sets the migration movie apart from the "ship of fools" conjunction of people on a short cruise, or trip, or holiday. In *The Big Trail*, the heroine conducts a school for her young sister, making life as "ordinary" as possible in the hard conditions of migration. The message is: "Life goes on, even in these trials."

3. *Physical obstacle course*. This is the excuse for the am-

bitious outdoor photography in these films—spectacularly achieved by cameramen Karl Brown *(The Covered Wagon)*, George Schneiderman *(The Iron Horse)*, and Arthur Edeson *(The Big Trail)*. [12] Storms, river crossings, extremes of heat and/or cold, failed supplies—all these test the endurance and temper of the migrants. Walsh outdid his predecessors with a huge wide-screen lowering of wagons and bulls (in slings) down a sheer cliff face.

4. *External opponents.* Indians must be fought in both the silent films. Walsh, however, *prevents* Indian attack by sending out the pacific scout Wayne. In his early travels, Wayne's character has achieved a peace with the land that makes him share the Indian's respect for nature. When the children of the wagon train ask if he has killed an Indian, he answers:

> You see, the Indian was my friend. They taught me all I know about the woods. They taught me how to follow a trail by watching the leaves, how to cut your mark on a tree so you won't get lost in the forest, and they taught me how to burrow in the snow so you won't freeze to death in a storm, and they taught me how to make a fire without even a flint. And they taught me how to make the best bow and arrow.

Wayne carries no pistol. Though he never uses a bow, we are made to understand that he can and has. For him, even the external threats of nature (snow) can be used as protection. Wayne's hero is in the tradition of Fenimore Cooper's Hawkeye, a between-cultures figure, one who wants to cooperate with nature and the Indians, not exploit and displace. But, like Hawkeye, he draws corrupt white elements in his train, along with the nobler settlers.

5. *Internal opponents.* There are saboteurs in the migrating band, trying to cheat their own kind, prevent completion of the journey, or seize control of the train for selfish purposes. In *The Big Trail*, the gambler and the bull whacker collaborate in several attempts on Wayne's life, to prevent the mission of the wagon train.

6. *Separation of the hero from the train.* The combination of external and internal threats draws the hero away from the train, damaging morale and breaking off the love affair with the heroine. In Walsh's movie, Wayne's missions to the Indians leave the wagon train prey to faltering resolve.

7. *The crisis.* Attrition and opposition finally break the spirit of the adventurers, and they begin to turn back or turn aside (to a gold rush rather than their distant farmlands). The hero must come to the rescue. Wayne arrives back as the wagons are stalled in a snowstorm and the leaders are calling it quits. He rallies them with a call to higher responsibilities.

8. *The higher goal.* In order to press on through every obstacle, it is not enough to hope for gain. The hero must articulate some altruistic motive for persistence. In *The Covered Wagon* it is the Mormon hope of establishing a heavenly community. In *The Iron Horse,* it is a Lincolnian vision of national union, tying East and West together by rail as Lincoln had preserved the union of North and South by warfare.[13] The higher goal Wayne offers in his snowstorm speech, shouted through the wind, is the European race's manifest destiny, its "civilizing" imperialism:

> We're blazing a trail that started in England. Not even the storms of the sea could turn back those first settlers. And they carried on further. They blazed it on through the wilderness of Kentucky. Famine, hunger, not even massacres could stop them! And now we've picked up the trail again. And nothing can stop us—not even the snows of winter, not the peaks of the highest mountains. We're building a nation!

Walsh improves on his predecessors in every category of this genre. His visual effects are more stunning, his villains more menacing, his humor less racist (though still lame), his treatment of Indians more nuanced, his heroine more beautiful and skilled as an actress, and his hero far more convincing than either Cruze's J. Warren Kerrigan or Ford's George O'Brien.

All this was accomplished under truly harrowing conditions. The crew and equipment, the cumbersome wagons and bulls, covered almost as much territory as the party it was portraying —from Yuma, Arizona, through sites in Utah, Wyoming, and Montana, reaching a grand climax in Sequoia National Park. Not only was Walsh doing a pioneer sound Western outdoors, he was supervising three different camera teams—one filming in 70mm, one in 35mm, and one with German speakers for foreign exhibition. Logistics, equipment failure, squabbling extras, drunks, and lecherous principals—all added to the stress of this grand-scale project.[14] Walsh said that Wayne, the newcomer, was the most professional person in the cast, the one he could rely on not to be drunk, womanizing, or lazy. He was ready to lend his great strength to difficult physical sequences (he was, after all, a trained mover of prop equipment). "I had found a leader."[15]

It is true that Wayne delivers some of his lines in a stilted way—as many did in those early sound efforts. But his moments of comic ineptness come when he is given terrible lines, lines any actor would find it hard to deliver convincingly. Praising the valley the settlers want to reach, Wayne says *"Fish,* you ask, and *game?"* Dialogue writing had not entirely escaped the style of intertitles in 1929.

One reason for Wayne's stiffness is that he had four major speeches to deliver stock still in the great outdoors, since he could not move away from the primitive mike emplacements.[16] For the most part, Wayne's lack of polish adds to the effect Walsh was aiming at. Though the scout can banter with the heroine, he is also quickly embarrassed by her. When he kisses her by mistake and she sweeps out of the room into the yard, he skips comically out in front of her, trying to explain, unable to stop her as she swerves this way and that to avoid him. Wayne makes a flighty series of moves, too vulnerable and undignified for the later Wayne, but entirely winning in this scene.

Wayne's ease with the villains and shyness with "the girl" helps Walsh achieve his most important effect in this movie. Though the Wayne character gives an imperial justification for the westward migration, his own motives are pure. When the heroine asks Wayne if he is not afraid to go west into the wilderness, with no one beside him, he says that he is only at peace out under the stars. They keep watch over him. Wayne expresses a nature mysticism that is the true religion of the West, the yearning gaze westward of the transcendentalists. He describes the "trees out there, big tall pines, just a-reachin' and reachin' as if they wanted to climb right through the gates of heaven."

As the train nears its chosen valley, Wayne leaves it to hunt down the fleeing bull whacker. Once again the heroine is afraid for him, clinging to the wagon train, unable to imagine going off into the wilderness. But after the settlers have been in their valley for a season, Wayne's comic sidekick hears his friend's bird call from far off. He sends the heroine to find a "surprise" he has planted in the trees. She is unafraid now, though dwarfed by the huge sequoias. Picking her way into the shadows they cast, the filigree of light they weave, she sees Wayne's twinkling motion in the depths of the glen, his white buckskins glowing in the intervals of light as he climbs a rise. The lovers come together silently, then the broad-spanned 70mm camera moves up the apparently endless trunks of the trees. This is as close as the worldly Walsh ever came to spiritual vision in his work. It is the seal on a forgotten masterpiece.

Why was such a stunning film forgotten? It was hit by a series of crippling blows—to the national economy (1929 was the year of the Crash), to the movie business in general, to William Fox specifically (he went into bankruptcy), to Fox Studios (which went into receivership), to Fox actors (who faced reduced film production and unrenewed contracts).[17] The very thing Fox had gambled on to save his teetering business—the multiple project of *The Big Trail*'s simultaneous domestic/foreign, 70mm/35mm production—helped push the whole parent enterprise over the brink. Because of the Depression's arrival, theaters already converting to sound had no money for the further adaptation to 70mm technology. Only two movie houses showed the picture in its intended form—the Roxy in New York, Grauman's Chinese in Los Angeles. Others played the inferior 35mm version shot by Lucien Andriot, not the cinematographic tour de force of Arthur Edeson. Film scholars in later years saw mainly the Edeson version cropped on both sides, the worst of both worlds. Not until the 1990s did the Museum of Modern Art restore the film to its pristine form and brilliance. It has to be seen on the big screen there to make its intended impact—which is overwhelming.

In the accounts of Wayne's career, there was a special reason to downplay *The Big Trail*. After the myth of Ford's importance to his career was entrenched, the orthodox view became that Walsh had used Wayne before he was ready, that Ford watched his faltering efforts until he saw that he had matured enough to be used in a major role—nine years after *The Big Trail*. It was assumed, by many who had never seen the movie, or seen it in a decent print, that Wayne failed here because of his performance.

But Marguerite Churchill, a haunting beauty whose performance is flawless, also failed to become a star after doing *The Big Trail*. The studio was struggling to survive; it could afford no strategy to develop promising actors. Churchill, like Wayne, was shoved into small roles. Fox, in its nosedive, had to jettison players without any nice calculations of their future promise. The present was all that mattered. There might be no future. *The Big Trail* was a bad memory. Having had any part in it was no recommendation. This was the movie that helped break the company. For a while, too, it broke Wayne's career.

□ 3 □
YEARS WITH YAK

THE GENERAL VIEW is that movies flourished during the Depression—and, after many adjustments, they did. But the initial impact was devastating. Four thousand theaters were closed in 1931 and 1932. Workers in surviving theaters were cut back— 43,000 were out of jobs at the exhibition end of the industry. Back at the studios, there was a 20 percent layoff of personnel. Those who stayed had their wages cut (extras went from $2.00 a day to $1.25). Theater attendance fell 12 percent despite a 30 percent cut in ticket prices.[1]

This was the climate in which Wayne had to find his way after Fox lost its gamble on *The Big Trail*. Fox had to keep making movies, in the hope of scraping through; but it made them as cheaply and quickly as possible, to get some product out as the other studios' output was shrinking. Wayne was thrown into two cheap movies of this sort before his contract was up for renewal. Inevitably, the contract was not renewed.[2]

Some have wondered why Ford, who was still at Fox and was supposed to be Wayne's patron, could not find something for him to do. But Ford himself was loaned out in 1931 to MGM, the only major studio still doing well (thanks to the strength of its parent company, Loew's, and its efficiently run theater chain). Ford was to make *Arrowsmith* at MGM; but when he failed to finish the movie, the financially struggling Fox had to give back $4,100 of the fee MGM was paying for his services. Fox fired Ford in December of 1931. Far from being in a position to help

55

Wayne, Ford needed help himself. His agent had to scramble to get him accepted back in April of 1932, under humiliating conditions (no script approval).[3] Everyone at Fox was in trouble.

Other majors were in no condition to hire actors still making their way, so Wayne had to go downscale. The minor studios were profiting from the trouble of the majors. Fewer A pictures meant a greater demand for B pictures economically produced. Theaters were running more double features to make people feel they got their hard-held money's worth. Doubling the product meant diluting quality. The pressing need was for seven hundred features a year.[4]

Below the "Big Five" major studios were the "Little Three" minors—Columbia, Universal, and United Artists. Wayne went in 1931 to the most productive of the three, Columbia, run by the gleeful cost-cutter Harry Cohn, whose creed, as he later voiced it, was already in place:

> Every Friday the front door opens and I spit a movie out into Gower Street. . . . I want one good picture a year [usually made by Frank Capra]. That's my policy. . . . And I won't let an exhibitor have it unless he takes the bread-and-butter product, the Boston Blackies, the Blondies, the low-budget Westerns and the rest of the junk we make.[5]

Wayne was picked up to make the junk, playing second banana to Cohn's fading Western stars Buck Jones, Tim McCoy, and Jack Holt. After a year of work on various quickies, Wayne's contract, renewable every six months, was dropped. He later said Cohn hated him for wooing an actress Cohn wanted—everyone who worked for the hated "King" Cohn had to have a story of personal enmity.[6] But Wayne had little to offer Cohn, whose interest in his budget exceeded even his interest in the bedroom. The fresh-faced young Wayne was taller and handsomer than the aging Western stars. He was no more stilted in his acting than these veterans of the silent era, who had been hired in the first place for their horsemanship. But the old guys still had name recognition and nostalgic audiences. They were realistic about what they had to do (and what they could get) in this minor market. Wayne got in the way of such geriatric, but still marginally profitable, exercises. He had to go, and would have gone, actress or no actress.

From major to minor, and now (in 1932) from minors to "poverty row," to the specializers in lowest-budget films. They,

YEARS WITH YAK   57

too, had profited by the troubles of their betters. Wayne went to Mascot, a studio that cranked out serials on a production line. Serials, called "chapter plays," had been popular in the twenties, when Frank Ford, John's older brother, made a successful run of them (starring his wife, Grace Cunard). But the luxury of the twenties became a necessity of the thirties, as quantity replaced quality in the theaters. Serials were added to double features, just as china giveaways and "bank night" lotteries were thrown in—anything to lure back the small spenders who made up the mass of moviegoers.[7]

Nat Levine presided over the serials operation at Mascot.[8] He had two crews working simultaneously. His veterans could do several tasks in those weak-union days. His stunt organizer, Yakima Canutt, could also act, double other actors, or direct a scene while the nominal director was elsewhere. The whole thing was a race against the clock, since time was money and projection rooms were clamoring for the next "chapter." It was physically grueling work, but Wayne was young and strong. He made three Mascot serials—thirty-six episodes—in a little over a year.[9]

At least he was being paid, in the worst of the Depression. There was little else of value to the experience. The episodes' breathless race from crisis to crisis left no time to develop character, make an impression, achieve anything subtle. For Wayne, whose power came from understatement and slow purposefulness, the frenetic pace, the silly reaction to new threats every two seconds, was frustrating. He built so little box-office appeal in the format that, though he stayed in the lead role, he was billed sixth in the third film's promotion.

In 1933, Wayne got back into the majors (Warner Brothers) —but only into the basement, and by way of a back door. Warner's, whose A product was itself comparatively low-budget (crime films, sub-MGM musicals), had to make even lower-scale films to keep going in 1933. Since the studio owned old silent Westerns starring Ken Maynard, it decided to redo those stories in sound, using stock footage of Maynard's trick rides on his superb horse, Tarzan. All that was needed was a large handsome horse that resembled Tarzan and a large handsome man to resemble Maynard.

Thus was born the "Four Star" series of films that opened with a close-up of John Wayne, the horse-hater, nuzzling his "wonder horse," Duke. Wayne had become Duke, as a boy, because he had a dog of that name; now, cast as "John," he passed the other name off to an animal. Since the original silent films had some interesting plot turns, these films were a step up for Wayne from Mascot (anything would have been). But he and his horse were pale imitations of the first electric pairing of "Ken and Tarzan."[10]

Wayne had to drop back into poverty row by 1934—this time to Monogram, where a little ensemble group made the most watchable of all Wayne's B Westerns. Much of the credit for this goes to Archie Stout, the cameraman who had worked with DeMille on *The Ten Commandments* (1923) and would win an Oscar for his work on *The Quiet Man* (1952). Like many people in these early days of the Depression, when there were too few A movies to work on, Stout was reduced to making B films; but he did so with distinctive touches—sparkling river crossings, latticed shadows in the woods, horses drawn at odd angles across a hillside. Wayne's later B Westerns for Republic usually get more attention, since they had higher budgets, better "production values." But they are visually less interesting than Stout's Monogram films.[11]

The third member of the ensemble team (after Wayne and Stout) was Robert North Bradbury, the father of Wayne's Glendale friends, Bob (Steele) and Bill. Bradbury, the man who made the 1926 Alamo film, created his own stories for the Western series. The plots were tailored to the skills of his actors and the locales available. They stay within convention, but with some ingenuity. The basic device is mistaken identity. Wayne comes into a community as a stranger. He is taken for another man, or pretends to be another man, in order to infiltrate the "gang" or expose a "respectable" person. Though the heroine is torn by suspicion that Wayne is a criminal, he cannot tell her the truth. The climax unmasks the real villain and vindicates Wayne. This is an Ur-plot, abounding in Aristotle's favorite devices, "recognitions" and "reversals." What varies in it are the stunts, heroines (they come and go while the male cast is stable), and different locales (mines, ranches, forests, rivers, etc.).

The heroine's father—or the sheriff, or a judge—is usually George Hayes, the fourth member of the ensemble. He would later be "Gabby" Hayes, the old-coot sidekick to cowboys like Roy Rogers; but in this series he is more dignified and not an appendage to the hero (Wayne is mercifully without a "sidekick" in these movies).

The fifth member of the series usually played the villain (or, more often, the villain's henchman). But he was much more. He conceived the action sequences, since he alone knew what he and others could do with the properties and sites given him. Yakima ("Yak") Canutt was the genius who created modern stunt work as a profession. He was a hero to Wayne, a mentor, a model of professionalism and male pride without swagger. Canutt and Wayne had worked together on the Mascot series, but the hectic pace of those episodes had not given them the time to become intimate co-workers as they were for Monogram.

The best place for us to meet Canutt is in one of the Warner's Westerns he made with Wayne in 1933, *The Telegraph Trail*. A Ken Maynard remake, this film tells the story of telegraph wires being strung through hostile Indian territory. The leader of the Indians is Yak, riding bareback and wearing only a loincloth (front and back panels on a thong). It is one of the few times he bares any part of his body, and the muscular frame shows why he impressed other athletes. Not even Cliff Lyons, whom Yak trained as his helper and successor, dared to take on Yak, though Lyons fought at the drop of a hat with anyone else.[12] In a world of tough men, he was the epitome of toughness. It radiated from him. In Wayne's autobiographical tapes he explained Yak's influence on him:

> I spent weeks studying the way Yakima Canutt walked and talked. He was a real cowhand. I noticed that the angrier he got, the lower his voice, the slower his tempo. I try to say my lines low and strong and slow, the way Yak did.[13]

Canutt won the world rodeo championship three years in a row. His real name was Enos, but he came from near Yakima, Washington, so a sportswriter gave him his nickname on the rodeo circuit.[14] When Canutt was inducted into the Cowboy Hall of Fame, so was Tipperary, a horse that had thrown eighty other men—until Yak became the first to ride him.[15] Yak was the only man who could perform horse tricks harder than Maynard's.[16] It was said that he could do anything with a horse. Some thought he could do anything, period.

In the Bradbury-Stout films for Monogram, there is a great moment one waits for when, all of a sudden, Wayne takes wing and does something impossible—comes out of a saloon, hops with one foot onto the horse rail, with the other foot onto the back of a horse, then flies over that horse into a farther one's saddle. Or he runs toward a horse like a high jumper approaching the pole and then—leaning back as he leaps, with a scissors-spread of his legs—throws his right leg over the saddle, gets his left hand on the saddle horn, and is seated upright as he lands.[17] It is not Wayne, of course, but Yak doubling Wayne.

Wayne and Yak formed such a partnership in this series as to blur their identities. Yak, as the villain, fights Wayne; but if Wayne takes a dangerous fall during the fight, Yak has to switch clothes and, after the cut, take Wayne's fall. It can get complicated at times. Yak, playing himself, gets laboriously onto his horse and rides clumsily away, only to be chased by Yak-as-Wayne doing a crisper mount (leapfrogging over the horse's rump) and tearing off with superb dash and ease.

When, in a fight, Yak had to flip Wayne in the air, another stuntman had to flip Yak-as-Wayne. When Wayne leaped onto an open little railway repair car and knocked Yak off, it was Yak who jumped onto the car as Wayne. It was the real Wayne who fought him, dressed as Yak. But it was the false Wayne again who fell off the car. It took two costume changes for one scene.[18]

In *The Lawless Range* (1935), done for Republic, Wayne is chasing Yak the villain. Yak shoots back and hits Wayne's horse. Cut. Now Yak, as Wayne, falls off the horse. Cut. Now Wayne rolls up on one knee and shoots at Yak. In *Randy Rides Alone* (1934), Yak as Wayne is riding at full gallop over a wooden bridge with a high railing on each side. He launches himself out of the saddle and *clears the railing* before falling to the water. In *Blue Steel* (1934), Wayne-Yak jumps onto a runaway wagon to rescue a young woman in it, then Wayne helps Yak (in the woman's clothes) jump to her horse, which is patiently running alongside the wagon.

Part of the fascination of watching these Monograms is to see how many variations the two men can play on their games with each other. Yak chases Yak. Wayne fights Wayne. Wayne-Yak circles Yak-Wayne. As Humbert Humbert put it: "I rolled over him. We rolled over me. They rolled over him. We rolled over us."[19]

It is a wonder—given the pace at which these films were made, their stunts invented and filmed, with little or no rehearsal —that the whole effort was not stalled more often by injuries. Wayne did many of his own stunts and all of his own fights—a director's nightmare. Any slipup can leave the leading man with a cut on his face, a sprained ankle or wrist, a black eye—enough to keep him off-camera for some vital day or more of the short shooting schedule. Wayne and Yak worked out their routines, and Wayne would teach other stuntmen, all during his career, how to make fights dramatic. He put his whole body in his fake punches, not showing the slight hesitation, the unsureness about missing, that plagues otherwise skilled actors who do not know how to "fight" hard without hurting. It is a stuntman's specialty, but Wayne acquired it and insisted on using it even when he was the kind of star denied that indulgence.

Wayne's riding improved immensely because of Yak's example and admonitions. He no longer slouched in the saddle, as in *The Big Trail*, but leaned into the gallop, like Yak. (The two men had to ride the same way, to make Yak a convincing double.)[20] Wayne developed a great respect for the discipline and skills of the stuntmen and riders who made their dangerous and underpaid living in Westerns. It was a respect they reciprocated. The riders are the secret judges on a Western set. They nod their approval or scorn of the star's achievements or pretensions. They admire the actor's willingness to *try* hard things. They admire even more the ability to *do* it. When Charlton Heston had occasion to work with Canutt in *El Cid*, he noticed how quickly Yak chose riders from the Spanish applicants. "I suppose you can tell how well they ride before they've gone very far." Yak answered: "I can tell if they can ride at all by the time they put a toe in the stirrup."[21]

Canutt's professionalism showed in his businesslike approach to stunting. He did not do it for the thrills, or think it manly to take chances. He studied the mechanics of every task, just as he studied the habits of every bronco he rode—what it did on the first jump, the second, the third; how and when it turned; how it responded to different uses of the reins or spurs.[22]

Canutt went on to a brilliant career even after he had retired from doing stunts himself. He was such a student of safety procedures that producers sought him out to oversee stunt work. He invented many devices for making tricks safer *and* more convincing—ways to make wagons fall apart without risk to the rider. He could also handle animals of all sorts. He doubled Clark Gable to control the skittish horses in the burning of Atlanta for *Gone With the Wind*. He shot the African animal scenes for the safari film *Mogambo*. Eventually, Canutt became the most respected director of action sequences in film "epics"—*Ben-Hur* (he filmed the chariot race), *El Cid, The Fall of the Roman Empire, Khartoum*.[23] His sons, Tap and Joe, became leading stuntmen after him—Wayne used them in his own production, *The Alamo*.

Canutt demanded total control of the scene when he was stunting. He needed to prepare the ground for falls, create machinery (he used many different chariots of his own design in his historical epics, each made specially for one trick), and dictate camera angles (to maintain the illusion while he used safety equipment not meant to be seen).[24] It would be hard to exaggerate the importance to Wayne of these years with Yak. At Mascot, Warner's, Monogram, and Republic, the two spent five years working long hours in each other's company, on location and in studios, growing in affection and respect for each other. From Yak Wayne learned the importance of making difficult things look easy. Yak was like other artists of the moving body—like Fred Astaire, like Gwen Verdon—in his conversion of hard discipline into apparently effortless feats. He flowed from point to point, and so would Wayne. Though director William Wyler might say that Wayne walked "like a fairy," Yak was living proof that grace can go with manliness, that competence is not swagger, that the securest pride is in professionalism.[25]

All those who worked with Wayne were impressed by his sense of responsibility on the set. No matter how undisciplined or hard-drinking when not making movies, he was always early to a shoot, sober, his lines learned, his attention fully engaged even when he was not in the scene being filmed at the moment. Like Yak, he studied the whole process, treated every day of filming as a school assembled for his instruction. No wonder Wayne was held in awe by the wranglers, riders, and stuntmen on later movies. He was honored as one who had passed the test of the best man in their field.[26]

In 1935, Monogram and other small studios were merged with Wayne's old serial-making company, Mascot, to form Republic Pictures. Herbert Yates, who effected the merger, owned a film-processing laboratory whose services would be available to the new studio. For Wayne this meant better pay in better-financed films.[27] His Republic pictures made more money, for him and for the new studio. But they are less interesting than the Monogram work done with Stout, Bradbury, Hayes, and Canutt between 1933 and 1935. In 1936, Wayne jumped at a chance to leave Republic and make six non-Westerns for Universal, which hoped to create a "nervous A" line of films budgeted a bit above B fare.[28] The project failed and Wayne had to go back to Republic. There, his principal duty was to serve in a long-running series of films that were audience pleasers of the most calculating sort, the "Three Mesquiteers" pictures. Fifty-one of these shows were made between 1936 and 1943. Wayne played in numbers 17 through 24, eight films in two years (1938–1939).[29]

The three title characters are drifters who get into trouble and have to solve a community's problems in order to get themselves free again. Though they ride horses, the scenes are set in the modern West (like most of Gene Autry's and Roy Rogers's movies). Wayne, as "Stony Brooke," is a person forever flirting and falling in love—this is what causes the trouble needed for plot purposes. His partners help him out—Tucson (played by "Crash" Corrigan, a popular B cowboy) and Lullaby (played by ventriloquist Max Terhune). There was too much clowning by Terhune for adults, and too much love interest around Wayne for kids; but the series seemed to hit some middle group that made it a surefire thing, its success guaranteed by its faults. Wayne ended his decade of cowboying in the most gimmicky contrivance of them all.

Looking back on the thirties, Wayne could be proud of the fact that he had survived the Depression while remaining an actor. That was no small achievement. Even stars had been struck down by changes, cutbacks, the new priorities of sound movies. Marginal actors had to shift about to keep finding work. Wayne had scrambled from studio to studio, seven of them in eight years—Fox, Columbia, Mascot, Warner's, Monogram, Republic, Universal, then back to Republic.

Five of those years he had worked with Yak Canutt, equipping him in ways he could not even guess for the movie work that lay ahead. But he could have little pride in the work he had done, little hope for anything better. After a misleading start, in which the promise of *The Big Trail* led nowhere, he had done year after year of hack work—hard work, honest and honorable; skilled work, with its own integrity and discipline. Still, on the scale of artistic endeavor, hack work. It was time for a movie-style rescue of Wayne, the cavalry arriving at the last minute. Enter Ford, offering him *Stagecoach*.

Part Two

JOHN FORD

*S*tagecoach (1939) is always considered Wayne's pivotal Ford film, but it took on much of its mythic status in the light of later work. At the time, it did not seem to set either man on the course of making classic Westerns. Ford, who had not filmed a Western in thirteen years, thought of *Stagecoach* as an art film, much like the next one he made with Wayne, *The Long Voyage Home* (1940), an adaptation of Eugene O'Neill's sea stories.

Stagecoach is the first Ford film to give Wayne a major part, and the first to use the magical locale of Monument Valley. The two men later claimed that it sealed their special relationship —an exaggeration, as we shall see, but one that needs careful investigation here (Chapters 4 through 7) because this is the point of origin for their close but tortured relationship.

That relationship was severely strained by World War II, in which Ford served as a combat film director while Wayne nimbly maneuvered to avoid volunteering or being drafted.

Though these years separated the two men, this was just the time when Wayne was wound more tightly into Ford's Hollywood circle through friendship with Ford's earlier cowboy star of the silent era, Harry Carey. Carey and his family deserve separate treatment (Chapter 9) because of their influence on Wayne and the way Carey served as a link to Ford's past as well as Ford's future.

□ 4 □
SADIST

BOOKS ABOUT JOHN FORD and John Wayne tell a warm story of their personal and professional relationship in the 1930s. It is a good story, and no wonder. It was invented, retrospectively, by a master storyteller. The tale goes this way. Ford had spotted Wayne on the Fox lot, in 1927, and tested him with a physical challenge. Wayne passed the test, and the two were friends ever after. Ford recognized raw talent in Wayne, but waited until it had matured and he (Ford) had found the right vehicle for Wayne's launching. Then Ford fought to cast Wayne, against producers' skepticism, as the Ringo Kid in *Stagecoach*. It had taken twelve years, but the wisdom of Ford's timing was vindicated by Wayne's "overnight" stardom in 1939.

The tale is equally satisfying and false. Take their famous meeting on the Fox lot. Ford is supposed to have said, "So you're the football player?" and asked him to prove his prowess: Can Wayne stop *him?* Accounts differ on the way this proof was offered. Sometimes Wayne sets himself in lineman's stance and Ford kicks both Wayne's hands out from under him with one sweep of his foot (try it sometime).[1] In other versions, Ford acts like a runner and breaks Wayne's attempted tackle—whereupon Wayne kicks Ford in the chest (imagine the physics of that).[2] The two men are fast friends ever after. It sounds like any number of male bonding scenes in Ford movies. Ford plays McLaglen to Wayne's "quiet man." Blows make them buddies, and they stagger off to a bar to celebrate.

What is wrong with that picture? Well, in the first place Wayne's college football career was ended or ending (depending on whether the two met in 1926 or 1927). There were other football players, probably less marginal, who worked around the lots in those years. Wayne was hardly *the* football player. The myth depends on the *other* myth of Wayne's football prowess.

It is true that Ford resorted to physical intimidation on the set—kicking John Wayne, even in his star period; knocking a young Robert Wagner to the ground; punching Henry Fonda; throwing rocks at actors (hitting Pedro Armendariz with one).[3] There was verbal abuse. Ford deliberately called people by the wrong name, or by humiliating nicknames he invented.[4] But there is no record, in all this long career of assault and insults from Ford, of anyone responding physically to Ford's aggression. Even the few who responded verbally were punished. Ben Johnson talked back, and was banned from future Ford projects for thirteen years.[5] When Ford told actors to "assume the position," established stars, even Wayne, did so—to be kicked in the rump, not to engage in any physical struggle. Ford wanted no challenges to his authority, not even advice, much less physical contest. The story of the Wayne-Ford meeting is a little movie Ford later ran in his mind, not a real encounter with a property-moving nobody on the Fox set.

Despite the friendship supposedly formed in 1926 or 1927, Ford gave Wayne only unimportant bit parts in a few early movies. Even Ward Bond, whom Ford met at the same time, was given a bigger part in 1929. This apparent lag in their relationship is also filled with apocryphal services Wayne rendered to Ford films. Did Victor McLaglen hesitate to wrestle a huge opponent in *The Black Watch* (1929)? Ford shamed him by having Wayne serve as his double—though Wayne at the time was thin as a whippet, hardly a convincing double for the fortresslike McLaglen.[6] Did stuntmen hesitate to jump into choppy water for the film *Men Without Women* (1930)? Then Wayne leaped in.[7] Yet the picture clearly shows nonathletic actors like J. Farrell MacDonald tossing in the choppy waves. Could middle-aged MacDonald do what stuntmen feared to do?

Though Ford did not trust Wayne with any but the smallest extra or bit work, we are told that he relied on him to arrange for USC football players to make the movie *Salute* (1929). But then, for all this growing chumminess, Ford suddenly refused to talk to Wayne for three years. Wayne charitably supposed that

Ford was just testing him, seeing if he could take it. But Ford elsewhere showed his anger at people too ready to work with other directors. Wayne's sin was making *The Big Trail* with Raoul Walsh.[8] The great silence began then, the kind of exile Ford's actors came to expect when Ford was not recognized as the proper determiner of their careers.[9]

Though Ford finally started talking to Wayne again, and welcoming him onto his boat, along with companions like Ward Bond, he did nothing to use Wayne or help his career until, twelve years after their meeting, he bestowed the part in *Stagecoach* as a great gift. In later interviews with Ford, the director skips over the thirties entirely and represents Wayne as still moving props when Ford decided to make him the Ringo Kid.[10]

The centerpiece of this whole Ford-Wayne romance is the making of *Salute*—a neat little myth within the larger Ford myths. Ford wanted to film a football tale at the Naval Academy (Annapolis), but the Navy would not let its midshipmen act in it. Ford needed to cast young men who could play football on-screen—so he asked Wayne, who knew the USC team, to pick out the actors, and Wayne did so. Not qualified (in Ford's eye) to be an actor himself at this stage, he was trusted to be a casting director.

When USC refused to let the players leave before the end of term, Wayne, it is said, negotiated early exams for them. He chose many of the players from his own fraternity, Sigma Chi; but a member of Sigma Tau, Ward Bond, heard of the project and showed up at the train uninvited. Wayne tried to prevent him from boarding, but Ford saw "the big ugly guy" and was intrigued by him. To irritate Wayne, he made Bond his roommate on the train (the players had *rooms*, not just a Pullman car).[11]

What is wrong with this story? Fox Films had difficulty getting permission from Annapolis to film at all. Its executives applied to the Navy Department.[12] Is it likely the studio would rely on a lowly extra to negotiate with the University of Southern California? Wayne had no relationship with the university, which he had left two years earlier. He was not a football player there —as Bond *was* in 1929. We get a different (and more expectable) picture of the process from a letter in the Ford files. The university's Bureau of Employment asked for a return of pictures, describing how they had been acquired by a studio representative (not Wayne): "During the casting of the picture *Salute* Mr. Odell came to the University and secured about thirty pictures of the football boys."[13] The cast was being chosen from pictures, not by Wayne's promotion of his fraternity brothers. Bond's last-minute choice by Ford also neglects the fact that Bond had already done a bit part in James Tinling's film *Words and Music*. Ford claimed he invented Bond's part as he came to use him in Annapolis, but the cocky character he is based on exists in the script James McGuinness had earlier submitted to Annapolis for approval.[14] Ford's whole tale is a confection.

Why would Ford make up such a tale, and why would Wayne and Bond endorse it? Well, this tale is not isolated. It can be paralleled in many of Ford's rearrangements of his own history. Much of this fabulizing was useful to his art. He tried to weave his movie-making troupe into a family with a strong authoritarian structure. He sincerely felt his fatherly role, however he explained it. His anger at rebellious actors arose precisely from this paternalistic conception of his position. His actors belonged to him, and to each other. When they came on the set, Danny Borzage played each one's "theme song" on his omnipresent accordion.[15] The company gathered for tea every afternoon. Ford liked to have everyone in the cast present on the set, even in scenes where some actors had no part. He forged a mystique of tough love like that he created in the cavalry camps of his films. Military veteran Jack Pennick drilled actors and extras in horsemanship, in martial exercises, and in military etiquette.[16]

Ford was the caring father, and in fact he *did* care. He was deeply, ludicrously sentimental—a fact that came out in his sloppily drunken gestures. He tried to cover up this "unmanly" tenderness with a gruff manner—which explains the fact that he was often harshest toward those he liked best.

Ford tried to seal others in a special relationship by a kind of sacramental gift. George O'Brien was stunned when, early in his dealings with Ford, the director suggested they exchange ties.[17] When Ford put a scarf on a man or woman on the set, it was a bond, making them part of him. He was still at this even on Wayne's *Alamo* set when he had cloth insignias made for select extras and called them "John Ford's group."[18] Anna Lee remembers, from her work on *How Green Was My Valley:* "He took this grubby handkerchief that he carried, which he chewed the corners of, and he tucked it in my apron. I knew that was his mark of approval, a sort of good luck token. In all the things I've done for him, I've had that handkerchief tied around me in so

many strange places."[19] These handkerchiefs became famous to-
kens. Ford gave one to his chauffeur, Bob Stevens, which Denver
Pyle asked for—it now hangs, framed, in Pyle's office.[20] Wayne
no doubt accepted the story of Ford's care for him in the thirties
as a form of scarf or pledge put around his neck—one it would
be ungracious to refuse.

One reason actors put up with Ford's abuse was their generally subservient position at the time. Ford's autocratic air on
the set was a rebellion against producers' power that the actors
appreciated. Stars were ornamental but not independent in the
1930s. They were cosseted but captive. The standard contract

> gave the studios control over the star's image and services;
> it required an actor to "act, sing, pose, speak or perform in
> such roles as the producer may designate"; it gave the stu-
> dio the right to change the name of the actor at its own
> discretion and to control the performer's image and like-
> ness in advertising and publicity; and it required the actor
> to comply with rules covering interviews and public ap-
> pearances. Another restrictive clause concerned picture as-
> signments. If the aspiring star refused an assignment, the
> "studio could sue for damages and extend the contract to
> make up for the stoppage."[21]

One aspect of Ford's control over his own set was his exclusion
of studio officials from visible interference. This did not stop a
producer like Darryl Zanuck from viewing Ford's "rushes" and
demanding changes, but Ford kept that to himself. To his actors,
he seemed to have formed an autonomous enclave from which
other powers at the studio were excluded. This explains all the
gleeful stories, relayed by actors, of Ford kicking vice presidents
off his set, defying their instructions, stopping work until they
left. The actors were participants in this rare defiance of their
overlords. Ford's domineering ways were those of a leader with
a rebel band.

The roots of Ford's attitude lay in his early experience as a
film-maker. He worked first for his brother Frank, who was given
broad directorial responsibility by the pioneer producer Thomas
Ince. Then Ford moved over to Harry Carey's special team of
Western film-makers at Carl Laemmle's Universal Studios. Olive
Carey has described in various interviews how Carey and Ford
camped out in a house at Newhall, improvising their own films
their own way.[22] By the time Ford was making his successful

films in the thirties, studio control had become strict; the Depression made producers cut back on the improvising and impose accountability. Ford's sensitivity to criticism, his need to seem independent, made Fox officials humor him so far as appearances went. But they really had control, and this made his gestures of defiance all the more theatrical. The reminiscences of many actors show that they were fooled—and thrilled—by Ford's gestures. In a sea of oppression, they entered an island of defiance when they heard Borzage's accordion escort them onto Ford's sealed set.

Arenas of control were important to Ford. He could discipline himself only when he was disciplining others. He insisted that his actors give up drinking while they made his films. It was his own sacrifice they were sharing. As soon as the movie ended (sometimes when it had almost ended), Ford went on a binge. He avoided his grand house on Odin Street, perched above Hollywood Bowl. He preferred his boat, the *Araner*, where, however much he drank, there were at least some elements of control —over the crew, over provisioning, over the destination, over scheduling of daily life.

In World War II, the Navy gave Ford his ultimate mission calling for self-discipline. He not only controlled his drinking, his anger, and his black moods, in those years; he dressed neatly for the only time in his life—the uniform must be honored. Ford could not wait for the war to start—he used the *Araner* to spy on Japanese merchants in Hawaii and Mexico even before Pearl Harbor.[23] And after the war he tried to prolong the experience, setting up a home for veterans of his combat film unit, where periodic celebrations were held in full-dress uniform.[24]

The Ford film set was war on a minor scale. He went off to battle every morning—which made him chew nervously on his handkerchief when under stress. Some people chew gum or candy when they quit drinking. Some smoke compulsively. Ford chewed handkerchiefs, to the amusement and puzzlement of his crew and actors, who had trouble deciphering commands that came filtered through the linen in his mouth.[25] Ford's cruel treatment of others also came from some obscure anger at himself. He was like any alcoholic separated for a time from the bottle. Doubts about his own performance were taken out on those who were innocently imperiling that performance. Even the joshing toughness covered an anguished toughness.

One reason Ford might fail, a reason he rightly feared, was

his own sentimentality, which does mar his work. He was afraid of his own tenderness. Women were especially resented as potential underminers of his manliness. He reduced them to tears, all but the tough ones. Katharine Hepburn stirred his torpid lust precisely because she was not "soft." She was tougher than Ford. Maureen O'Hara was best of all—she soared above sex with wit and professionalism. He liked to have her on any project—going so far as to miscast her as the prostitute in *What Price Glory?* (Zanuck, fortunately, blocked that one.)[26]

Ford's mixture of cruelty and tenderness showed up in his treatment of "Dobe" Carey, the son of Harry, his old partner, and "Ollie," Harry's wife and Dobe's mother—a woman for whom he had an early crush (wistfully, at times, renewed). The most sadistic act I know of on any Ford set is the way the director stepped with his whole weight on a hungover Dobe's chest, breaking his rib.[27] But Ford was dismayed at seeing his own faults destroying this adoptive son. His anger at Dobe's drinking turned to support when Dobe finally gave up the bottle. (Wayne, on the other hand, snubbed Dobe for ceasing to be a man who could down booze with the other men.)[28] The key to the matter is to be found in a phone call Ford made to Dobe after he failed to meet a cast call because he was drunk. Ford told him: "I'm an alcoholic. Your Aunt Mary [Ford's wife] is an alcoholic. Ollie's an alcoholic, and God knows Duke is one. When are you going to wise up?"[29] When Dobe broke the hold of alcohol, Ford was quick to offer him work, and he stopped riding him before other actors. The father had disciplined his son—but without showing much discipline himself.

Rebuff Ford's benevolence, and you released a demon. Dobe recalls how Ford, drunk and salivating heavily (as he did when he was drinking), leaned over at his home and gave Dobe a wet kiss on the cheek. When Dobe wiped off the slobber, a look of hate came into Ford's eyes.[30] This recalls the thing Dobe disliked most about Ford's ridicule in the first movie they made together. Signaling that Dobe had blown a scene, that he was "jerking off," Ford launched a stream of invectives at him:

> He was yelling all kinds of terrible things at me. He panto-
> mimed masturbation with an expression so loathsome that
> even in my teen years I could never have looked so de-
> mented.[31]

Dobe, who in fact loved his "Uncle Jack" (as Ford insisted that he call him), was more ashamed for Ford than for himself. "I died a little each and every day" when Ford was "making that awful face and gesture." No wonder James Cagney, asked what one word best described Ford, answered: "Malice."[32]

Yet those who stuck with Ford found the malice redeemed, at least part of the time, by funny loyalties, an endearing ceremonial formality about his set, and a perceptible weakness that made his tyranny less imposing. Ford insisted on absolute control because he was so clearly afraid of losing control, over himself as well as others. He brooked no criticism, no suggestions. Cameramen could not suggest a better angle for catching the light. Actors could not suggest a different reading for a line. Richard Widmark, though fond of the man, said, "He did not want to hear *anything* from you."[33] When Helen Hayes made a suggestion to Ford, he said: "Who is directing this picture? Get back on the set and stick to your acting—such as it is."[34]

Ford's famous grudges, which made him banish actors from the set—for a long time, sometimes forever—came from his fear of challenge. That is why Yak Canutt could never be welcomed back, why Ben Johnson was exiled, why Harry Carey (Senior), who had been such a great part of Ford's happy early years, was used only once after Ford came into his own position of power. Carey was unacceptable *because* he had been such a part of Ford's formation. When the two got together, in later years, Ford would say things like, "When I wrote *Hell Bent*, I was—" Carey would break in: "Jack, for Christ's sake, I wrote most of that."[35] It would be hard to maintain total control over one who had once controlled *him*.

Even more satisfying than banishment was the *retention* of a former benefactor, so long as current domination could be continually asserted. That was the case with Ford's brother. Frank had been a film pioneer, with the Méliès company in the East and with Thomas Ince in the West. He had played Lincoln and Custer and Crockett. Ince had given him extraordinary control over the films he made, even when they were credited to Ince's direction. There are "Fordian" touches in, for instance, *Custer's Last Fight* (1912) that people would later associate with his brother—as when cavalry crest a hill and slant down across the screen. This was the leader John Ford worked for, as property assistant and stunt extra, during his early days in Los Angeles.

But by the time John was in charge, Frank had succumbed to the family curse of alcoholism. John gave Frank steady work, but of a demeaning sort, regularly casting him as a silly old codger, shabby and bearded. With an almost fiendish ingenuity, John took his revenge on Frank in just that area where he had excelled. This silent screen star would usually be *kept* silent in John's "talkies," or given only brief echoes to others' comments. This was accomplished with great cleverness, where one would think Frank *must* talk. In *Stagecoach*, Frank is the host at the first stage stop. He welcomes people who are full of questions. But Frank only pantomimes his welcome, concern, and joy at seeing others. In *Young Mr. Lincoln*, Frank is a juror questioned by Henry Fonda. After two monosyllabic replies, he answers with nods and shakes of his head. (There is no court stenographer to ask, "Is that a yes?")

Other members of the family were also kept on the set— Ford's second brother, Eddie O'Fearna, his brother-in-law Wingate Smith, his son-in-law Ken Curtis. His son, Patrick, was sometimes used as a scriptwriter and a scout of locales. His daughter, Barbara, was a production accountant. If Ford tried to make family of his actors and crew, he tried to make employees of his relatives. He was an Irish "squireen" with his own fiefdom. The results were unhappy for his son, Patrick, who rebelled against his father's domineering ways.[36] His daughter, Barbara, chafed at her inability to enter the male Ford world (whose drinking and sexual freedom she tried to emulate).[37]

In fact, there is an eerie fascination to the spectacle of Ford making movies in a way that unmade him. He destroyed his family in the process of creating stories to glorify the family. He dreamed up, out of his own lack of discipline, paeans to military and frontier disciplines. He made beauty out of ugly humiliation. His love scenes were hatefully confected. The happy endings were elaborated out of his own unhappiness, which he spread to others. Katharine Hepburn, who loved him, was not surprised at this. She felt that suffering was the alembic from which he distilled his art.[38]

On the set of *Stagecoach*, Ford nagged mercilessly at Wayne. One of the persistent legends about that picture is that he did this simply to arouse sympathy for Wayne in the other actors, to break down any resistance they might be putting up against this newcomer. But Wayne was not really a "newcomer" ten years after he played the lead in *The Big Trail*. And Ford did not need reasons for his sadistic treatment of players—each of whom received this treatment, in unpredictable patterns, long after they had ceased to be newcomers. For reasons that remain mysterious, Ford at his most creative was often at his cruelest. As we shall see, Wayne's performance in *Stagecoach* exceeded in impact the role as it was scripted. That is what Wayne was punished for.

□ 5 □
ARTIST

ONE LEGEND about *Stagecoach* is that no one would produce it, at first, because Ford would not accept stars to make it commercially viable. Gary Cooper and Marlene Dietrich were suggested; but Ford, convinced that he at last had the right vehicle for Wayne, kept searching until he found an independent entrepreneur, Walter Wanger, who would back *Stagecoach* with the right actors for the film's parts—John Wayne and Claire Trevor.

Ford is supposed to have broken his decision to cast Wayne in a typically teasing way, partly cruel, partly pleased with the gift he was giving him. He had Wayne read the script, one day on his yacht, and asked him to suggest men who might play the Ringo Kid.[1] Wayne named Lloyd Nolan, a rising young actor.[2] Ford did not go for Nolan. He asked Wayne to keep thinking, and let the matter rest overnight. Only on the next day did he unwrap the gift and show that it had Wayne's name on it.

This story, if we can trust it, has an aspect that has not been pointed out. Wayne does not suggest Gary Cooper or a big star to play the Kid. He seems to assume the role would go to a minor actor—for a very good reason: it was a minor role. The Kid does not show up until fifteen minutes of a short film have gone by. Once introduced into the stagecoach, Wayne speaks fewer lines than other passengers. Indeed, if we except Wayne's two walks alone with Claire Trevor, every principal character says more than the Kid does.

No big star would want to play such a part and no producer

would want to "waste" a star on it. That is why Ford wanted Wayne. If he had accepted a Gary Cooper, the role would have been beefed up, the script rewritten—and Ford liked the script as he and Dudley Nichols had shaped it during a trip to Mexico on the *Araner*. The film is an ensemble piece, not a star vehicle. Its whole ethos depends on the interplay of nearly equal parts. Each character is wrought upon by all the others, as they rub up against each other in close quarters. In the event, Wayne leaped out from this ensemble in ways no one could have anticipated, including Ford. But the first imperative for keeping the script intact was to keep it *away* from any star, whose presence would alter its chemistry. Ford did not plan *Stagecoach* to make Wayne a star. He used Wayne as an anti-star to hold the Gary Coopers at bay.

The subsidiary nature of Wayne's role as written can be seen in the vague and misleading assignment of a musical theme to him and the prostitute. The other themes introduced while the opening credits run are clearly attached to each subject on its first appearance. The stagecoach motif goes to a jaunty version of "Oh Bury Me Not on the Lone Prairie." The gambler and the army wife have a Stephen Foster theme, appropriate to their Virginian origin, and we hear it often. The Indians have the expectable two descending chromatic notes (emphasis on the first note). The fourth theme, played in a misleadingly martial way during the credits, is not keyed to the first appearance of Wayne or Trevor; and its later, soupier version is not connected to the "overture" except by people who go back over the film very carefully. Even the cavalry theme, introduced in the flow of the action, is more prominent and recognizable.

Wayne was so low in the order of actors, according to the parts assigned as well as the pay appropriated, that he barely edged the gambler (John Carradine) for his fee—$3,700 as opposed to Carradine's $3,666. Seven other actors got more than Wayne did for this picture—Thomas Mitchell $12,000, Andy Devine $10,124. This fits the number of lines given them in the script. Only Claire Trevor got paid an A-film recompense ($15,000).[3]

No wonder producers turned *Stagecoach* down. They had learned to be wary of Ford when he had the "art film" gleam in his eye. That usually meant that he had been talking too much with Dudley Nichols, a frustrated dramatist who idolized Eugene O'Neill. Ford and Nichols had enjoyed critical fame with their expressionistic *The Informer,* the movie about an Irish Republican Army informer. But the film was not a commercial hit. Neither were downbeat Ford-Nichols collaborations like *The Lost Patrol,* the story of a colonial outpost wiped out. Ironically, the very success of *Stagecoach* would confirm producers' suspicions. Ford and Nichols used that boost to get their way on *The Long Voyage Home* (1940), a moody Eugene O'Neill adaptation that also flopped. The word on Ford was that he could not be trusted to choose his own projects. He made money when given scripts by the studio, things like the Will Rogers hit *Steamboat 'Round the Bend* (1935). David O. Selznick, approached to back *Stagecoach,* voiced the common wisdom. He would be glad to use Ford, but only if he could assign the script: "We must select the story and sell it to John Ford, instead of having Ford select some uncommercial pet of his that we would be making only because of Ford's enthusiasm. . . . I see no justification for making any story just because it is liked by a man who, I am willing to concede, is one of the greatest directors in the world, but whose record commercially is far from good."[4]

This attitude of producers helps explain Ford's autocratic attitude on the set. If he could not always control *what* he made, he would try, at least, to control *how* he made it. His frustration with the lack of autonomy was countered by attempts at more complete power over his output—whence *Stagecoach.* The same attitude would lead him to other projects dear to his heart, notably *The Fugitive* (1947), Graham Greene's story of a whiskey priest, Ford's artiest film and one of his least successful. These forays into cherished projects sent him scurrying back to Westerns in order to recover his financial base.

Some modern critics agree with the producers of Ford's time. Even his grandson thinks that Ford operated best with some checks and guidance from smart producers and editors, like Darryl Zanuck (who was both). The *auteur* school, which wants to put the sole responsibility for a masterpiece in one artist's hands, does not fit very well into a collaborative social act of creation like movie-making. The director is important; but so is the camera artist, the writer, the set designer, the costumer, the musicians, the editor. Any one of these can sabotage the whole enterprise. And all make vital contributions to any successful outcome. That galled Ford, who, in his quest for domination, denigrated the contributions others were making. He claimed that actors were good only when he tricked something good out of them. That is why he would not consult them, just browbeat them. Producers got in the way; their representatives had to be banished from the set. Scripts he rewrote while filming them (though far less than he pretended), unless he told the writer what to say while working with him (the case with James McGuinness, Dudley Nichols, James Bellah, and Frank Nugent). Seen in these structural terms, Ford's striving to dominate, which had its psychological roots, also had an artistic basis. In the jumble and confusion of movie-making, one might never achieve total control. But unless one made yeoman efforts at control, the whole thing could escape *any* ordering grasp.

In fact, in the long history of art, the problems of authorship in cinema are less distinctive than they at first appear. In the Renaissance, artists rarely chose their subject matter. The patron did. Church authorities commissioned religious art, usually down to minute details of iconography, attributes, and theological interpretation of the saint or miracle or scripture event to be depicted. Secular authorities showed similar regard for the glorification of family, city, or class. Scale and style were determined by the locale of the work. Michelangelo had to satisfy Della Rovere family pride, the demands of the Sistine Chapel's physical space, the theological program already in place on the walls of the chapel, and the function of a papal chapel, when he painted his famous ceiling frescoes. Modern architects work under similar restraints—from the commissioning agent, the function of the building, the site available, the surrounding artifacts or scenery, the needs of those who will use the building. The great artist is not one who lacks all such restraints, but the one who can work best under them and still convey a personal vision.

Ford was always under constraint, and always chafing under it. He sometimes profited precisely from that struggle. He is not necessarily at his best when at his freest. Many artists are goaded into achievement by a recalcitrance of the stuff they work in—as Michelangelo was by the flawed marble for his *David*. With the artist, less can often be made more. For *Stagecoach*, Ford accepted some restraints in order to avoid others. He would work with no commercially important actors. He would rely on Yakima Canutt for action-sequence expertise. He would work with a budget approaching the B-movie level.

Some critics think it no burden that *Stagecoach* was budgeted as a B picture. For them, it *is* a B picture.

> For all of Ford's innovative techniques, however, *Stagecoach* is at its core a B Western all the same. Based on a piece of pulp fiction, it had a B Western plot and B Western characters, and although Dudley Nichols's script added characters to and deleted characters from Ernest Haycox's short story, it did not change the overall B quality of the tale.[5]

It is true that Ford and Nichols use a Western setting and stock characters—the good-hearted whore, a drunken but wise doctor, the dishonest gambler with a quirk of honor, the hero strong in his very naïveté. There are standard elements here—pursuing Indians, rescuing cavalry, a shoot-out on the town street. But attempts to treat *Stagecoach* as a "typical" Western run into endless difficulties. Will Wright, in his exhaustive typology of Westerns, finds nowhere to squeeze it but into the "revenge" plot, since the Ringo Kid has broken out of jail to avenge his brother's death.[6] Yet the villains show up only at the end, and have nothing to do with the images of the coach's travel that dominate the movie. The reason for the Kid's revenge is sketchily referred to, and Ford actually omitted parts of the script that made it clearer.[7]

What matters in *Stagecoach* is not what put the characters on the coach, or where they are going, but how they are altered by dealings with each other once inside. *Stagecoach* belongs to the "ship of fools" genre, which isolates strangers in a transient condition for an intense time of confrontation. They might be traveling on a boat, or on a train *(Murder on the Orient Express)*. They may gather at a hostelry *(Grand Hotel)* or a country house *(Rules of the Game)*. When this form is taken seriously, it almost always exposes human pretensions. When strangers are forced together, their masks become obvious and must be lowered. The "everyday" cracks open and light or darkness breaks in—or both.[8]

Ford and Nichols show the level of their concern with the genre's possibilities by the thoroughgoing way they alter society itself, as in a laboratory experiment, inside the stagecoach. Characters are pushed into new positions like parts of a Rubik's Cube being shifted. They acquire new values by a changed relationship with what is next to them. They enter the coach with this social standing (in descending scale):

1. Banker (social pillar)
2. Army wife (transient but respectable)
3. Gambler (partly a gentleman)
4. Whiskey salesman (transient, barely acceptable)
5. Doctor (drunk and disgraced)
6. Prostitute (driven from town)
7. Kid (escaped convict)

By the end, the order of our esteem has turned the social order on its head. Now, by a precisely symmetrical inversion, they rank this way:

7. Kid (hero)
6. Prostitute (heroine)
5. Doctor (redeemed)
4. Whiskey salesman (dignified)
3. Gambler (past revealed)
2. Army wife (needing all the above)
1. Banker (thief)

This emphasis on social class indicates that Ford was telling the truth, not just being pretentious, when he said that Nichols's script was based on Guy de Maupassant's short story "Boule de Suif."[9] An English equivalent for this title, a whore's nickname, would be "Suet Pudding." Maupassant told the tale of an 1876 coach trip from Rouen to Le Havre, in which the passengers' attitudes toward a prostitute on board alter their behavior from station to station. This tale is clearly a ship-of-fools type. Unlike the *Collier's* story credited as the source of *Stagecoach*, Maupassant's story has no hero and heroine; it is an ensemble piece, where even the eponymous prostitute is more a touchstone for the hypocrisy of others than the protagonist.

This tale, too, exactly reverses the characters' rank in the course of the voyage. They enter by order of their social position. They exit in the order of their honor. The hierarchy is, at the outset:

Two nuns
A count and countess
Two merchants and their wives
A hedonistic radical
"Suet Pudding"

Nine of the ten travelers are initially united by their contempt for the whore. But when the coach is stalled, and it turns out that she alone has food, all nine (even the nuns) grow respectful toward her. They congratulate her when she patriotically rejects the sexual overtures of a Prussian officer at their first stop. But when they discover that the officer has power to hold them until she gives in, the company (even the nuns) persuade her that it is her duty to ease their journey onward. Once she has done this, of course, and the voyage is resumed, they revert to their earlier contempt for her—all but the dissolute radical, who despises the hypocrites and respects her honesty. The nuns now rank at the bottom of the human scale, along with the count and countess, who should have shown higher standards.

Maupassant's tale is called radical, since he had clear class structures and the Church to castigate. But Ford and Nichols (and the politically conscious Walter Wanger) invent class attitudes from their Western materials. The banker represents the hollow social claims of Tonto, Arizona (the tale's point of origin). His wife is prominent in the Law and Order League that is driving the whore out of town. The gambler and the army wife are former aristocrats of the Confederacy, she now married to a Union soldier, he descended to the level of a cardsharp fast with his derringer. The doctor was an army surgeon before he yielded to drink. The Ringo Kid is a dirt farmer framed for murder.

None of this social complexity is in the film's "official" source —Ernest Haycox's "Stage to Lordsburg," in which a ranger-gunman falls in love with a prostitute while taking a short coach ride to kill a man who has insulted him.[10] Haycox is imitating the Western stories of Bret Harte and O. Henry, which reversed the formula for sugarcoating a pill. Those authors wrapped a gooey center in a cynical outer crust. In this case, the cynical exterior reaches only to the choice of a gunman and a whore as lovers. The tale has none of the real cynicism about society's structure that Nichols shared with Maupassant. Of course, Ford and Nichols had every reason to hide their "arty" source, given their reputation with Hollywood producers. It was important to present their biting comedy of social manners as a modern Western.

Some critics, far from thinking this a typical B Western, find it too neat in the economy of its moves, in the way it remakes the entire social arrangement. Tag Gallagher condemned it for being too "self-conscious" rather than naive, and Robert Warshow, in a famous essay on Westerns, regretted the film's "preoccupation with style."[11]

One sign of *Stagecoach*'s departure from the typical Western is the fact that it had no real imitators—this despite the fact that it is often said to have revived the Western as a genre. In fact, the year 1939 saw a flood of Westerns, all conceived before *Stagecoach*'s release, and these films had many imitators. Tyrone Power in *Jesse James* helped create a fad for outlaw films in the early forties. Errol Flynn in *Dodge City* renewed the town-taming plot—so definitively that when Mel Brooks wanted to parody the "typical" Western in *Blazing Saddles*, he chose *Dodge City*. James Stewart's *Destry Rides Again* became the model for other comedy Westerns.[12] All these were imitated because they were imitatable —tales of pioneer treks, range wars, cattle towns, scouts, cavalry missions. *Stagecoach*, though it borrows some elements from such tales, is put together in a way that makes it resist assignment to any one type.

Ford's own later Westerns fit the established categories. Certainly the cavalry stories did. Even the apparently "offbeat" *My Darling Clementine* and *The Man Who Shot Liberty Valance* were variations on the "town-taming" story familiar to moviegoers from the earliest days.[13] But the closest analogue to *Stagecoach* is Ford's next work with Nichols, a non-Western, *The Long Voyage Home* (1940). That, too, is an ensemble play of travel, this time by boat, structured around calls at different ports (like the coach's trip from stage to stage). In that movie, Wayne again plays a naive young man who does not recognize the prostitute for what she is. For the second and last time Wayne was playing the Ringo Kid type—a role he never repeated in Westerns. This was not simply because he was getting rather long in the tooth to play a "kid." He is a kid, but a superstitious and hateful one, in the non-Western *The Shepherd of the Hills* (1941). In the Western roles that followed, Wayne was always tougher and more knowing than the Ringo Kid.

André Bazin, despite his love for *Stagecoach*, has misled generations of film critics by making the film a classical embodiment of "the Western."[14] It is not archetypal but atypical. The classic Western has a hero who forges his own and others' destiny (as Wayne did in Walsh's *The Big Trail*). The Ringo Kid is surprisingly passive (in all but his determination to avenge his father and brother). He is disarmed when he enters the stagecoach. He gives up his freedom and his loved one at the end—it is the marshal who determines that he should escape. Wayne is neither hero nor antihero, but part of the complex social weave accomplished by Ford in this Renoir-like "game" of social rules.

Yet Wayne does fairly leap off the screen in *Stagecoach*, in ways that a prior reading of the script would not make one expect. That is because of the way Ford shot the film. The handling of space—of interiors, of a suggested vastness around the cramped little coach—pits foreground intimacy against background immensity. And Wayne is the "space traveler" who provides the visual link between these poles. He brings the outside into the coach—and he stands up against outside menace when this enclosed community is threatened. Ford exaggerates his size by having him duck under low doors and climb around the coach as if it were a toy. He makes Wayne's graceful motion a sign of power, as when Wayne swings around on the swaying platform of the coach's roof. None of this is in Nichols's words. But Ford got it all into the camera. He did not give Wayne a starring script, but he gave him space to star in. He gave him Monument Valley.

□ 6 □
RHYTHMED MOTION

IF YOU COME toward Monument Valley from the northern (Utah) side, you see them twenty miles off—the high flat mesas and sharp-profiled buttes. Prehistoric glaciers swept by these formations, scraping away all softer rock, leaving only hard extrusions, too tough to be bullied by Nature itself. At first glance, they seem huge and near. Though they get higher as you drive toward them, they do not seem to come nearer. Not till you are almost upon them do you realize that you have seen only the upper parts poking up from a deep basin, the Valley, where their broad foundations have been hidden from you.

If you come from the southern (Arizona) side, you pass a rock tower (El Capitán) standing sentinel outside the Valley. Such a spectacular locale could not be kept secret. But the Valley lacked water, electricity, and other amenities, so early visitors took an awed look and moved on—until, early in this century, John Wetherill and his wife set up an Indian trading camp near the Valley (at Oljeto) and tried to supply visitors with a base for staying overnight. This proved too isolated and vulnerable a spot. So the Wetherills moved twenty-five miles south of the Valley, to Kayenta, Arizona. This became the place where visitors—including Theodore Roosevelt—stayed when they looked at the Valley. One of those who lived regularly with the Wetherills was George Herriman, who drew the comic strip *Krazy Kat*.[1] Much of that strip is set in the Valley, lending the panels their eerie, surreal character. A cast of decidedly urban characters—a cop, an amorous mouse, an oblivious alley cat—play out their little dramas, of affection posing as aggression, in what might be a vast moonscape, a setting of cosmic indifference to their emotional sputterings.

Zane Grey knew the Valley, too, along with the entire Arizona region where he set many of his wildly popular Western novels. When he sold rights to his stories to Paramount, it was with a proviso that they be filmed in the locale where they were set. The actors and crews on these movies became acquainted with the Valley, and some gorgeous views of it are seen in the prologue to *The Vanishing American* (1925).[2] An assistant cameraman on some of these films was Bert Glennon, who would shoot *Stagecoach*. George O'Brien, Ford's star from the silent days, made movies around Kayenta in the thirties, and John Wayne claimed to have seen the Valley while visiting an O'Brien film.

The studios always used the Wetherills' inn and trading post when working in this area, and that is where Walter Wanger's preproduction crew went in 1939 to arrange for the hiring of Indians, extras, horses, and equipment for *Stagecoach*. While making the film, Ford and other principals stayed at the Wetherills' (fourteen people), while twenty-two people bunked in a Civilian Conservation Corps barracks, and twenty-six camped at the Valley's edge by a trading post run by Harry and Leone ("Mike") Goulding.[3] There was water and food, and that was about all, at the Gouldings'.

In the John Ford mythology, the Gouldings have completely displaced the Wetherills, who were there before them and first brought film companies to the area. It seems clear from Wanger documents that the Gouldings made their contact with the Wanger company through the Wetherills, and offered quarters to crew members that were closer to the Valley (if more primitive) than the established Wetherill post.

In the subsequent, self-aggrandizing legend, Harry Goulding became the first person to bring movies to the Valley. He did it by taking still photos to Hollywood, where he asked to see someone at the Wanger office. (How did he know Wanger was about to make a Western? Not from the Wetherills, of course. Goulding lamely explained that he heard something about it on the radio.) In this version, worked out in later years with Ford himself, Goulding agrees to build a barracks on his property to handle the whole expedition (the CCC camp is totally forgotten).[4]

After *Stagecoach* other movies were made in Monument Valley, movies like *Kit Carson* in 1940 and *The Harvey Girls* in 1946. But Ford did not return to the Valley for eight years. By the time he came back, to make *My Darling Clementine*, Goulding had expanded his facilities and Ford began staying with him. Between them, they conveniently remembered themselves as the sole discoverers and developers of the Valley for cinematic purposes.[5]

Actually, very little of *Stagecoach* was filmed in the Valley, though scenic views were taken to be used in process shots. Even the scene where the stagecoach drives toward a distant and sky-filling El Capitán is a process shot. In 1939 there were few roads in the Valley where a horse could gallop or a coach be driven. The land is creased and deeply ridged with irregular rock surfaces. Later, crews would have lanes smoothed for them, but in 1939 the stagecoach moved, most of the time, on other sites. Even *Kit Carson*, made just a year later, used more actual footage shot in the Valley. The six pictures Ford made later at the Valley will forever associate him with it. (Goulding helped, by giving exotic names to the rock formations—one of them called John Ford Point.) But in *Stagecoach* the Valley is as much an idea as an actuality.

Still, the idea is what counts. The movie continually pits the cramped little stagecoach against the cosmic vault through which it moves. The banker takes up so much of his seat that the two women on either side of him are squeezed in and pushed down. He is a mini-Capitán in this closed-sky world drawn by horses. A constant pressure is built up, urging those inside to break out of the coach's confines. Yet outside there is not just empty space. There is danger.

Ford's use of the Valley is not far from Herriman's *Krazy Kat*, where tiny figures dance out their concerns in a cosmic theater. Ford makes the galloping coach crawl past huge emblems of menace. This is not the rich land toward which pioneers strain in *The Big Trail*. It is not good for farming or founding a community. It is a place to be got through, to be endured. It is a forge of souls, a test of valor, a passageway to the unknown.

Each of the characters in the coach has been *compelled* to undergo this testing journey. The whore is marched down the street by a troupe of respectable ladies driving her out. Just as they pass a boarding house, the doctor is literally thrown out by his landlady. The driven nature of this exit is contrasted with the free scamper of a colt down the street in the wake of the arriving coach—it has broken from its mother out of sheer exuberance.

The compulsions exerted on the other passengers are internal. The banker has to escape before his theft is discovered. The marshal has to leave his post when he hears that the Ringo Kid is loose and headed toward Lordsburg. The wife must join her husband, a cavalry officer. The gambler leaves his card game when he hears that the army wife (a fellow Virginian) will be in danger. The driver is forced to go on, even after he tries to quit rather than run into Geronimo's warriors. Wayne, when he stops the coach, is made to disarm himself before he enters the coach (later he is manacled by the marshal).

The displacement of people entering the forced intimacy of the coach is glimpsed in the separate scenes where the marshal and the gambler rise to go. The camera has looked down on each, his posture carefully composed in the "pocket" of his own arena—the marshal lounging back near a rack of carefully arranged rifles, the gambler at a window where he sees the action outside and inside, perched to have the advantage against all comers. Each must give up his carefully constructed "home advantage" to be dragged along, with others, exposed to a perilous trip outside their cocoon of the accustomed.

Passage through the Valley is punctuated by three stops, each a further step into devastation. At the first one, Dry Forks (a name suggesting barrenness), the travelers are told their cavalry escort is leaving them. They must go forward, if they go at all, alone. They will be hurtling through emptiness sealed up in their coach as in a space capsule. The vote to go on is tensely arrived at.

At the second stop, the very name, Apache Wells, tells them they are deeper into Indian territory. The innkeeper's Indian wife signals to the mestizo laborers to steal the stagecoach's relay team. The travelers will go forward with no spare energy source should any horse fall. The third stop, Lee's Ferry, no longer exists by the time they reach it. The Indians have wiped it out. The gambler covers up a raped woman (the glimpse of her cut down by the censors)—an omen of what will happen to his charge, the army wife. There is no further stop, just the last stretch taken at breakneck pace, with the tired horses, through a swirl of attacking Indians.

The closing in of menace is suggested by the quickening tempo as they move from station to station of their ordeal. The trip to Dry Forks takes 8.17 minutes on screen. The second leg, to Apache Wells, 6.13. The third only 2.14.[6] At the first stop, the hosts were all Anglo. At the second, Mexican and mestizos. At the third, no one. Ford emphasized the fixed gauntlet they must run by having Andy Devine, the driver, sing out the stops when people board the coach. (The script simply has the driver give the final destination.)

The changes in external geography are played against alterations in the social geography inside the coach. Nichols made charts of the occupants' positions after each stop. The opening arrangement looks like this:[7]

		DOCTOR		WHORE
	DRIVER			
HORSES		SALESMAN		BANKER
	MARSHAL			
		GAMBLER	KID	WIFE

When Wayne stops the coach—an escaped convict whose horse has died—he is disarmed by the marshal and seated on the floor, his back to the door, between the gambler and the wife. His large torso increases the crowding. Yet he has brought some of the largeness of the Valley into this stifling space.

The shot that introduces Wayne has become famous. Edward Buscombe, of the British Film Institute, calls it "one of the most stunning entrances in all of cinema."[8] We hear a rifle report. The cavalry escort, still riding behind the coach, splashes at quickened pace through a stream. We see Wayne standing alone against a mesa.[9] For many, including most critics, it was their first look at Wayne. Few saw *The Big Trail* in 1930, and even fewer had seen the B movies that intervened in the nine years since then.

Wayne's image had changed since 1930. He is still slim but more heavily built and more toughly costumed than he was when Raoul Walsh put him in skintight buckskins and moccasins.[10] When Wayne moves to the coach and stands beside it, we see how tall and solid he is—no longer flexible and soft. Much of that has to do with the high boots he wears instead of moccasins. Wayne always gave an impression of great size, but the endlessly repeated description of him as standing six-foot-four is false.[11]

He stood that *in his boots*, which made a subtle change in his whole body's configuration. Dan Barden, who grew up knowing Wayne (his father worked for and with Wayne on real estate ventures), points out to me that Wayne had a long torso above the waist, broad shoulders, large hands. But he had comparatively short legs and small feet. When he is not wearing cowboy boots he is no taller than Ward Bond or many others. The boots extend the legs, restoring proportion. They also disguise the small feet.

We get only a short look at Wayne's full body. Then the camera tracks quickly to him while he is twirling his rifle as easily as a pistol, to end in a close-up as Wayne does a "take"— he has recognized the coach's drivers, including a marshal who has left his own town headquarters. Renowned as this shot has become, it is deeply flawed. It is a process shot done in the studio. It would have been far more impressive if Wayne were standing in real space, with Monument Valley around him.[12] Furthermore, this seems to be a one-shot—or at least the editor had nothing better to use than this one, where the camera loses focus and fumbles back into it as it tracks forward. And Wayne's "take" is crude, easily improved if Ford had had the patience to reshoot. It looks as if Ford did not realize how important this shot was—not what one would expect if Ford had planned the movie as a vehicle for launching Wayne as a star.

When Wayne gets into the coach—sitting on the floor, across the line of the other bodies—he should crowd the little container more than anyone else does. But unlike the banker, who elbows others aside, Wayne seems to lounge at ease in the space that would actually double his legs up against his knees.[13] Ford can play tricks with space since he uses a breakaway set for all the interior shots of the coach.[14] He can make people look pent-in or expansive without regard to actual conditions in a four-walled space. Wayne's freedom and power are suggested by the ease with which he controls any space he is in.

At the stops, Wayne *flows* out of the coach—still seated on the floor, he reaches up outside the coach to its roof, pulls himself up, and swings his legs out. The contrast between his fluidity and the cramped moves of other passengers speaks of the different world he inhabits. One deft touch emphasizes the point: after getting out at Apache Wells, Wayne offers to help the gambler climb down, an effort haughtily brushed aside before the gambler helps the wife out.

Even inside the coach, Wayne sprawls at cross-purposes to the others' properly seated postures. They are "ticketed." They have a proper place. He is a loose item, not relegated to any pigeonhole. This choreographed set of meanings is continued inside the first post station, where everyone else has entered and taken his or her place before Wayne ducks his height under the door, steps to its side, and leans by its border. From there he can sweep the company with his glance. We look, through the arranged group, at Wayne gracefully lounging by the door. He interrupts the vote already in progress to ask why the lady (the whore) has not been consulted. He is ignorant of the protocol that assigns her a place—a fact confirmed when he seats her at table near the army wife. The gambler comes to the wife's rescue, moving her to the other end of the table, where the banker follows her. The seating is as much a confinement here as in the coach. Even the outside can be imprisoning.

After the passengers reenter the coach, the cavalry escort peels off, and a colt from the military's remuda frisks playfully behind the departing guards—the same contrast with the *compelled* nature of the voyagers' travel that we saw in the early scene, contrasting a colt's lone scamper with the prostitute's driven passage down the street. Tim Holt, the young son of a cowboy actor who plays the officer in charge of the cavalry, tries to smile encouragement to the army wife as the troopers pull away from the coach; but when she turns her head, his concern for the abandoned party shows on his face.

Leaving the next stop, where the army wife has borne her child, the passengers' attitudes are sharply altered—something I discuss in the next chapter. To reflect the changes in their relationships, the interior geography of the coach is recast.

		W	KID	WHORE (holding baby)
DRIVER		I		
		F		
HORSES		E		BANKER
MARSHAL				
		GAMBLER	DOCTOR	SALESMAN

The doctor, who sobered up to deliver the baby, is now on the floor with Wayne, not clinging to the whiskey salesman and sipping continually from his samples. The salesman now sits by a window, indicating his new assertiveness and manhood (he will be exposed to an arrow that wounds him in the Indian attack). The prostitute is now part of the community, since she assisted at the birth and has taken charge of the baby. The wife, still recovering from the delivery, lies with her head in the gambler's lap (she is slipping down the social scale). Only the banker remains an outsider, concerned only with his bag of money.

When the attack comes, the little internal community rallies to acts of mutual defense. The doctor knocks out the banker and tends to the wounded salesman. Wayne, doing his own stunt work here, clambers onto the top of the coach while the horses are at full gallop. On top, he commands a view to all sides, and shifts about to fire at the nearest menace. He sprawls gracefully (most of the time in process shots), writhing around this endangered platform as artfully as Michelle Pfeiffer squirmed on her piano top in *The Fabulous Baker Boys*. Wayne's ease on the pitching surface makes him freer than those inside, at one with the speed of the horses and the omnidirectional chances offered for his rifle fire. The "outsider" fights for the community in most Ford films, a concept given its visual representation in this scene.

The chase brings Yak Canutt into his own. He has been a recurring presence in this film. He even had a small speaking part. When riders come at us in the film's opening scene, one of them is Yak. Dismounted, he reports that Geronimo is in the area. Later, when the stagecoach is floated over the river on logs, Yak doubles Andy Devine in order to handle the horses. (He also contrived the log floats.) Later still, Yak doubles Wayne when the Kid leaps from the coach to the horses' harness (retrieving the lead rein dropped when the driver was shot). But mainly Yak plays several Indians in the chase scene. First he is seen on his pinto galloping full speed along the starboard side of the coach, the reins of the horse loose while Yak uses both hands to reload his rifle. Since he was directing everybody's stunts, Yak can be seen looking back, at one point, to see if an Indian fall behind him has gone safely.

His most famous appearance is as the Indian who leaps on the horse team, gets shot by Wayne, then falls between the horses' hooves and passes under the stagecoach—all this last sequence in one take so we can see him struggling to get up at the end, proving that no dummy has been used. Edward Buscombe calls this "Canutt's most difficult stunt," and Charlton Heston (who worked with Yak on *Ben-Hur*) said it had never been done before and was never repeated afterward.[15] Actually, the Olympic track star Dean Smith repeated the "gag" (as stuntmen call it) in the weak 1966 remake of *Stagecoach*, and Yak had done it earlier in the B movies critics knew nothing about. In fact, Yak had done something even more amazing in an earlier film. Passing under the coach, he grabbed its undercarriage, pulled himself up, and *climbed back on* the hurtling vehicle. This is the stunt Yak rightly boasts of as never tried again.

Yak, as usual, took control of the scenes where he and his men were at risk. And Ford, as usual, resented anyone else asserting himself on *his* set. This, the first, was also the last time the greatest director of Westerns would work with the greatest Western stuntman.[16]

When the stage finally reaches Lordsburg, its destination, the whore, stripped of the baby she nurtured, loses the respect she had temporarily won—just as "Suet Pudding" does in Maupassant. But the Kid, like Maupassant's hedonistic radical, still looks at her with admiring love. Wayne offers to take the woman "home"—something she opposes as long as she can, lest he see the "red light district" where her only friends are. Their walk toward the rather surreal honky-tonk area, where brothel pianos are tinkling sad gaieties, is kept vague, at the censors' insistence that no identifiable whorehouse be fully visible.

But Ford ignored Joe Breen's other directive to alter the script. Breen, the censor in chief, had said that the marshal could not abet the flight of an escaped convict, so Nichols wrote into the script a pardon for the Kid, worked out when new evidence showed the Plummers, Wayne's prey, had been guilty of the crime he was charged with. In this version, when the Kid and the whore escape to Mexico, the doctor (Thomas Mitchell) asks the marshal: "You dad-blamed fool, why didn't you tell 'em Luke [Plummer] confessed to killing his foreman?" The marshal (George Bancroft) answers: "If you had the brains of a tadpole, Doc, you'd figger out why they're better off without knowin'— headin' over the Border." The escaping couple will stay away from "the curse of civilization" out of ignorance that return is possible. The Kid, passive through much of the movie, is manipulated to the end.

Ford ignored this attempted intervention of the censors. There is no talk of a confession, of a pardon, or the marshal's observation of the rules. In fact, Ford had the marshal *take off his badge* as the Kid disappears and offer to buy the doctor a drink. The two turn away together like Humphrey Bogart and Claude Rains at the end of *Casablanca*—the beginning of a beautiful friendship.

But first the marshal puts the Kid and the whore on an open buckboard and shies rocks at the horses to make them bolt away, relieving the Kid of responsibility for his flight. The horses run free with their light open carriage, more like the scampering colts of earlier scenes than like the laboring team that dragged the stagecoach away from pursuing Indians. The couple who earned respect in the coach's confinement now move into a welcoming, not a menacing, space. The alternations of confinement and release that ran all through the picture, in a rhythm of enclosure and exposure, are resolved at last in the union of intimacy and immensity—Wayne moving with his loved one toward a huge but friendly horizon. Vast spaces had, during the long stagecoach ride, made people cower in their little corners. Now they beckon Wayne out toward freedom.

INNER SPACES

IN ITS GENERAL PATTERN, *Stagecoach* counterpoints the crowded interior of the coach against a vast circumambient landscape. But the principal break in that pattern takes the movie's characters into inner spaces, at the coach's second stop, Apache Wells, where enclosure opens the characters up to each other. This is a place of shadows, where people learn respect for each other's mystery. The social masks slip, and different persons emerge. This sequence is the still axis, at the very center of the film, around which everything turns. The episode at Apache Wells takes up twenty-four minutes of the film—about seven minutes more than the climactic scenes at the destination (Lordsburg).

We know that we are in a different atmosphere, at this second stop, when the marshal, coming through the door, sees that the pregnant wife has collapsed on the floor. Dropping his rifle, the marshal leaps forward in concern, and his shadow is cast on the wall beside him. This is a device from silent pictures for showing inner division or opposed promptings. A good example occurs in William S. Hart's *Hell's Hinges,* where a gunman hired to drive social reformers out of town is smitten by the preacher's sister. He walks apart from the crowd and stands at the corner of a barn. The screen is neatly divided in half—on the right, a plain expanse of wall, on the left, Hart musing as he leans on the wall, his fragmented shadow cast on various surfaces as he debates with himself, within himself.

It is often said that Ford used "innovative techniques" in

Stagecoach.[1] Actually, he went back to the style of his early Westerns, telling a story in visual images more than in words. This was, after all, Ford's first Western of the sound era—his last one had been made thirteen years before (*Three Bad Men,* 1926). He would fill the central panel of this sound film with silences and crossing shadows. When the army wife is carried down a dark hallway, the light from a room on the right throws bright squares on the left wall. Sharp-profiled shadows cross and recross that bright patch. In a hushed awareness of crisis, the doctor and the prostitute go in and out of the room where the travail of a baby's delivery is played out in remotely signaled urgencies. People forget their poses, the simple front they put up to each other, as they become aware of their own and others' depths.

While the pains of delivery intensify at the building's hidden center, menace closes in from outside. The host's Apache wife sings a song to gather the mestizos of the post. At her signal that the coast is clear, they steal the relay team of horses. The coach must now go on with the tired horses and no replacements. The men rush out, too late, to fire after the escaping thieves. The marshal does not know whether to arm the Kid for help against the Indians or to manacle him—*he* could easily slip away in the night.

Inside again, the five men of the party—all but the banker—arrange themselves around the one lamp in this dark room. Shot from above—as the isolated marshal and gambler had been in their daylight "lairs" of the early scenes—the men form patterns of community, leaning toward the light. The driver even tells the gambler what card to play in his unsolitary game of solitaire—and the gambler is too worried to take offense. The sounds of danger and community mingle when, for a moment, we cannot tell the difference between a coyote's howl and the baby's first cry. The men crowd the entry to the dark hall as the prostitute brings out the infant girl. All the others stare at the baby, but Wayne stares at the whore holding her.

Changes in the people standing there become evident at once. The mousy salesman becomes assertive, ordering the marshal to be quiet, to think of the woman down the hall. The marshal lets the driver get whole statements out, without silencing him (as he normally does).

After the delivery, Wayne goes down the dark hall for the first time, following the prostitute as she goes to a back door that opens on the stable. When he is halfway down the hall, the

Mexican host comes out of an unsuspected door on the left. He is carrying a lamp as he whispers a friendly warning about the men waiting for Wayne in Lordsburg. Wayne tilts his white hat brim down to the lamp, lighting his cigarette. Intimate gestures multiply in these dark recesses. The inner spaces of this inn open hidden places in the characters. A community is born from danger. Human warmth replaces the stifling proximity of strangers jammed into unwelcome proximity. All this is reflected in the new social arrangements inside the coach as the party faces its last string of ordeals—the destroyed third post, the perilous river crossing, the flat-out race through encircling Indians.

When, fleeing the Indians, the coach's party runs out of ammunition, Ford pays a silent tribute to D. W. Griffith: the gambler's gun, with one bullet saved for the wife, enters the frame almost entirely filled with her face—a scene repeated from Griffith's *Battle at Elderbush Gulch* (1914). But then rescue comes, with another ambiguous mingling of sounds—this time of muted trumpets through the noise of battle. The cavalry has returned. The coach sweeps into town. The banker is arrested. The Kid goes after his father's murderers.

The sheriff of Lordsburg is played by Duke Lee, Ike Plummer by Vester Pegg—both veterans of Ford's early Westerns. Two cowboy stars of the twenties, Buddy Roosevelt and Bill Cody, have bit parts in the town—as does Steve Clemente from B cowboy pictures. One of the bar girls is played by Western actress Helen Gibson. Tim Holt, the young cavalry officer, was the son of cowboy Jack Holt, with whom Wayne played a bit part in *Maker of Men* at Columbia (1931). Luke Plummer, the principal villain, is played by Tom Tyler, who followed Wayne as "Stony Brooke" in the Three Mesquiteers series. The coach, when it enters Lordsburg, is going back into movie history, to a place haunted with the ghosts of a hundred shoot-outs.[2]

Ford's silent technique is most evident in the scene where Luke Plummer, playing cards in a saloon, is informed that the Ringo Kid has reached Lordsburg. Plummer rises. His face, above the hanging lantern, turns into a black silhouette-shape as the dread knowledge fills his mind. He moves to the bar, where his spiritual isolation is enacted by the motion of others away from him. An innocent gesture by the bartender almost makes Luke draw on him. The others edge off, afraid of Luke's fear. The only continuing sound is the saloon player's nervous tinkling on his piano—itself a suggestion of the piano music that accompa-

nied silent films. When Wayne walks toward his shoot-out with
the Plummers, we see him from the back. He cradles his rifle in
his arms—exactly the way Harry Carey paced to the showdown
in *Straight Shooting* (1917). Probably, if we had more of Ford's
old Westerns, we would see more references to his past in this
section of *Stagecoach*.

Yet these devices were not specific to Westerns as a genre.
They reflect the whole "expressionist" range of Ford's work from
the silent era. In fact, we learn little by comparing *Stagecoach*
with other Westerns. Its natural companion is the next movie
Ford made with Dudley Nichols, again using Wayne—*The Long
Voyage Home* (1940). Nichols, Ford's best prewar collaborator,
made no other Western with him. Instead, the two men turned
to a favorite of their Irish hearts, Eugene O'Neill, stitching together four of his one-act plays about the sea. This is another
ensemble piece, with no stars. It is not, technically, a ship-of-
fools story, since the merchant crew lives together from port to
port. They are not temporarily *wrenched* from normal society.
This *is* their society, such as it is.

Ford again conducts his narrative by manipulation of
spaces, shadow, and shifting groups of bodies. Making a virtue
of necessity—there is no real ship, just partial sets—Ford does
not ever show us the whole boat. We see men scramble through
divided spaces, compartmentalized, cut off from each other. In
the first episode, a triple horizontal division is emphasized, as
firemen swarm up, officers rush down, to grapple with rioting
sailors on the deck.

In the third episode of *Long Voyage*, the suspicions that divide men, even in close quarters, are played out as an alcoholic's
furtive acts make others think him a spy. The alcoholic is seen in
misleading glimpses through the upstairs window, the darkened
wheelhouse, his cramped bunk. The spying men are severed
from each other spiritually, their views only partial, their lives
fragmented. The obstructive partitions of naval architecture
speak of thwarted lives. The steersman is literally in the dark as
he guides the ship through the night, everyone steering for
"home"—as O'Neill calls death.

In the final sequence, the shallow bonhomie of the men on-
shore leads to a betrayal of the naive Swedish farmer trying to
leave the ship. Wayne is the farmer, once again too innocent to
recognize a prostitute. He is deserted by the men who claim to be
celebrating his escape from seafaring. Ford uses a dark alleyway

crisscrossed with light as he had used the hall in *Stagecoach*—
only this time the hall leads back to profane mystery (the prostitute's quarters), not to a holy mystery of birth. When Wayne tries
to go out that alley toward the ship, a prostitute plucks him back,
her form just a dark silhouette in the door. She looks like the
slim black devil who puts his hand on Judas's cloak in Giotto's
Arena Chapel. It is an extension of the same device Ford used
when he blanked out Luke Plummer's face.

Ford's cameraman on *Voyage* was the great Gregg Toland,
with whom he had just made *The Grapes of Wrath* (1940).
Though Toland always had his own magic to bring to a film, it is
striking how much Ford gets stylistic uniformity from different
cinematographers. *Voyage* has many points of visual continuity
with Joe August's filming of *The Informer* (1935) as well as with
Bert Glennon's *Stagecoach*. Toland went directly from this experience with Ford to his work on Orson Welles's *Citizen Kane*.
Dark silhouettes, like the whore's in *Voyage*, are used—indeed
overused—throughout *Citizen Kane*. The scene in a projection
room (after the opening newsreel has been run) is entirely a
shuffling of dark profiles. Welles said that this, the first scene
shot, was acted by his Mercury Theatre players, more of whom
would show up, later, in different roles. (One of the disembodied
voices—the one telling where Kane's second wife is—is Welles's
own.)[3] But the most fascinating aspect of the episode is the way
it reuses vital elements from *Voyage*'s wheelhouse scene—a dark
enclosure slashed across by a great diagonal of light glowing
square in the back (through which, in *Voyage*, the shape of an
officer on watch suggests how near to all others, but how far
apart, is everyone on O'Neill's merchant ship).

Yet the most effective use of a dark silhouette in *Kane* does
not resemble anything in *Voyage* as much as it does the Luke
Plummer scene in *Stagecoach:* Welles, playing Kane, stands writing his "Declaration of Principles" up against a darkened window, the reflection of a gas light wriggling on its panes. When
Kane turns and says he wants his new paper to be as vital to New
York "as this gas light," he paradoxically turns the light *off* before
reading his statement—his head now just a silhouette. Even
while he claims to be bringing the light of truth, he is "darkening
counsel." *Stagecoach*'s real effect in movie history was not, as
legend would have it, on other Westerns, but—through Welles—
on the camera as an explorer of inner spaces.

The movie's meaning for Wayne was not, yet, that his future

lay in Westerns. His only other work with Ford before the war was on the O'Neill project. And even after the war, Ford's first Wayne film would be the Navy story *They Were Expendable*. Wayne's fate was still unsettled, even after his supposed breakthrough. He would not be comfortable with the prospect of remaining a cowboy until he met and worked with Harry Carey.

□ 8 □
WAR YEARS

THOSE WHO THINK John Ford put John Wayne in *Stagecoach* in order to make him a star should reflect on the fact that Ford's next three movies were star vehicles—*Young Mr. Lincoln, Drums Along the Mohawk,* and *The Grapes of Wrath*—but Ford did not use Wayne in them. He gave the leading part in all three to Henry Fonda. When Ford did use Wayne again, it was in an even smaller role than that of the Ringo Kid—as "Oley" Olsen in *The Long Voyage Home* (1940), another ensemble play without a star part. Other actors got more lines than Wayne did. Thomas Mitchell had the most dynamic role in the movie, and Ward Bond had the juiciest single scene (a long deathbed speech). Wayne is even more passive here than in *Stagecoach*—a man things happen to, not who does things. Wayne is drugged and unconscious at the climax of the film when Mitchell leads the crew to rescue him from being "shanghaied."

Though Ford later claimed he did not know Wayne could act, he seems to have considered him in 1940 as a character actor—much what Ward Bond would remain. Ford had to have some confidence in him at that level, since the small part he gave him was not easy (it called for a Swedish accent), and this movie meant a lot to Ford, who thought of Eugene O'Neill as a brother artist in the ranks of Irish creativity.

Wayne performed creditably—his accent is subtle, more a matter of lifts and dips in pitch than of pronunciation. The only time he actually uses Swedish, it is to count under his breath, so the exact sounds are not clear. Wayne is innocent and likable, enough to create the pathos of his kidnapping scene. He could have matured into an actor of secondary parts, another of Ford's big palookas (Bond, McLaglen, George O'Brien, Woody Strode); that was the direction Ford was taking him in. Why else demote him from the Ringo Kid, a part that played bigger than it was written, to a small part that could *only* work if it was *under-played*? Luckily for Wayne, who meant to be a star, not an actor, Ford went off to war the year after making *The Long Voyage Home*.

Nor did Wayne's masters at Republic have any obvious plans for making Wayne a star. They released four more films in his Three Mesquiteers series after *Stagecoach* won good notices—a way to cash in on Wayne's improved status, not a way to build him up for bigger things. Even when Wayne was given better roles, it was on the basis of his pairing with Claire Trevor, whose name was still the bigger "draw." After all, Wayne's performance in *Stagecoach* might be a fluke; but she had more than a one-shot record. She had been well received in *Dead End* even before she made *Stagecoach*. She got top billing, above Wayne, when RKO used him in the Revolutionary War film *Allegheny Uprising* (1939), and Republic used him in *Dark Command* (1940). This latter film was directed by Raoul Walsh, ten years after he had given Wayne his name in *The Big Trail*. Walsh again plays two styles of manhood off against each other—Walter Pidgeon as an educated but insecure man, Wayne as an illiterate but cocky son of nature. Wayne is engaging in the role, which presents him as more confident than bright. Not much of a schemer himself, Wayne does not defeat the cleverer Pidgeon. The villain's own mother kills him at the end of the movie.

Wayne was not soaring, in other words, but rising slowly when he began what would turn out to be a series of three films with Marlene Dietrich. This was not as great a step up as it might seem now. Dietrich's career had just been shakily reborn after serious decline. Distributors made a famous declaration that she was "box office poison" in the late 1930s.[1] Her exotic roles as a European temptress had proved boring to the public. Further-more, her German accent was an embarrassment at a time when Hitler was pushing the world into war. She was "un-American" in ways that were no longer alluring.

Dietrich was nursing her show business wounds on the Rivi-era, waiting for calls that did not come, when she was offered a new gimmick by her agent, Charles Feldman, working with the producer Joe Pasternak: take the glowing marble face out from behind the veils and lattices in which Josef von Sternberg had shadowed her, and rub the marble nose in the dirt. She would become a "regular" out on the frontier, where she could be earthier, not otherworldly. Running a western saloon, she could be presented as tarty and French, not slinky and German.

Dietrich thought the idea vulgar and absurd, but her friend Joseph Kennedy, vacationing with his large family on the Riviera, asked what alternatives she had. The old no longer worked. Why not try the new?[2] *Destry Rides Again,* the resulting spoof Western, came out the same year as *Stagecoach.* It was a pleasant change of pace, and Jimmy Stewart played with quizzical virtue the man trying to tame Marlene and the town that supports her saloon. The tart was not good enough to marry this paragon of nonviolence, so she had to die for him in the end—a surprising twist on an otherwise lighthearted story. Dietrich acquired another signature song in the process: "See What the Boys in the Back Room Will Have."

Having purged Dietrich of European pretensions and dignity, her handlers could think of nothing to do but repeat the *Destry* formula. In *Seven Sinners,* a comic-rueful "Sadie Thompson" tale of the South Seas, she is made a traveling floozie, kicked out of island after island, who again sacrifices herself for a sample of pure American manhood—not by dying this time, but by renouncing her love rather than ruin his Navy career.

Who was to be the male this time? Jimmy Stewart was not available. Her agent wanted Tyrone Power, but he was too big a star to risk on a still-shaky Dietrich project. The myth is that Dietrich chose Wayne. In an anecdote often repeated, director Tay Garnett claimed that he arranged for her to see Wayne in the Universal commissary, where she whispered to him (Garnett): "Daddy, buy me that."[3] If she said it, she was remembering it from a Somerset Maugham play *(The Circle)* she had acted in on the German stage.[4] But even if she said it, the choice was not hers to make. The studio did the pairing, and Wayne was as good as they could find for her at this stage.

The attempt to repeat *Destry* extended to use of the same comic actors (Mischa Auer and Billy Gilbert) and to double entendre songs from the same musical team (Frank Loesser and Frederick Hollander). But the light *Destry* touch is gone—mainly because Jimmy Stewart's part is gone. Destry was a man who must tame a town without wearing a gun—a cool observer, not blindly infatuated with Dietrich, as Wayne must be in *Seven Sinners*. Wayne's assignment is to go instantly gaga for Marlene, to be instantly resigned when she says It Must Not Be, and to look decorative in the interval. Meanwhile Dietrich's brassiness began to wear as thin as her earlier *hauteur* had. In *Seven Sinners*, she alternates broad comic "takes" with exaggerated leers.

The formula clearly had to be varied. In 1942, Randolph Scott was brought into *The Spoilers* in order to compete with Wayne for Dietrich's favors—Scott as a claim jumper on Alaska gold mines, Wayne as the man defending his claim. Dietrich does not have to give up Wayne this time, since the "good girl" he thinks he loves turns out to be conniving with Scott's thieves. By comparison, Dietrich looks pure enough to win the hero.

Wayne's third film with Dietrich, *Pittsburgh* (1942), uses Randolph Scott again. This time the men clash more over business policy than over Marlene. She recedes in importance (and dies again) while the men, partners in a coal-mining operation, fight for control of it. Scott is the "straight arrow" who thinks of the miners' safety, while success makes Wayne become arrogant and greedy. The men are reunited by the war effort, as the movie turns into propaganda which looked blatant even to the Office of War Information.[5] Dietrich delivers the film's message:

> This is no time to think of personal feelings and personal grievances. The only question that should guide each of you and every one of us today is devotion to your country —that's the one thing you should think about. Your country needs you.

Dietrich did less for Wayne's wartime movies than for his personal life. She was an experimenter with people, and sex was the laboratory instrument she used on her co-stars, male and female. Wayne accepted with alacrity this "perk" of his rising status.[6] He told his third wife that Dietrich was a torrid lover.[7] But Dietrich's daughter, Maria Riva, who was a close observer of all her mother's affairs, said that Wayne dropped Marlene. When, later, Riva asked him why, he said: "Never liked being part of a stable."[8] Wayne liked submissive women—the very opposite of Dietrich. Her bitterness about him was in marked contrast to the fond recollections she had for most of her lovers—many of whom were content to wait with masochistic devotion for her to bestow some new attention on them. That was not Wayne's style, and Dietrich took revenge on his imperviousness by ridiculing him ever after. She told her daughter: "Those long drinks of water, like Cooper and Wayne, they are all alike. All they do is clink their spurs, mumble, 'Howdy, Ma'am,' and fuck their horses."[9] She told John Ford's wife that Wayne was stupid and conceited: "I tried to help him. I knew he couldn't act without being coached. He said Ford took him home at night and helped him with his next day's scenes. I tried that too, but it didn't work."[10] That was said in 1943, just after Wayne had dropped Marlene for Esperanza Baur, the woman who became his second wife.

Though Marlene thought she failed to "educate" Wayne, he learned from her what was important at the time—and it had nothing to do with sex. Wayne was coming into sight of stardom in the war years, and he meant to reach that goal. In Marlene he had a complete example of discipline devoted to "the career." She had been a star on two continents a decade before she and Wayne met, and in all the vicissitudes of her life, onstage or onscreen, she summoned an iron control over what was needed to keep coming back. She would forge two later careers— as character actress, and as concert performer—after World War II.

Dietrich had worked out a way of surviving her possessive manager and self-proclaimed "discoverer," Josef von Sternberg (for whom Wayne later acted in *Jet Pilot*).[11] When von Sternberg said he taught her all she knew (sounding a lot like Dietrich posing as Wayne's educator), she responded with expressions of gratitude that took the wind out of his sails, killing him with kindness. This was all the more galling to von Sternberg because he saw what her tactic was, and that it was working:

> In the beginning the defensive maneuver was most proba-
> bly an instinctive measure, if it was not genuine humility,
> but as soon as it was evident that it produced additional
> admiration [for her], there was no good reason to refrain
> from earning a few plaudits on her own account.[12]

That is not a bad description of Wayne's later relationship with John Ford—a man Wayne had problems with during the war years, the time when he was observing Dietrich's conduct on and off the screen. She tried to exert total control over her image. She used people with a severe economy, always keeping in mind her professional goals. Wayne, who had spent ten years laboring in the lower ranks of Hollywood, now saw a chance for something much better. He was in his early thirties, at the peak of his physical attractiveness, and the need for male stars was increasing as those in Wayne's age bracket went off to some form of military service.

There was tremendous pressure, in public and in private, for Wayne to join them. But if he did, his opportunity, sought for over a decade, might slip away forever. He would return from war older, with not much made of his post-*Stagecoach* roles, to a glut of males returning from war, competing with all the young stars who moved up during the war. Wayne was prepared to do anything to avoid such a fate. He wrote tortuous excuses to John Ford, who had rushed into military service. He had his studio contrive ever-new exemptions for him.[13] He hoped to substitute morale work with troops for joining the troops. As he told the daughter of his friend and fellow actor, Paul Fix: "I better go do some touring—I feel the draft breathing down my neck."[14] As far as careerism went, Marlene had a very good pupil in Wayne.

Wayne's fans have tried to make excuses for his absenteeism from the war. They even bring up the mythical "football injury" that supposedly cost him a scholarship fourteen years before the war. Wayne, to his credit, never did that. They point out that he was thirty-four in 1941, still married to his first wife, with whom he had four small children—enough to get an exemption in the war's early years. But other stars were as old or older, and some of them had children.

Clark Gable was forty-one when he entered the service, Tyrone Power forty, Henry Fonda and Robert Montgomery thirty-seven, Jimmy Stewart thirty-three, Ronald Reagan thirty-two. Reagan did not serve abroad because he was practically blind without his contact lenses—but his military film work for the Signal Corps kept him from commercial movie-making and definitely hurt his career. Like Wayne, he had just completed a breakthrough performance (in *Kings Row*) after years in B movies and matinee series. By the time he returned to the studio, Reagan had lost his romantic boyhood, his stock in trade, and his acting career spiraled down into TV, radio, and a Las Vegas act before he discovered politics.

Perhaps the most galling newspaper item for Wayne appeared in 1942, when Gene Autry gave a widely reported interview about his own enlistment. (Autry was just four months younger than Wayne.)

> I think the He-men in the movies belong in the Army, Marine, Navy or Air Corps. All of these He-men in the movies realize that right now is the time to get into the service. Every movie cowboy ought to devote time to the Army winning, or to helping win, until the war is over—the same as any other American citizen. The Army needs all the young men it can get, and if I can set a good example for the young men I'll be mighty proud.[15]

Wayne knew, of course, that failure to serve in the military would lower him in John Ford's esteem. Ford had always admired war heroes. His friendly professional relationship with producer Merian Cooper, begun in 1934, was largely based on Cooper's record as a World War I ace flyer and German prisoner of war. Cooper's World War II work with the Flying Tigers further impressed Ford. It always counted with him that George O'Brien had been in the Navy, Jack Pennick in the Marines. Ford's own personal hero was Frank ("Spig") Wead, the World War I flyer and naval reformer. (Ironically, Ford would later, in 1957, have the noncombatant Wayne play Wead in *The Wings of Eagles*.) Ford, wounded in combat at the Battle of Midway, honored a whole gallery of heroes from "his" war—including John Bulkeley and Douglas MacArthur, commemorated in *They Were Expendable*, or William ("Wild Bill") Donovan, Ford's superior at OSS, about whom he later tried to make a movie.

Wayne could not just ignore Ford. He was caught in a web of Ford's friends and professional colleagues. Ward Bond, who had a genuine exemption because he was epileptic, became a kind of surrogate father to the Ford children while Ford was in the OSS.[16] Wayne met and worked with Harry Carey during the war, which introduced him to a large part of Ford's past life (Ford got Carey's son shipped out of a battle zone to ease his mother's mind).[17] Wayne was living in the house of a fellow Western actor, Paul Fix, at the very time when Carey's son wooed and married Fix's daughter.

Even if Wayne had wanted to ignore Ford, Ford's wife was urging her husband to intervene in Wayne's life. Wayne's new affair—with Esperanza Baur (known as "Chata")—was making reconciliation with his first wife impossible. Mary Ford wanted to save Wayne's marriage for the sake of the four children. She wrote her husband: "It's a damn shame that with a war going on he has to think about his lousy stinking tail. I only think of those gorgeous kids. It's really tragic."[18] She asked her husband to do something.

Ford, whose male circle boasted of "conquests," found it hard to preach to Wayne about chastity. He was forced to try awkward and indirect joshing: "If you can take enough time from playing with those Mexican jumping beans, I would be very much interested in knowing what's cooking, good looking."[19] Ford did arrange to get Wayne out of Hollywood—for an OSS-sponsored "inspection tour" of the Pacific to report on morale. Wayne admitted he found nothing to report.[20]

The obvious way to get Wayne out of Hollywood was to get him into uniform. But he was determined to avoid that. His excuses were varied and contradictory. He wrote to Ford that he was trying to fill out the proper forms to enter the military, but he had no typewriter on location; that he left forms with Ward Bond, who couldn't fill them out; or that his wife, from whom he was separated, would not let him get essential documents he had left at home.[21] In short, the dog ate his homework.

To others he claimed that Herb Yates, the head of Republic, threatened that the studio would "sue you for every penny you hope to make in the future" if he walked away from his contract.[22] But no studio took action against the actors, directors, and cameramen, all under contract, who went to war. Given the patriotic atmosphere of the time, that would have hurt the studio far more than the loss of even a big star—Gable, or Ford himself, or Fonda. And Wayne was not yet in their league.

In later years Wayne had a new excuse. He told Ford's grandson, Dan, that he would have been a private in the military (an absurd supposition), so he could have more influence through the war films he did as a star.[23] By the time of that interview, Wayne had, indeed, acquired the reputation of having won World War II single-handedly on the screen. Wayne even expressed astonishment when the Emperor Hirohito, visiting America in 1975, asked to meet him—"I must have killed off the entire Japanese army."[24] But Wayne's identification with World War II came mainly from movies made after the war—especially *Sands of Iwo Jima* in 1949, after Wayne's 1948 breakthrough into superstardom (with *Red River*). During the war he wore a uniform in only four pictures—as opposed to nine other pictures (Westerns, Marlene vehicles, etc.).[25] None of the four was an important contribution to the war effort, and Wayne was not a great hero in them. In two he is a cocky fellow who loses the girl to a more stable patriot. In one (*Reunion in France,* 1942), he does not even appear until the film has run a full forty minutes —the reunion of the title is Joan Crawford's reunion with another man. In *The Fighting Seabees* (1944) he is a hothead who imperils his own men and has to die to redeem himself.

Wayne was not a model hero in World War II. Humphrey Bogart (who had served in the Navy during World War I) was the leading war hero of the movies. We remember him, now, for his civilian role in *Casablanca,* but he was in the uniformed services for *Across the Pacific* (1942), *Action in the North Atlantic* (1943), *Sahara* (1943), and *Passage to Marseilles* (1944).

Not that the Office of War Information wanted independent heroes in the movies. The message was to be one of teamwork. "Grandstanders" are routinely punished in films of the time, and "kids" in the ranks win by pulling together (a whole crop of new stars played these roles—Van Johnson, Robert Walker, Richard Conte, John Garfield). What Washington most wanted from Hollywood were stories of fighting *groups (Wake Island, Guadalcanal Diary, The Story of G.I. Joe).* Wayne was in none of these films that made a difference to the war effort.

He worked steadily, he continued to rise, during the war. His real breakthrough was still ahead of him; but he was making it clear that if single-minded careerism would get him there, he was bound to make it. This cost him the chance to serve his country at its time of greatest unity against worldwide foes. Some in Hollywood never forgave Wayne for that. Part of John Ford never forgave him. A few even claim that Wayne did not forgive himself—that the compensatory superpatriotism of later years, when he urged the country on to wars in Korea and Vietnam, was a form of expiation. If so, it was not enough. This is a man who called on other generations to sacrifice their lives, and called them "soft" if they refused.

Wayne's uncertain relations with Ford became clear on the set of *They Were Expendable* (1945), the story of John Bulkeley's PT boat services to General MacArthur in the early days of the war. Bulkeley's boat had been put at Ford's disposal as a kind of water taxi during the landings at Normandy. (Ford's photographic unit was covering the operation.) Maneuvering in the Channel, Bulkeley was hailed from a boat by another veteran of the Pacific PT group, the actor Robert Montgomery. Montgomery did not know that the man standing next to Bulkeley was John Ford; but Ford was already casting Montgomery to play Bulkeley in a script that Ford's other hero, Spig Wead, had worked up from the bestselling tale of Bulkeley's boats. Ford could not wait to get released from war service to make this picture. He mobilized officials to give him orders that would let him defy Zanuck and his Fox contract so he could work with MGM, the studio that owned the script.[26]

Ford, who meant the movie as a tribute to the Navy, made it with fellow veterans, a point made in the list of credits, where rank and service are put after each officer's name:

> SECOND UNITS DIRECTED BY
> James C. Hoven
> Captain U.S.M.C.R.
> DIRECTOR OF PHOTOGRAPHY
> Joseph H. August, A.S.C.
> Lt. Comdr. U.S.N.R.
> DIRECTED BY
> John Ford
> Captain U.S.N.R.
> SCREEN PLAY BY
> Frank Wead
> Comdr. U.S.N.R.

There was one great exception to this list of proud service connections. It came second in the roll of actors:

> LT. JOHN BRINKLEY—Robert Montgomery, U.S.N.R.
> LT. RUSTY RYAN—John Wayne

Ford's annoyance with Wayne's avoidance of war came out on location (Florida serving as a tropical Philippines). This is the place where Ford, knowing what would rankle most with Wayne, told him he could not even move well. He was particularly critical of his salutes: "Duke, can't you manage a salute that at least *looks* like you've been in the service?" Wayne was so hurt and angry that, for the only time in his life, he stalked off the set.[27]

This was too much for Montgomery, who went over to Ford and told him, sailor to sailor, that you do not dress down a man that way before the troops. Ford was so shocked by the rebuke from his hero that he wept, and had to apologize to Wayne. Not only could Montgomery get away with things no other actor did on the set, but when Ford fell off a gantry and was sent to the hospital, he told Montgomery to finish directing the picture. He felt Montgomery understood what he was trying to do—as Wayne, for instance, could not. Montgomery said: "I felt so in tune with the way Jack thought and felt that it didn't seem difficult. I just tried to imagine how he'd have done it. When he saw the first edit—all the material strung together—Ford said 'I couldn't tell where I left off and you began.' I couldn't have asked for more."[28] Montgomery liked this first experience of directing and went on to direct five films on his own, beginning with the well-received *Lady in the Lake* (1946).

Montgomery says that Ford was trying to apologize for his own blowup at Wayne when he gave Wayne his most effective scene, the one where he recites a poem over a fallen comrade. Montgomery would have been particularly sensitive to any advantage given Wayne, since the second-billed actor was overshadowing the star. This was not Ford's intent; but he treated Montgomery so reverentially that the Bulkeley/Brinkley figure is frozen in rectitude, too perfect to be interesting.

The tone of *Expendable* is odd. It is eerily personal to Ford. Made between V-E Day and V-J Day, the movie was released just after the war ended, and it has an elegiac atmosphere in that time of triumph. Ford accepts the propaganda line of the early days in the Pacific, that the fragile little PT boats were important offensive weapons after Pearl Harbor, when the regular fleet was all but nonexistent. When the big ships arrived, the PT boats were consigned to ignoble courier service. They, too, were "expendable."[29] Ford has his actors give the ships lugubrious farewells, as if the boats were Conestoga wagons disappearing from the Old West. Ford was, in effect, saying goodbye to the war, which had been an exciting and fulfilling time for him. The man who could not stay disciplined away from movie sets had at last found a cause and the right company for bringing focus and purpose to his life. He would try to prolong the experience by using the proceeds from *Expendable* to set up a retreat for fellow veterans of the Field Photographic Unit.[30] Called the Field Photo Farm, this retreat became a place of military ceremony and memories, where Ford insisted that men wear their old uniforms to the celebration of Memorial Day or the Fourth of July. When Dobe Carey said he was getting too fat to fit into his wartime uniform, Ford told him to rent one from a costume shop.

Wayne went to the Photo Farm for the annual Christmas parties (with actors like Andy Devine playing Santa Claus for the children) or events like Harry Carey's funeral, conducted there. But he tended to avoid the occasions for which the Farm was set up, where war memories were tended.[31] He could not, like Dobe, go to the costume department for a uniform to wear. Though Ford and Wayne came professionally to depend on each other during the fifties, there was one very important part of Ford's life Wayne could never share. Wayne was even ill at ease, at times, aboard Ford's yacht, the *Araner*, where Navy terminology was used. Ford's screenwriter James Warner Bellah remembered a time when Wayne was criticized, on the boat, for never having worn a *real* Navy uniform.[32] Though Wayne's personal character came to approximate the roles he played on-screen, they could never merge in this area. There was nothing in his actual life to resemble the blank bullets he shot at fellow actors in feigned combat. He would forever be the warless "war hero."

□ 9 □

HARRY CAREY

ONE THING that eased the estrangement of Ford from Wayne during the war years is the fact that those same years brought Wayne into a close association with Harry Carey, Ford's first cowboy star. That complicated triangular relationship, of Ford with Carey and Wayne, calls for separate treatment here, though it goes back in time to Ford's earlier days. Ford's 1948 film with Wayne, *Three Godfathers,* cannot fully be understood without a separate consideration of Carey's place in the careers of his old colleague, Ford, and his young disciple, Wayne. The movie *Three Godfathers* is really about *these* three men.

Between his work on Ford's *The Long Voyage Home* (1940) and Ford's *They Were Expendable* (1945), Wayne made only one film of any real distinction, *The Shepherd of the Hills* (1941). It was his first Technicolor movie, and the first time he worked with the director Henry Hathaway, whose *True Grit* would later bring Wayne his only Oscar. It was photographed by Charles Lang, whose eighteen Oscar nominations are the highest number ever won by an artist in a single category.[1] It has an engaging performance by Betty Field, fresh from her first screen triumph in *Of Mice and Men.* Marc Lawrence, who normally played slit-eyed mobsters, is brilliant as the retarded mountain boy "Pete."

But more important than all these new elements to Wayne's career was his first chance to work with Harry Carey, the star of Ford's early silent films. Wayne grew up watching those films in Glendale, and he often said that Carey was the only cowboy he found convincing, the one who needed no fancy costume, horse tricks, or heavy weaponry. Apart from Yakima Canutt, Carey was the only actor Wayne called an important influence on his own acting.[2] Carey had a quiet strength, an informed authority.

Will Rogers had sensed those qualities in Carey. Working with Ford in 1934, Rogers said, "Jack used to direct Westerns [in the silent era], and made great ones with Harry Carey, the most human and natural of the Western actors."[3] In fact, Rogers had some of Carey's mannerisms—like pushing a cowboy hat back with the first three fingers of his right hand, to scratch his head with the other two. Both had tousled hair with one lock falling over the forehead. They had similar crinkly-eyed grins, as they looked up from under their hats. Ford, directing Rogers in three films during the thirties, probably brought out resemblances to his star of twenty years past. When one looks, now, at later character parts Carey played—e.g., the President of the Senate in Frank Capra's *Mr. Smith Goes to Washington* (1939)—it looks like Carey is imitating Rogers. What influence there was probably worked in the other direction. When Rogers was opening in New York vaudeville, he would have seen the successful Ford-Carey Westerns he later praised.

Carey, despite his "authenticity," had invented his own West as an aspiring New York playwright. The son of a well-to-do merchant and judge, Carey gave up the study of law to write, produce, and act. Though he had never left the East Coast, his first play, a Western melodrama called *Montana*, filled the house at every production, according to the New York *Telegraph*.[4] Carey rode his own horse, Dolly Varden, onto the stage every night, and drew attention to his walk (the *Mirror* called it a "swagger") and his well-staged fights. He took the play on tour—Boston, Toledo, Milwaukee, Philadelphia, Louisville.

For his second play, he created a Klondike tale *(Two Women and That Man)* and brought a real wolf and sled dogs onto the stage. To create a woodland atmosphere, he had the stage sprayed with pine scent before the doors were opened. This was too corny even for 1910. When he took this play on tour, the Chicago *Tribune* said only the dogs were convincing.

Between his stage efforts, Carey had been working in D. W. Griffith's New York studio, where his friend Henry Walthall was already employed. Carey made his first film *(Bill Sharkey's Last Game)* in 1909, when he was thirty-one, about Wayne's age when he played the Ringo Kid; but Carey, like Wayne, looked much younger and would star as a cowboy well into middle age. He played a thug in Griffith's drama of urban gangs, *The Musketeers of Pig Alley* (1912), and a treacherous young man in the biblical epic *Judith of Bethulia* (made in 1913 but released in 1914). Carey, who had gone to California with Griffith, left Biograph at the same time Griffith did (1913). At Universal Studios, which had just been moved to California from New York, Carey was allowed to write, direct, and star in his own films.[5] The director of shorts and serials at Universal was Frank Ford, whose younger brother Jack had just arrived from Maine and was doing menial jobs on the set.

Division of labor had not yet entrenched itself at Universal, so Jack Ford was allowed to do some writing and directing on his brother's multiple projects. Carey got to know Ford through Olive Golden, an actress he met when they were both still working for Griffith in New York. "Goldie," as she was known in those days, was part of the younger set at Universal, like Jack. They were eighteen and nineteen, while Carey was thirty-five when they all met. Two years later, when studio boss Carl Laemmle gave Carey authority to form his own production team for making two-reeler Westerns, Carey chose Goldie as his heroine, Jack as director, George Hively as writer, and Hoot Gibson as stuntman. Together with a cameraman, they went up to Newhall, for its colorful locations, rented a little house, and turned out Westerns in four or five days.

"Ollie," as she was later known to all her friends except Harry and Jack (who called her "Goldie"), remembered those idyllic days with affection. The house they rented was too small for any but her to sleep in, so the men "slept out in the alfalfa patch on bedrolls."[6] Harry and Jack would sit up late into the night, around the kitchen's wood stove, creating scenes to be shot the next morning, drinking their favorite rye (Melwood), "talking, talking, talking." Jack, ever the late riser, could not be dragged from his bedroll in the morning till Harry turned his dogs loose (Carey always had dogs about him). They would swarm all over Ford, licking his face. George Hively, supposed to be creating scripts, wrote down what Harry and Jack had already shot as a result of their late-night sessions. Everyone did everything—except drive. Ollie was the only one who could drive in 1917 (Harry never did learn). The 1917 car was so temperamental they often had to use a horse, pulling it, to get it started. Stunts, props, sets all had to be improvised. "Jack would make bullets and let Harry fire them, and sometimes just the opposite.

They worked together. It was very strange. They had a great, funny, wonderful relationship."

None of the team's two-reelers have survived. But two five-reelers were found not long ago, and they show how thoroughly Jack Ford's later work was shaped by his experience with Carey —just as it had been shaped, earlier, by apprenticeship under Frank Ford. Carey plays "Cheyenne Harry," essentially the creation of his own earlier plays. In *Straight Shooting* (1917), he is the only one free to mix with all four of the warring factions in the movie. He is at home with the virtuous farmers, the imperial cattle ranchers, the corrupted townspeople, and the thieves hiding out in a neighboring canyon. At the climax, a Griffith ride-to-the-rescue, Harry brings the bandits out of their lair to thwart the cattle baron. The broad social sweep of the story is astonishing for its limited playing time.

Despite their extraordinarily close collaboration in the teens of this century, Ford and Carey worked together only once after 1921—Ford gave Carey a small part in *The Prisoner of Shark Island* (1936). Carey's son Dobe blames the break on a troublemaker who bore tales of reciprocal criticism between the two men. Ford also seems to have had a crush on Ollie, which made him jealous of Carey.[7] But Ford's resentment of dependency on others meant that he *had* to part company with Carey, precisely because of Carey's influence on him at the outset. When they made *Straight Shooting*, Carey was thirty-nine and Ford was twenty-two. Carey had been with Griffith, had mounted his own plays in New York, had a circle of writers and artists as his friends. He was the authority figure at Newhall, the one Goldie fell in love with, the one whose dogs made Jack get up. Harry chose Jack to direct the pictures, but Harry was directing the director.

Despite Ford's refusal to employ Carey (even when Carey had financial problems later on), the personal ties were kept up. Dobe remembers Ford's visits to the Carey ranch several times a year, and going to visit Ford at his Odin Street house above the Hollywood Bowl, or on Ford's ship, the *Araner*. The meetings were prickly until booze softened the two men. At one memorable reunion, Ollie remembers, Jack and Henry

> got pissy-ass drunk (ah Jesus, and I mean *drunk*) . . . Harry passed out and I got him to bed. Ford was sitting out there in the kitchen . . . I can't get Ford to go to bed. Mary's gone to bed [Ford's wife], she's passed out, too. [Ollie did not

drink in those days.] So I go into the kitchen and there's Jack, and he's got a crying jag on, drooling all down his chin, and crying his eyes out about Barbara [Ford's daughter] and Dobe should get married—that's all there is to it, got to carry on the tradition, got to combine the Fords and the Carey family.

When Ford sobered up, he would be compensatorily harsh to make up for these breakthroughs of nostalgia for the good old days with Harry and Goldie.

The professional separation of Ford from Carey explains why Wayne had not yet become a friend of the actor whose Westerns he watched as a schoolboy in Glendale—not, that is, until they were cast together in *The Shepherd of the Hills*. But Wayne's admiration, and his liking for Ollie (whom everyone liked), led to a friendship that ripened during the war years, while Ford was away. When the Careys' son married the daughter of Wayne's friend Paul Fix, Wayne gave them their reception ceremony. When Ollie died, she willed Harry's memorabilia to Wayne—they are now in the National Cowboy Hall of Fame. Wayne had been taken into the Careys' extended family. They gave him, as it were, a back door into Ford's past, and he entered it while Ford was off to the war. Ford's first cowboy and his last one were forging ties that created a legacy almost despite Ford.

In *The Shepherd of the Hills*, Wayne actually plays Carey's son. The Wayne character does not know, at the outset, that Carey is his father, though others see a resemblance in the set of their eyes, the authority of their carriage. The scenes between the two lift the movie above its sentimental plot. The film was based on a popular novel that had been brought to the screen twice in the silent era. It deals with a poisoned knot of relatives, clustered on a remote Ozark mountain, who are forced by an outsider to open up and let in some light of sanity, some warmth of humanity. Hathaway plays off against each other the idyllic mountain scenery and the festering human relationships. This film attacks the iconographic assumptions of a film like *The Big Trail* (or, for that matter, of paintings by Albert Bierstadt)—that going out into nature is a way of returning to some primal innocence and purity.

There is nothing innocent about Hathaway's Ozarks, though the opening scene briefly tempts one to think so. The camera pans over a picture of forest tranquillity. But the beauty is quickly disturbed by shotgun fire. "Revenuers" have wounded the lookout for a hill distillery. The camera goes into the fastness where the liquor is made and we see Wayne thrusting jug after jug down a long wooden shoot—the illegal operation is obviously mounted on a large scale. When he hears the shot, Wayne starts off to help the lookout, though an imperious woman (Beulah Bondi) orders him to stay.

The scene shifts to a mountain cabin where perky Betty Field is singing merrily while her father plays his accordion. When the revenuers show up, Field and her father welcome them; but, just as she has shown them out the door, a wail from the accordion accompanies her father's slide to the floor. He is the lookout who was shot. Frightened by another knock at the door, Field opens to admit a stranger, in a place strangers never penetrate. It is Harry Carey, who says he has come to buy land in the area. When he sees her father on the floor, he helps him to bed and tends him—to Field's puzzlement. She thought he was allied with the government men.

Wayne arrives to ask what happened to the lookout. He is surly and suspicious toward Carey, who looks at Wayne intently as if memorizing his face. To allay Wayne's concern, Field claims Carey is a visiting cousin. After Wayne leaves, Field says she will help Carey look for land. But when he says he wants to buy some from the Gibbs family, the superstitious Field tries to discourage him. The Gibbs family, at the center of the liquor trade, is sealed up in its fortress home, and Aunt Mollie (Beulah Bondi) is a woman whose curses have made Bald Knob a haunted place. Nonetheless, with Field's help, Carey penetrates the Gibbs territory (running the gauntlet of a fierce watchdog), where he asks to buy "Moanin' Meadow." When he takes possession of that property, the idiot Pete takes a shot at him, one that misses only because Carey leans forward just as the bullet passes him.

As Carey is looking over a grave on his new property, Wayne comes striding through the woods toward him. When he sees Carey, he orders him off the property. The grave is that of Wayne's mother, who died here, abandoned by her husband. Wayne has been raised by Aunt Mollie, who imposed on him a "blood oath" to kill his unknown father. Betty Field has guessed —from an accidental gift, and from the command in each man's bearing—that Carey and Wayne are father and son, but she has given Carey her word to wait until he finds the right time and place to reveal himself. The Gibbs family conceives a deep hatred for Carey as he teaches the mountaineers how to build other forms of business than the liquor trade. Only Wayne, who is Aunt Mollie's nephew, breaks with the Gibbs hostility, yielding to Field's plea that Carey means well. Once again he is seen pacing, rifle in hand, onto Carey's property—but this time to accept an invitation to go fishing.

Seated on the pond's bank, Wayne goes into an almost fetal crouch, his fishing line untended, his hat tipped to cover his face, as he tries to get up nerve to tell Carey about his troubled conscience. After a first bit of bravado—"Seems like some things just come natural to mountain men, and *I* might be able to teach *you* about them"—Wayne confesses he does not know how to go into the outside world to seek the man he is sworn to kill. Carey asks how he will be able to live with himself after killing a man. Wayne shows reluctance to give up everything, including his love for Field, to destroy himself by destroying another, but he is bound by the mountain code and his oath. We are teased with suspense—will Carey choose this, Wayne's first vulnerable moment, to reveal himself? But Carey's gentle assurance goes no further than a promise to help Wayne find the man. It is a delicate scene beautifully played and photographed—at one point, the camera goes up to shoot down over the two men, showing the sky reflected in their quiet pond.

After a hokey scene in which a woman, blind from birth, recovers her sight and blurts out that Wayne must be Carey's son, Wayne stalks one last time into Moanin' Meadow, all business now, not to be deflected from his task. Carey comes out to meet him—they approach across the meadow, Carey unarmed. Wayne stops, lifts the rifle to his eye, and the camera veers up as a shot is heard. Then we see Carey, armed after all—he has drawn, from under his coat, the pistol in his belt (a reminder of the holsterless Cheyenne Harry). We cut back to Wayne, still sighting down his rifle, then see his eyes flutter up, his limbs go slack, as he twirls slowly down—our surprise turning to shock as we realize that the father has just shot his son.

This scene was carefully prepared—not only in all the earlier times when Wayne strode toward Carey vindictively, but in an earlier brawl Wayne had with his Gibbs cousin, Ward Bond. Field tries to hit Bond with a heavy sack of grain twirled in the air, but hits Wayne by accident. We see his eyes flutter and go blank as he falls backward in a swoon, a comic variant of what occurs in deadly earnest at the climax.

While Wayne is coming out of a coma in a hospital tent, he overhears Carey tell Field why he could not let Wayne kill a man and go to prison for decades—exactly what had kept Carey away from his wife in her time of need. As Wayne stirs, Carey comes to his bedside and the two show an affection that was developing off-screen as well as on in 1941. Carey's concerned watchfulness over Wayne all through the movie makes a wonderful performance.

After this, the two would act together in only three more movies before Harry's death in 1947. They do a blackface scene as night raiders in the Dietrich film *The Spoilers*. Then Wayne cast Harry in the first movie he produced himself, *Angel and the Badman* (1947). The last of their films to be released was *Red River* (1948), in which the ailing Carey has a small part as the buyer at the end of the cattle drive. This picture is the only one where Wayne played with both the Careys, Dobe as well as Harry. By this time Wayne was so close to the entire family (including Ollie, with her genius for friendship) that *Red River's* director, Howard Hawks, had trouble getting Wayne to play his own part in the scene with Dobe. Wayne was observant and solicitous about Dobe's performance. Hawks, shouting "Cut," told him it was not in the despotic nature of "Dunson" to be smiling at Dobe as he talked to him. "I wasn't smiling," Wayne responded. "Yeah, you were." Wayne shrugged, "I guess it's because I'm glad the kid's doing a good job." Dobe, who was in a major picture for the first time, says Wayne's words made him think he had the world by the tail.[8]

Wayne's silent tribute to Carey in *The Searchers* (1956) has become a part of film lore. Though Harry had been dead for eight years, Wayne was working in that film with his son and widow. In the final scene, where Wayne is silhouetted in the doorway, about to be shut out from the family, he looks in at Ollie's character and strikes a pose associated with Harry, his left hand grasping his right forearm. Actually, that pose was part of the repertoire of melodrama and the early silents. It signified things like inner struggle, or being wrapped up in thought. Ford had Buck Jones strike it in *Just Pals* (1920), and the Lincoln character in *The Iron Horse* (1924) holds the pose. But Carey's frequent use of the device made those around him remember it as his signature gesture. Ford knew better, but he was hardly the one to discourage any gesture of respect for Carey, once he was safely dead. Ford had hastened, right after Carey's funeral, to pay his own tribute, remaking an early Carey film, *Three Godfathers*, with a flamboyant dedication to Carey just after the opening credits.

Ford promised Carey's wife, after they witnessed Carey's death, that he would use her son, Dobe, in his next film. Ford had cried and reminisced with Carey as he was dying, and the loss seemed staggering—in part, no doubt, because Ford had self-defensively frozen Carey out of his professional life for decades. The fear and resentment of Carey's early supremacy were wiped away by death. Ollie remembered the scene:

> I went out on the patio—it was at 1920 Mandeville where we were living then—and was just standing there, and I was terribly skinny, and I had on a red sweater, a beige pleated skirt. And I remember Jack came out and he took ahold of me and put his head on my breast and cried—and the whole front of my sweater was sopping wet, all the way down the front . . . and the more he cried, the stronger I'd get. It was very good for me. It was wonderful. Oh God, he shook and cried. He was very young then, and cold sober.

Ford put on an emotion-laden funeral for Harry at the Photo Farm. Carey's horse, Sunny—the spiritual descendant of the "Dolly Varden" he had ridden onstage in the first years of the century—was hitched outside the chapel. Danny Borzage played "Red River Valley," and Wayne read the poem he had recited over the dead comrade in *They Were Expendable*. George O'Brien's son remembered a bugler sounding taps, as in a cavalry film by Ford.[9]

The emotions of Carey's death and burial carried over into the film Ford made for Carey. In the dedication shot, stuntman Cliff Lyons rode Sunny up to the horizon line and, against a setting sun, imitated Carey's way of lifting his hand to scratch his head, then leaned on one arm propped against the horse's rump.

Everything about the film took Ford back into the past he had shared with Carey. The tale is one they had told in several variants—one of tough cowboys who take it on themselves to save an orphaned baby. Ford first made the story as an actor in his brother Frank's film, *Three Bad Men and a Girl* (1915), where the brothers played two of the bad men.[10] Bret Harte's "The Outcasts of Poker Flat" has a similar plot, with an all-male town adopting a baby—and Jack made that story with Harry in 1920, the same year they filmed Peter B. Kyne's version of this sentimental myth. Kyne's tale was called "The Three Godfathers," though Ford's movie title was *Marked Men*. Ford made another variant in 1926 as *Three Bad Men* (with George O'Brien rather than Harry).

Ford was in such a charitable mood when he made the film that he forgot to put in any *human* conflict. All the struggle is against physical difficulties, the ordeal of men stranded in the Mojave Desert. *Three Bad Men* had rough ethnic humor, some plausibly bad traits in the title characters, and an even worse villain from whom the baby and her mother must be saved. In that 1926 film, the three bad men are killed while protecting the child who will bear their names. In the 1948 film, there are no villains—the pursuing sheriff is a kindly Ward Bond (who will try to adopt the baby). No one kills anyone. Though "the Kid" in the three-man gang is wounded during a bank robbery, he dies of exposure. The Mexican thief, played by Pedro Armendariz, breaks his leg and kills himself. The movie ends in a competition of kindliness around the baby.

No wonder the film was dismissed as gooey "holiday fare." It has the atmosphere of a Christmas party at the Field Photo Farm. Ford's troupe is on hand for the festivities—Hank Worden, Jack Pennick, Frank Ford (given a few lines to speak for a change), Jane Darwell (the earth mother from *Grapes of Wrath*), Mildred Natwick (the prostitute from *Long Voyage Home*), and Mae Marsh (Griffith's star from *Birth of a Nation* and *Intolerance* whom Ford started using regularly after *Fort Apache*). It is as if they were gathered to welcome Dobe into their company. Wayne's character is protective of "the Kid" from the very outset. Hawks had told Wayne that Dunson in *Red River* cannot show affection for his adoptive son; but in *Godfathers* Ford *instructs* Wayne to be a sheltering figure. The real baby being adopted, long before the actual infant has been discovered, is Dobe. It is as if Wayne were watching over his own earlier self. The Abilene Kid is the Ringo Kid redivivus. But this Kid must die.

Ford, with his proprietary air, put "And introducing Harry Carey, Jr." in the credits. Hawks had already let Dobe—whose vocal training had been suggested by Kurt Weill, a friend of his father—sing a song in *Red River* (1948). Ford lets him sing *two* songs in *Godfathers* (1948)—though he kept shooting the scene over and over (not Ford's normal way) trying to improve it, with the result that Dobe's voice got husky and sank lower, to Dobe's dismay.

Even as Ford was showering Harry's son with professional

kindnesses, favoring him in camera angles, making Wayne and Armendariz show him affection, he was berating Dobe off-camera, covering his own feelings with taunts and insults. This is the film where he embarrassed Dobe with repeated "jerking off" gestures. At one point, disgusted with Dobe's first playing of his death scene, Ford walked off and let him lie without water on the floor of Death Valley. (Dobe is a redhead, very sensitive to the sun and to sand's abrasion.) Dobe charitably supposed that Ford was trying to torture a good performance from him. But Hawks had got an affecting performance in *Red River* without all the abuse. Dobe was experiencing what Uncle Jack's own children did, that Ford punished people for eliciting his love. He could not perform an act of love without some attempt to abjure it. When Goldie tried to thank Ford for getting Dobe removed from a war zone, he just said, "Oh go fuck yourself."[11] (Ollie could repay Ford in kind. Richard Widmark cracked up when Ollie called Widmark by the wrong character's name while filming *Two Rode Together* and Ford shouted at her, "Goldie, you're the worst goddamned actress I ever directed." She replied, "Oh go fuck yourself"—a liberty no other actor could take on a Ford set.)[12]

While Dobe Carey was being chewed up in Ford's own little psychodrama, the movie was made with touches of Ford's normal sensitivity to a story. The birth of the baby could not take place in the shadows and depths of *Stagecoach*'s central episode. How was Ford to build a sense of mystery on the baking Death Valley basin? He does it by striking fear in the three dismounted men. When they hear noises over a rise in the desert, Wayne goes alone, pistol in hand, to scout. Returned, he refuses to get near the birth process. "Pedro," presumed to know more about nature's mysteries, is sent over the rise, but the others keep their distance. Only as night is falling, and the covered wagon is lit from within by a reddish lantern, do the two men creep near it, awed—Wayne makes the Kid drop his gun belt, and performs a hasty self-grooming himself, before they enter the arena where death hands over a life into their keeping.

The Magi theme has been attacked as superstitious, but Ford unobtrusively contrives a natural explanation for all its elements. Nothing miraculous occurs. Even the donkey that turns up to support a hallucinating Wayne is the obstreperous animal Hank Worden could not control in several comic scenes near the start of the film—it has simply wandered off again. The destroyed waterhole that strands the woman and child was dynamited by the "damn fool" brother-in-law Ward Bond railed against at the outset. The men's literal readings of the woman's Bible are set up by the painfully literal reading they gave to the baby-care book they found along with the Bible: "Oil the baby" leads to smearing him with axle grease. Wayne sees the others' ghosts while hallucinating—he almost sings "They'd *string* ya" (F up to A, back to F-sharp) when he thinks of taking someone's mule.

Some who ridicule *Three Godfathers* accept without question the evil coincidences that plague three men in the desert for John Huston's *The Treasure of the Sierra Madre*, made in the same year as *Godfathers*. Walter Huston says, at that film's end: "It's a great joke played on us by the Lord, or Fate, or Nature, or whatever you prefer . . . the gold has gone back to where we found it." This is an example of a tendency Gilbert Chesterton noticed—that intellectuals are willing to accept the contrivances, no matter how artificial, of a malevolent fate, but not of a benevolent one.[13]

For all his ranting at Dobe, Ford was in the mood Chesterton describes as Dickens's "happy occultism" when he made *Three Godfathers*. Whatever limits one must place on *auteur* theories, no film was ever more entirely a personal expression of its director than this one, made up of Ford's memories, affections, and involvement with Harry and Goldie, Frank and Dobe—and, yes, with John Wayne. This movie healed some of the resentment left over from the war and from the fact that Wayne had just made his breakthrough film, *Red River*, with Howard Hawks. By 1948, Wayne had become a superstar, and Ford obviously decided to accept that fact and attribute it all to his own earlier formation of the man. By making Wayne's character in *Godfathers* a surrogate to express the love for Dobe that he could not show himself, Ford created a new relationship with Wayne. Dobe describes how the two of them came over to him after the death scene was completed. "Duke lifted me to my feet. He had his arms around me, holding me up. Ford took my face in his hands. He was smiling. 'Why didn't you do that the first time? See how easy it was? You done good.' "[14]

Wayne had played Harry's son in *The Shepherd of the Hills*. Here Ford makes him play Dobe's father, putting him in Harry Carey's shoes. He was also bringing out aspects of Carey in the Wayne performance. For the first time, Ford concentrates on Wayne's huge hands—dangling in front of him over a railing, lighting cigarettes, holding the lantern near the dying woman's face. Carey had always been good at "business" using his hands and his muscled forearms (with sleeves rolled up). In almost every posed still shot, Carey is doing something interesting with his hands.

Even Wayne's slow but emphatic ways were traits Ford had seen in Carey. In 1946, as Carey was nearing death, Ford wrote in an essay, "The Man's Story," that "I learned a great deal from Harry. He was a slow-moving actor when he was afoot. You could read his mind, peer into his eyes and see him think."[15] Carey, older than Ford, more experienced, more important in their early days, had influenced him in ways Ford could not bring himself to acknowledge until their last days together. Carey had never been "his" cowboy. But Wayne, the new Carey, could be considered Ford's very own invention—a claim that would get exaggerated through the years. This Carey would be dependent on him, which made him an improvement (in Ford's eyes) over the original. The Ford Cowboy was dead. Long live the Ford Cowboy.

Part Three

INVENTING ANOTHER COWBOY

The naive "Ringo Kid" of *Stagecoach* was just one version of the conventional young hero Wayne played until 1946, when Howard Hawks persuaded him to take on an older, darker role in *Red River* (made in 1946 but not released till 1948). This established the kind of role Wayne is mainly remembered for from his superstar days, which began in 1948—the authority figure, the guide for younger men, the melancholy person weighed down with responsibility. The most influential example of this new type is his Sergeant Stryker in *Sands of Iwo Jima* (1949).

□ 10 □
HOWARD HAWKS

THE BREAKTHROUGH YEAR for John Wayne was 1948. He appeared in three pictures that year, all first-rate films by first-rate directors—Howard Hawks's *Red River,* and John Ford's *Fort Apache* and *Three Godfathers.* This year moved Wayne onto the actors' top ten list of moneymakers in 1949. He would not be off that list for the next quarter of a century.

Although *Fort Apache* was the first Wayne film to be released that year (in March), and *Red River* did not come out until September, Hawks had made the latter picture in 1946. Its release was delayed by financial and legal problems.[1] Ford had helped Hawks in the editing of *Red River,* and saw what a powerful performance Wayne gave, before he even began filming *Fort Apache.*[2] If Raoul Walsh was the discoverer of Wayne, Hawks was the one who made him a superstar.

Red River was Hawks's postwar attempt to become an independent producer—an ambition shared by Ford and many others. He took many risks with the film, since it involved long and expensive location work in Arizona—work that in fact strained his resources beyond his ability to pay his workers. It is significant, therefore, that he cast Wayne in this crucial endeavor, since Wayne was not a great commercial property in 1946, when filming began. Only two years before, MGM had treated him as a minor player in *Reunion in France.* His best-received work so far had been in his three films with Ford—and *Stagecoach* was seven years in the past; *Long Voyage Home,* six years in the past, had given Wayne only a small segment of the film to shine in; and *They Were Expendable* was not a favorite with the public.

It might be thought that Hawks chose Wayne simply because he was making a Western—he called it his first Western.[3] But, in 1946, only eight of Wayne's last twenty-one movies had been Westerns, and only one of those, *Tall in the Saddle*, had been impressive. None of Wayne's prior roles was anything like the older, meaner part given him in *Red River*. Here Wayne would have no romantic partner—which was almost unprecedented for him.[4] Hawks obviously saw something he could shape for his own purposes in Wayne's ability to convey control and menace. What were Hawks's purposes? Why did he start his independent producing with an ambitious Western? He was best known for urbane movies with sly dialogue. His outdoor stories had mainly been aviation films (reflecting his own interest in flying, and that of his frequent producer, the millionaire aviator Howard Hughes).

But Hawks had filmed much of an ambitious Western in 1941, *The Outlaw*. That movie was very important to him. He had bought a story from one of his favorite writers, Ben Hecht, and worked on the script with another favorite writer, Jules Furthman, shaping the project very much to his own intentions. He later flatly claimed, "I wrote *The Outlaw*."[5] He wanted to produce it himself, but he did not have the money, so he brought in Howard Hughes as co-producer.[6] Hughes called the production back from the Arizona location, pleading economy, but in fact to keep the filming under his control—for he had developed a fierce obsession with it, based largely on the casting of his own "discoveries," Jack Buetel and Jane Russell.

Hawks and Furthman had written a wittily sexy script, most of whose double entendres they thought they could sneak by the censors. But Hughes added a heavy-breathing score (Tchaikovsky belabored by Dimitri Tiomkin) and hired a flamboyant publicist, Russell Birdwell, to mount a publicity campaign devoted mainly to the young Jane Russell's breast measurement. The result, despite Gregg Toland's moody cinematography, was a badly edited travesty of the original project.

But, in a curious way, Hughes's long fight with the censors over Jane Russell's breasts distracted the censor, Joe Breen, from more outrageous things in the script—especially the sadomasochism that permeates it. *The Outlaw* also contains some of the more blatant homoerotic scenes put in a commercial Hollywood product by that time. The heterosexual panic over La Russell blinded the Hays office to the fact that the real sex object in the picture, photographed as seductively as the woman, is Buetel as Billy the Kid, a pouty young gunman.

According to Lucien Ballard, the assistant cameraman who filmed the first test shoots with this Hughes protégé, Hughes was not sleeping with Russell, but with an unwilling Buetel.[7] The script, as Hawks was developing it in those days, may have reflected slyly on the Buetel-Hughes relationship. At any rate, the center of the story is not Jane Russell but a romantic triangle of Billy the Kid, Doc Holliday, and Pat Garrett. Billy steals Doc's horse and defies him to take it back. When Pat, as sheriff, tries to intervene, Doc sides with Billy, making Pat respond like a jilted lover. Thomas Mitchell, playing Pat, has speeches like this:

> I might have known you'd do this to me. . . . Ever since you met him, you've treated me like a dog. . . . You stand there, side by side with that little snip of a kid, against me, me, who's always been the best friend you ever had. And I still would be if it wasn't for him.

Doc, played by Walter Huston, masochistically lets his young lover exploit him, stealing not only his horse but his "girl" (Russell), and trying to get one or the other back in a fair swap. Their union is consummated when Billy becomes the masochist, letting Doc shoot chunks out of each ear and crease the back of his gun hand rather than draw on him. At the end, Doc takes a bullet from Pat that was intended for Billy, and Billy leaves Pat bound to a post for respectable people to discover.

Jane Russell is a pawn in the men's power-and-love games with themselves. She is as masochistic as Doc, who lets Billy steal her and a horse. She loves Billy though he has killed her brother, raped her at their first meeting, and strung her up in the desert, abundantly pendulous, to die in a classic bondage posture. The Breen office thought it could morally disinfect this tangled scene if it made sure Russell was married to Billy before she got into bed with him, to warm him in his delirium. (We are later *told* that a priest married them, but we never see that happen—a scrap of dialogue that pacified guardians of the marriage bed.)

Though Hughes is rightly blamed for *The Outlaw* as it appeared, much of it is clearly by Hawks. One of the torture scenes was made by Hawks as a test shot—the one where Billy threatens to kill Russell and asks if she will watch the process. She answers in a parody of sexual surrender; he is repeating her rape, but this time with a gun:

—Will you keep your eyes open?
—Yes—yes.
—Look right at me all the time?
—Yes—yes.[8]

Every Western Hawks made, after the abortive attempt at *The Outlaw*, contained elements, scenes, and dialogue modeled on that first endeavor, which remained close to Hawks's heart. *The Big Sky* (1952) has the woman giving her body to warm a delirious man. *The Big Sky* and *El Dorado* (1967) both have a woman trying to kill a man and being wrestled into the hay. All of the films have male triangles, a humiliated woman, and a "pretty boy" gunman.[9] *The Outlaw*, which was not widely released until 1943 because of its troubles with Joe Breen, was clearly vivid in Hawks's mind as he made his own Western in 1946, his first attempt at the genre since 1941. He went back to Arizona, where he had begun filming *The Outlaw* five years earlier.

He developed the script much as he had Hecht's story for *The Outlaw*. Having bought a Western tale by Borden Chase, he had shaped a script from it even before Chase sold his tale to the *Saturday Evening Post* for serialization (from December 7, 1946, to January 11, 1947). Hawks even tried to get the magazine to change Borden's title, "The Chisholm Trail," to "Red River"; but the *Post*'s editors liked the original better. The story had an historical theme—the first drive of cattle from Texas to Kansas. But Hawks wanted a more local and lurid accent. His first title was *The River Is Red*, from a piece of dialogue (later cut) referring to an Indian's blood floating in the water.[10]

The Chase short story has a male triangle:

1. *Tom Dunson* is a brutal Texas cattle owner, an immigrant sailor from the Liverpool area who served in the British navy, where he received the lashes he gives out to rebellious drovers on his cattle drive, teaching them "the obedience I learned as a boy aboard a British man-o'-war."[11] Dunson heeds no one, even when men describe a shorter route for getting the cattle to mar-

ket. "A hell of a man. A brute of a man. Thick-necked, low-jowled, with eyes that looked out at you like the rounded grey ends of bullets in a pistol cylinder." [12]

2. *Matthew Garth* is a man Dunson found as an orphan and raised to be taller and tougher than he is. After Dunson whips drovers, and is shot by one, Matt takes the herd from him, to follow the shorter route. Dunson vows to stalk and kill Matt.

3. *Cherry Valance.* A Creole gunfighter, a seductive Latin lover constantly singing "Chacun vit à sa guise," Valance has joined the cattle drive as a rival to Matt. He goes with Matt when the herd is taken from Dunson, but leaves it to stay with a traveling brothel (on its way to service gold-rush miners). From that base he makes a night raid to steal the herd from Matt. Failing in that attempt, he returns to the brothel, where Dunson arrives and engages Cherry in a gunfight (since Cherry helped Matt steal the herd). A prostitute jostles Cherry's elbow as he draws, so he only wounds Dunson (though the wound will prove mortal). Cherry dies as the prostitute tells him, "Chacun vit à sa guise."

Hawks's first step was to make the male triangle resemble more closely that of *The Outlaw.* The "pretty boy gunman" in the Chase story is the Creole Cherry. Hawks changes that, making Chase's tall and tough Matt the short and slight Montgomery Clift, whom Hawks had seen in New York doing a Tennessee Williams play. Clift was his discovery, as Buetel had been Hughes's, for the central role in the movie as it was first planned.

Matt and Cherry team up against the rejected Dunson, just as Billy and Doc made common cause against Pat Garrett in Hawks's earlier script. In this script, the two younger men have the same kind of erotic competitiveness that Billy and Doc had. The two men compete for a girl and a horse in *The Outlaw.* The two compete for a girl and for ownership of the other's gun in *Red River.* Much of the gun rivalry is cut in the final script, but not the opening of the contest, when Cherry asks to heft Matt's gun:

> If you'd like to look at mine. . . . Nice, awful nice. There's only two things more beautiful than a good gun, a Swiss watch, or a woman from anywhere. You ever had a good Swiss watch? [13]

This bit of dialogue is the basis for later references in the original script. After Cherry rescues Matt during a stampede, he says he acted only because "That gun of yours—I want it all in one piece." [14] After Clift is kissed by the prostitute, she asks, "Well, Matt?" and he answers: "I'm thinking about a good Swiss watch." [15]

In the story as Hawks reshapes it, Cherry does not leave Matt to stay with the brothel; nor does he try to take the herd from Matt. He stands with Matt against Dunson, and takes the bullet when Dunson is trying to kill Matt, as Doc takes Pat's bullet meant for Billy in *The Outlaw*. Much as Doc shared his girl with Billy, Cherry tells the prostitute, whom he first slept with ("Back for more?" she says when they meet again): "I like him. And he needs some of you." [16] During the drive, Cherry keeps up an erotic observation of Matt:

> —Down Valverde way, they would call you "El Lobo."
> —"El Lobo"?
> —Yes. You have the look of a man with the need of a woman. [17]

When Matt, in an early script, goes to kill the prostitute's pimp, she and Cherry confide their fears for him, confessing a shared love. [18]

In Chase's original story, Matt is the center of the action. He has a life away from Dunson's ranch that is more than glanced at (as in the final movie). We first encounter him, after the Civil War, in Memphis, where he meets the prostitute Therissa Mullay, "Tess of the River, who set men mad in Jackson and Natchez, Cairo and St. Louis." [19] Matt watches her humiliation as one pimp kills another pimp to take her away. He learns on the drive that Cherry has been Tess's customer. When they meet the brothel on its way to the gold towns, the two have a prior history with her that intensifies their erotic competition.

As the scripts were developed, Cherry's role shrank drastically. Borden Chase, who was on the set to rewrite scenes at Hawks's command, but who did not get along with Hawks, later claimed that Hawks cut Cherry's part out of dislike for the man playing him, John Ireland. The dislike was real—Hawks said because of Ireland's drinking, Chase said because Ireland took Joanne Dru away from Hawks. (Dru and Ireland later married.) [20] But the scripts show an inexorable process at work, cutting back on Cherry's part no matter who played it.

The need for dramatic economy took away some of Cherry's

action sequences—the raid on Matt's herd, the separate duel with Dunson in Tess's camp. The censors cut many of his erotic comments with Matt or Tess. The larger role for Dunson shouldered him aside—a shift away from the male triangle was occurring (one traced in the next chapter). Cherry's main role in the final script is to keep up suspense about a shoot-out with Matt that never occurs.

Tess's profession had to be changed, of course, because of the censors. She is a singer-prostitute in the Chase story. Hawks has changed her to a gambler by Script 2, but the nature of her associates is still clear enough. When she tells Matt's friend Nadine Groot (played by Walter Brennan) that her skill with cards protects her and he asks why, she says:

> —There's no [other] part of me I ever have to sell. Not when there's a deck of cards to hand.
> —'Pears to me you ain't thought that sellin' idea through.
> —Why not?
> —You figger, bein' a woman, when you're leanin' over like, a man ain't gonna be lookin' at your figure.
> —[Laughing] Right.
> —You're sellin'. No diffrint from other wimmin.
> —You caught me shy my ante.[21]

Humiliating the woman is a regular feature of Hawks Westerns. Though Groot's rebuke is not as harsh as the original story's scene of pimps squabbling for her, even this scene was given up under pressure from Breen's censors. So was the way Tess fondled and practiced with Groot's whip during this same scene. Even the "cover" of making her a gambler rather than a whore is only wispily referred to in the final product—mainly when Tess uses one hand to deal cards during her scene with Dunson. She cannot use the other arm since she was hit by an Indian arrow. The way Matt sucks out the blood, leaving some on his face, offended Breen—but the scene was kept by moving the arrow up from her breast toward her shoulder.

In Script 2, Tess is humiliated by Matt's suspicion that she does more for a living than deal cards. To get even, she has Cherry bring Matt to her, then introduces him to a whore in the camp for his entertainment. Later she admits this was "cheap." All this fell before the Breen assault. In fact, no whores were left in the camp. They had *all* been turned into gamblers, like Tess. Any sadistic elements persist in the story only by implication. It is amusing to wonder what some Wayne admirers, who think of him as the embodiment of "basic American values," would make of the truly kinky story that created his superstardom, if they knew how that story was gestated.

Joanne Dru, playing Tess, is often considered the film's weak point. Hawks stumbled frequently in his casting of women. Dru says this was her first movie, and he gave her little help.[22] She was a model, married to the singer Dick Haymes, and Hawks was in effect repeating Hughes's effort to take two beginners and launch them in his Western. Dru and Clift were the Jane Russell and Jack Buetel of 1946.

Hawks had taken an inexperienced model and launched her spectacularly in 1944 when he introduced Lauren Bacall in *To Have and Have Not*. Hawks's wife of the time, better known in her later social incarnation as "Slim" Keith, saw Betty Bacal's picture in *Harper's Bazaar* and brought her to his attention. Bacal (with one *l* at the time) bore a striking resemblance to the woman who found her, and Hawks labored to make the similarity more complete. He had her work her voice down from the chirpy to the husky. He renamed her—from Betty Bacal (née Betty Perske) to Lauren Bacall.

His success as a Pygmalion in this case led to many doomed efforts, later, to take a model or starlet and refashion her as a new Slim-Betty. Joanne Dru was one of the first in this long line. He told her to lower her voice. When she could not, he told her to go outside and shout until she was hoarse.[23] Her problem in *Red River* was not of her own making. The story kept changing, as the Tess figure became sanitized, not only by the Production Code but by Hawks's own shifting of the center of gravity from a Matt-Cherry-Tess involvement to the story of Dunson. His many changes of the ending confused her, though she was called on to play the key role in the scene finally chosen—where she had to talk with a nervous involuntary compulsiveness. This was one of Hawks's favorite ploys to show the humiliated woman at the end of her endurance, and few could do any better at it than Dru. The list of victims to this quirk of Hawks includes Angie Dickinson, Elsa Martinelli, Paula Prentiss, Charlene Holt, and others. They cluster in the Westerns, where Jane Russell had set a pattern of female humiliation as the price of male companionship. The weakness was not in Dru, but in the plot manipulation

Hawks had to resort to when he tried to make a better *Outlaw* out of Chase's story. It was the price he paid for the creation of a new role for Dunson/Wayne—which is the real point of *Red River*.

THE NEW WAYNE

FOR HOWARD HAWKS, the most important thing about an actor was what he called his "attitude." When an interviewer mistook "attitude" to mean the actor's "outlook" or mental state, Hawks corrected him: he meant his *physical* attitude, his bodily carriage —how he walks and how he moves. He felt that Humphrey Bogart radiated insolence by his whole manner, and Cary Grant moved like one watching himself move. Gerald Mast knew that "for Hawks, to walk is to be."[1] That explains his interest in Wayne.

Wayne's generally graceful movement was most evident in his walk, though not much had been made of that until 1944, when he made *Tall in the Saddle*. Actor Paul Fix, who claimed to have invented Wayne's walk for him, wrote the screenplay for that movie (with polishing that gave Michael Hogan a co-credit). The walk preexisted the film, but Fix did emphasize it for the first time—in the scene where Wayne comes down the town's main street toward a drunken gunman, not bothering to draw his own gun, intimidating the other man just by the easy purposefulness of his stride.

Wayne was living with Fix and his family while they worked on the script of *Tall in the Saddle*. The two men were acting together in *War of the Wildcats* (originally called *In Old Oklahoma*). They went to the set, every day, with sandwiches packed for them by Fix's wife. This was just the period, late in the war, when Wayne was growing self-confident—Mary Ford said he "has gotten too big for his britches."[2] He stayed at the Fixes' with his Mexican lover "Chata" (Esperanza Baur).[3] His close working relationship with Fix proved useful over the years. Fix, though only a B actor in 1944, had started (like Harry Carcy) as a dramatist and director—he had been a close friend of Clark Gable during his early stage career. Fix had ideas about Western movies and their heroes, and he scripted *Tall in the Saddle* to express them. But while Wayne was learning from Fix, Fix was imitating Wayne's illicit attachment—Fix began an affair with the heroine of *Tall in the Saddle*, Ella Raines, one that led to his being thrown out of his own home, along with Wayne and Chata.[4]

Tall in the Saddle gives us—as, no doubt, it gave Hawks—a first glance at what would be Wayne's later persona. His whole character seems to be an extension of the calm authority of his walk. Early in the film, villains beat up a stagecoach driver so they can replace him. Wayne, a passenger, says with quiet finality, "I'll drive," and the villains are as paralyzed as the drunken gunman when he walked toward him. After Wayne is cheated at cards, he goes upstairs in the hotel to put on his gun. The mere assurance of his carriage as he comes down the stairs makes the cheater hasten to return the cash.

In Ella Raines, Wayne also gets his first tough-opponent lover, just the kind of woman-in-a-man's-world that Hawks liked. Clad in leather chaps that emphasize her derrière, Raines wields a whip—as Tess will do in the first script for *Red River*. This is the first Western in which Wayne chooses the "bad girl" in cowboy outfit over the "good girl" in crinolines.[5] Wayne is no longer the young idealist but a mature man powerful enough to "handle" the spitfire played by Raines. Never before had Wayne exuded the air of indomitable will that was to become his trademark—precisely the quality Hawks needed for his Dunson.

There is even a scene in the film that Hawks had put in *The Outlaw* and would use again at the end of *Red River*. When Raines thinks Wayne has cheated her brother at cards, she shoots at him repeatedly, trying to make him draw. Doc had done that to Billy, and Wayne (Dunson) would do it to Clift (Matt). Hawks was so taken with this device that he kept it in *Red River* even after Howard Hughes threatened to sue him over it. Hughes claimed the *Red River* scene was plagiarized from *The Outlaw*. In his response, Hawks cited six films that used it, including *Tall in the Saddle*.[6] The tougher Wayne of *Tall in the Saddle*, the emphasis on his walk, the touch of sadism in Ella Raines's leather and whip—no other film of Wayne's had the elements that would interest Hawks when he was looking for a Dunson. There is even a line of dialogue taken over from one film to the other. When the stagecoach driver offers Wayne's character a suggestion in *Tall in the Saddle*, Wayne tells him, "I'll do the thinking"—exactly what Dunson tells Matt in *Red River*.

Dunson in the original magazine story was a character practically unplayable. He is such an unsympathetic figure that it is hard to understand why Matt does not shoot him at the end. Chase wrote that Matt tried to shoot, but his hand froze—presumably from a parricide taboo. This does not expose Matt to death, in the *Saturday Evening Post* version, since Dunson is already collapsing and cannot aim at him. Chase could describe Matt's inner state. If the actor playing him just froze on the screen, it would look ridiculous.

Hawks began by inventing for Dunson some human ties. Chase sent him off alone to start his ranch, but Hawks gives him a friend to travel with him, Nadine Groot (Walter Brennan).[7] This is the key change in the plot. Groot is the figure connecting Dunson to normal human feelings—something made more evident in the first script than in later ones. In that version, Dunson, lacking a ring to engage the woman he leaves behind, takes Groot's bracelet and gives it to her. When the bracelet is found on the Indian who killed the woman, Groot reclaims it. When he sees that Tess loves Matt, Groot gives her the bracelet as if it came from Matt. In later scripts, the familial ties between Dunson and Matt will be emphasized: it is *Dunson's* bracelet, given him by his mother, which he offers the woman. Then, when he finds it on the Indian, he gives it to Matt. So Matt personally hands it over to Tess. When Dunson finds it on her wrist, the plot is given a roundelay shape, as in *La Ronde* by Ophuls.

In the scene where the boy Matt is found, Groot's presence means that he is joining a family, with Groot in a maternal role. If Matt is puzzled by Dunson, Groot can explain the older man's troubled past. After the war, Groot is the chronicler of what went on in Matt's absence. When Matt takes the herd away from Dunson, Groot, by siding with Matt, legitimizes his rebellion in family terms.

Hawks was so urgent about giving Dunson an inner life, and some reason for Matt to be attached to him, that the early scripts are far too explicit in spelling the matter out. Groot admits that Dunson is hard, but only for Matt's sake:

> Who's he been doin' it for? Fightin' rain 'n muck, an' tyin' the drive together with the linin' of his gut? You, Matt! All for you! Some day the whole shootin' shebang, it'll all . . .[8]

Dunson is explicit, too, not the inarticulate brute of the Chase story, but not yet the stoic of the movie. Getting ready to begin the drive, he says:

> —This is it, Matthew. My last silver dollar. And the last ten years of my life. They tell me this drive can't be made.
> —We'll make it.
> —I couldn't work it alone, Matthew.
> —Neither could I.
> —Start them for Missouri, Matthew.[9]

Matt tells Tess beforehand that he could never draw on Dunson (this would have taken suspense from the climactic scene):

> I'd seen my folks killed, Millay [her name in this script]. Half skinned alive in front of my eyes. I'd walked till I couldn't feel my feet touch the ground. I'd've kept on walking, yes—till I dropped. He took me in. Brought me up. For ten years he called me "son"—and he meant it. Millay, if you were me, could you draw on him?[10]

Not only does Matt settle the matter beforehand with Tess. She goes back to Dunson and tells him:

> He won't draw on you. He's the kind who'd walk his shoes through to pay off a debt. And you're the one he owes. He's determined that.[11]

The script states, restates, and overstates the family affections. Matt, discussing Dunson with Groot, says:

> —Sometimes it's like he's a kid. A kid with a chip on his shoulder. A kid who needs taking care of.
> —Could be he figures the same about you.[12]

Having created an interior life for Dunson and Matt, Hawks then cut out the explicit statements about the relationship, so his actors would suggest it. Is there a deep tie between the two men? It comes out, not in words, but in one little gesture. Verbally fencing with Cherry, Matt rubs his thumb alongside his nose. Only later, when Wayne does the same thing, do we see where he got the gesture. It is a mark of Hawks's subtlety that he does not give us this pattern in its expectable sequence—Dunson doing it first, then Matt imitating him (which could be happening for the first time). We have to infer a long-standing relationship, seeing the results before we see the cause.

In the first script, Dunson states his dependence on Matt. ·That is not in the character as Hawks is reshaping it—he told Wayne not even to smile in this Dunson role.[13] But the fact is signaled in Dunson's acting. After the war, when Matt has returned, Wayne slumps, dispirited, as he talks of his financial plight. When he is ready to rise, he reaches instinctively for Matt's help, which is given. This is not Wayne of the determined walk. When Wayne, thirty-nine years old, asked Hawks how to move like an old man, Hawks joked, "Just watch me" (Hawks was fifty in 1946).[14] Wayne moves in a gingerly way, lets Matt light his cigarettes for him, pulls himself heavily onto his horse. Hawks told him to show fear in this scene, but Wayne refused.[15] Wayne was right. Dunson, even if he felt fear, would not show it. As soon as Wayne goes off-camera, Matt says, "He's afraid!"— another sign of how close they are, how well Matt knows Dunson.

Hawks said Wayne refused to do one other thing on the film. All the scripts show a concern for handicapping Dunson before he goes into the final struggle. Chase's story had wounded him just once, but mortally (when Cherry shoots him in Tess's camp). The scripts wound him more superficially, but twice—each time by gunshot. Looking for some variety, Hawks says he wanted Dunson's finger to get caught in a rope during his punishment of the man, leading to its amputation. Hawks may have made this up later on, but it does seem to reflect his taste for sadistic tortures—he finally used the amputation in *The Big Sky* (1952): "I did it with Kirk Douglas, who isn't nearly as good as Wayne."[16]

If the beginning of the drive shows us a physically deteriorated Wayne, the running of the herd shows a spiritual deterioration. This is not so much a matter of aging as of Wayne's growing gaunt, hollow-eyed, semi-insane with worry. Dunson broods in the camp, drinking too much, sleeping too little, driving others so they will be too tired to rebel, but driving himself so hard that he suspects rebellion all around him. In Script 2, a drover whose identity is never discovered shoots Dunson when he forces them to make a river crossing at night. That was changed in the final version, where Dunson is wounded by the man he is about to whip. The man draws, but Matt shoots him in the shoulder. It is made clear, in several places in all the scripts, that Matt is now faster on the draw than Dunson; but he defers to the older man as long as he can, in the classic situation of a son replacing the father, but not wanting to make that obvious. (In *The Odyssey*, Telemachus is about to succeed where the suitors had failed, since he is strong enough to string his father's bow—but he refuses to do it in his father's presence.)

Left behind by the herd, wounded, Dunson has to heal while he collects gunmen to ride with him and fulfill his oath to kill Matt. Rested, he begins to heal spiritually as well as physically. This, too, is spelled out in the first script. When Dunson meets Tess, and sees she has the bracelet, he recalls his own lost love— the wagon train he abandoned (unlike Matt, who risked the herd to come to the rescue of Tess and her gamblers). The tie between first love, bracelet, and Matt had been underlined almost mawkishly in Script 1. Discovering Matt so soon after the loss of the woman he loved, Dunson connects his appearance with hers. Groot asks, "He'll do?" (two words later changed to a statement and given to Dunson). Dunson answers: "Maybe. But I wish he didn't have yellow hair." Groot brushes the hair out of his eyes, to make the style less like hers: "From now on, Matthew, maybe you better keep it slicked back out of your eye."[17]

In Script 2, Wayne refuses to judge Tess (who is still clearly a prostitute), admitting there were things in his own past no one (not even, presumably, Groot) will ever know about.[18] The two become friendly. Dunson even lends her his horse to go see Matt before he kills him.[19] All this is made implicit in the final version. The two reach their unspoken accord when Tess does not try to use her hidden derringer on him. (In the second script, Tess had returned from her night with Matt ready to kill Dunson—until the latter says, "You'd lose him." She admits he is right: "You're in the part of him I must never touch.")[20]

How to end the story was always its great problem. The unsatisfactory "freezing" of Matt's arm was what Hawks addressed in most of his major changes to the plot. But that still left him in a quandary. If Dunson was no longer to die, how could he and his son have their showdown and still be reconciled? Cherry is still involved in the final script, since Dunson no longer kills him in Tess's camp.

An early solution was to have Cherry draw on Dunson, forcing Matt to shoot the gun from Cherry's hand. Then, after Matt refuses to use his gun on Dunson, Dunson beats him to a pulp, taunting him with the challenge to "Use your left." Only when Groot turns Matt's inert body over does he notice that Cherry's bullet had entered Matt's left shoulder. But Dunson knew it—hence his taunt: "Do you think I'd have fought him with fists if he hadn't [been shot]? He'd have killed me. Don't forget, I taught him to fight. Get me a bucket of water."[21] The father can, in effect, step down from his superiority only after beating Matt to satisfy his own oath to kill him. Few can regret the loss of this ending.

In the far better resolution of the film as it stands, Cherry calls out to Wayne, is shot by him, but wounds Dunson (not Matt) in the exchange. This settles one thing. After Cherry's erotic byplay with Matt was almost entirely eliminated, Cherry's one function was to keep up suspense over a showdown with Matt to prove who is faster. Since Matt is faster than Dunson, and Dunson beats Cherry, even from the disadvantaged posture of having to turn completely around as he draws, that makes Matt the fastest man on the field. Earlier, when Groot had shouted, "Draw!" in a game of long standing, Matt had been the one who must turn around while drawing, and he still beat Dunson, exactly as Dunson now beats Cherry. The two men perform each other's feats, moving with a common impulse.

In the situation as Hawks had reconfigured it, it is clear why Matt does not draw when ordered to by Dunson. He knows Dunson too well to believe that Dunson could kill him. Dunson takes the gun from Matt's holster, throwing it aside: "You once told me never to take your gun away from you." That recalls the first meeting between Dunson and Matt, when the orphan's gun was wrested from him without warning. "Don't ever trust anybody until you know him," Dunson says—then returns the gun and turns his back on him, showing that he trusts the boy. The whole of that interchange lies behind Dunson's reference to the boyish threat: "Don't ever try to take it away from me again." This time, Matt trusts.

In a scene right after that early one, Dunson sees that a Mexican is on the point of drawing his gun and shoots him first. The boy asks how he knew what the man was doing. "By watching his eyes. Remember that." In the buildup to the final fight scene, as Dunson shoots at Matt, Hawks does repeated close-ups of Matt's eyes, confident above his slight grin. As Dunson knew the Mexican would draw by "watching his eyes," he knows that Matt will *not* draw.

In *The Outlaw*, Billy also knew that Doc would not kill him, even as Doc's bullets were nicking his ears and creasing his gun hand. When Howard Hughes claimed that this scene was taken outright from his picture, he had a point too good for either man to make explicit. Hawks ridiculed the idea that shooting at someone to make him draw was unusual in Westerns—he claimed he got telegrams from friends saying they were going to take out a patent on things like "They went thataway" or "We'll head 'em off at the pass." But this scene *was* a duplicate of the other, in that the bullets are frustrated expressions of love in either case. But Hughes could hardly argue that position in court —proclaiming the homoerotic nature of his own movie.

In *Red River*, the love is not homoerotic, but familial, as Groot makes clear by cheering Matt on, legitimizing the rebellion—the son must challenge the father in order to be mature, to resume relations with him as an equal. What has happened, almost against Hawks's first intentions (signaled by his making Matt the pretty boy gunman), is the replacing of the first male triangle (Matt-Cherry-Dunson) with a different one (Dunson-Groot-Matt). The external challenge, of saving the Dunson ranch financially by means of the drive, has gone along, step by step, with an internal challenge and development, that of securing an orderly succession to the ranch's regime—something finally settled when Dunson reshapes the Dunson brand to give Matt an equal "M" on it. When Dunson says, "You've earned it," in this roundelay-story of continual recurrences, we are taken back to the scene where Dunson promised Matt a place on the brand "when you earn it."[22]

When Matt refuses to answer Dunson with his gun, repeated blows make him fight back with his fists. There was understandable concern that the matchup would not be convincing. Wayne, after all, was a beefy six-foot-three, and Clift a willowy five-foot-ten. Hawks had created the problem for himself when he was still thinking of the first triangle, with Cherry the antagonist-lover of Matt. Now, with Cherry a peripheral figure, an imbalance between Clift and Wayne was disturbing.

Hawks later emphasized the imbalance by telling one of his

favorite stories about the movie, one surprisingly accepted by interviewers and those who depend on them. The difference between Wayne's authority and Clift's tentativeness is supposed to come out in the scene Clift considered his major one, where he tells Wayne they are leaving without him, but Wayne just stares off, away from him, before saying, "I'm gonna kill you, Matt." Hawks claimed that he was amused at Clift's presumption that he could take a scene from Wayne:

> Monty didn't know what to do. Finally he came out of the scene and came around to me and said, "My good scene certainly went to the devil, didn't it?" I said, "Any time you think you're gonna make Wayne look bad, you've got another think coming."[23]

Anyone who has ever seen the movie should know that Hawks is fabulating. The scene where Wayne looks off into the distance was never a big one for Clift. Hawks set it up so Wayne could dominate.[24] We first see him from behind, up on his wounded leg, leaning against his horse in a monumental pose (emphasized by the low camera angle). Matt comes over to say, apologetically, that he will get Dunson his money—an overture, not an ultimatum. Dunson stares off, impassive, he and the horse a rock formation of unyielding bulk. There was no way Clift could have expected from the scene, as it was written or shot, anything but what Hawks wanted to get out of it—the beginning of The Hunt, in which Matt will become almost as fearful, haunted, and aware of danger as the paranoid Dunson had been in the first part of the drive.

Hawks's story is a parable for what he felt about Clift's problems in general, and specifically in the fight scene. He later claimed that "my arm is still sore from trying to show Montgomery Clift how to throw a punch."[25] Even an admiring biographer of Clift has to admit that "Monty, as every director who attempted to choreograph one of his fight scenes soon discovered, 'punched like a girl.' "[26] Hawks tried to even the odds by having Cherry's bullet wound Dunson, not Matt, just before the fight begins. (In the earlier script, Matt's wound makes it easier for Dunson to beat him into the ground.) Then, before the fight can be resolved decisively in either man's favor, Tess fires a gun and trains it on them both, breaking up the brawl and babbling compulsively that they love each other, though they won't admit it.

One way to ease his problem was available to Hawks, but he

wisely refused to accept it. He could have kept Wayne deteriorating through the movie to the point where he was a shell of himself, easily handled by Clift. He did just the opposite. Wayne is never more commanding than when he moves inexorably through the milling cattle, the beasts he and Matt are contending for. Gerald Mast wrote some famous words about this scene:

> It may seem a hyperbolic claim, but no star in the history of film other than John Wayne could play the role in *Red River* and make it mean what it does and make the story mean what it does. But then the same would be true of Cary Grant in *Bringing Up Baby, His Girl Friday,* and *Monkey Business,* or of Humphrey Bogart in *To Have and Have Not* or *The Big Sleep.* The complexity of Hawks's narrative puzzles requires the solid sense that these archetypal stars make of their roles. Think of Gary Cooper marching toward Montgomery Clift at this climactic moment (too soft and loose; Cooper doesn't march, he saunters—hence his appropriateness in *High Noon* or Hawks's *Sergeant York*). Or James Stewart (too calmly reasonable). Or Henry Fonda (too sweetly mysterious). None of these stars can ever walk the way Wayne does, devouring space with his stride.[27]

To show a weak Wayne at the end would betray the subtlest, deepest pattern in this film. At every level the plot has a "ring composition." Dunson deteriorates in the first half of the play, then heals—both physically and spiritually—in the second. The wagon train of Tess recalls to him the woman he left on the first wagon train, when he had been "wrong," as both the woman and Groot told him. The softening toward Tess, the bracelet's memories, take Wayne back to his youth. He is being rejuvenated as Matt is reaching his maturity—just as Odysseus is restored to vitality when he sees his son show manhood. They have both traveled to this joining of their forces. In *The Odyssey,* not only does Athena give Odysseus back his strength—even Odysseus' father, Laertes, goes out again in armor and, by Athena's aid, throws the first lance with a force that breaks the enemy's spirit. The young man (Telemachus) prevails by the power of those who preceded him and live on in him.

Hawks solved the problem of making Wayne a member of the older generation without making him powerless or "fatherly" in a condescending way. The Wayne only partly glimpsed in *Tall in the Saddle* comes into full view in *Red River*. In that sense, "John Wayne"—all we make of that name from this time on— was Hawks's invention. He may or may not be the *auteur* of the movie. He authored the star.

□ 12 □
AUTHORITY FIGURE

AFTER 1948, his breakthrough year of three powerful movies, Wayne went on, in 1949, to give his most influential performance, that of Sergeant Stryker in *Sands of Iwo Jima,* a role closely modeled on the one Hawks had fashioned for him in *Red River. Sands* brought Wayne his first Oscar nomination and Stryker entered the mythology of right-wing America. Right-wing candidates and their followers have used Stryker's rallying calls "Saddle up!" and "Lock and load!" Such cries were natural to the Senate campaign of ex-Marine Oliver North, though they seemed anomalous on the lips of presidential candidate Patrick Buchanan, who had no military experience himself. Newt Gingrich performed no military service either; but he was able to apply "Strykerism" to his battle-style politics. He told author Elizabeth Drew that *Sands of Iwo Jima* was "the formative movie of my life." He explained his tough discipline over Republican insurgents as inspired by Stryker's determination to shape his men for battle, even if that involved making them hate him.[1] Oliver Stone, when he filmed *Platoon* (1986), had his psychopath, Sergeant Barnes, use both the Wayne calls: "Saddle up! Lock and load!"

Marine recruiters have said that enlistment goes up when *Sands of Iwo Jima* is revived.[2] When I lectured on Navy films to the Naval Academy in Annapolis in 1995, a midshipman told me that he had a videotape of *Sands* that he played almost every Saturday to a roomful of classmates. He said he gets choked up every time. The emotional climax of the film is the raising of the American flag over Mount Suribachi. That was the scene that led Ron Kovic to volunteer for service in the Marines during the Vietnam War.[3]

Sands was made while the cult of the Suribachi flag-raising was still being formed. The cult found its ultimate shrine five years later, with the unveiling on the Potomac of the one-hundred-ton bronze sculpture group of the raising, one of the patriotic sites visited by tourists to Washington. The movie was drawn into Marine efforts to promote the Suribachi myth, and it helped entrench certain elements of misinformation in an irrevocable way. (How can history contradict the *movie?*) There were two Suribachi campaigns—one waged on the island, the other carried out on propaganda fronts. Students of both efforts conclude, of *Sands,* that it "fostered virtually every distortion embedded in the heroic myth, including the misimpression that the flag-raising represented America's first victory over the Japanese on Iwo Jima."[4]

The controversy over the flag-raising, that iconic image of Marines in action, stems from three still photographs.

1. *Louis Lowery* took the first shot of a flagpole being secured on the rim of Iwo Jima's volcanic mountain. This occurred on February 23, 1945, four days after the landings at Iwo Jima. The flag's appearance told those on the beach and in nearby ships that United States forces now controlled the heights and only "cleaning up" operations still faced them (extracting the remaining Japanese from caves where they were hidden). General Holland (Howlin' Mad) Smith was just landing when he heard the cry, "There goes our flag!" He later wrote: "This vision of triumph had an electrifying effect on all our forces ashore and afloat." In what turned out to be a lucky break for the Marines, Secretary of the Navy James Forrestal accompanied General Smith. Pointing to "the tiny speck of red, white and blue," Forrestal—later to be Secretary of Defense—told Smith: "Holland, the raising of that flag on Suribachi means a Marine Corps for the next five hundred years."[5] This was the first American flag to be raised over Japanese home territory. The emotion of such a moment was treasured by those who saw it. Needless to say, it was doubly treasured by those who actually raised the flag, and by Lowery, who caught it for posterity on film. Nonetheless, it *was* a "tiny speck," not visible to some without field glasses. Marine officers below decided that a larger flag was needed.

Commandeering the flag from a nearby shop, they sent it up the slopes, along with a higher pole, to replace the lower, smaller flag.

2. *Joseph Rosenthal*, an Associated Press photographer, was in the journalists' pool that accompanied this second flag to the top. His picture caught the group of six men struggling with the big flag, only halfway raised to the perpendicular. The surge of one effort through the compacted body of men is easily read. The faces of some are hidden in the communal endeavor. Limbs overlap; some are barely visible; one cannot tell, without careful scrutiny, exactly how many men are wrought into this unit. The *New York Times* ran Rosenthal's photograph on the front page of its Sunday edition, two days after it was taken. A caption assured readers that it was taken with "battle still raging" around the Marines—a misimpression the Wayne movie would indurate. It is easy to read the men's struggle with difficulty as a struggle with danger. They go forward, resisted but irresistible. It is a vivid image of accomplishment against the odds. This *looks* like an act of valor—yet it does not show Marines killing other human beings. These men are accomplishing a joint patriotic act of celebration. They are doing something constructive in the midst of destruction, bringing order out of chaos, life out of death.[6] The photographed men already seemed sculpted. The photograph would "translate" into a statuary group with little effort at composition. It is almost too good to be true—so its truth would be called into question.

3. *Rosenthal* took another photograph, after the flag was raised, asking the bystanders in front of the flag to wave helmets or rifles, and shout their joy at the accomplishment. This was a "posed" shot, in the sense that everyone was looking at the camera and cooperating with it. Rosenthal called it his "gung-ho shot." But later, when controversies arose over the whole sequence of the flag-raisings, this "composed" shot would be confused with Rosenthal's earlier picture of the six men raising the flag. That, too, was called "staged," though a movie camera running at the time proves that this is a false charge.[7]

The appearance of the first Rosenthal picture in the *New York Times* guaranteed its immortality. Even those who knew about the first raising had to admit that Lowery had not shown the *drama* of the flag raising. Though the first event was exciting when taken in context, Lowery's picture of it was boring. Rosenthal's was the more desirable "record," and those who wanted to emphasize its importance tried to minimize, overlook, or forget the first raising.

All this was natural. The best action photographs from the war were not necessarily taken of the most important or exciting events. If it were just a matter of preferring one picture, Lowery had little reason to grumble. But the outburst of patriotic enthusiasm over the photograph created a chain reaction of after-effects that ran far beyond anyone's ability to foresee.

A first effect of the picture was the call to identify and glorify the half-hidden men who created this glorious moment. There is an ironic twist in this. The point of the picture was the *sinking* of individual effort into the communal act; yet people wanted to disentangle the group and shine a separate light on each individual's face. The Marine Corps complied with this call for celebrities. Such publicity helped them oppose the long-standing call for the submersion of the Marines into the Navy. Besides, the Corps felt a patriotic duty to help morale, both in the service and on the home front. The six flag-raisers came home to sell war bonds. They gave Americans an anticipation of victory. The men were ordered to perform in publicity tours, on radio shows, at celebrity gatherings.

This creation of instant heroes naturally made the raisers of the *first* flag wonder what their successors had done that was so wonderful. Their only feat was the luck of being caught in a photographable position. What danger there was in the flag-raising (not much) was obviously greater for the team that raised the earlier flag. (Actually, the danger was greatest for the patrol that was sent up to reconnoiter *before* the first flag-raising patrol).[8] The Corps was caught in a delicate task of publicity-maintenance. It could not deny the earlier raising, or disown the men who did it. But the Marines wanted the focus to remain on Rosenthal's photograph, that godsend to the Corps. Attention to others would fuzz the effort, take some of the glow off the appearance of a unique act that fairly leaped out at one from Rosenthal's photo. The first raisers, those in the Lowery shot, were heroes, perhaps; certainly the men who led the first assault on the beaches were incredibly brave. But none of them were starred in an action shot like Rosenthal's. In the Rosenthal six, the Corps had stars on its hands, and it meant to use what it had been given.

The publicity effort did not end after the war. The Corps used the surviving flag-raisers to help lobby for a great monument based on the Rosenthal picture. The Corps had rapidly chosen a sculptor for this project, Felix de Weldon, who prepared a life-size model of the six for celebration of the first postwar Veterans Day, November 11, 1945— just nine months after the photo was taken and three months after the war ended. The painted plaster group was installed on Constitution Avenue.

This temporary version of the statuary group stood prominent on the avenue for two years, while controversy raged around it. If the Marines were given a Washington site for their glorification, the other military branches would demand similar showcases. Other causes and groups competed for the precious public spaces. The artistic community did not think de Weldon was up to the job of creating the group on a colossal scale.[9]

In 1947, the Marines moved their plaster monument to the entrance of Quantico Marine Base outside Washington, where it stood for another two years. But they kept de Weldon at work on a larger limestone group, and they were sending plaster casts of the original on tour for recruiting drives. They were still agitating for a colossal bronze work in or near Washington.

That was the situation when Republic, the poor sister of the "Little Three" studios, approached the Marines for assistance in making *Sands of Iwo Jima*. Without the considerable help of loaned military equipment, uniforms, and base locales, the studio could not make the ambitious war film. The Corps responded enthusiastically—on the condition that the Suribachi flag-raising would be prominent in the film. Marine publicity went to work. The second flag, the larger one, was taken to the set, to be raised again. The surviving flag-raisers were brought to the base and given minor parts in the film (many publicity stills of the "real" heroes with Wayne and other stars suggested that they would have major roles). "Howlin' Mad" Smith was in attendance as a technical adviser for the Marines.

The Corps's use of Ira Hayes, a Pima Indian who helped raise the flag, led to unintended consequences. When Hayes died at age thirty-two, an alcoholic who drowned in his own vomit, he was portrayed as a victim of the celebrity the Corps had thrust upon him. The author Merle Miller wrote an hour-long television show in 1960 that made Hayes the victim of his casting in *Sands of Iwo Jima*. Lee Marvin, playing Hayes in the Miller version, tries not to take part in the Wayne movie's flag-raising—he says it is all a lie.[10] Hollywood followed this up the next year with a movie *(The Outsider)* about Hayes, written by novelist William

Bradford Huie and starring Tony Curtis as Hayes. This film makes racial prejudice the cause of Hayes's disintegration.[11]

None of these problems were foreseen when the Corps participated in making *Sands*. Missing no trick, the Corps used this occasion to promote de Weldon and his scheme for the giant monument. De Weldon, consulting with Rosenthal, was sent out to ensure that the poses of the actors raising the flag corresponded exactly to his monument (rather than to the picture on which it was based). The monument was now the authentic event to which a representation must conform.[12]

Despite all the Marines' ballyhooed assistance in achieving authenticity, the movie-makers were allowed to tamper with the story. The two earlier patrols up Suribachi, and the earlier flag-raising, are omitted.[13] For extra drama in the film, Wayne's men *battle* their way to the mountaintop to plant their flag. The Corps, like Hollywood, wanted the second flag-raisers to be seen as heroes. When the Marines won their second battle of Iwo Jima, in 1954, unveiling the huge bronze monument just west of Arlington Cemetery, the statuary group confirmed the legend enshrined in the movie—which was often shown at the Marines' basic training camp, Parris Island.[14]

Though the movie prospered on the growing legend of Mount Suribachi, its long life in the Wayne legend comes from the character he was given in the script, and from the way he performed. It shows how eager the Corps was to promote the Suribachi myth that it gave in to Hollywood pressures for dramatic license.

Sands reflected a trend, in the war's aftermath, to present war films as psychological studies of men under stress. The Cold War was taking shape in 1949, a time of protracted conflict, with the emphasis on discipline, on *organization* needed to sustain pressure on the Soviet Union. A new wave of Second World War films was the result. In 1949 alone, *Sands, Battleground, Twelve O'Clock High, Home of the Brave*, and *Task Force* came out.[15] The year before, *Command Decision* had its premiere. In these films, the World War II enemies rarely appear. The drama lies in the neuroses of individuals, the tensions between men "on the same side," the difficulty of maintaining the military as a social structure. Though these films were putatively concerned with World War II, the real unseen enemy was Communism, and the real battle was to impose the psychological conditioning necessary for a new kind of "war." By "winning World War II" in 1949, Wayne was really waging the Cold War.

The principal writer of *Sands* was a precursor of this wave he now participated in. Harry Brown, a Harvard-trained reporter for *Time* and the New York *Times,* had served in the Army as a writer for the service's official paper, *Yank,* and he wrote a taut little novel, heavily influenced by Hemingway, that appeared in 1944: *A Walk in the Sun.* The enemy is absent from that story of a platoon landing on Italian shores and nearly disintegrating as its lieutenant dies, the sergeant replacing him cracks up, and others talk in inconsequent snatches, disoriented, unable to see the war all around them. Since Brown was still in the service, Robert Rossen (who later wrote *All the King's Men*) adapted the novel for the screen, keeping most of the dialogue verbatim from the book. The movie appeared at the same time as *They Were Expendable,* and—like it—was a meditative, not a triumphal movie. There are signs that Brown wanted to strike a similar note in the script for *Sands,* with the brutal conditioning by the Wayne character added to the internal dynamics of the squad. The script gives as much time to the Tarawa landing, which is grim and nontriumphal, as to the Iwo Jima operation. But the studio's economic need for Marine support, and the Marine need for a glorification of the flag-raising, led to the Suribachi scene at the end, which has the air of something tacked onto a story whose ethos it violates.

Brown had already tried once to write a story for Wayne that would use the manic edge of his Dunson character. His second postwar screenplay was for *Wake of the Red Witch* (1948), Republic's effort to give Wayne a mini-epic patterned on his appearance in Cecil B. DeMille's *Reap the Wild Wind* (1942). In DeMille's flamboyant tale of crooked sea salvagers, Wayne—still playing second lead (this time to Ray Milland, to whom he loses the heroine)—is a bitter man who becomes the cat's-paw of the villain (Raymond Massey). He deliberately wrecks the ship of which he is captain, and makes only partial atonement by dying in the red rubber tentacles of an octopus.

In *Wake of the Red Witch,* Republic's cheaper sea tale, Wayne is again a troubled captain who deliberately wrecks the ship to get revenge on its owner. He fights another octopus (but wins this time). Then he dies at the end, to be reunited with his dead lover, Gail Russell.[16] Wayne has a protégé (Gig Young) who does not understand his dark angers and compulsive drinking. Only when he hears the story of his earlier romantic disappointment does this younger man see the humanity within the brute—as the John Agar character will in *Sands.* The "crazy" scene—which was at this point in danger of becoming a Wayne trademark—comes when Wayne thinks Russell has betrayed his love and comes close to strangling her in a drunken wild-eyed rage.

Sands of Iwo Jima was concocted out of all these elements—the Cold War movie finding its shape, the Marine mythologizing of Suribachi, the Wayne persona created by Hawks, Harry Brown's use of that persona in the DeMille rewrite, Republic's need for a larger-scale film than it could make without military help, and the Wayne box office resulting from his three hit films of 1948. The film made its long-lasting impact because of the fortuitous conjunction, partly calculated, partly accidental, of such ingredients. Wayne's later war movies would succeed to the degree that they rode on the effect Sergeant Stryker had on audiences. The movie merged the legend of the Marines and the legend of John Wayne. From now on, the man who evaded World War II service would be the symbolic man who *won* World War II. Its contagious delusions were registered not only in the lives of Ron Kovic, Newt Gingrich, Pat Buchanan, and Oliver North, but of countless unknown Wayne surrogates who strut about with a need to be tough, to think of life as warfare.

The dynamics of the Stryker role would affect Wayne's nonmilitary movies, too. This film confirmed the success, for Wayne, of the two-generation plot that Hawks had crafted in *Red River.* Wayne, at forty, became an authority figure, and he would remain one ever after. He is a lonely man burdened with responsibility. His wife or lover he has lost to death, divorce, or estrangement—and with her he has lost potential or actual sons (daughters don't count). This character will find in a follower the son he never had. The "son" at first resists Wayne, but finds maturity in coming to understand the responsibility he bears, the reasons for his strictness, his emotional stuntedness. An affective link is formed precisely from the refusal to display affection. The love interest in such stories is restricted to the younger generation, or focused on it. In *Red River,* Montgomery Clift wins Joanne Dru. In *Sands,* John Agar wins Adele Mara. (Wayne is disgusted by the prostitute he meets, until he finds she has a baby boy—repeat, boy—whom he cradles in his arms.)

Tag Gallagher opined that one reason Ford movies have so many celibate heroes is Ford's Catholicism, which honored celibate priests.[17] But Hawks created the womanless-man role for Wayne, and Brown broadened its impact. Besides, Ford's love for male societies—the Navy, the OSS, the cavalry, his yachting companions—was not a religious taste. Male ritual handles the tensions of competitive equals by creating authority figures to whom one can defer without losing one's manhood. Submission to one who is partly above the conflict takes away the fear of giving in to rivals. The rivals make peace around a respected elder.

It is easy to see why so few women are fans of John Wayne. His character has been schooled by adversity to do without them. They must seek tenderness in his "softer" protégés. It is just as easy to see why the Wayne mystique has such an allure for males, especially young ones still forming their own character. Wayne is the ideal to which no boy's father, or coach, or teacher, or scoutmaster, or religious minister can quite live up. Yet even the ideal figure is flawed, which offers a partial justification for the actual fathers, a way of understanding *them*. Newt Gingrich is almost a laboratory case of this effect. Too young (five years old) to take in the message of *Sands* when it appeared, he went four times to a revival when he was in his teens. Gingrich and his mother had been deserted by his natural father, and Gingrich was trying—not very successfully—to win the esteem of his step-father, who was a career Army man. Wayne was both an alternative to that parent and an excuse for him. If the Army toughens men only to make them survive, then to be affectless is to show the highest affection. You can live with emotional stuntedness by this logic of Wayne-olatry. Moving under a variety of masks, Sergeant Stryker is still with us to this day—out on the hustings with Pat Buchanan, presiding over the House of Representatives, and lurking in thousands of men's own adolescent pasts. This was, until *The Shootist* (1976), the most famous of the films in which Wayne died. But he only seemed to.

Part Four

EMPIRE

John Ford had come out of World War II in love with the Navy, with military units in general, and with America's new imperial role in the world as the asserter of freedom everywhere. The three "Seventh Cavalry" films he made with Wayne from 1948 to 1950 reflect this attitude, and put Wayne at the center of a Cold War sensibility striving for social discipline in time of trial. In 1949, the Soviets exploded their first atom bomb and Communists won their war for China. In 1950, President Truman escalated the nuclear competition by deciding to create the hydrogen bomb. The image of cavalry units surrounded by hostile Indians echoed the fears of Americans trying to remain steady as peril increased. Wayne became the cool but determined model for Americans living with continual danger.

□ 13 □
CUSTER AND COLD WAR

JOHN FORD always considered himself a radical. In the 1930s he occasionally acted like one. When the Spanish Civil War broke out, he extended his earlier sympathy for the rebel Irish Republican Army to the Communist-supported Lincoln Brigade in Spain, praising a nephew who joined it and contributing to the cause after he met Ernest Hemingway.[1] He could even be considered a maker of leftist pictures (insofar as the studio system permitted such a thing). With the Irish republican Liam O'Flaherty and the committed liberal Dudley Nichols, he made the IRA film *The Informer*. With Richard Llewellyn and the committed liberal Philip Dunne, he revealed the anguish of Welsh miners in *How Green Was My Valley*. With John Steinbeck and Nunnally Johnson, he celebrated displaced agrarian workers in *The Grapes of Wrath* (a novel whose leftist reputation made Hollywood's money men especially nervous).[2] Ford's collaboration with Nichols was a defining element in his work of the thirties, both because of the two men's professional success and because of their pictures' political drift. Theirs has been called, by a student of screenwriters, "the most successful collaboration of screenwriter and director in Hollywood's history."[3] Murray Kempton wrote, "Dudley Nichols, who was never a Communist, contributed a larger number of socially conscious scripts than all [Communist screenwriter] John Howard Lawson's revolutionary cadre together."[4]

It comes as a surprise, therefore, that the "liberal" John Ford worked after World War II with a reactionary writer like James Warner Bellah and joined a repressive organization like the Motion Picture Alliance for the Preservation of American Ideals. On the other hand, when Cecil DeMille tried to drive Joseph L. Mankiewicz out of the presidency at the Directors Guild, Ford rose to defy DeMille, and he carried the day. People ask, "What happened to Ford?" There is no mystery. He was a typical Democratic cold warrior. Before the war, liberals entertained some radical thoughts. Dudley Nichols chaired a Hollywood meeting to be addressed by Vice President Henry Wallace.[5] After the war, screenwriter Philip Dunne and others formed the Americans for Democratic Action in order to oppose Henry Wallace's 1948 presidential campaign as too soft on Communism.[6] These liberals maintained "leftist" credentials by attacking Joseph McCarthy. But it was the Democratic President, Harry Truman, who gave McCarthy the tools for his extreme tactics—the Attorney General's List of subversive organizations, the classification of secrets, and government security clearances. As Truman's adviser Clark Clifford admitted, the internal threat of Communism was deliberately exaggerated by Truman in order to win the 1948 election.[7]

Ford was an honorary member of the Cold War elite that forged such policies. He had been very close to his hero, "Wild Bill" Donovan, during the war, when Donovan ran the intelligence operations of the OSS. Ford traveled with Donovan, and received special treatment from him for his film projects. After the war, he reserved the master suite for Donovan at his quasi-military reservation, the Field Photo Farm. He kept hoping to make a movie of Donovan's life.[8] Ford's admiration was expressed in his swaggering description of his friend: "Bill Donovan is the sort of guy who thought nothing of parachuting into France, blowing up a bridge, pissing in Luftwaffe gas tanks, then dancing on the roof of the St. Regis Hotel with a German spy."[9]

Donovan had collected for his wartime unit an extraordinary group of talented, learned, eccentric, privileged, and influential people. He inspired them with a grandiose conception of their own capabilities. As his best biographer puts it, "Donovan welded them into a brotherhood."[10] For many of these people, service with Donovan was the high point of their young lives, introducing them to a heady atmosphere they wanted to keep on breathing—the air of that "remarkable institution [the OSS], half cops-and-robbers and half faculty meetings."[11]

When the veterans of adventure with Donovan went back to their Wall Street investment firms, their Ivy League faculty posts, their senior law partnerships, their publicity jobs on Madison Avenue or in Hollywood, they felt they were the bearers of a special knowledge. They had been the people most "in the know" as America became the world's dominator during the war. They felt the nation still needed them if it was to remain the world's dominator in peacetime—if it was to bring order out of the war's chaotic aftermath, to manage with wisdom the contest with Russia, to allocate resources with theoretical and technological expertise. Who better for this task than Donovan's veterans, along with their pupils, colleagues, or protégés?

America, selectively "isolationist" before the war, felt an urgent need to understand the world it was being called on to manage. The best universities set up "area studies" programs for crash courses on geopolitics—and McGeorge Bundy, the head of the Ford Foundation, funded them, happy that they tended to be "manned, directed, or stimulated by graduates of the OSS."[12] This new cadre of intellectuals had a quasi-monopoly on the data America would need in its role as leader of the free world. Britain had for centuries absorbed a familiarity with far-flung outposts of its empire. As that imperial system evaporated, America had to acquire overnight the kinds of knowledge needed to replace it.

Yet the action officers of Donovan were not content to study the world. They wanted to change it, to intervene with "surgical precision," as they felt they had during the war. Night raids in war would be replaced with quieter manipulation of foreign governments. Despite America's twin traditions—of demobilization after war, and of keeping no peacetime intelligence agencies— the OSS veterans pressed for an activist elite to *apply* the lessons being learned by the scholarly elite. America needed secret planners and protectors. Nuclear research and development called for tight security arrangements around the academic study of the atom, around geographical places of experiment and storage, and around all the military services meant to deliver nuclear weapons. The need for American bases abroad meant that friendly and unfriendly elements in the countries of deployment had to be watched constantly, assessed, quietly encouraged or discouraged. Communist propaganda, infiltration, or intimidation must be met, overtly or covertly, with carefully calibrated countermeasures. Foreign aid could be used dexterously only if continuing surveillance assured America's rulers of the recip-

ients' trustworthiness. Loyalty tests at home had their equivalent abroad. Allies had to establish and maintain firm anti-
Communist credentials. All this effort would be, in effect, a series
of shots in the dark if observation and testing of worldwide attitudes were not reduced to some kind of systematic monitoring.

These arguments made the adoption of a worldwide surveillance apparatus seem inevitable, however unprecedented. Donovan's men responded to this situation with alacrity. Ivy League
recruiters for the CIA, the successor to the OSS, were active on
all the major campuses. Former intelligence officers sought out
the best and brightest of their pupils for this new crusade—the
CIA called it "the P source" (P for Professor).[13] Early organizers
of the CIA created an esprit based on Donovan's. William Colby,
who later became a director of the CIA, thought he was joining
"an order of Knights Templars to save Western freedom."[14]

Ford felt himself a vicarious participant in all this. He was
proud of what his fellow Donovanites were up to, so far as he
knew about it. When war came to Korea and Vietnam, he made
propaganda films for the Pentagon, as he had made *December
7th* and *The Battle of Midway* in "his" war. He was flattered with
intelligence briefings and naval promotions. In time he became
a rear admiral, and flew his admiral's flags on his limousine and
his yacht (receiving naval salutes when he sailed past military
ships).[15] He was a conscious part of America's postwar war.

Not that one had to be an OSS veteran to join in that effort.
Historian Michael Sherry has demonstrated how, by converging
pressures, American culture was thoroughly militarized in the
Cold War years.[16] Larger social trends, not quite militarizing in
themselves, contributed to the nation's new conception of its role
in the world. A kind of imperial literature grew up celebrating
America's epic destiny. The clearest example of the genre was
Bernard De Voto's series of books celebrating the Manifest Destiny that drove America to its western empire in the mid-
nineteenth century. Beginning this series on the eve of World
War II, De Voto took west with him for research a young protégé,
Arthur M. Schlesinger, Jr., who would later celebrate a "*new* frontier."[17] Though De Voto's first book appeared during the war
(1942), his later volumes made their impact during the Cold War
period. A great American historian has told me that he was
moved to become an historian by the grand vision De Voto
opened up to him in *Across the Wide Missouri* (1947) and *The
Course of Empire* (1952).

This was not the first time that a moment of imperial breakthrough made Americans look back to the West as their pledge of an expansionist destiny. At the end of the nineteenth century, when the absorption of Cuba and the Philippines was advocated by neo-imperialists such as Theodore Roosevelt, John Hay, Alfred Thayer Mahan, and Henry Adams, Roosevelt's own four-volume saga on the "taming" of the West was supplemented by the work of his friends, the novelist Owen Wister and the painter Frederic Remington.[18]

Another experience Americans have turned to when bracing themselves to a sense of world mission was the Civil War. The costs of that fierce internal struggle were interpreted as an investment in the united and disciplined nation able to expand west and then move outward to the rest of the world. John Hay's volumes on Lincoln were a complement to Roosevelt's long western history.

In the Cold War, too, there was a fascination with the Civil War, measured in the tremendous popularity of Bruce Catton's volumes of narrative and biography.[19] Douglas Southall Freeman, who was a military adviser to the Pentagon in World War II and a radio commentator on that war's strategy, continued his series of volumes on *Lee* and *Lee's Lieutenants* with attention to the disciplines of patriotic duty. Dan Ford says that his grandfather read and reread *Lee's Lieutenants.*[20]

The connection between America's modern mission and its expansion of the western frontier was felt with special intensity by James Warner Bellah, on whose work Ford based his three cavalry pictures of the late forties. Bellah claimed descent from a Confederate cavalry officer and service with the British Empire —an empire whose burden, he was certain, America must now assume. Bellah's story, as he told it to his son, was of a life filled with adventure. Born into comfort in New York, he lost his father when he was ten, and joined the Royal Canadian Flying Corps in his teens. This was during World War I. Between the wars he joined that nursery of aspiring writers, the copywriters' crew at an advertising agency. An Anglophile of very conscious elegance, he married an Englishwoman (the first of several wives) and became a successful writer of magazine stories.[21]

During World War II, he told an interviewer for the *Saturday Evening Post,* he served with General Wingate's British troops in Burma and on His Majesty's Ship *Illustrious* under Lord Mountbatten. He was back in advertising, of a sort, when he did promo-

tional material for war bond drives.²² After the war, he wrote a
novel, *Ward Twenty*, to expose the inadequate care given veterans
in military hospitals.

Bellah was a sardonic man, one who was (or who posed as)
a disappointed romantic. In love with the military, with power,
with discipline, he nonetheless felt that the keepers of duty's
standards were dolts. Asked about his service in Burma, he said
Merrill's Marauders did a better job. His son notes that all his
cavalry stories have a hero who must disobey commands in
order to save the command *structure*. Bellah was a rebellious
authoritarian.

So, in his own way, was Ford, who responded to Bellah's
stylish cult of power. Behind Ford's back, Bellah called him a
"shanty Irishman," and "not a gentleman." He called Wayne, for
whom he wrote the movie *The Sea Chase* (1955), "a phony," making continual fun of Wayne's refusal to wear any uniform not
supplied by the wardrobe department.²³ In line with his adopted
British mannerisms of the Empire, Bellah had contempt for all
"wogs," for what Kipling called "lesser breeds without the law."
This self-proclaimed descendant of Confederate heroes thought
of blacks as those who had brought down a southern order of
discipline. The Indians in his cavalry stories live only to commit
atrocities—their specialty is imaginative forms of rape.

As an Irishman who, at least occasionally, talked like an
Anglophobe, Ford might have been expected to bristle at such
lord-of-the-manor ways. But Ford's old associates from the OSS
were also ardent Anglophiles. Trained, many of them, at Groton
and other prep schools modeled on English public schools, graduated from Ivy League institutions, these men admired the British intelligence tradition formed by the Empire.²⁴ They, too, as
they moved into Third World counterinsurgency activity,
thought of their charges abroad as "wogs," imperial pawns to
be manipulated.²⁵ The odd willingness of prep school "straight
arrows" to engage in dirty tricks is explained by their attitude
toward inferior human types, whose best use was as unwitting
sacrifices to the gentleman's ideals. As Bellah's stories continually emphasized, one must break rules to keep up a benign ruling
order.

After World War II, Bellah began to do research for his Seventh Cavalry stories. Despite his own sympathy for the Confederacy, he wrote about the Army of the Union. But this was the
army of the 1870s, in which former Confederate soldiers could

unite with their northern counterparts to oppose a common foe —the Indians lying athwart the spread of civilization. Bellah took real events and fictionalized them. The four of his tales used by Ford all deal with Fort Clark, in southwest Texas, thinly fictionalized as Fort Starke. From these tales Ford created *Fort Apache* (1948), *She Wore a Yellow Ribbon* (1949), and *Rio Grande* (1950), all starring Wayne.

The first Bellah story Ford used (in *Fort Apache*) had appeared in the February 22, 1947, issue of the *Saturday Evening Post*, where it was called "Massacre." Bellah wrote his own version of George Armstrong Custer's death, giving his Custer character the name Owen Thursday. Bellah neither accepts nor rejects the Custer legend. On the one hand, he admits that Custer was glory-hungry, that his attack on the Indians was risky, his preparation inadequate to the point of dereliction. On the other hand, his main character, Lieutenant Flint Cohill, who knows all this about his superior, promotes the myth of the innocent victim of Indian savagery in order to maintain imperial morale. Cohill even gives the false details of Custer's "last stand" to a painter who immortalizes the lie. Bellah explains Cohill's code:

> There are ways of living that are finer than the men who try to live them, and a regiment has honor that no man may usurp as his private property. Glory is a jade of the streets who can be bought for a price by anyone who wants her. Thursday [Custer] wanted her, but his pockets were empty, so Cohill lent him the two dollars for posterity.[26]

This mixture of idealism (the honor of the regiment) and cynicism (glory as a two-dollar whore) is typical of Bellah. Cohill acts for the good of the service—which, he knew, might mean performing low deeds to uphold high standards. The last words of the story are these:

> Even when he was very old, Cohill always looked sharply at anyone who said, "for the good of the service," and he always said, "What, exactly does that mean to you, sir?"[27]

Cohill might have been an Ivy League recruiter for the CIA.

Earlier, Cohill shows his idealistic side when preparing to make what he believes will be his own "last stand"—after Major Thursday [Custer] has left his supply team stranded. These thoughts run through his head:

It is not always in the book. It's a hundred thousand years. It's a heritage and a cause and the white man's burden. It's Cannae and Agincourt and Wagram and Princeton, and it's the shambles of Shiloh. With Flint Cohill it was thirty-one men on a hogback ridge and the thought in his angry mind that he'd never live now to be a general officer, but he'd die the best damned first lieutenant of cavalry that the world could find to do the job that morning![28]

Bellah is not ashamed to quote Kipling's racist definition of empire, "the *white man's* burden." He is clear-eyed about what is at stake—empire. In a later story, used by Ford to make *She Wore a Yellow Ribbon* (1949), Bellah writes: "The ends sometimes justify any means, when the odds are twenty-three to one and an empire hangs in the balance."[29]

Ford liked what Bellah gave him in "Massacre." He promoted Owen Thursday from major to colonel, but retained all the tics Bellah had given him—his insistence on the uniform, on unquestioning obedience, on military etiquette. Ford gives Henry Fonda all these, along with much of Bellah's dialogue.[30] But the short story was not enough to fill up a movie. There are no women in any of the Bellah stories Ford used for his cavalry films—and Ford knew from sad experience what the studios thought of all-male casts. He and Dudley Nichols had used such a cast in the British-empire film of 1934, *The Lost Patrol*. The two men's first film together, *Men Without Women* (1930), had proclaimed in its very title the problem it would have at the box office. Bellah was clearly no good at imagining or inventing (or even recognizing the existence of) the minds of women. So Ford brought Frank Nugent and Laurence Stallings in to expand the story. Stallings was an old favorite of Ford's, the author of the hit play *What Price Glory?* Stallings was another writer who specialized in male dialogue. Nugent was something else. As a movie critic, he had raved about Ford's work, calling *Stagecoach* "a motion picture that sings a song of camera."

Ford later pretended that he paid no attention to critics (sometimes claiming that while talking on the set to critics like Lindsay Anderson or Peter Bogdanovich). But in the earlier days he had cultivated them with all his tricks and blarney—especially the most influential critics on the *New York Times*, Bosley Crowther and Frank Nugent.

Nugent, asked to introduce women into an imperial tale,

drew on an earlier Ford picture about the British Empire, one Nugent not only saw but reviewed in the *New York Times, Wee Willie Winkie* (1937). The film is often dismissed, since Ford had to accept the studio's decision to turn Kipling's boy "soldier" into a girl, making it a vehicle for the magically popular tot, Shirley Temple. But the movie has wit and flair. A rigid officer's sterile discipline is undermined by the women in the regiment after his son's widow brings her daughter to the camp. Shirley not only charms her Colonel Blimpey grandfather, but melts the "wog" adversary—Khoda Khan, played by a stunningly beautiful young Cesar Romero—into a brotherhood that reaches across cultures.

Nugent's review, "Imperialism Claims Shirley Temple," put it mildly when he called this "not an entirely credible story," but he admitted it was "likely to win the grudging approval even of those who, like myself, are biding their time until she grows up, becomes gawky, and is a has been at fifteen."[31] Nugent and Ford (who remembered reviews very well) must have chuckled over that line when, later, they prepared the script for a twenty-year-old Shirley Temple in *Fort Apache*.

However it came about, there is something very fitting in the use of motifs from Kipling for Ford's tale of empire in 1948. Evan Thomas has noticed that key officials in the CIA, like Richard Bissell, had been brought up loving Kipling and saw him as a mentor for their imperial tasks. Bissell's mother read him Kipling stories: " 'Take up the white man's burden; I still read it,' he would later say."[32]

> As a young boy touring Europe with his parents, Bissell had stood in the Colosseum in Rome, dreaming of lost glories. The experience, he recalled, "gave me an early interest in empire." At Groton and Yale, Bissell's academic interest had been in empires, particularly those of Rome and Britain. At the CIA, he would often think of that history as he surveyed his own domain.[33]

The favorite book of Frank Wisner, the CIA covert operations guru, was Kipling's *Kim*. One reason he trusted the British traitor Kim Philby was an admiration for the man's first name.[34]

In Nugent's reworking of material from *Wee Willie Winkie* for *Fort Apache*, the daughter who is brought to a severe officer's post is that officer's own child, now a young woman. Bellah's Major Thursday would never allow a woman into Indian territory, but Nugent's Colonel Thursday does. Once his daughter is there, however, he tries to discipline her, just as he does his men, telling her not to mix with the Irish canaille of the regiment. When Ford wishes to brand a man a racist, at this stage in his career, it is not for any inhumanity to Indians. The officer is marked with infamy because he thinks all Irish names interchangeable and shows an obvious distaste for having to dance with the Irish Sergeant Major's wife.

Though Ford is rightly condemned for a general insensitivity to women in his films, Nugent provided him here with a whole gallery of down-to-earth but noble women drawing strength from each other's company. They make up a kind of Greek chorus commenting, often wryly, on the men's posturings. Ford plays up this choral role in stylized shots of them lined in a row against the sky—a female counterpart to the dusty ranks marshaled below them on the parade ground or to the "chorus" of earthy sergeants lined up at a hitching post. These women entirely alter the chemistry of Bellah's story, whose plot line is retained but transmuted. The women's gallery is made up of four portraits.

1. Mrs. Collingwood, played by *Anna Lee*, is the wife of the post commander replaced by the arrival of Colonel Thursday. Her husband came late to an engagement in the Civil War because of his drinking. Thursday remembers this and refuses even to shake his hand when they meet. Though Collingwood, played by George O'Brien, has been on the wagon ever since that episode, Thursday sadistically offers him a drink early in the morning. Collingwood is tortured by the thought that some of his brother officers think him a coward. His supportive wife is joined in sympathy by the other women of the camp. Just as Collingwood is riding out of camp on Thursday's doomed Indian raid, news of his long-desired appointment as an instructor at West Point comes into his wife's hands. But she, knowing he would not miss another appointment with danger, refuses to send a messenger to recall him. She is the one who, as the women strain forward for a last glimpse of their men, says, "All I can see is the flags." Lee was wearing under her costume the handkerchief Ford gave her when they made their first film together, the Welsh tale *How Green Was My Valley*.

2. Mrs. O'Rourke, played by *Irene Rich*, is the wife of the camp's Irish Sergeant Major (Ward Bond), a man whose medal of honor, won in the Civil War, secured his son an appointment to the Military Academy at West Point. That son, now a graduate

of the Academy, arrives at Fort Starke just as Fonda does, causing a confusion in their escorts, one haughtily resented by
Fonda. Mrs. O'Rourke is the person all the other women turn to
for practical counsel and support. She is loyal to her husband,
but ready to correct Fonda when he gets too pompous, and quick
to shut her husband up when he tries to interfere in their son's
romance with Fonda's daughter.

3. Mrs. Gates, played by *Mae Marsh*, the heroine of many
D. W. Griffith classics. Mrs. Gates is the oldest woman on the
post, one who looks with tragic eyes on Mrs. Collingwood when
she lets her husband ride off to his death. Ford, who tried to use
Griffith veterans, had not employed Marsh before this, but *Fort
Apache* became the first of five pictures she would do with Ford.

4. Philadelphia Thursday, played by a twenty-year-old *Shirley Temple*, is the loving but rebellious daughter of Fonda, the
martinet. She repeats her role from *Wee Willie Winkie* as the cute
but unmanageable troublemaker at the post. Here, as then, she
is abetted by an avuncular sergeant—in both cases Victor
McLaglen. An indication that Ford and Nugent had the Kipling
movie in mind is that Ford ended the punitive exile to which he
had condemned McLaglen since the making of *Wee Willie Winkie*
eleven years before.[35] Ford seemed to be in a forgiving mood at
the time—he also welcomed back George O'Brien to play Collingwood, the disgraced officer. O'Brien had been Ford's star in
the silent days, when he made him the hero of *The Iron Horse*
(1924), but he had been in Ford's doghouse even longer than
McLaglen—seventeen years. Once back, he would act in three
more Ford pictures.

The family spirit was completed by Ford's giving Shirley
Temple's husband, John Agar, his first screen role. Agar, the heir
to a Chicago meat-packing fortune, met Ford when the director
was getting off a cruise ship from Hawaii. Ford had struck up a
shipboard acquaintance with Agar's widowed mother, and she
pointed out her son on the dock. When Ford saw his smooth
good looks, he asked him to call at his office.

When the office interview took place, Ford asked what Agar
had done during the war. "Air Force, sir." To which Ford said,
"Oh yes, 'Off we go into the wild blue yonder'—CRASH." The
unintimidated Agar asked Ford where *he* served—Navy? Agar
said, "Oh yes, 'Anchors aweigh, my boys'—SINK."[36] Ford liked
the feistiness, but he would test it. Could Agar ride? Yes, he had
spent childhood summers on a dude ranch where each boy was

given his own horse to groom, care for, and ride. Ford told him to report to Jack Pennick for advanced lessons. Pennick had Agar out at dawn every day taking fence jumps bareback—skills totally useless in the role Agar played.

Ford was creating the esprit of a military camp for his set. Pennick drilled infantry troops as well as the horsemen. McLaglen fit right in, since he had played British imperial soldiers for Ford in *The Black Watch* and *The Lost Patrol* as well as in *Wee Willie Winkie*. He had also been an imperial officer in World War I.

Wayne, though he was working with Fonda, Ford's star from great films like *Young Mr. Lincoln* and *The Grapes of Wrath*, was in the same enviable relation he enjoyed with Robert Montgomery in *They Were Expendable*. As the warmer subordinate to a tense superior officer, he inherits the sympathy the superior rebuffs. Richard Dyer has noticed how important to the film is the contrast in body language between Fonda and Wayne. When the two men are side by side on horseback, preparing to go meet the Indian chief Cochise, Fonda sits rigidly upright, while Wayne is more pliant and mobile.

> When Fonda announces that he will be deploying his troops to the North, the placing [by Ford] means that he has only to make a slight turn of his body round in the saddle, whereas Wayne has to turn the whole of his body round in the saddle [as he had to turn all the way around to shoot Cherry in *Red River*]. This he does very swiftly and easily. The placing demands the larger movement, but this performance of the movement both suggests a sense of urgency (Fonda is making a disastrous decision) and, because it is so easily done, signifies again Wayne's total at-home-ness in the saddle.[37]

Throughout the movie, Fonda moves stiffly, almost leaning backward in his finicky distaste for the people and things before him. His slow and resisting movements when he has to dance with the Irish wife of the Sergeant Major—the excessive formality with which he tries to cover, but actually reveals, his disdain—prepare us for the scene where the rigid man breaks. In the climactic battle he is unhorsed, stumbles clumsily, falls into the last redoubt in a stagger of disconnected limbs, all of these contrasted with Wayne's economical and graceful moves under pressure.

The contrast is played out in the two men's vocal delivery. Fonda could work his warm baritone up to whiny and clipped tones when conveying the pinched nature of his character. His voice gets an extra nasal quality on rising notes of asperity, as in his refrain, "Any questions?"—which means "Don't dare ask any questions." The Wayne delivery is slower and gets its authority from falling cadences, not rising. The two create a duet of contrasts when Fonda repeatedly overrides Wayne's orders for numbers of men, ammunition, and supplies, and Wayne echoes Fonda's amended orders with a dull, flat compliance not indicating approval.

The contrast between the two characters is at the heart of the final battle scene, one of the greatest sequences Ford ever created. Ford had set this scene up with an earlier one, where he used dust to obscure a conflict and make it mysterious. In that scene, a cavalry detachment approaches a stagecoach from the front while Indians pursue it from behind. When the two forces meet around the stagecoach, the combined dust kicked up by the horses erases all sight of the stagecoach and its fate—until, finally, the coach's dim silhouette emerges from the hazy scene.

Archie Stout at the camera turned the dust into veils by shooting it with infrared film.[38] Thus the final clashes of the cavalry and Indians are hidden from us in mysterious scrims. We do not see the death of Fonda and others at "the last stand," just the clouded approach and obliterative passage of the Indians as they sweep away the regimental flag that stood higher than the men in their little ring of death.

Fonda faced to the right as the Indians approach. Breaking film conventions of "directionality," Ford makes Wayne face to the left as the same band of Indians sweeps up to the ridge where Fonda posted Wayne, along with the supply train. The diptych formed by this symmetrical and literal "face-off" is completed when Wayne walks into the dust that swirls around and before the Indians. Lost in the cloud, he speaks to the Indians words we cannot hear. Like the men he left behind, we are kept in suspense —until the noise of the wheeling Indians is succeeded by a clearing of the dust, and Wayne's silhouette is seen beside the regiment's pennant, stuck in the ground beside him.

On the left of this diptych, Fonda, the man who tried to control every detail of his own and his men's lives, had lost control over his own limbs. He had to be propped up, given a revolver by the despised Irish sergeant, after he apologized to the disgraced Collingwood (O'Brien's line is: "This time *you* were late, Owen"). On the right side of the diptych, Wayne is the prop to his men—and he drops his revolver belt as he goes forward, placing himself in the Indians' control, but rescuing the situation by that very trust.

I do not know whether Ford, or Nugent, knew about the miragelike atmosphere over Custer's actual approach to his own death. But it, too, appropriately baffled visual comprehension:

> By some trick of the atmosphere, common in that region, the air above the regiment acted as a mirror so that two regiments—one real in the dust of the river bank, one mirage in the air above—appeared to be marching westward. The Seventh Cavalry and its commander, both reality and image, were marching to their apotheosis.[39]

History is made in a confused murk of humans' conflicting volitions.

Ford has moved Bellah's plot toward humane views of war distant from Bellah's own attitude. There was no respect for the Indians in "Massacre," and any lie to them was justified. The movie meeting with Cochise, in which Wayne tries to soften Fonda's contempt, is simply a scene of contempt in Bellah:

> Major Thursday saw their impassive Judaic faces, their dignity, their reserve. He felt the quiet impact of their silence, but, being new to the game, he had no way of knowing that they drew all of it on as they drew on their trade-goods blankets—to cover a childish curiosity and the excitability of terriers. Stone Buffalo. Black Dog. Pony That Runs. Running Calf. Eagle Claw. Chiefs of tribes in the sovereign nation of Stone Buffalo—a nation under treaty of peace with the United States. A nation, in effect, held as prisoners of war, so that it would keep that peace.[40]

Ford is often criticized for insensitive treatment of American Indians. But the Wayne figure in *Fort Apache* is a defender of their rights. He criticizes Fonda not for military failings but for breaking the whites' pledged word to the Indians.

The character of Bellah's Thursday is also softened. In the magazine story, Thursday is caught with his men, but slips away with a few survivors after the Indians' assault. Cohill comes down a hill to help him and Thursday orders him to move his supply train. Objecting that this would be suicidal, Cohill gives

Thursday his pistol and says he will have to arrest him to make him obey. Thursday, confused and defeated, turns back toward the dead, and shoots himself. Cohill arrives later and hides the gun, inventing the fiction that he died by an Indian bullet. The censors of the 1940s did not approve of "honorable suicide," but Ford and Nugent would probably have changed the plot anyway, to give Fonda a belated recognition of his errors—he apologizes to Collingwood and Mulcahey (McLaglen) before he dies with them, this time by an Indian bullet in fact.

After the battle scene, Ford goes back to Bellah's ending, where Cohill endorses the lie of Thursday's glory. Wayne approves a romantically false painting of Thursday's end ("Correct in every detail"), and says that the cavalrymen are better today than in the past ("Thursday did that"). In a final touch, Wayne turns to a group of journalists with Thursday's own trademark cutoff: "Any questions?" Then he puts on Thursday's hat with the white desert veil behind it.

This is a formulaic ending for stories of a strict officer whose merits are recognized belatedly by the men he served in shaping them up. But that is not Thursday's situation at all, at least in Nugent's movie to this point. Fonda had resented being shunted to a backwater, among Indians not even warlike, "mere" Apaches. Shirley Temple informed us that her father (Thursday) was in Europe for several years (like his model, General Philip Sheridan), to explain his ignorance of frontier conditions. When Thursday hears that Cochise is a worthy opponent, he decides that he can win back his wartime commission as general if he provokes the chief to a fight in which he can defeat him. The fatal remark is Collingwood's, when he tells Thursday that Cochise "outgeneraled us" in earlier engagements (before the treaty was signed that Thursday will break).

There is nothing but ambition and vanity behind Fonda's doomed raid. To suggest otherwise at the end is to belie everything we have seen before, and to insult the men who died as his victims—Collingwood, Mulcahey, O'Rourke, the men we have been made to care for, seeing them through the eyes of the fortress's women. When Wayne turns to the window in which passing troops are reflected, and says the cavalry will live on, he is implicitly justifying his lie about Thursday to maintain morale.[41] But a passive or minimal acceptance of the Thursday legend is one thing. To take on his persona, his characteristic sayings and garb, is quite another. They are the things we have been taught to resent, in contrast with Wayne's more humane bearing. We are led, now, to think that Wayne may also take on Thursday's attitude toward Indians.

The acceptance of official lies, the covering up of blunders, the submission to disciplines of secrecy—these were attitudes being developed in 1948. And Wild Bill Donovan's old pal John Ford was ready to join this Cold War boosterism. The Cold War would take many more casualties than artistic integrity, but in this case it also victimized art.

WASHINGTON AND SHERIDAN

JAMES WARNER BELLAH believed, with many in the military, that soldiers are undercut by politicians, who do not understand battle conditions. In "War Party," which appeared in the *Saturday Evening Post* on June 19, 1948, Bellah tells the story of "Fort Starke" left helpless as tribes of Indians are gathering to prepare an assault. Officers in the fort want to go out and skirmish with bands of Indians, divide them before they coalesce, whittle at their numbers. But they are under orders to make no offensive move. They can only send out scouts, who watch helplessly as the Indians' numbers grow.

One officer at the fort, Captain Nathan Brittles, is retiring. On his last day of service, he goes to the scouts watching the Indians and writes them an order to shoot or drive off the Indians' horses. The order is valid for only a few hours, while Brittles is still an officer. It evades instructions from Washington by targeting no Indians themselves, just their horses. But Brittles knows he will be court-martialed if the raid results in an engagement with the Indians. Luckily, no casualties occur, so Brittles does a final service to the command structure by circumventing a specific command.

Wayne plays Brittles in *She Wore a Yellow Ribbon,* the second of Ford's cavalry pictures. Hawks had aged Wayne for *Red River* in 1946, making a thirty-seven-year-old play a forty-two-year-old when he had been playing twenty-nine-year-olds. Ford makes Wayne a man in his sixties for *She Wore a Yellow Ribbon,* shot when Wayne was forty-two. Hawks is supposed to have encountered Wayne's resistance when he asked him to play an older man; but Wayne would later say that his favorite role was the grizzled man of retirement age in *Yellow Ribbon*.

He walks stiffly, stretches, blows on hands cold with age, sucks in his belly before going out before the men, and wears a Lincoln shawl for warmth. This is very far from the repressed and hard Brittles of the Bellah story. That officer will not even go near the cemetery where his wife is buried, for fear of yielding to sentiment. Wayne's character goes twice to his wife's grave, to water flowers there and talk to her as if she were alive.

Bellah's Brittles is given a watch as his men's farewell gift. He is standing before them at morning inspection, looking at "the fifty-cents-a-day faces that he had seen all his life." He would like to say something more, but all his rigid code will allow him is: "Thank you, sergeant. Thank you. B Company's a good company. Best I've seen in all my time. Tough in the rump, but good. Good luck, all of you."[1] He strides away.

Nugent and Ford make a bigger scene of this. Wayne is on horseback reviewing the troops. This watch, unlike the one in Bellah, has an inscription, and Wayne must take out his glasses to read it. This recalls the famous scene where George Washington, at Newburgh, New Jersey, put down an officers' rebellion by reading a special message to them. He said, as he took out a new pair of glasses: "Gentlemen, you must pardon me. I have grown gray in your service, and now find myself growing blind." Wayne says nothing to excuse the glasses, but he looks furtively to the side as he pulls them out, as if embarrassed by the move. When he reads the inscription, the watch held out for focus in his big paw, he chokes back tears.

This is not just a stray sentimental touch in the picture. Ford and Nugent evoke the Father of His Country because Brittles is made a father-figure to his men and the civilians at the post. He pats people on the head or back, hugs sorrowing women to comfort them, toughens up his subordinates with a forgiving eye. When he comes across an Indian atrocity, it affects him so deeply that he says, "Maybe I *am* getting too old for this."

The captain is in danger of coddling his men (never a problem with Bellah's officers). When Wayne asks to spend his last day leading a relief mission, to spare a spoiled rich kid (Harry Carey, Jr.) from the dangers of taking out his first command, Wayne's superior (George O'Brien) tells him the young lieutenant must learn the hard way, just as he and Nathan did. Wayne admits that is true—but he later goes out to the relieved troops and their relievers, and gives the order to attack Indian horses.

Ford and Nugent had to add episodes to Bellah's thin short story to create a movie. They do this in four ways. Instead of just sending troops against the horses, Wayne first goes into the Indian camp under a flag of truce, so that his adjutant (Ben Johnson) can scout out the vulnerabilities of the horse picketing. This sequence is more than a filler, since it allows Wayne to speak with the aging Indian chief whose peaceful efforts have been overridden by a hotheaded young warrior. The image of Wayne as father to his troops, but keeping them in line, is played against the affectionate memories he shares with his counterpart, the old chief who wants to go fishing with Wayne, smoke, and share old men's memories of a world that is disappearing. Wayne sympathizes with the mood. It is a wonderful vignette, captured perfectly in the picture frame when Wayne and the chief reach to each other, their hands touching behind a young man's rifle that cuts across the screen.

The second way the plot is fleshed out is by using elements of another Bellah story, "The Big Hunt," in which a cavalry officer who cannot punish an Indian agent maneuvers a buffalo herd into a stampede that tramples the agent to death. Ford keeps the buffalo and the agent, but has Indians kill the agent. Nugent's Brittles is a figure too benign to resort to such devices.

The third expansion introduces women into the camp. This time there are only two—the fort commander's wife (Mildred Natwick) and her visiting niece (Joanne Dru). Two lieutenants (John Agar and Harry Carey, Jr.) compete for Joanne Dru's attention, giving Wayne the opportunity for some kindly intervention as father-confessor to Dru and controller-of-the-competition with his subordinates. But the real plot function of the women is to give Wayne a "last mission" before he rides out to give the order to attack the Indians' horses. He is delegated to take the women to a stagecoach, so they can escape the oncoming Indian attack. But his caution for the women's safety makes him take a long route to the stage stop, which has been wiped out by the time he reaches it. This lends support to Brittles's own feeling that he is going soft. He fears that he must end his days of service with a failed mission.

Mildred Natwick, the "old soldier" of the post, pooh-poohs such fear. When Wayne leaves the fort, apparently forever, she reminds him that "we in the cavalry" never say goodbye. With a kiss on the cheek, she corrects him: "To our next post, dear." Natwick is a solid support to the community, while Dru is a flirtatious disturber of young men's composure. Natwick's authority is confirmed when she goes to the barroom where seven men are trying unsuccessfully to arrest Sergeant Quincannon (Victor McLaglen) for being out of uniform. The overtowering McLaglen sheepishly obeys her words—in a scene that anticipates Fellini's *Amarcord,* where a crazed man in a tree ignores all efforts to get him down until a dwarfish nun comes and takes command of him with her orders.

The fourth addition to Bellah's plot is thematically the most interesting, and politically the most important. Running all through the film is a theme of reconciliation between the veterans of the Civil War. Wayne, O'Brien, and McLaglen are Union veterans—Wayne recalls the days of Bull Run with McLaglen. In line with his fatherly care of others, Wayne has tricked McLaglen into being out of uniform so he can be locked up where no booze will tempt him into trouble before his own retirement. Wayne has extracted a promise from O'Brien to retire McLaglen with a top sergeant's pension.

But other officers and enlisted men (all at reduced rank) fought for the Confederacy. Pedro Armendariz plays a Hispanic Texan who is now a drill sergeant. Ben Johnson, now Sergeant Tyree, used to be a captain. When Wayne's troops find the obliterated stagecoach post, they learn that a former Confederate was mortally wounded defending the position. When he dies, Natwick uses her red flannels to make a Confederate flag for Tyree to put over the body, and Wayne refers to "Captain Tyree," his Confederate rank. At the end of the movie, when Wayne receives a commission as head of the scout service and boasts that it is signed by Sherman, Sheridan, and Grant, Tyree says that it would be a full house if Robert E. Lee's name had been added. Wayne nods reflectively and says, "Wouldn't-a-been bad."

National unity for the great Cold War effort was a theme of growing insistence by 1949. Internal differences must be sacrificed for the sake of putting up a united front as the "leader of the free world." People as different as Robert Kennedy (for a while) and William F. Buckley (for an extended period) argued that civil rights protestors should refrain from raising doubts about freedom within a country playing the role of "leader of the free world." Critics of the national security program—Robert

Oppenheimer, for instance, opposing the development of the hydrogen bomb—were considered traitors to the great joint endeavor. It was not a time for division or dissent. Social criticism in the movies, what little of it there had been (dealing with American racism), was branded as red propaganda by the investigators and blacklisters. Ford's movie puts a benign and fatherly face on this search for national union. Wayne's trusted adjutant —his eyes when he cannot see far enough, the man courageous enough to ride alone with him into the Indian camp—is Ben Johnson as Lieutenant Tyree. The two embody the fusion of different elements in American society—North and South, old and young, experience and energy, Father of His Country and rebellion restored to loyalty. This resembles the "songs of social harmony" advanced as propaganda in World War II—the movies encouraged by the government in Hollywood, the radio shows produced by Norman Corwin. In the Cold War, Ford volunteered his service, needing no censor's promptings.

Wayne himself criticized the ending of *Yellow Ribbon*. He thought that Brittles should serve his men one last time and then go off, unappreciated, to obscurity, completing a characterization heavy on pathos. Instead, in the movie as in Bellah's story, he is intercepted as he rides toward a private citizen's life, to be recalled as a leader of scouts—which obviates the retirement age for regular officers. Since Brittles was conceived as a Washington figure, it is best to have the father of the country still riding out from the main force to make things safe, to find new paths. The mythic stature of Wayne as an authority others can rely on, even while they shape their own lives, is important to the logic of this picture. Wayne's fatherly yet vigorous air of authority makes him indispensable, first in peace as in war.

The last of Ford's three pictures made from Bellah stories was *Rio Grande*, released in 1950. It was even more closely based on fact than was the Custer film, *Fort Apache*. It gives a softened version of an actual raid made out of Fort Clark in 1873, executed on the direct order of General Phil Sheridan, President Grant's commander of western operations against the Indians.

Sheridan was a great hero to James Warner Bellah, who believed in Sheridan's charges that an "Indian ring" was responsible for the military's ineffective response to the Indian peril in the West.[2] Bellah's material was used in *Fort Apache*, where Wayne denounced the ring to Fonda, saying it was "the dirtiest, most corrupt group in our history," a conspiracy of politicians, merchants, and Indian agents to flatter, provoke, and abuse the Indians for profit. Sheridan thought it was cruel to promise Indians what they could not have. His own policy was for rigorous treatment impartially applied, with no interference from the bureaucrats. Though he denied saying that "the only good Indian is a dead Indian," contemporaries thought that he did. Certainly some of his actions seemed to reflect that attitude—one that Bellah heartily concurred with.

Sheridan's favorite officer on the frontier was Colonel Ranald Mackenzie. Mackenzie graduated first in West Point's Civil War class of 1862 and rose rapidly to major general's rank under Sheridan. Wounded five times during the war, and once more on the frontier, he was known to the Indians as "Bad Hand" because two fingers were shot off his right hand.[3] A grim and antiromantic officer, the very antithesis of Custer, Mackenzie had absorbed the doctrine of total war under Sheridan, Sherman, and Grant. He had some of the same objections to fighting a limited war against Indians that modern generals had to "fighting with one hand tied behind our backs" in Korea or Vietnam.

Sheridan had explained his western policy to Sherman, his military superior, in these words:

> In taking the offensive, I have to select that season when I can catch the fiends; and if a village is attacked and women and children killed, the responsibility is not with the soldiers but with the people whose crimes necessitated the attack. During the war did anyone hesitate to attack a village or town occupied by the enemy because women or children were within its limits? Did we cease to throw shells into Vicksburg or Atlanta because women and children were there?[4]

Sheridan got a chance to put his doctrine to use in 1873, when a number of Kickapoo Indians left their reservation in the Indian Territory and went across the Rio Grande into Mexico. From that base, they made forays across the river, hitting white installations and drawing back across the border, where the cavalry could not follow them.

Sheridan made a trip to Fort Clark, near the Rio Grande, to give a personal (but unwritten) order to his trusted ally, Colonel Mackenzie, telling him to stop those raids by whatever means necessary. If this involved violation of an international boundary, Sheridan would do everything he could to support Mackenzie with General Sherman and with Secretary of War William Belk-nap (whom some considered a member of the "Indian ring," but who was Sheridan's ally).

Mackenzie told his adjutant, after the meeting with Sheri-dan, that he had been ordered to conduct "a campaign of annihi-lation, obliteration, and complete destruction." Sheridan never mentioned crossing the border, but he had to know that would be necessary to the execution of his order. He predicted to an associate at his base of operations in Chicago that Mackenzie would in fact cross the border.[5] That was on April 12, 1873.

It took Mackenzie a month to perfect his plan. Rather than pursue Indian soldiers and wage direct war with them, he sent scouts to tell him when the warriors had left the village of Remo-lino, one of the principal launching points for Indian raids. Then, in a night crossing of the Rio Grande, he went on a sixty-hour raid to destroy Remolino and two neighboring villages. He took forty noncombatants (after killing nineteen resisters), and brought them back onto American soil as hostages. The hostages were sent back to the reservation, and Mackenzie told diplomats negotiating with the Mexican government that there would be no trading for them. Those warriors who wanted their families back would have to disarm and rejoin them on the reservation.

General Sherman was angered at this operation planned behind his back, but the popular rush of praise for the raid made him acquiesce in the fait accompli—though he warned that he would tolerate no repetitions. He told an officer who wanted to pursue Indian raiders into Canada: "Because as you explained General Sheridan and Mackenzie once consented to act unlaw-fully in defiance of my authority in a certain political contin-gency is no reason why I should imitate so bad an example."[6]

In his magazine version of the raid on Remolino, Bellah gave Mackenzie the fictional name "Colonel Massarene," keeping the dour and ascetic nature of the original: "A frigid shadow of a man, D. L. Massarene—living in Capuchin solitude with one chair, one cat, one table."[7] Sheridan, in this telling of the story, openly orders a crossing of the border:

> Grant and I will take personal responsibility in Washing-ton, but we want no official paper record to exist. My job is to protect Texas. You cross the Rio Grande and smash 'em, Massarene. . . .[8]

Bellah gleefully makes the raid more savage than it was. His colonel does not go to take hostages. He re-creates, on a smaller scale, Sherman's obliterative "march to the sea." Once they are across the Rio Grande, Massarene's surprised men are given these instructions by their commander:

> Gentlemen, the direction of march is south by west, magnetic. I'm burning out everything in my path—everything Kickapoo, Lipan, and Apache, and anything else that darkness fails to distinguish. I'm going through like a scourge —in column at the gallop, so that the next five hours will be remembered for twenty years to come. If I'm opposed by troops, I'm still going through, for a recrossing at Paredes at six a.m. You will leave your dead, shoot wounded horses, and lash your wounded in their saddles. There will be no dismounted action.[9]

The raid destroys seven villages. The narrator describes it with relish:

> See the reprisal raid for a red beast in the night, clawing on a forty-seven-mile arc of the world like the devil in white-hot armor. See the spoor of dead in its pathway, hacked open and gaping, and the crimson flowers of flame that burst in the darkness and guttered in the echo of ruthless hoofs.[10]

Massarene makes clear his contempt for those who would question his methods. He tells his men: "You are operating under my orders. You need, therefore, have no thought for the consequences of tonight's work. That will be thrashed out thousands of miles away by men who wear clean clothing and sit in comfortable offices."[11]

Bellah's protagonist is given only one softening touch. Alone at night, he plays the violin in memory of the wife who could not share his hard vocation. When General Sheridan tells Massarene that his son, who has grown up without knowing a father, flunked out of West Point, Massarene feels that the son has been corrupted by his wife's soft ways. His greeting to the boy he has not seen since he was an infant is this:

> There are two bloodstreams coursing in you. One is deeply ingrained in a way of soft and moneyed living—so deeply that pride of oath and commitment is secondary to its continual necessity. . . . My father shot, for cowardice, at Chapultepec, the officer son of a United States senator with his own hand. . . . You have chosen my way of life; I shall

see that you attain to it with its deepest essence or leave
your bones to bleach under the prairie moon.[12]

Of course, the son proves himself in battle. Both men are
wounded. When Massarene sends his son off to the regimental
surgeon, the two salute each other with manifest respect. That is
all the affection such stories will indulge.

Bellah's tale gave Ford a perfect opportunity for making
Wayne repeat his successful role of the preceding year, as Sergeant Stryker in *Sands of Iwo Jima.* Bellah describes just such a
man—one so hard on his subordinates that they have trouble
seeing how it could all be for their own good.

> They hated Colonel Massarene because he hewed so close
> to the line that no humanity ever got between, only an
> immaculate military justice that was machine-made and
> icy as the fingers of death. They hated him because he was
> ever right, and they hated him because they knew they
> could never love him.[13]

Ford could never care for such a monster. Only once would he
make Wayne so hard—as the hateful hater in *The Searchers*
(1956)—and even then he makes him relent at the end, surrendering his hate.

In *Rio Grande,* Ford takes Wayne's character as far as possible from the principled thuggishness Bellah admired in "Massacre." Wayne is first humanized by giving him a sentimental
companion, Victor McLaglen (again called Quincannon), as his
aide from the war days when they rode down the Shenandoah
Valley under Sheridan. When Wayne's son arrives at the fort,
Wayne uses the same line about an officer who shot a senator's
son to indicate there will be no favoritism. But under the gruff
exterior he is clearly moved to see his son grown up tall and
handsome (Claude Jarman, Jr.). After Jarman leaves Wayne's
tent, Wayne goes over to the point where his son's head hit the
canvas and compares the height of father and son (it is equal).
When his son is earning the other men's respect by dangerous
stunts—riding "Roman style" (standing on the saddles of two
horses), or fighting a tough old-timer and not "snitching"—
Wayne betrays his concern. When a man given a dangerous mission asks for Jarman as one of his two assistants, Wayne is forced
to acquiesce, though he is visibly uneasy.

But the real humanizing of the Wayne character is achieved

by bringing his son's mother into the camp. She is not simply a "soft" aristocrat, as in Bellah, but a Southern lady whose plantation Wayne destroyed, under General Sheridan's orders, destroying their marriage. She has come to buy her son's way out of the Army, and she is willing to ingratiate herself with "Kirby," if that is necessary to getting his signature. This is the first of Maureen O'Hara's five films made with Wayne, and their mutual respect contributes to quietly powerful performances. When she seems to relent, he must resist, and vice versa, as they grope their way to honest statement under all the fencing they do over their son's future, their own past, and the peril that surrounds the fort after her arrival.

This is the most beautifully filmed of the cavalry pictures—Archie Stout, as the second-unit director, doing the stunning Moab, Utah, landscapes, and Bert Glennon (the cameraman for *Stagecoach*) doing intimate scenes between the principals. In fact, the pivotal scenes in Wayne's officer's tent are the equivalent of the interior scenes at Apache Wells in *Stagecoach*. The translucent canvas of Wayne's small tent cocoons the characters in face-offs that are charged with emotion. There are four main scenes in the tent, each played with two characters putting up masks over their real feelings, which nonetheless shine through.

The first scene takes place in full day, Wayne's son reporting to him, their dark uniforms silhouetted against the bright canvas. (There is a colorized version of the movie that totally cancels the brilliance of the black-and-white photography.)

The next scene is played in the soft light of the afternoon—Wayne confronting O'Hara as they conduct their first argument over their son. She is stiff and stubborn, he relaxed and stubborn. When he leaves, she opens his old war chest and finds the music box that plays "I'll take you home again, Kathleen" (Kathleen is her movie name). As her rigor softens, the camera does a melt, fuzzing out her features in a wave of emotion. This is an expressionist device Ford was using as early as 1917: in *Straight Shooting*, we see a funeral through Harry Carey's eyes, and the scene blurs as emotion makes him teary.

In the next scene, the tent is black with the outside darkness and only a candle-lamp lights Wayne and O'Hara as they have dinner—the closing in of the two around the lamp recalls the clustering of the men around the light in *Stagecoach* as outside danger forces them toward intimacy. When, after dinner, the regimental chorus shows up to serenade the visiting lady, they sing "I'll Take You Home Again, Kathleen," and Wayne says with embarrassment that he had no part in choosing this song. He is the stiff one now, shifting uncomfortably and playing with his cigar, while she relaxes with memory and leans imperceptibly toward him. The whole wordless sequence, as the two listen to the singers, is a masterpiece of subtle action, each achingly aware of each other's presence, but looking at the singers with a resolution to hide their emotions, sneaking rare glances at each other, their bodies touching each other at times, then tautening away.

The fourth scene occurs when Wayne, returning from a patrol, goes wearily into his dark tent, strikes a match off the canvas side, and lights a lamp whose flame turns him into a pitch-black silhouette (like the prostitute in Ford's *The Long Voyage Home*). When he turns, light hits O'Hara as she rises toward him out of the dark. He impulsively spins her into a passionate kiss—then draws away, since he knows she is "seducing" him to get her way on their son. Though she has planned this, she is flustered—not by his rejection, but by her emotional response to him, which goes beyond her calculation. Wayne grabs his military blouse, says she can have the tent, and blunders out to find a wagon he can sleep in. His walk off into the night is the very opposite of "the Wayne walk"—uncoordinated, disoriented by conflicting emotions.

Ford could not make his Wayne character act with the ruthlessness of Bellah's "Massarene." In the movie, Sheridan (played by J. Carroll Naish) visits "Fort Starke" twice. The first time, he and Yorke (Wayne) complain about their weak position with regard to pursuing Indians. This is mixed up with comments on the weak coffee they are drinking. On the second visit, Naish talks in a code of "stronger coffee" as necessary for dealing with the Indians. He says he is making the recommendation on his own, but that if there are repercussions he will stack Yorke's court martial with men "who rode with us down the Shenandoah."

Wayne agonizes over the charge he has been given, walking by night along the Rio Grande (actually the Colorado River) while the Sons of the Pioneers sing around a campfire. The river is a glittering symbol of division—what divides him from his target enemies, but also from his family, his feelings, his principles.

Sheridan has told Yorke to send the women and children

farther north before leaving an undefended fort to pursue the Indians. Wayne sends his son with the wagons of women and children, thinking he will be safer guarding them; but they are the ones ambushed by the Indians. All the children and several women are snatched away. O'Hara, among those left behind, sends her son to summon Wayne.

The Indians take their hostages into Mexican territory—exactly reversing the historical event. Colonel Mackenzie kidnapped Indian women and children in Mexico and carried them over the river border into the United States. Wayne faces a situation in which his foes are the abductors. Wayne sends his trusted scout (Ben Johnson, again playing Sergeant Tyree) to find out the hostages' whereabouts while he makes a secret night crossing of the river.

The moral objections that could be raised against Mackenzie's raid have been artfully avoided. Wayne goes, not in "hot pursuit" of Indian warriors, but on a mission of mercy. As if that were not enough to blunt misgivings about breaking international law, Nugent invents an earlier meeting for Wayne where a Mexican officer borrows the services of a surgeon for his men. He, too, complains about the Indians' raids back and forth across his border and says that *his* government's hands are tied. Implicitly we are being told that the Mexican government will not really mind, and will make no international protest, if Wayne removes the thorn from a neighbor's side. (In fact, Mexico *did* protest Mackenzie's raid, energetically—it knew the United States had seized border territory in the past and could use excuses to take more.)

It is noteworthy that the censors of the Production Code did not object to the crossing of an international border. But they were disturbed by Wayne's complicity in the escape of Sergeant Tyree from a Texas marshal come to fetch him for murder.[14] Tyree had earlier killed a man who dishonored his sister. The script was altered to show that Tyree was not running from the law for good, just until his sister, about to wed, leaves Texas with her new husband—Tyree does not want unpleasantness with another man to mar her marital prospects.

Johnson's Southerner, Tyree, has the same function in this film as in *Yellow Ribbon*—showing how the South has rejoined the North in the national enterprise. Wayne's son, the heir to his mother's Southern plantation, is taken under Tyree's tutelage ("Get her done, Johnny Reb"). The Southerners working with

Wayne are an implicit rebuke to O'Hara for still holding out, harboring grudges from the war. When she arrived, she still thought of Victor McLaglen as the "arsonist"—who burnt her ancestral home. But as she sees him caring for the fort's children, sees the work of the other women to keep this frontier society together, she is slowly brought into its social weave. After cleaning Wayne's uniform in order to undermine his refusal to release their son, she soon joins other women in washing the men's clothes.

In the opening scene of the movie, a line of seven women stand inside the gate of the fortress as men ride wearily in from a patrol. As faces emerge from the dust kicked up around them in the gateway, the women react either with relief, when they see their husbands still mounted, or with anxiety, when they see horse-sleds dragging the wounded. One man on such a slanted cot, dragged behind a horse, puts his hand up for his child to walk along beside him.

When Wayne and his troops bring back the children from captivity, O'Hara has joined that line, watching for her son and husband. The son walks behind the husband on the sled-cradle, and she takes Wayne's hand, to walk beside him as the wounded man's relative did in the opening scene.

No matter how Ford humanized the brutal Bellah story, he did justify breaking international law to protect one's own. The picture was released on November 15, 1950. The Korean War officially had begun on June 27, 1950, when the U.N. authorized support of South against North Korea—but the full-scale war was preceded by two years of northern incursions into the South, followed by retreats back across the Thirty-eighth Parallel. In the course of the war, "hot pursuit" of the enemy into China would become an inflammable issue. The same problems would arise in Vietnam—in fact, Wayne would have trouble with the Pentagon when he made *The Green Berets,* since he wanted to show Special Forces acting like Colonel Mackenzie as they crossed borders to retaliate for raids. Beautifully crafted as *Rio Grande* is, simply as a story, it also resonated with Cold War concerns, with the duties of empire when the leaders of the free world had a global mission that refused to observe national borders. Wayne put a human face on empire—which did not make it any less an empire.

Part Five

PROPAGANDA

In the early 1940s Wayne avoided the ideological conflict over Communism just as he avoided physical combat with the Axis powers. But by 1948 his symbolic status as a patriot on the screen drew him into anti-Communist activities in Hollywood. (By that time, the most bruising ideological battles were over.) Wayne made "patriotic" movies for billionaire Howard Hughes in the 1950s, and launched his own efforts at defining the duties of Americanism in the 1960s: *The Alamo* (1960) and *The Green Berets* (1968). The last two films, though ridiculed by critics, earned back their considerable production costs and confirmed Wayne's hard-core fans in their belief that he represented the power and resolution of America.

Wayne in 1929, in costume for Raoul Walsh's *The Big Trail*. Walsh told him to let his hair grow long.

Harry Carey, circa 1917. Wayne's model of a cowboy.

Wayne in *The Man Who Shot Liberty Valance*. The Harry Carey image.

Carey and Wayne in their first film together, *The Shepherd of the Hills* (1941).

Yakima Canutt, rodeo champion and stuntman, who taught Wayne how to fight and ride. From *The Telegraph Trail,* starring Wayne (1933).

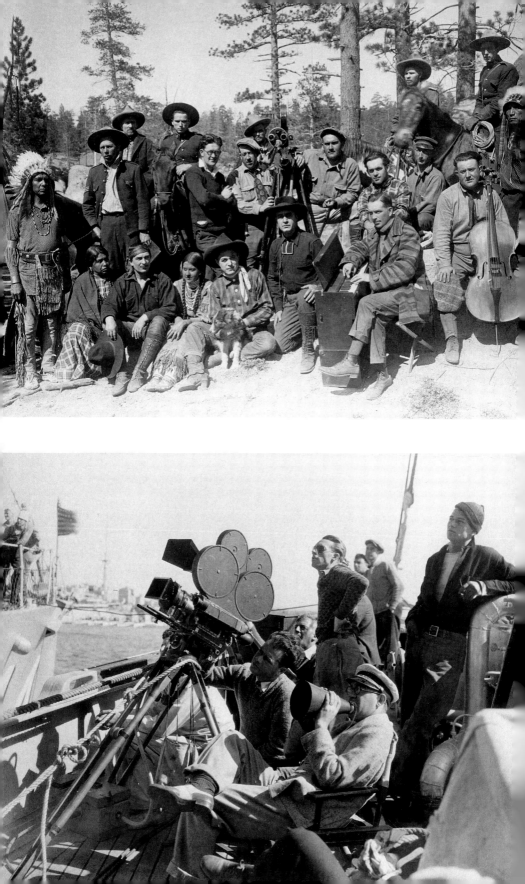

OPPOSITE TOP: The John Ford set, I, circa 1917: Harry Carey seated in center with dog, Ford behind him with arms crossed. Note the silent-film musicians for setting the mood of a scene.

OPPOSITE BOTTOM: The John Ford set, II, 1930: Shooting *Men Without Women,* Ford with megaphone, Wayne a bit player in stocking cap.

BELOW: The John Ford set, III, 1957: Ford wets down Ken Curtis and Maureen O'Hara, with Wayne watching in baseball cap.

ALINARI/ART RESOURCE

Michelangelo's *David* (1501–04).

Wayne in his customary Michelangelo contrapposto pose.

© PHIL STERN PHOTO

Donatello's *David* (1440–42).

Wayne in his Donatello contrapposto pose (on the *Stagecoach* set, with Ford seated by camera platform, 1938).

Ford's *Fort Apache* (1948), with Wayne in his relaxed contrapposto pose, Henry Fonda in stiff frontal stance.

Wayne visits Vietnam in 1966—a rare shot without his toupee (as if to say he really *was* too old to serve in this war).

□ 15 □
FORT HOLLYWOOD

THE YEAR WAYNE BECAME a superstar, 1948, was also the year when he became a political activist.¹ In the late 1930s, when Henry Fonda was sailing with Ford on the *Araner*, and the two men were airing liberal views with Dudley Nichols, Wayne was not interested. He could not even spell politics, according to Fonda.

Wayne, a careerist in the forties, had not played a role on either side as the conflict over Communism in the movies intensified between 1939 and 1947. In 1939, the House Committee on Un-American Activities, chaired by Martin Dies, went to California to investigate Communist influence in the film industry. In 1947, suspected Communists in the industry were summoned to Washington, to answer questions from the same committee, now chaired by J. Parnell Thomas. The movie industry filled the intervening years with efforts to keep government out of the hiring and firing practices of the studios. These efforts were not primarily political but (on the part of the executives) a matter of business and (on the part of screen workers) a matter of professionalism. Even most anti-Communists took the position Ronald Reagan later espoused when testifying before the Thomas Committee—that if there were any loyalty problems in the Hollywood community, the producers and the various guilds could handle the problem without external interference.

The movie colony was especially nervous about charges of "radicalism," since it had been treated like a resented enclave in

193

a state and locale historically conditioned to oppose the alien. California, with its thousand-mile stretch of ocean and foreign border, with its flood of immigrants, felt a need to define itself in the midst of flux. The California labor movement was born as part of an effort to keep out Chinese workers.[2] But when the unions began to gain power, strong forces led by Harrison Otis's Los Angeles *Times* branded its organizers foreign agitators. When those agitators blew up the *Times* building in 1910 (killing twenty and injuring seventeen), a hysteria was unleashed that the *Times* maintained for decades—a legacy the even more powerful Hearst papers in California accepted and intensified.

The Hollywood community lived apprehensively in this atmosphere. Producers who came to Los Angeles for the climate, for year-round filming possibilities, were "migrant workers" of a different sort from coolies and Mexicans, but they were resented the more for the differences. A heavily Jewish circle of producers was said to be bringing in actors with bohemian lifestyles. Foreign artists were attracted by Hollywood money. The film companies, to show that they were respectable and super-American, suppressed or harshly punished scandals, accepted voluntary censorship (the Production Code), and wooed religious groups like the Catholic Church's Legion of Decency, which forbade Catholics to attend movies it condemned. When the California establishment balked at the thought of Upton Sinclair, a dreamy socialist, becoming governor in 1934, MGM came to the rescue with a series of fake documentary movies showing trainloads of radicals arriving to support Sinclair.[3]

It was not surprising, then, that the studios told actors to cooperate with Congress in 1939, when investigators went to California looking for reds. Humphrey Bogart, James Cagney, Fredric March, and others dutifully went before the Dies Committee to say they were not secret Communists.[4] They cooperated, but with contempt—a contempt generally shared by the movie community. During the war, the studios submitted, like the rest of the country, to patriotic discipline, seeking and following governmental directives on the making of propaganda vehicles, overt and covert, and surrendering personnel to military service. Ironically, this involved some government-sponsored movies that praised our wartime ally, the Soviet Union.

A few hard-core anti-Communists in the industry thought the government was all too ready to sponsor, and the studios to accept, such "pro-Soviet" assignments. Screenwriter Ayn Rand resented the fact that Russians smiled in the 1943 *Song of Russia,* a favorable treatment of the Soviet ally.[5] The direst suspicions were entertained by director Sam Wood, who attributed his loss of an Oscar for *Goodbye, Mr. Chips* (1939) to a leftist cabal trying to discredit accusations that fellow film workers were Communists.[6] During the war, he became even more apprehensive that Roosevelt was in cahoots with Stalin, and that Hollywood was softening America up for a Communist "takeover" of this country.

Wood was treated as a fanatic by most of those who knew him, but he had a circle of friends sympathetic to him (though less overheated than he was). He had broken into movies as an assistant to Cecil B. DeMille, cooperated with writer Morrie Ryskind on Marx Brothers pictures, and become a friend of the anti-Roosevelt newspaper giant, William Randolph Hearst, while directing two pictures that starred Hearst's mistress, Marion Davies.

When Dudley Nichols chaired a 1944 rally for Vice President Henry Wallace, Wood, along with friends like Ryskind and Walt Disney, announced a countermeeting to set up the Motion Picture Alliance for the Preservation of American Ideals. This organization did the one thing guaranteed to make the rest of the movie world hate it. It openly invited the House Committee on Un-American Activities to come back to California and take up where the Dies Committee had left off five years earlier. When representatives of the committee came to Los Angeles for preliminary investigations, they worked closely with the amateur sleuths of Wood's world (Wood had endless lists of suspected "reds") and talked with "friendly witnesses." From this groundwork subpoenas issued for nineteen "unfriendly witnesses" who resisted the committee. Of these, the famous "Hollywood Ten" were called to testify in Washington late in 1947. Even those agnostic about the Ten's Communist background (real enough, though in the past for most of them) felt that they had not made Hollywood a vehicle for Communist propaganda. Hollywood's artistic sin, as any observer knew, was conformism, an eagerness for acceptance as *super*-American, a willingness to adhere to voluntary censorship. Had the Production Code been approving anti-American movies all those years? The "evidence" offered for Communist propaganda in the movies was laughable. Lester Cole was criticized for making a rabbi tell Jews facing a death camp, "It is better to die on your feet than live on your knees."[7]

That is the kind of thing John Wayne would say when he made *The Alamo.*

Support for the Ten ran high in 1947. Sam Wood's group was considered a band of traitors to the industry. Inviting the government to run one's business is an odd position for "conservatives," who professed a fear of big government. Since the original strategy of the Ten was not to invoke the Fifth Amendment, but the First (their private opinions were free by constitutional guarantees), a Committee for the First Amendment was formed, with a galaxy of names familiar to the public—Walter Wanger, Humphrey Bogart, Myrna Loy, Katharine Hepburn, Danny Kaye. These celebrities were opposing obscure men like Wood and Ryskind. Did people really trust the latter more than the former? A chartered plane of the stars carried Bogart's merry band to Washington, to serve as a cheering section for the Ten. (This is the episode treated fictionally in the Robert Redford and Barbra Streisand movie, *The Way We Were.*)

But 1947 was the year of the great domestic Communism hunt initiated with Truman's internal security program—a program Clark Clifford said Truman was blackmailed into by J. Edgar Hoover, even though he abhorred it himself. Things in Washington went poorly for the overconfident Hollywooders. The Ten got off to a faltering start when John Howard Lawson, the head of the Communist writers' cell in Hollywood, filibustered pompously. As Murray Kempton wrote:

> Just this once he could enjoy a fling at freedom. "I am an American," said Lawson, "and I am not at all easy to intimidate, and don't think I am." He had forgotten in the splendor of this hour all those shabby nights in 1945, when he had allowed the bravoes from the Party headquarters to pommel him at their pleasure.[8]

Lawson did not come across like Jimmy Stewart's "Mr. Smith," crying for justice in the halls of Congress. He seemed to think himself an aristocrat dealing with bumpkins. But his dignity was hard to maintain when the Capitol police hustled him off while he kept trying to shout defiance. While the stars watched these goings-on with some dismay, the movies' money men, whose offices were in New York, went into panic. When the Ten were cited for contempt, the studio heads called a hasty summit conference at the Waldorf-Astoria in New York and promised to fire anyone who defied a congressional committee or refused to establish his or her non-Communist credentials. As usual, the Hollywood managers were willing to please the audience. Members of the Ten like writers Lester Cole and Dalton Trumbo had been assured by their Hollywood bosses that their contracts were safe. But contracts had a "morals clause" and other protections for the studios, to make sure they were not asked to offer a product grown unpalatable to audiences. As silent comedian Fatty Arbuckle was dumped by his studio when accused of sexual deviance, the Ten were dumped for intellectual deviance. The norm was commercial, not political. Ronald Reagan, as head of the Screen Actors Guild, turned down Gale Sondergaard's request for support when she took the Fifth Amendment before investigators. This was his justification:

> If any actor by his own actions outside of union activities has so offended public opinion that he has made himself unsalable at the box office, the Guild cannot and would not want to force any employers to hire him.[9]

Reagan's guild stance explains Wayne's later claim that there was no industry blacklisting of suspected Communists.[10] He felt there was just a box-office judgment on who was saleable in a particular climate—a view to be expected on the employers' side but unusual in a workers' spokesperson like Reagan, who was a union leader. After the producers' capitulation to the red scare, actors made what peace they could in the hostile climate. The Committee for the First Amendment was dissolved. The Ten switched their strategy to the Fifth Amendment. Humphrey Bogart confessed he had been "duped" by the Communist Party. One of the Ten (Edward Dmytryk) repented in prison, and was employed on his release. Some of the rest wrote again, but for years under pseudonyms. The surrender was made, and one had to put the best face possible on it.

In that whole period, from 1939 to 1947, Wayne's name does not appear on any side of the struggle. A noncombatant during the physical shooting of World War II, he was also a noncombatant in the ideological war. The same careerism that kept him from wearing a uniform kept him from taking a stand. His role, finally, was to emerge after the battle and shoot the wounded. He became "outspoken" only after the Waldorf conference had ended the war and the industry was voicing *only* one side.

Wayne's long reticence is remarkable when one considers that the Motion Picture Alliance was set up with some of the people close to him—Ward Bond, Ford's screenwriter James McGuinness, and *Red River's* author, Borden Chase. When Wayne finally did join the fray, it was to act as president of the Alliance, in succession to Ward Bond. It would have taken some courage, even if wrongheaded courage, to assume that office before 1948, when the whole industry resented the Alliance for calling in the House Committee. But by 1948 the Alliance had won, Congress was calling the shots, the studios had capitulated, and actors were making overtures of preemptive cooperation. To step in then was joining a bully, not an underdog.

Wayne would swagger in his new role, taking credit for wounds he never dealt: "I'll never regret having helped run [Carl] Foreman out of the country."[11] He had nothing to do with expelling Foreman, the screenwriter for *High Noon* (1952). By the time Foreman took the Fifth Amendment before the House Committee, blacklisting was automatic, and he went to England looking for work (which he found). Foreman never consulted with Wayne, as Wayne claims. Wayne entered the ideological wars as he did World War II—retrospectively, and with compensatory bravado. He seems to have felt that a man about to put Sergeant Stryker on the screen should stand somewhere in the great struggles of his time—though he had trouble formulating the issues at stake apart from his screen symbolism. He was not as clear as Reagan on the grounds for denying that there had been any blacklisting of suspected Communists: "There was no blacklist at that time, as people said. That was a lot of horseshit. . . . The only thing our side did that was anywhere near blacklisting was just running a lot of people out of the business."[12]

The only blacklist in Hollywood, according to Wayne,[13] was created by "Communist sympathizers" like the liberal producer Dore Schary, who did not use McGuinness after he took charge of MGM.[14] It is true that many hated Ryskind, McGuinness, and other Alliance founders—but they did not have to be Communist sympathizers to feel that way. The martyrs' list was a lot shorter on the right than on the left—though Wayne included himself as one of the martyrs. Asked by an interviewer if he agreed that criticism of *The Alamo* was "inspired by the Communists," Wayne said: "Well, there's always a little truth in everything you hear. The Alliance thing was used pretty strongly against me in those days."[15]

The Alliance wanted Wayne's prestige in 1948, not his dialectical skills, and he rarely got into the details of names to be named and reputations to be restored. A rare exception was his publicly expressed view that actor Larry Parks, having repented and named names, should be reemployed. Columnist Victor Riesel shouted back at him, "To hell with Larry Parks!" Columnist Hedda Hopper said, "We must be careful lest we give sympathy to those who do not deserve it."[16] Wayne had not participated enough in the dark struggle to know just the right degree of vindictiveness and absolution to grant the victims. He made the tactical mistake of trying to remove Parks from a blacklist he said did not exist.

Despite Wayne's image as a nonconformist, one who goes his own way for his own reasons, nothing was more conformist in the Hollywood of the 1950s than to berate Communists and to call oneself brave for doing so. Wayne, after all, could not take credit for his one truly nonconformist act in the 1940s—his defiance of all the pressures to join the military. Nor was he known as a rebel or nonconformist in the studios he worked for —no Jimmy Cagney or Bette Davis, who attacked unjust contract conditions. His docility with Ford was almost childlike. Wayne the late-arriving anti-Communist cut no profile in courage.

But when, at last, Wayne stepped forth as an Alliance president, he showed a growing interest in making Cold War propaganda movies. His first one was filmed the same year as his first World War II movie of the postwar era, *Sands of Iwo Jima.* In 1949, the flamboyantly anti-Communist Howard Hughes hired Josef von Sternberg and cinematographer William Clothier to remake *Ninotchka* as an aviation picture, *Jet Pilot.*[17] But the movie was not released until Hughes sold RKO in 1957. Hughes gave the young and shapely Janet Leigh the same treatment he had given Jane Russell. Playing a Russian jet pilot who has strayed into American-controlled territory, the dangerous spy takes off her flying suit in a long striptease scene, with passing jets making *woo-woo* noises, while Wayne gets improbably shy and embarrassed by the lengths she goes to prove herself unarmed because unclothed. Later Wayne begins her conversion to the capitalist system by taking her to a lingerie shop where Hughes's fixation on Jane Russell's breasts gets a replay at the brassiere counter.

The Outlaw's release had been delayed by censorship problems. *Jet Pilot's* shooting and editing were extended by Hughes's attempt to make the last word in aviation films. He had made what was in some ways the first word in such movies with *Hell's*

Angels (1930). But it is harder to create aeronautical ballets with jet fighters than with the biplanes of Hughes's young flying days. Jets go too fast to be engaged with each other in swirling arabesques. Besides, the technology was changing rapidly during the Korean War. Every year he spent trying to perfect the film made the planes used in it look more obsolete.

Wayne and Hughes became friends, united by anti-Communism and their enthusiasm for Mexican vacations. But none of their professional collaborations was an artistic success. *Flying Leathernecks* (1951), done by the cult director Nicholas Ray, was a formulaic repeat of the Sergeant Stryker story— Wayne as a tough flight commander, Robert Ryan as the subordinate who resists him but learns to admire him before taking up his responsibilities himself. Another Hughes project, *The Conqueror* (1956), with Wayne as Genghis Khan, is best passed over in silence.

Wayne was not content to wage the propaganda war through Hughes films. In collaboration with Robert Fellows, he produced a piece of Cold War agitprop called *Big Jim McLain* (1952), written by James Edward Grant. Jimmy Grant was a poor man's Ben Hecht, another tough-talking, hard-drinking Chicago newspaperman who came west to create film scripts. He and Wayne had become friends by the time Wayne let him direct as well as write Wayne's own production, *Angel and the Badman* (1947). Over the years Grant had more to do with Wayne's blustery style of superpatriotism than anyone else. He became Wayne's favorite screenwriter, the abettor of his dream that *The Alamo* would be a knockout blow to Communism.

Their 1952 opus, *Big Jim McLain*, takes Wayne to Hawaii as an investigator for the House Committee on Un-American Activities. Wayne's assistant is played by Jim Arness, the tall and tongue-tied hero of TV's longest-running series, *Gunsmoke*.[18] Ayn Rand, who hated the fact that Communists smiled in *Song of Russia*, would have loved the Communists in this movie. They not only abjure smiles, they cannot speak without sneering. An evil doctor controls Communists and their forces with his truth serum, and accidentally kills Jim Arness with an overdose. When Wayne runs him down, he regrets that he cannot pulverize him because he is too small: "That's the difference between you people and us, I guess. We don't pick on little people." It is a chastening reminder of the overheated red scare of that time to read the praise given *Big Jim McLain* by the trade press. *Variety* thought it achieved a "documentary-styled account of the Communist peril."[19] More astounding is the fact that a similar, and similarly unsophisticated, film called *I Was a Communist for the FBI* was used in training sessions for the CIA.[20]

Wayne's next Cold War film was *Blood Alley* (1955), in which Wayne, playing a happy-go-lucky ship's captain, takes onto his boat little children escaping from Communist China. Originally, Wayne was to produce the film but not act in it. Robert Mitchum, however, was invited to lunch on a Navy ship, where he drank so much that he punched an extra on his return and insulted the director, William Wellman.[21] "He goes or I go," said Wellman, and a call to Wayne in New York brought the unwilling actor back to learn his lines in a hurry. Use of the ship and of merchant marines was already scheduled and the clock was running. Wayne talks throughout to "Baby," a fantasy guardian angel he invented to stay sane in a Chinese prison. Mitchum might have given a slightly deranged comedy to these scenes. They are painful to watch as Wayne delivers them after leering at a puzzled young Lauren Bacall.

In the 1960s, Wayne joined the John Birch Society, Robert Welch's group that suspected the United States government was secretly run by Communists. Welch embarrassed Barry Goldwater with a smothering embrace in 1964. Richard Nixon had denounced the society in 1962—how could he not, when the society claimed that President Eisenhower, Nixon's patron, was a dupe of the Soviets? Nixon paid for this in the loss of Orange County votes for his gubernatorial race that year. Chastened by that example, Goldwater would not publicly denounce the Birchers in his 1964 race, but he privately tried to purge his campaign of its members. Unknown to Goldwater, this discreet dekooking was assigned to campaign director Denison Kitchel, who had to cover up the fact that he had been in the John Birch Society himself. As Clif White, the head of the Draft Goldwater movement, later said: "If Kitchel's former membership had been made known during the 1964 campaign, it would have blown everything to smithereens."[22]

Wayne was a good friend of Goldwater, whose interest in Arizona's Indian art had taken him to locales where Westerns were being filmed in and around Monument Valley. Goldwater's wife, Peggy, became an intimate drinking partner with Olive Carey, the den mother of Ford's circle. In fact, one of the women's New York shopping trips threatened to cause a scandal during the 1964 campaign, until emergency calls led to their quiet removal from public view.[23]

Wayne's other political activities in the 1960s were concentrated on public endorsement of conservative Republicans at election time. He backed Nixon for President in 1960 and attacked John Kennedy for having his daddy buy the election that year. Advertisements for *The Alamo* (1960) took sly shots at Kennedy for using helpers to write his Pulitzer Prize–winning book, *Profiles in Courage:* "There were no ghostwriters at the Alamo." Kennedy was asked questions about the ad at a campaign press conference.

Wayne himself felt that the greatest service he could do his country was to make the story of the Alamo, a story that had mysteriously become his touchstone of all the essential American values. After Ford set up his Argosy production company with Merian Cooper, Wayne tried to get their backing for such a film. Title rights were secured, and Patrick Ford drafted a script in 1948.[24]

When Wayne and Ford went to Texas to scout locations for *Three Godfathers* (1948), they stopped at the Alamo, where Wayne was photographed holding Davy Crockett's rifle, and the two told reporters they planned to make a movie about the Alamo. But Cooper and Ford decided the commercial promise of the film did not warrant the grandiose scale Wayne desired for it.

Wayne also tried to get Republic, where he was still under contract, to back his effort—a doomed attempt, given Republic's stingy budgets. After Wayne left Republic in 1951, the studio chief, Herb Yates, did make a version of the Alamo story, *The Last Command* (1955). Wayne hangers-on said this was done in spite, to preempt Wayne's grander scheme. Jimmy Grant, screenwriter for *The Alamo,* even claimed that Yates had used an earlier script he had written at Republic for Wayne.[25] But the Yates movie makes Jim Bowie (played by Sterling Hayden) the hero, and Wayne focused always on Davy Crockett, as the Patrick Ford script demonstrates.

Those who want to personalize all Wayne's unhappy experiences with producers or directors (Harry Cohn, Cecil DeMille, Edward Dmytryk, John Huston) understate the financial considerations that weigh more than individual likes or dislikes. Yates did not "rush out" an Alamo picture, four years after Wayne left Republic, as an act of pique. Spitefulness that costs money does not get approved by the head office. Yates was responding to the sudden Alamo fever that swept the nation in 1953–1955 as a result of the Disney television series, *Davy Crockett, King of the Wild Frontier,* starring Fess Parker. This series was done in Technicolor to promote one of the first television shows regularly done in color. Then the Crockett story was sent out as a feature film in theaters. Clamorous children drove up the suppliers' price of raccoon for coonskin hats.

This mid-fifties saturation in the Alamo led to the expectable collapse of interest. Raccoons were safe again. Fess Parker, who *was* Davy Crockett for a whole generation, subsided into obscurity. Through all these fluctuations in the marketability of the Alamo, Wayne was undeterred in his resolution to make the ultimate in patriotic statements. He and Jimmy Grant brooded over the story. He and Alfred Ybarra incubated design schemes. This was not, for Wayne, a business prospect, but a cause, a crusade. It was something he *had* to do for his country. For him, Fort Hollywood had been transmuted into the Alamo.

□ 16 □
ALAMO: LEGEND

THE CLOSEST WAYNE CAME to having a real religion, one for which he would sacrifice himself, was his devotion to the Alamo. How he came by it remains something of a mystery. There would be no problem if he were a Texan. President Lyndon Johnson, carried away while talking to troops during the Vietnam War, blurted out: "My great grandfather died at the Alamo."[1] It is a common enough delusion in Texas. But why should Marion Morrison, of Winterset and Glendale, have become obsessed with the old mission compound where Texans fought a Mexican army on Mexican territory?

Wayne may have heard from Frank Ford how he made the first film about the Alamo, and made it in San Antonio.[2] But John Ford was never one to celebrate his older brother's achievements. A more likely factor in Wayne's growing awareness of the Alamo was a movie made by his Glendale friend, Bob Bradbury (Bob Steele), the year after the two boys had left high school. *Davy Crockett at the Fall of the Alamo* was directed by Bob's father, Robert North Bradbury, who would, not long after, be directing Wayne's B Westerns at Monogram.[3] The Alamo film was a breakthrough for the Bradburys, both father and son. The director was given a more ambitious set (the chapel façade replicated near Santa Barbara) and a wider range of extras (though some shots of the Mexican army for the movie are taken from stock). This hour-long ambitious film was a far cry from the "Bill and Bob" shorts the Bradburys were making when Wayne first met them. No doubt Wayne was impressed by his friends' step up in the movie world (a world Wayne was getting his early glimpses at on the Fox sets). Young Bob, who was twenty at the time, played the horseman-courier of the Alamo—a role Wayne later cast with Frankie Avalon, who was also twenty when Wayne chose him in 1959.

Bradbury's film was the first to emphasize Davy Crockett's own version of his double personality, the Congressman too idealistic to succeed in politics, and the rough frontiersman who hides his sensitivity. That is the way Wayne conceived his own Crockett. It coincides with aspects of his own self-image, of the way he "put on" his cowboy persona, learned to say "ain't," and feigned a liking for horses. Much of the dialogue for Wayne's character in *The Alamo* is autobiographical. Wayne himself crafted and kept shaping the script, along with his sycophantic personal author, Jimmy Grant. Wayne is trying to speak through his work in lines like these: "It seems like, you added up my life, I spent it all either stomping other men or, in some cases, getting stomped myself." Now he (as Crockett) wants more.

Wayne's sense of personal destiny about making *The Alamo* would be hard to exaggerate. In this film, he would not only be acting, but producing and directing. He would demonstrate that there was a mind behind his much-photographed body. He would manipulate others instead of being manipulated by John Ford or Howard Hawks. When one considers what became of all these hopes, nurtured for years and brought to fulfillment through heroic effort, the movie acquires an unintended pathos. Wayne tried to raise a great monument to his own idealized self, and it came close to crushing him, to marking his artistic burial site.

He began making plans for *The Alamo* in 1948, the year of his new political activism. The man who had avoided any sacrifice during World War II now felt ready to make his contribution. His growing involvement in the anti-Communist politics of Hollywood made him feel as if he had joined a struggle greater in significance than the war with fascism. Wayne was ready to preach national preparedness and discipline. While making his Cold War films of the 1950s, he began denouncing young people's hedonism. He had found a mission. As he says in his Crockett role:

When I came down to Texas, I was looking for something,
I didn't know what. . . . Had me some money, had me some
medals; but none of it seemed a lifetime worth the pain of

the mother that bore me. It's like I was empty. Well, I'm
not empty any more. That's what's important. I feel useful
in this old world—to hit a lick for what's wrong, or to say
a word for what's right, even though you get walloped for
saying that word.

Wayne would get walloped by critics for the words he spoke in
making *The Alamo,* and he would conclude that the world was
not ready for a message of self-sacrifice. When the nation wanted
sacrifice from him in 1941, it did not fit his career plans. Now
that he was ready to offer his services to the world, it no longer
wanted them. That is why there is a great sadness under all the
bombinations of his Alamo film. Wayne was trying to make sense
of his own life, but his quest met the demands of the Alamo
itself, which imposes falsehood on all its celebrants; and the
result was a great big Todd-AO lie told from the best of intentions.

Truth is not an item easily smuggled past the customs officers who keep guard on information at today's Alamo. As we
have seen, Lyndon Johnson instinctively resorted to a lie when
he wanted to deploy the Alamo for use in Vietnam. It is a habit
ingrained in Alamo devotees. Journalist Ronnie Dugger was surprised, during an interview with Johnson, that the President
could still quote from childhood memory two stanzas of a poem
about the Alamo. Here is the second stanza:

> And thirty lay sick, and some were shot through,
>> For the siege had been bitter, and bloody, and long.
> "Surrender or die!" — "Men, what will *you* do?"
>> And Travis, great Travis, drew sword, quick and strong,
> Drew a line at his feet . . . "Will you come? Will you go?
>> I die with my wounded, in the Alamo."[4]

Most people who discuss the legend that William Travis drew a
line in the sand discuss the historicity of this later invention.
Fewer address the larger assumption on which it is based—that
all 180 or so inhabitants of the Alamo chose to sacrifice themselves to certain death in order to give Texas time to create an
army to support its revolution.

This theme is struck over and over in Wayne's movie. Sam
Houston (Richard Boone) appears early on to tell William Travis
(Laurence Harvey) that he needs time to form an army, so Travis

must buy that time by holding out at the Alamo in suicidal dog-
gedness. In fact, Houston had earlier sent orders that the Alamo
be abandoned and destroyed.[5] Houston did not want to fight
from fixed places but in a mobile campaign of maneuver, the
kind he used for his victory over Santa Anna at San Jacinto.[6]

In Wayne's movie, Frankie Avalon rides to Houston's camp
and tells him that the men in the Alamo are buying him the time
he asked for. In fact, Houston was not raising an army at this
time. He had taken leave from his command and gone off on a
diplomatic mission to the Cherokees.[7] Not even pop singer
Frankie Avalon could have crooned him back into communica-
tion with the Alamo.

It is true that Travis sent out missives from the Alamo saying
that he would die there if he had to—but those missives contained appeals for reinforcements that he hoped would arrive. It
makes no sense to say he was holding Santa Anna at bay so
Houston could gather an army elsewhere, if *at the same time* he
was summoning the elements of such an army away from Houston and back into the post Houston wanted abandoned.

It goes against the whole Alamo myth, but accords with all
the evidence, to conclude that Travis and the others held on to
the Alamo, against Houston's earlier orders, because they
thought it was a place where they could *win*. The Alamo had
twenty cannon, the largest artillery battery west of the Mississippi. The man who placed the guns, Green Jameson, wrote to
Houston that they would allow defenders to defy ten times their
number.[8]

Jameson claimed that the Alamo had only one hundred or
so men in it. The letter was sent to summon more men to this
spot as the *best* place for their use. Although the Alamo was only
a makeshift fort (as was every other fort in the vicinity), its main
weakness turned out to be the small number of its defenders. An
ideal number would have been five hundred men—a goal that
seemed easily reachable with the bands of volunteers forming
and itching for a fight all over the territory early in 1836.

When people get their first glimpse of the Alamo today, they
are expected to say (and many of them do), "How small it is!"
How could 180 defenders find room for themselves in the little
church and L-shaped building that make up the shrine? They
would be like sardines in a can. And anyone told that there were
twenty cannon would have to wonder where they could all be
put to use.

Well, the remains of the mission *are* small, because they represent only a fragment of the original compound—half of the wall on one side, and an excrescence beyond that wall (the church). In 1836, the mission enclosed roughly a third of an acre within a walled perimeter of a quarter mile.[9] The wall was only twelve feet at its highest point, but it was of thick adobe, resistant stuff for a siege. It had been built to protect the mission monastery, schools, gardens, and workshops, with room to bring in the Catholic Spaniards of the town when Comanches were raiding. With its thirty adobe houses and a number of huts, it was designed to serve a large population in time of peril.

That population was what the Alamo lacked as Santa Anna approached it. The defenders thought they had more time to raise troops. Santa Anna reached San Antonio a month before he was expected. His six thousand men struggled through a freak snowstorm that killed mules and crippled the men, who lacked doctors.[10] Santa Anna was obsessed with the Alamo, which had been wrested from his brother-in-law General Cos—along with those twenty cannon now bristling in all directions from the mission walls. Santa Anna was the first man to act on the principle of remembering the Alamo.

Santa Anna considered himself a true republican in Texas. Trained in the Spanish army, he had fought in the rebellion that first declared Mexico a monarchy independent of Spain, and then a republic (1824) of federal states (like those of the United States). The new government could not contain the conflict of Mexican autocrats and democrats, of church and republic. Siding with the republic, Santa Anna nonetheless seized dictatorial powers in 1834, claiming they were necessary to give a stumbling new country the order needed for its survival. He liked to compare his role to that of Napoleon, bringing order to France after its revolution of the preceding generation.

The Mexican province called Teja provided an instance of the misrule Santa Anna said was plaguing Mexico. This Texas province was so sparsely inhabited and economically unproductive that it had been incorporated into the federal union as a dependent part of another province, Coahuila. The Texas war of independence began as a move, led by Stephen Austin, a Mexican citizen, to make Texas an independent state (independent of Coahuila) *within* the Mexican republic. That is why early flags of the independence forces showed two stars (for the separated provinces) and "1824" (for the republican constitution Santa Anna was abusing).[11]

Stephen Austin was a Mexican subject because his father had bargained with the newly independent (but still monarchic) Mexican government of 1821 to settle the Texas area with colonists who would serve as a buffer between the hostile Comanches and more densely populated parts of Mexico. In return for land grants, the settlers would become Mexican subjects, Catholics, and nonslaveholders. (The Mexican revolution had freed the slaves held under Spanish law.)

The settlers given grants began as law-abiding Mexican subjects. But they evaded certain parts of the contract—becoming nominal Catholics (if that) and keeping slaves they brought to work their land under a fictitious form of contract or indenture. Though they were now fellow citizens with the Mexicans already resident in Teja, these former American citizens, most of them Southerners, held racist views of Mexican inferiority.[12] Though the two groups collaborated at the beginning of the war (to win independence for Coahuila, to lower taxes, to restore republicanism), they fell out in the course of the war, and Mexican allies like Juan Seguin (a supporter of the Alamo's defenders) were driven back to Mexican allegiance.[13]

As disaffection with Santa Anna's government grew among the land-grant settlers, they began to welcome "squatters" from America, who seized control without the formality of grant, or "filibusterers" who came to take advantage of the unrest. These were allies who made no pretense about their noncitizenship, non-Catholicism, and possession of slaves.

Whatever else, they swelled the number of white resisters to Mexican authority. A lawyer named Travis led a revolt against a former American serving in the Mexican army who was collecting taxes at the port city of Galveston. Armed conflict was breaking out in different spots, with different goals. Some wanted to filibuster into Spain, some to win concessions from Mexico City, some to set up their own country at once.

The elders were embarrassed by the "crazies" who came along at this opportune moment. When Stephen Austin went to Mexico City in 1833 to negotiate for provincial independence within the Mexican federation, he was seen as acting in bad faith, since Texans were already resisting authority in armed clashes. Austin was imprisoned for a year and a half. On his return, he had to join the effort to set up a provisional government working for—what? The members of the "government" were still divided on the best course. Meanwhile, they established a provisional (regular) army under Sam Houston. But

volunteers, voting for their own officers, deciding which commands to obey, took de facto leadership from him.

In the fall of 1835, a hodgepodge of regulars and volunteers
milled about San Antonio, where a Mexican army had been sent
under General Cos to subdue the province. Cos held the town
and the mission (Alamo). Outside, the regulars were unsure of
their authority to engage Cos, but volunteer troops prompted a
rush on the town that others had to follow.[14] A house-by-house
struggle led to Cos's surrender. He turned over the Alamo, along
with the town and all his cannon. Cos was allowed to depart
under "parole," his word not to engage in war against Texas; but
his brother-in-law Santa Anna said that a word to outlaw rebels
was not binding, and he came north to reinstall Cos in the
Alamo.

Santa Anna's own officers thought his focus on the Alamo
insane.[15] He should have gone north along the Gulf of Mexico
coast to seize Goliad, the key town being held by James Fannin.
Even after Santa Anna arrived at San Antonio, and the town
surrendered to him, there was no reason to attack the Alamo. It
was not important in itself, as Houston had realized. Santa Anna
had only field guns. He could not make a real breach in the walls
until he received siege guns from the south. But that wait would
make it possible for more men to come to the Alamo's defense.

Santa Anna determined to take the mission by storm. In the
predawn darkness of March 6, he mounted massive assaults
from all four sides of the Alamo. When his ranks wavered, he
sent his crack reserves into the melee.[16] It was ruinously expensive—he lost perhaps sixteen hundred men, taking losses of almost nine to one. The defenders had never thought it would
come to this—they expected a siege, not an assault, with time
for help to arrive.

Santa Anna meant to cow the whole province by his ferocity.
He had flown the flag, had played the ceremonial song ("De-
güello"), that meant "no quarter." When, during the assault, several inside the walls surrendered themselves to an officer, Santa
Anna had them butchered before his eyes when they were
brought to him. He spared one woman and several slaves, including Travis's "Joe." He still upheld *that* part of the Mexican constitution.

It is a good story, of the bloody sort martial legends are
made of. But it soon got taken up into legend, tearful celebration,
and the rituals that govern Alamo observances. The three princi-

pal figures inside the Alamo became the center of intense admiration. They were, in fact, representatives of the various forces in play at that confused moment in the rebellion. Bowie was a type of the original land-grant settlers, Crockett of the last-minute military "filibusterers," and Travis stood somewhere in between them. It did not hurt the myth-making process that two of the three, Bowie and Crockett, came to the Alamo with reputations already established as hunters and Indian fighters.

James Bowie, played in the movie by Richard Widmark, was known for his ferocity in knife fights (not the most glorious form of combat).[17] He was born in Georgia (1796), grew up in Louisiana, and came to Texas to prospect for ore when he was thirty-two years old. Two years later he became a Mexican citizen, a Catholic, and the son-in-law of the provincial vice-governor, Juan Martín de Veramendi of San Antonio. He fought in a tax-resistance campaign at Nacogdoches in 1832, and was part of the rebels' regular army. But when militia men in San Antonio resisted the regular command of Travis, Bowie let himself be elected commander of the volunteers. The schism was resolved when a violent illness (emphysema?) made Bowie turn his command over to Travis before the final battle.

Bowie's wife had died of plague in 1833, and his ties with the Mexican community had been strained by his land-grabbing policies and high-handedness—while on a binge in San Antonio, he had freed men from jail, defying the local government.[18] This event is turned by Wayne into a celebration of the defeat of General Cos at San Antonio, which occurred three months before the famous binge of history. Wayne also made Bowie's wife die during the siege, three years after the actual date. He gives to Bowie a slave (Joe) who was actually owned by Travis, and ages the slave into "an old black Joe" who is manumitted by Bowie so he can escape, but who chooses to die with his massuh. Wayne makes the personality clash between Bowie and Travis turn on Bowie's down-to-earth resentment of Travis's spit-and-polish manner. Actually, Bowie seems to have picked up some grand manners of his own from wealthy in-laws. He was bedridden at his death in the Alamo, and wishfulness has made him die wielding his famous knife, but there is no real evidence for his last moments.

William Travis (played by Laurence Harvey) was born in South Carolina (1809) and raised in Alabama. He did not come to Texas as a land-grant settler but in a service industry to the landed men—a lawyer who helped them resist Mexican taxes. He had left a failed marriage behind, and he indulged in Byronic musings about a military career. A leader of spontaneous resistance by volunteers, he served as a scout in the defeat of General Cos at San Antonio. The provisional government made him an officer, first in the artillery, then in the cavalry, before putting him in charge at the Alamo, where he reported the drunken binge of Bowie to his superiors. A charming and ingratiating lawyer, he was at least as good at addressing common folk as Bowie—though no one except Sam Houston was Crockett's equal at such cracker-barrel oratory. Wayne dresses Travis in a spiffy uniform, though he never owned one (he had ordered a uniform that never arrived). He wore jeans.[19] Wayne makes him die wielding his sword in a dazed condition, a not-so-distant memory of Henry Fonda's Colonel Thursday in *Fort Apache*. In fact the whole Bowie-Travis relationship is close to the Wayne-Fonda conflict in that movie. Wayne does forswear myth in one respect. He omits the legend that Travis took his sword and drew a line in the dirt, asking those who would die to step across. But he does not challenge the *basis* of the myth—that the band of defenders was deliberately suicidal, a kamikaze team. Wayne could challenge the frill around the myth, but not the central myth itself.[20]

David Crockett (Wayne's character) was born in Tennessee (1786). He is shown in the movie arriving with a loyal band of old Indian fighters pledged to him. He asks the female lead:

> Do you like my Tennesseans, Flaka? You could shake ten thousand and not come up with twenty-three better. Most of them have been at my elbow whenever some "difficulty" arose.

In fact, Crockett had left Tennessee disgusted with the state's residents for voting him out of Congress after he attacked the Tennessee hero Andrew Jackson. He was seeking a new political base, to be earned with military exploit. But only three Tennesseans left with him. In San Augustin he joined a previous body of volunteers who called themselves Tennessee Volunteers, even though only three of them were from that state. None of this latter group had known Crockett before, and they continued to be commanded by a Captain Harrison from Ohio.[21]

Asked to swear allegiance to the provisional government at Texas, Crockett did so, with a strong hope he would be joining it. He wrote to his son: "I have but little doubt of being elected a member to form a constitution for the province."[22] He apparently either inserted or underlined the word *republican* in the oath he swore. His most respected biographer thinks this was because of the resentment of the "despotism" he felt that Jackson had made in the *United States* government. He feared that Jackson's friend and fellow Tennessean Sam Houston might try to do the same in Texas.[23] Starting from that single reported reference to Crockett's republicanism, Wayne gives his character this rhapsody:

> "Republic"—I like the sound of the word. . . . Some words give you a feeling. Republic is one of those words that makes me tight in the throat. Same tightness a man gets when his baby makes his first step, or his boy first shaves, makes his first sound like a man. Some words can give you a feeling that makes your heart warm. "Republic" is one of those words.

That speech makes the movie Travis say that Crockett is a sensitive man who hides his idealism under uncouth externals. The same discovery is made by "Flaka," Wayne's Spanish love interest awkwardly added to the story. When wooing her, Wayne's Crockett wears immaculate formal clothes. Wayne-Crockett is supposed to be many-sided. He plays rough games of punch-face with "his" Tennesseans, but is a shrewd diplomat making peace between Bowie and Travis.

The real Crockett lacked the shrewdness of the movie character. Semiliterate, defensively absolutist, he had destroyed his political career after two terms in Congress. Opposed to the Jacksonians who were his natural allies, he had little chance for the new political career he was seeking in Texas. Unable to live up to early legends about his backwoods exploits, which had taken on a life of their own in stage plays and phony "biographies," he was moving on a slope of inevitable decline until he was rescued by a heroic death—and even that death was not legendary enough for his cultists, who injected what they considered more appropriate. The cult has Crockett die as he swings his "Ol' Betsy" long rifle (which he had left back in Tennessee).

The only eyewitness to have left an account of his death, a trustworthy witness to things he actually saw, wrote in his campaign diary:

> Some seven men had survived the general carnage and, under the protection of General Castrillon, they were

brought before Santa Anna. Among them was one of good stature, well proportioned, with regular features, in whose face there was the imprint of adversity, but in whom one also noticed a degree of resignation and volubility that did him honor. He was the naturalist [i.e., woodsman] David Crockett, well known in North America for his unusual adventures, who had undertaken to explore the country and who, finding himself in Bejar at the very moment of the surprise, had taken refuge in the Alamo, fearing that his status as a foreigner might not be respected. Santa Anna answered Castrillon's intervention in Crockett's behalf with a gesture of indignation and, addressing himself to the sappers, the troopers closest to him, ordered his execution. The commanders and officers were outraged at this action and did not support the order, hoping that once the fury of the moment had blown over these men would be spared, but several officers who were around the president and who, perhaps had not been present during the moment of danger, became noteworthy by an infamous deed, surpassing the soldiers in cruelty. They thrust themselves forward, in order to flatter their commander, and with swords in hand, fell upon these unfortunate, defenseless men just as a tiger leaps upon his prey. Though tortured before they were killed, these unfortunates died without complaining and without humiliating themselves before their torturers. It was rumored that General Sesma was one of them; I will not bear witness to this, for though present, I turned away horrified in order not to witness such a barbarous scene.[24]

This detailed contemporary report by a trustworthy and intelligent officer in Santa Anna's army was not published until 1955 (in Spanish) and it did not get much attention until it was translated into English in 1975. Then cultists of the Alamo exploded. Texans would not have *their* Crockett surrendering, giving a false story, denying his Texas citizenship. A flood of denunciation led to a book that tried to prove the de la Peña manuscript a forgery.[25] The translator of the manuscript was given a "Bum Steer of the Month" award by *Texas Monthly* magazine (February 1976).

Yet the president of the Texas State Historical Association, Dan Kilgore, pointed out, in his inaugural address, that other eyewitness accounts, not written down, had been spread from the moment of Crockett's death and were widely accepted in the nineteenth century.[26] Even Theodore Roosevelt's admiring portrait of Crockett had him die in captivity. And why not? There is nothing wrong with living to fight another day. Crockett had not come to Texas to "buy time for Sam Houston." He meant to be a *political* leader in Texas; and though dead people vote in Texas elections, they are not normally *elected* there. When he had to die, he did so with a noble stoicism. De la Peña admired the man, and used his death to indict his own leader, Santa Anna.

It was only in the twentieth century that the story of Crockett's dying without surrendering became dogma. It became fixed in order to prop up other myths. *If* Crockett crossed Travis's famous but mythical line, he pledged himself to die—then how could he hope to escape dying by his surrender? *If* the choice were liberty or death, how could he give up liberty in order to live? The legends became a cage from which no evidence can "spring" the historical Crockett. You are still asking for a fight if you say, in San Antonio, that Crockett died in a captivity he chose.

Needless to say, Wayne did not challenge the orthodoxy on this point. In fact, he went the myth one better. He not only had Crockett die fighting; he had him "win" by denying Mexicans the gunpowder they were about to capture. Wayne's wounded Crockett will die by no hand but his own as he swings a torch into the powder magazine and expires in a blaze of fire bursting from the shrine itself, the mission church, the place that people still visit.

This has symbolic force. It brings together the image of Crockett's sacrifice and the remaining part of the Alamo. It makes Crockett's death an assertion of will, not the obliteration of it. As Crockett blows up a building that, nonetheless, survives, so his own death is transformed into a cleansing apocalyptic fire in which he will live forever.

On the other hand, to be prosaic, this final scene makes nonsense of much that precedes. The church is, in the movie, the refuge of women and children as well as a hospital for the wounded. To put all of them together with the powder magazine would not be a rational choice. The movie's Crockett is blowing up his own survivors. Logic, history, symbol sharing, and bluster are all thrown together in this film, as indiscriminately as women, wounded, and powder were crammed into the little church. The end was supposed to be a fiery apotheosis of the Alamo's gods. Instead, it was just a bomb.

□ 17 □
ALAMO: ORDEAL

IT MUST BE SAID for Wayne that he faced daunting obstacles in bringing his dream to fulfillment. For one thing, he had to tiptoe through and around Texas pieties connected with the Alamo. He did not realize this when he began. He was naive enough to think he might make the movie in Mexico, where extras were cheap and union restrictions lax (at that time). That is: he wanted Mexicans to celebrate their own defeat, and to do it at cut rates. Wayne also explored sites in Panama, where he was hoping to make movies on a regular basis.[1] But that angered Texans, who wanted their sacred story told on their sacred soil. Wayne's first financial backers would not undertake an "epic" film made in America—all such films had to be made in (and largely for) foreign markets, for economic reasons. To escape that problem, Wayne went to Texas oil millionaires like Clint Murchison, who "angeled" the film for patriotic as well as investment motives.[2] This first pommeling from place to place, under joint economic and ideological pressures, was typical of the forces that would beset him throughout the project.

When it was decided to film in Texas, areas close to San Antonio (of the sort Francis Ford's Méliès team had used) were ruled out by the need for unpopulated stretches of land around a reconstructed Alamo (the third-of-an-acre mission) and for a token "San Antonio" of 1836. The natural place to look was Brackettville, a hundred miles southwest of San Antonio, since Republic had made its Alamo film there in 1955.

But Republic had thrown up only temporary sets of selected parts of the mission. James "Happy" Shahan wanted something more permanent raised at his own Brackettville ranch, to serve as a regular film-making site. He showed Wayne's scouts a flat open space where they could build an "authentic" Alamo out of the original adobe. His workers would supply much of the labor. His land they could use for free, if they would just leave him the permanent Alamo and "San Antonio."

Happy Shahan was, like Monument Valley's Harry Goulding, a self-promoting promoter of his area. Perhaps Wayne, trying to establish his own identity as a director, saw the possibility of becoming the John Ford of this godforsaken corner of Texas, returning to make films with a stamp of place created by the director's vision. If so, the dream faded fast. The difficulties of building the Alamo in Brackettville jinxed the place in Wayne's mind. Others would make Westerns there, using some of the facilities created by Wayne. But Wayne never went back.[3]

The first stage of the project was washed out, after thousands of adobe bricks had been made, by a flash flood.[4] The needs of workers and staff called for miles of water pipes, huge electrical installations, a flying shuttle to get film back and forth (or for actors needing doctors). The expenses mounted dizzily, even before completion of preproduction work.

There were intellectual problems, too. The designer Al Ybarra had to reconstruct the lost parts of the Alamo mission from guesswork. He could get the general design right—Franciscan missions were simple in principle, arranged according to the function of such a religious complex, adaptable to local materials and building habits. But Hollywood likes to claim an "authenticity" that is perfect. Ybarra promised to show *exactly* what the Alamo looked like before its crumbled walls were built over by "Wendy's" and other stores on the current Alamo Plaza. He claimed that he went to Spain to look in the Franciscan archives for a copy of the Alamo's design.[5] Fortunately for him, that was not true. It would have been wasted effort.

A major problem, curiously, was not with what is lost of the Alamo but with what remains. The current shrine is so stamped on the public mind that any change in it is bound to be resented. Yet what exists now is not what was visible in 1836. The current "Long Barracks" is a low one-story structure; but in 1836 it had a second story, much of which survived into the twentieth century. The keepers of the Alamo, the Daughters of the Republic of

Texas (DRT), had the second story razed, to give greater prominence to the church's profile. The so-called preservationists mutilated the historically most important part of the complex.[6] The mission church was never completed by the friars or used for religious service.[7] Its functions, and other business of the mission, took place in the monastery building, of which the barracks is the only remaining fragment. Ybarra kept the stone structure of the barracks low, as it is today, though he put a wooden office on it, to serve as Travis's headquarters.

Then what was Ybarra to do with the church itself? Though incomplete in 1836, it was altered and roofed by the United States Army in 1850–1852.[8] That is when it acquired second-story windows on the façade and the curvilinear gable that is now its most identifiable feature. Ybarra kept the anachronistic windows but he could not retain the most desirable thing of all, the famous scroll-shape on top, since that was widely known to be a later addition. His solution was very clever. He kept a ragged irregular line of bricks on top, but with a slight swell in the middle. To those who do not know better, it looks like a ruination from the known outline—as if the scroll top had existed *before* and had been rubbed down by time, instead of having been added afterward. This stratagem kept the general outline of the façade familiar enough to be shown constantly through the movie—outlined against the dawn, shadowy in the dusk—as the sacred place it has become. Wayne added his own touch by having Ybarra put an outsized wooden cross, knocked sideways, on the top, to indicate that a larger structure had crumbled.[9] This, too, made the "little" Alamo seem part of something greater that had been violated. The cross form shows up everywhere in Wayne's film, a device he took from Ford—who overdid it almost as much as Wayne does.

The church is so important to the Alamo cult that, even though Wayne built the whole mission complex (in replica), almost all the film's important action takes place on, in, or around the church.[10] For the movie, the mission's big gun, which threw an eighteen-pound ball, is put on the church's roof (which did not exist in 1836). "San Antonio" is placed on the set so that the church is the part of the mission closest to it, though it was actually the farthest. As we have already seen, Wayne puts the hospital, the children's sanctuary, the powder magazine, all in the church. Also Jim Bowie's room, where he is killed.

This central role for the church has nothing to do with the

events of 1836. But it reflects the centrality of the church to modern civic rituals in San Antonio. A professional anthropologist born in San Antonio, Holly Beachley Brear, studied the city's rites as if approaching a foreign religious culture. She found that the calendar of San Antonio revolves around the liturgy of the shrine, and prominent citizens rank themselves by their membership in its cults of preservation and celebration.

Presiding over the calendar, and over the general management of the shrine, are the Daughters of the Republic of Texas (DRT), descendants of Texans who took part in the Revolution. They exclude from the sacred ground any unholy intruders— even the Mayor of San Antonio was forced to withdraw when he tried to film an ad for historic preservation on the lawn-apron of the church.[11] The Daughters have their own little army of Alamo Rangers to guard the grounds.

Besides the DRT, the only groups authorized to meet in secret session inside the church are the Texas Cavaliers and the Order of the Alamo. The first group chooses the King of the annual Fiesta honoring the Alamo, the second chooses the Queen. The King is a socially prominent Cavalier. The Queen— young enough to be his daughter rather than his wife—is also from a prominent family, as one can see from the fact that she is expected to spend at least $25,000 on her fiesta gown. Wealthy young women from all over Texas aspire to join her court. Ross Perot's daughter made it in 1989.[12] A fourth group with strong ties to the Alamo is the Battle of Flowers Associates (BOFA), a group that gives the King and Queen another event to preside over.

The initiation of members into these select groups, their meetings and awards ceremonies, fill the year with Alamo-oriented rites. The activity has traditionally been Anglo, leaving Hispanics out or taking in a token few. Some Hispanics have demonstrated and protested at the Alamo. Others have formed an alternative fiesta with their own King (Rey Feo) who is included in some Fiesta events but does not have the access of Cavaliers to the inner sanctum.[13] The Alamo has a prickly sacredness. Though the Alamo was originally built to be a Franciscan church mission complex, Catholics were not allowed to celebrate Mass in it during an historic anniversary when the four other San Antonio missions held special Masses.[14] The Alamo's rites are specific to its martyrs. It is not surprising, then, that Wayne did everything he could think of to play up the church's centrality to his movie. He could not genuflect or bow his head deeply enough. His movie's potential contribution—the suggestion of what the *whole* mission might have looked like—was overshadowed by an unhistorical prominence given to the church.

Yet the larger mission complex posed its own problems for the kind of film Wayne was making. A third of an acre is not much as the arena of an action epic. Wayne was telling the story of all thirteen days of the siege, during which nothing much took place in terms of splashy external action. Santa Anna's gun emplacements crept forward by night while the defenders inside sent out desperate messages calling for help. One band did race to the rescue—thirty men from Gonzales (whose overnight march was duplicated by thirty young Marines for the premiere of the movie in San Antonio).[15] But even the final assault, on the thirteenth day, took place in the darkness just before dawn.

Wayne obviously felt he had to "open up" the action. He could not just have people mill around inside the palisade, stare out from the walls, and fire the occasional cannon. So he sent out large forays to destroy the Mexicans' large siege gun (an impossible task in history, since the Mexicans did not yet have a large siege gun) or to capture a herd of beef for provisioning the mission. He also had the Mexicans stage *two* mass assaults instead of one, a first one coming ludicrously against just one side of the mission, the final one taking place in full daylight. Wayne did not want to waste the long vistas he had paid so much for, or hide the large number of extras he had assembled (large, but not the eight thousand he claimed), by staging a night battle. He had a fine team of stuntmen, including Yak Canutt's sons and Dean Smith, an Olympic track champion (who leaps onto a Mexican's horse from the ground). Their actions were coordinated by Cliff Lyons, the veteran of many Ford films.[16] The largest coordinated horse fall ever filmed was completed in safety.[17]

Wayne had to concoct ways to use all these stunts, the basic fare of his Monogram Westerns with Yak, in a story that was static. Three hours is a long time to have people sit around the campfire listening to Chill Wills sing "Here's to the Ladies" or Frankie Avalon sing "Tennessee Babe." To keep waking up the audience Wayne resorted to the episodic violence of his serial-making days. He not only blows up the powder magazine in the mission but comes close to blowing up another one in the town. Frankie Avalon, with the help of a stuntman, becomes a trick rider, mounting horses as Yak did in the thirties. Though Wayne made *The Alamo* to prove he was not "just a cowboy," he had to reach back into his cowboy repertoire to prod his lumbering story forward.

Added to all Wayne's other problems were casting difficulties. He claims he wanted to play a bit part (Sam Houston) so he could devote his main energies to direction; but the financiers would not back a film in which he was not starring. His drawing power depended on his being top-billed. Wayne was probably fooling himself if he thought seriously about not playing Crockett. The part was tailored to his idealized image of himself. If another actor took it, especially under Wayne's direction, he would have been reduced to imitating Wayne, and no one could play Wayne the way Wayne played Wayne. There was no other part for him in the movie. Travis is a martinet, and Wayne had played one in *Red River,* but it was not a role he wanted to repeat. Bowie is the opponent of the martinet, and Wayne had played *that* role in *Fort Apache,* when he stole the film from Fonda; but he did not want to steal the film from his own Crockett-surrogate in *The Alamo.* There was only one person who could play Crockett as he had—too self-indulgently—created him. Crockett is Wayne philosophizing about his own Wayneness. That is both a flaw at the center of the film and a gap only he could fill.

United Artists, the distributor, demanded that the film have other stars, and it put forward Richard Widmark, under contract to the studio, which wanted to showcase him. Widmark was not happy about the idea, though "I needed the work" (the perennial refrain of actors). Widmark belonged to a social circle that overlapped Wayne's. Thus, though they were far from friendly themselves, the two men were kept constantly aware of each other. Robert Ardrey, the anthropologist and playwright, was a friend of Widmark's from their shared New York stage days. As a screenwriter, Ardrey came to know Harry and Olive Carey well, and introduced Widmark to their home, which Wayne frequented because of Ford's close ties to the Careys. After Harry's death, Ollie was the object of both Wayne's and Widmark's solicitude. Widmark took her to the American Film Institute's tribute to Ford. When she died, Ollie left Harry's cowboy memorabilia to Wayne. None of these links softened the hostility that had been formed between Wayne and Widmark from the moment they met. Widmark and his wife went to the Careys' house for a party: "I opened the door, and there's this big guy in the corner, and he looks at me and says, 'Well, here's that laughing sonofabitch.' He was half potted, and that started it. So, just chemically, we were two guys who didn't like each other."[18]

Though Widmark acceded to the studio's pressure to play in *The Alamo*, he refused to accept Wayne's casting of him in the small role of Houston rather than as Bowie. "He said, 'You're not *big* enough for Bowie.' Wayne only liked big guys—smaller guys annoyed him. I said, 'I'll be big enough.' "

The actors' mutual dislike fostered a story that has entered Wayne lore and never been questioned. When Wayne took out an ad to announce Widmark's casting, one that said, "Welcome aboard, Dick," Widmark is supposed to have said, "Tell your press agent that the name is Richard"—to which Wayne responded, "If I ever take out another ad, I'll remember that, *Richard*."[19] Widmark says this is a total fabrication. He was always "Dick" in the circles he and Wayne shared, and though he was fighting Wayne over other things, like getting the Bowie role, "I would never have said that." Where did the story come from? Widmark thinks from Jimmy Grant, Jim Henighen (the movie's first publicist), or some other member of Wayne's entourage of sycophants, who blamed Widmark for adding to Wayne's problems on the set.

At one point, Widmark remembers, there was a potentially dangerous flare-up: "In a big scene—granted, he was tired—he screamed things to me in front of all these people. I told him: 'You no-talent sonofabitch, don't ever talk to me that way.' But I didn't say it before I had an iron bar in my hand, because if he had come at me, I was a goner. I didn't really think he had no talent, but I knew that would set him off." What happened after that? "We got along fine. He's like any bully. If you call a bully, it's over."

The other casting was not as difficult. For some reason Wayne decided on Laurence Harvey, the British actor, to play Travis. Admittedly, Harvey was raised in South Africa, but that is not quite the South that was supposed to be conveyed by Travis's accent. Some Texans objected to having a foreigner play *their* hero, but Wayne soothed matters by having Governor Price Daniel declare Harvey an honorary citizen of Texas.[20] Richard Boone, playing in the popular TV Western *Have Gun Will Travel*, could spare from his shooting schedule the little time needed for the role of Sam Houston.

Wayne yielded to financial pressures for including a youth idol in the cast, to bring in the teenage audience—the same marketing calculation that had put young singer Ricky Nelson in Howard Hawks's *Rio Bravo* the year before. Wayne himself, with his preference for Latin women, promised the part of his love interest to a young Argentinean, Linda Cristal, who had been promoted at Universal as "the Pepper Pot of the Pampas." Wayne was succumbing to the old producer's belief that "I can make you a star"—the urge Wayne had criticized when Herb Yates foisted his protégée, Vera Hruba Ralston, on Wayne in *Dakota*. Corseted and bra-lifted, Ms. Cristal bridged her age gap with Wayne by surrendering her youth to robotic stiffness.

With the example of Ford before him, Wayne made his set a family enclave. Ford usually had his brothers present (Francis acting, Eddie an assistant producer), along with his brother-in-law (Wingate Smith). Sometimes his daughter was there, with her husband (Ken Curtis). His son, Patrick, was used as a second-unit scout. But Wayne outdid Ford at this family game, assigning bit parts to his third wife (Pilar), his daughter (Toni), his granddaughter (playing Toni's girl), as well as speaking roles for his son (Patrick) and his daughter (Aissa). Another son (Michael) was the assistant producer. Wayne forgot the main thing about Ford's use of his family. Ford had them on hand to humiliate them. No one ever accused him of cosseting Frank or Eddie. Quite the reverse. They were there to testify to Ford's own patriarchal sense of clan. He was the successful one, the boss. Wayne was too indulgent to his family. The most useless and embarrassing part of the film is the birthday party for Aissa, where Ken Curtis sings her a birthday song and Chill Wills dances with her.

Wayne was indulgent in other ways. He had ingratiated himself with the Texas governor, Price Daniel, by putting Daniel's brother Bill in the film. That would not have mattered much had Wayne not given Daniel some important lines delivered in the very opening scenes—an amateur performance that stamps the film as less than professional when it is making its earliest impression.

The Texans who smothered Wayne with good will became more a nuisance than a help. One reason Wayne had gone to Brackettville was to get away from modern intrusions on the scene—no jet contrails or telephone wires or paved roads. But Texas millionaires in their private planes got into the habit of twirling over the Alamo set, to look at the interesting bustle below. Wayne threw rocks at them in frustration, and once grabbed a rifle and shot at a low-flying gawker. "They're only blanks," one of the cast reminded him. "I know; but it makes me feel better," Wayne growled.[21] Widmark says he also threw rocks at distant cameramen who did not respond fast enough to orders.

The toll of being everything to everybody on the set was a high one. As the producer, the director, the star, the diplomat solving personal problems, the father, the husband, the symbol, Wayne was on continual call, reworking his own lines and everybody else's, trying to keep on schedule and not too far over budget. Things great and small went wrong. The headquarters of Wayne's production company, Batjac, in Fort Clark's Officers Club, was gutted by fire. While Wayne was expanding the role of a promising actress, LeJean Ethridge, the actress's lover murdered her. Wayne was sorry, but he did not want to lose time by testifying at her murderer's hearing—not at the cost of losing a day of shooting. He used the Texas Highway Patrol to set up roadblocks in order to find the murderer's lawyer, who had subpoenaed him. Wayne was allowed to give a deposition, instead of testifying in court.[22]

As his difficulties mounted, Wayne's temper flared. Some flunkies blamed Widmark. Others, with better reason, blamed John Ford—since Ford, in an act both sly and cruel, had shown up unsummoned in Brackettville. He said he had come to "lend a hand," the last thing Wayne wanted or needed, someone looking over his shoulder, undermining his authority, suggesting to others that Wayne was not up to his work—or laying the suspicion, if things turned out well, that part of the credit was Ford's.

An officer's house at Fort Clark had to be given over to Ford. He took up his station, on the set, near William Clothier's camera. Ford had just used Clothier to film *The Horse Soldiers* (1959), and he annoyed the cameraman by assuming his former proprietary air over the camera in Texas.[23] To old associates on the set, Ford made denigrating remarks about the crew or the production. "The waste!" he would mutter.[24] He gave Wayne gratuitous advice before the cast and crew. At one point he sat watching Wayne and Widmark do a scene together, just the two of them. By that time, the men had reached a working accommodation, to get the job done as professionals. They finished the scene and, as Widmark remembers: "He [Wayne] said, 'Is that O.K. with you?' I said, 'Yes, is it O.K. with you?' Then we heard Ford growl, 'Do it again!' Wayne asked, '*Why*, Coach?' ' 'Cause it was no damn good.' " It was a typical ploy on a Ford set—to make people do something again if they seemed too complacent. But this was not a Ford set—or was it?

Wayne was partly to blame for having given the idea that he needed the real Ford. Much of the set looked like imitation-Ford. Clothier was at the camera. Ken Curtis was singing a ballad. People were doing for Wayne what they had often done for Ford —Jack Pennick drilling the troops of military extras, Cliff Lyons supervising the stunts, Hank Worden doing his eccentric-preacher turn. Minor technicians who had cowered on Ford sets now came under his glare again. Perhaps most redolent of all was the presence of Danny Borzage, playing his accordion, the very essence of Ford atmospherics while shooting.

Wayne complained to Denver Pyle: "What am I gonna do with the Old Man? I gotta get rid of him."[25] Of course, Wayne should have told Ford, the minute he showed up, that he could not have him anywhere around. That is what Ford would have done to any intruder on his set. But Wayne was not ruthless. The screen disciplinarian—Sergeant Stryker whipping his troops into shape, Dunson of *Red River* telling Montgomery Clift's character he is soft—was, off-screen, too nice a guy to be the boss in a situation calling for tough treatment of others. Wayne had always taken Ford's orders submissively, off the set as well as on. Marilyn Carey remembers him grumbling when the Old Man ordered him to drop everything else and go over to his house to play cards—but Wayne went.[26] And now, with the largest project of his life at stake, and money bleeding from it every day, Wayne continued to humor Ford and defer to him.

To get Ford some distance off from his own activities, Wayne gave him one of Clothier's precious Todd-AO wide-screen camera crews. For tricky shots, Clothier had come with six cameras to be stationed around the set, coordinated for big battle scenes— it was these far-flung cameras that Wayne threw rocks at in his frustration. Now one of them was given to Ford, to go out and to do second-unit work with the army of extras massed to attack the Alamo.

Denver Pyle, who was assigned to Ford's unit, says Ford went enthusiastically about his task. He chose fifty or so of the best-looking troops, got red cloth medallions made by the prop department, and stapled the medallions to the turned-up brims of the extras' hats, telling them, in halting Spanish, that they were now Ford's crack troops. Ford was doing what he did best, creating an esprit among those he directed. Another scene Pyle watched him film was of men charging forward with a cannon. It looked too dull, so he had one of Cliff Lyons's stunt experts rig a way to pull one wheel off as they labored forward, so they had to lift the gun in their blind rush. Not an inch of film separately shot by Ford got into Wayne's film.[27] Wayne did not want to leave any basis for people to say, "The only good stuff, or the best stuff, is Ford's." One still reads suggestions of that sort. But an indication that they are not true is the way Ford tried to take quiet revenge on Wayne the next time they worked together, on *The Man Who Shot Liberty Valance* (1962).

If Wayne could have rejected Ford, he might have done more decisively what he showed some signs of attempting. He might have drawn more on the director of the first ambitious epic he played in, *The Big Trail*. That, too, had involved great physical problems on location, temperamental actors, multiple-camera work, evil villains, and hokey comedy. But Raoul Walsh forged something larger than life from all those things, and some memory seemed to linger in Wayne's mind from that formative first experience with large-scale film-making. The clearest example is the use of the tree in Wayne's farewell scene with Linda Cristal's "Flaka." A large tree, with limbs writhing an arabesque, draws Wayne's attention as proof that even barren-looking Texas can produce greatness. Clothier's camera rises slowly up the trunk, into the air, and then—in the most stunning crane shot of the movie—looks down at the lovers through the widely spaced limbs. It recalls the two lovers seen through the frame of redwoods at the end of *The Big Trail*. Even the dialogue in this scene echoes Wayne's major speech in Walsh's film. As Crockett, he says that he can now fight for a purpose ("To hit a lick at what's wrong, or to say a word for what's right"), and concludes: "There's right and there's wrong, you gotta do one or the other. You do the one and you're living, you do the other and you may be walking around but you're as dead as a beaver hat." Wayne's scout in *The Big Trail* says: "No great trail was ever blazed without hardship, and you've got to fight—that's life. And when you stop fighting, that's death. What are you gonna do, lay down and die?"

The most interesting possibilities of *The Alamo* seem made for Raoul Walsh's treatment—the contrast in styles of masculinity between the three leading characters. Wayne makes Bowie and Travis pair off against each other while Wayne circles around and between them, much as Walsh had pitted Wayne against the smooth gambler and the rough bull whacker of *The Big Trail*. The choreography of the triangular male relationship is the best thing in *The Alamo*—Wayne poised skeptically to the side of the clashes, or moving in between the others as mediator, conciliator, referee. The other two are touchy, Travis too rigid, Bowie too unfocused; only Crockett's devious manipulation of them and others can keep peace. But these possibilities are not developed in a satisfying way. Wayne is too busy with his message of final Alamo solidarity. The tensions between the men are dissipated by their joint submission to the sappy myth of holding out for Sam Houston's sake. Walsh was working, within commercial restraints, to create. Wayne, within even greater restraints, was trying to create *and preach*.[28] That rarely works in movies, as Ford found out with *The Fugitive,* his film about Catholic priesthood.

Wayne's popularity was such that even *The Alamo* regained, gradually, its huge costs. But that was little comfort to Wayne, who had to sell his part in the film to Universal, to pay the personal debts he had incurred while making it. More important, the film did not give Wayne the basis for a whole new career as a director. No one wanted him in that capacity after *The Alamo*. He would only get one more directing credit, a shared one, for his other big ideological project, *The Green Berets*—which sank even deeper his credibility as a director. In those terms, the biggest gamble of his life was a great setback. Though the movie won several Motion Picture Academy nominations (including two for Dimitri Tiomkin's music and one for best picture), the Academy gave it only one Oscar, and that on the technical side (sound). The whole Oscar nomination process was soured by Chill Wills's injudicious private campaign to win the Best Supporting Actor award, and by publicist Russell Birdwell's claim that true patriots would never criticize the film. That was Wayne's view, too. He felt that the movie was victimized by the left, by all those who were soft on Communism.

Wayne was done in by many things in the making of this film. Some of them were out of his control, like fire and murder. Others showed an admirable side to the man, if not to his professionalism, like his inability to treat Ford with the toughness he deserved. Others were things he asked for, like coping with Alamo zealotry in darkest Texas. There were many things working to make the movie fail. But commies were not among them.

□ 18 □
GREEN BERETS

EIGHT YEARS AFTER *The Alamo* (1960), Wayne again felt the urge to save his country with a movie. His ardor for the Vietnam War was a match for his listlessness toward World War II. Protests against the Vietnam engagement infuriated him. He felt he was an expert on the area, since he had made a celebrity visit to cheer up the troops. The continuity between *The Alamo* and a movie on Vietnam was so obvious to him that he quoted the former movie when asking President Johnson for Defense Department help in making the latter. He knew, of course, that Johnson also equated Vietnam with the Alamo, where his grandpappy supposedly died:

> Perhaps you remember the scene from *The Alamo*, when one of Davy Crockett's Tennesseans said: "What are we doing here in Texas fighting—it ain't our ox that's getting gored." Crockett replied: "Talkin' about whose ox gets gored, figure this: a fella gets in the habit of gorin' oxes, it whets his appetite. May gore yours next." Unquote. And we don't want people like Kosygin, Mao Tse-tung, or the like, "gorin' our oxes."[1]

Wayne thought the perfect vehicle for talking about the war would be Robin Moore's collection of short stories called *The Green Berets*, which was a bestseller in 1965. Wayne, the longtime supporter of Nixon, the critic of the New Frontier and the Great Society, could use the Alamo to woo Lyndon Johnson,

228

and use the Green Berets to woo the legatees of John Kennedy. President Kennedy had set up the Special Forces (the Green Berets) and celebrated them as "a symbol of excellence, a badge of courage and a mark of distinction in the fight for freedom."[2] "Bobby" Kennedy, a name Wayne normally pronounced sardonically, had kept a Green Beret on his desk at the Justice Department.

Robin Moore's book was first optioned by Columbia and then dropped. Wayne snatched it up, thinking its bestseller status would be an automatic promotion of the film. When, in 1966, Barry Sadler's "The Ballad of the Green Berets" shot to the top of the music charts, he must have felt that his strategy was surefire. It was said that a movie about Vietnam could not succeed. Then why had the book and the song done so well? People were still proud of the crack Kennedy "counterinsurgents" in 1965 and 1966.

But Moore's *Green Berets* soon became a dubious blessing. The Defense Department did not like Moore's work, and the movie's connection with the book made the Pentagon specially wary of Wayne's project. The Department, vetting the script, demanded changes before giving Wayne access to Fort Benning, Georgia, with all its modern hardware. These conflicts, along with the normal problems of settling financial and distribution arrangements, delayed the movie's completion and release to July 1968—six months after the Communists' Tet offensive, which began the rapid crumbling of confidence in the whole Vietnam project. Even if Tet had not occurred just before the film came out, the three-year delay would have been damaging. The glamour had begun to rub off the idea of counterinsurgency. Trust in the military was evaporating. The Robin Moore tales, what parts of them the military would let Wayne use, had dated badly. And it did not help that Wayne was aging rapidly in the three years between inception and completion of the film.

It is a mark of Wayne's naïveté—and of the bad advice given him by people like Jimmy Grant and his son Michael—that he could even think the Army would be pleased to see Robin Moore's book given a wider audience. It was objectionable on almost all conceivable grounds. It portrays the Green Berets as lawless, sadistic, and racist. Moore, who claimed to have trained and served as a Green Beret while remaining a free-lance writer, considered such sadism the attribute of "real men."

Michael Wayne, who took credit for having read the book

and urged his father to buy the rights to it, was the producer who dealt with the Pentagon in wary exchanges over what the film could say while using taxpayers' military real estate and weaponry. He later claimed that the government's main objection to the book's use was a raid into Laos before that was authorized by the President. Michael defended Moore's accuracy, saying that Moore knew truths the Pentagon was trying to suppress. Michael even believed Moore's claims to a presidential blessing on his work:

> Robin in a sense was an expert. He had trained with the Green Berets and he was actually a Green Beret to all intents and purposes. They had tried to wash him out of the training because they didn't want him around. He had Bobby Kennedy's support in his research. He had been Kennedy's roommate at Harvard. Jack Kennedy was the one who got him in to the training at Fort Benning. Robin was tough and he stuck with it. So he wrote it the way it was.[3]

It is true that Moore overlapped with Robert Kennedy at Harvard (Kennedy was class of '48, Moore of '49), but he did not claim to have been Kennedy's roommate before auditors less gullible than Michael Wayne.

The family naïveté on this film equals Wayne's own belief that he could make *The Alamo* in Mexico, coaxing people to celebrate their own defeat. He went to the Pentagon expecting it to be happy with a book that contained the following things.

1. The Green Berets treat Vietnam allies (ARVN) as corrupt and cowardly: "There isn't a battalion commander in the ARVN that would take a chance on getting himself or his officers shot . . . [they] won't fight like men."[4]

2. Some ARVN members are praised for being torture specialists. A Sergeant Nqoc drives a heavy pin under a prisoner's thumbnail, then hammers at it when the man will not answer questions. He gets results by the end of the process, when he has driven the needle "all the way through the bent thumb-joint."[5] The "interrogation" is described with relish and the torturer admired for the aplomb with which he cleans the blood off the needle by wiping it on the collapsed victim's hair.

3. Those "do-gooders" who want to fight a war by social work are mocked: "Funny thing about Victor Charlie. He thinks Americans are dickheads for coming over here and trying to drill

water wells and build schools and orphanages. The only time he respects us is when we're killing him." The tough realists know they look silly when "we want everyone to love us."[6]

4. Even unwilling married men are encouraged to take native mistresses as a way of showing sympathy with America's cultural beneficiaries: "Arklen so thoroughly pleased and satisfied his young bride that the Meos, seeing her the next day, knew at once that the American was finally one of them."[7]

5. One story has a long leering sequence in which a young Vietnamese virgin, a grammar school teacher of French, is recruited to seduce a Viet Cong officer. She is shown pictures of her horribly mutilated parents, victims of the enemy officer, to ensure her cooperation. She says she will sleep with the man in order to get revenge, but she is afraid of having a Communist baby. She is Catholic and cannot submit to an abortion; but she is also ignorant about contraceptives, since the Vietnam Catholic regime keeps people innocent of such things: "Madame Nhu really had this country tied up."[8] A Green Beret is deputed to fit her with a diaphragm and show her how to use it—a task he performs with glee, to the envy of his fellows; they call him "the famous Hungarian pussy specialist."[9] When the victim is snatched from bed while they are making love, the kidnapping patriots are not too intent on politics to pause for some sightseeing: "They pulled Ling off Co Binh's naked young body. For a moment each of them almost lost his sense of mission as he stared down lasciviously."[10]

6. The raid into Laos that Michael Wayne says the Pentagon especially objected to is done with such panache in the book that there is time for recreational sex in the midst of it.[11]

7. The book presents Moore as a writer given war correspondent's status, but fighting as a member of the Green Berets —which is a violation of the rules of war.

One might well ask, having read the book, why the Americans in it are propping up a corrupt regime with cowardly soldiers and repressive Catholic rulers. The answer Moore suggests is that it is all an adventure. The Green Berets in the book are mainly soldiers of fortune from many different nations, men who enjoy their work, exulting in their skills and in the perks of the job (mainly sexual). The author cannot keep himself from joining in the fun. It is an adolescent's dream version of Gunga Din. No wonder the Pentagon hated it.

The first task of the scriptwriter, James Lee Barrett, when

revising drafts for the Army censors, was to clean up scenes in the book. The torture scene, for instance: the Americans in the movie do not want to know how the ARVN "interrogates" prisoners out of their sight. The racist implication here is that "wogs" can do to their own what Americans are too high-minded to do themselves. As Big Jim McLain might say, "Viet people are too small for me to pulverize." That task is left to despised allies. The use of a woman to seduce an enemy officer is cleaned up by not using an innocent virgin. The woman is a cabaret singer, and when a relative shows contempt for what she did, Wayne says that it was all in the line of duty.

The ARVN troops are uniformly bright, courageous, and freedom-loving in the movie, while social work is what the Americans do best, and most enthusiastically. Wayne had written Bill Moyers, President Johnson's aide, that he wanted to show the Green Berets as "diplomats in dungarees . . . [handing out] little things like soap, which can become so all-important."[12]

The journalist portrayed in the book, a free-lance author along for the ride and approving of everything, is changed for the movie's purposes into a prissy journalist critical of the war, one who takes Wayne's dare to go to Vietnam. Wayne tells him he can only be critical because he has not been on the ground to see what was going on. Wayne is reversing the actual experience of American journalists. The famous cadre of reporters who sent disturbing reports from Vietnam—Neil Sheehan, David Halberstam, Malcolm Browne, Charles Mohr, Mort Perry—all went to Vietnam thinking the war was worthwhile and winnable.[13] They began to doubt that it was winnable long before they concluded it was not worthwhile. Certainly they knew more about actual conditions than Wayne picked up on his VIP tour of the place. (Actually, Moore's novel makes fun of the official "tours" given to visiting celebrities in Vietnam.)[14]

Wayne's film begins with the prissy reporter (played by David Janssen) asking rude questions of Green Beret officers giving a demonstration of their skills. The Green Berets, with an answering rudeness, describe Communist atrocities, in a passage Wayne had already used in a letter to the Senate Foreign Relations Committee, urging Congress to stay firm in backing the war:

> Proportionally, the Vietnamese have lost twice as many fighting men in their battle for freedom as we lost in the

Second World War. . . . Imagine the equivalent percentage of our leadership being murdered. That would be around 250,000, which would be enough to include every Major, every Governor, every Senator, and every member of the House of Representatives and their combined families.[15]

It is not every citizen who can put his letter to Congress in the mouth of a character at the opening of a propaganda film.

Yet Wayne had promised Lyndon Johnson's aide, Bill Moyers, that he would get his point across in such a way as not to be "interfering with the entertainment."[16] To accomplish this, he drew on the comic conventions of World War II movies—especially the use of an irreverent character good at pilfering whatever his superiors or comrades want. This is the "Ensign Pulver" type played by Jack Lemmon in *Mister Roberts* or by Tony Curtis in *Operation Petticoat*. He also has the function given to Victor McLaglen's comic sergeants in the cavalry pictures—to play with the children, as someone not quite serious enough to be out of their mental sphere. The Pulver type in *The Green Berets* is played by Jim Hutton, whose career in light comedy pictures brought its own aura of whimsy to the unrealistic nobility of the warriors around him. After a period of exasperation with an orphaned little Vietnamese scamp, Hutton becomes his pal and surrogate father—which means that the boy is doubly orphaned when Hutton dies. But Wayne says he will take care of the lad, as the film ends with the sun setting in the China Sea to the east of Vietnam.

The picture is more absurd than *The Alamo*. Wayne is totally miscast as a tough combat leader rappelling down ropes with a rescued woman on his back. Yet, in another proof of Wayne's invincible popularity at the time, *The Green Berets* was a commercial success despite all critical ridicule. For Wayne fans, its very unrealism may have been its selling point. People who did not want to know about the actual Vietnam War could feel that the national unity and resolve of World War II might turn around this strange new conflict in the far-off jungles of the East. Wayne was fighting World War II again, the only way he ever did, in make-believe; and that make-believe was a memory of American greatness that many still wanted to live by.

Part Six

LATER FORD AND HAWKS

In the 1950s, John Ford made his two best films with Wayne, *The Quiet Man* (1952) and *The Searchers* (1956). But by the end of that decade Ford was faltering, and of his last three Wayne movies only one was an artistic success, *The Man Who Shot Liberty Valance* (1962).

The other man principally associated with Wayne's earlier career, Howard Hawks, made four of his last six films with Wayne (from 1959 to 1970), successful but formulaic and repetitive films of another great director in decline. Though still immensely popular, Wayne seemed to have reached a creative dead end by the end of the sixties.

□ 19 □
"IRELAND"

MUCH OF JOHN FORD'S Irishness was sham. It began with his name. To anyone he thought would swallow it, he claimed that he was born and baptized Sean O'Feeney. Critic Lindsay Anderson fell for that.[1] To those even less suspicious, he claimed it was Sean O'Fearna—the name his brother Eddie later adopted. Actually, John was born John, and the last name was plain Feeney. Though his actors used deferential-comic titles before him—Coach, Pappy, the Old Man—friends and equals, like Dudley Nichols or Lord Killanin, knew he liked to be called "Sean." That was his favorite identification until he won an even more welcome one—Admiral. Ford also claimed he could speak Gaelic, which he had learned as a boy when he spent a (nonexistent) year in an Irish school. In fact, he knew a few words, and he faked the rest with people like Maureen O'Hara, who knew as little Gaelic as he did.

Ford had a genuine interest in Irish literature, art, and acting—though his attempt to bring the whole Abbey Theatre to America was a well-intended but harmful idea that could kill Irish theater in its native place. He did lure to this country the experienced and influential Abbey player Arthur Shields—along with his brother Barry Fitzgerald. Ford was so impressed by Shields's directing record at the Abbey that he let him coach and rehearse his other actors, a privilege he granted no one else.

As usual, Frank Ford had anticipated his brother's later films when he made *The Cry of Erin* in 1916, the tale of an unjustly imprisoned man who escapes in disguise—a story echoed by younger brother Jack in *The Rising of the Moon* (1957).[2] Ford made a conscious effort to film the work of modern writers who were Irish—Liam O'Flaherty's *The Informer* (1935), Sean O'Casey's *The Plough and the Stars* (1936), Eugene O'Neill's sea stories as *The Long Voyage Home* (1940), Frank O'Connor's "Dan Bride" in *The Rising of the Moon* (1957), Edwin O'Connor's *The Last Hurrah* (1958). He was working on *Young Cassidy* (1965), a fictional version of Sean O'Casey's life, when his powers failed him.

But the Irish picture he most yearned to make was based on a 1933 *Saturday Evening Post* story, "The Quiet Man," by Maurice Walsh. Ford bought an option on the tale in 1935 for ten dollars, to be boosted to $2,500 and percentages if the film was made. Walsh had a long wait for something beyond his first ten dollars —sixteen years. He ended up with only $6,260 from a film that made millions.[3]

Ford could not interest backers in a tale that seemed narrow and somewhat nasty in its first form. A boy named Shawn Kelvin, raised in Ireland, goes to America, works in a Pittsburgh steel mill, makes some money boxing, and goes back to buy a farm in his home county. Liam O'Grady, a local landowner, wants to get rid of his thirty-year-old sister, Ellen, in order to welcome a rich widow into his house. Shawn accepts the "old maid," who does not love him. But in time she does grow fond of him, while resenting his self-contained indifference to the fact that Liam, disappointed that his rich widow got away, will not pay his sister's dowry of two hundred pounds. She demands that Shawn go get it. When Liam refuses, Shawn is willing to forget the matter. Ellen, now carrying Shawn's child, says her baby will have a coward for a father. Liam, a giant of a man, has been mocking the lithe but little Shawn at markets and fair meetings. So Shawn tells Ellen to stay home while he goes to make one last demand —he does not want her to see what lever he means to use for prying the money loose. But Ellen insists on going along. Shawn tells Liam he will give his sister back if Liam does not produce the dowry. Liam cannot hold out any longer, for fear of the shame and ridicule at his sister's being treated as a reject. He gives the money over, but with this consolation in his mind: now he can thrash the little nuisance, Shawn. Liam in fact never lays a hand on Shawn, who is an expert boxer, and who leaves Liam a bloodied mess. Ellen, who smiles and helps when Shawn throws the money into a threshing machine's boiler, says,

"Mother of God! The trouble I had to make a man of him!" But a friend of Shawn's gets the last word: "God Almighty did that for him before you were born."[4]

It is not much of a story—the adolescent dream of a little picked-on fellow who triumphs improbably over a towering bully. The larger social scene is one of tight-fisted concern for money, of the disposition of lands and women as interrelated possessions. There is no humor or forgiveness in the tale. No wonder others did not see any commercial possibilities in it. It was easy to imagine Ford making another moody Irish picture like *The Informer*.

Yet Ford kept hoping to film the story. He would later claim he had it cast by 1944, with Wayne, Victor McLaglen, and Maureen O'Hara playing the roles they ended up with.[5] This is unlikely on several grounds. Wayne was not a big star in 1944, and Ford was cool toward him for not serving in the war. McLaglen had been in Ford's doghouse for the preceding seven years, and would not be brought back till Ford and Frank Nugent got the idea of reuniting him with Shirley Temple in *Fort Apache*. Perhaps there was loose talk, as there always is among directors and producers and screenwriters, of the "Who could play this role?" sort. But the firm agreement, over a handshake, that Ford talked of is not probable.

Ford may have been making an excuse, in his own mind, for the apparent miscasting of the parts in the film when it did appear. In 1944 Wayne was thirty-seven, a little long in the tooth to be playing a young boxer retired at the peak of his game, but he still looked younger than his years in 1944. Maureen O'Hara was twenty-four, six years younger than her model in the tale, and thirteen years younger than Wayne. Victor McLaglen was fifty-eight, not an age to intimidate a trained boxer. By the time the film was made (1952), O'Hara had reached the right age and then some (she was thirty-two), but Wayne was now forty-five and McLaglen a lumbering sixty-six. McLaglen and O'Hara, playing brother and sister, had a difference in their ages of a third of a century.

Ford's difficulty in getting his project financed had a surprise ending. The notoriously stingy Herb Yates of Republic, trying to upgrade his studio's product, agreed to finance this "art film" if Ford would first do a surefire Western for him (*Rio Grande*, with Wayne and O'Hara). Ford, naturally, mythologized the process of wresting money from Yates. Lindsay Anderson describes a lunch-table conversation he witnessed between Ford and an MGM producer, Gottfried Reinhardt. Ford said:

> I took him [Yates] to the west of Ireland, to the most pictur-esque part of Connemara, and I showed him a little white-washed cottage, with shutters and a thatched roof. "There it is," I told him, with the tears running down my cheeks, "the house where I was born . . ." "And was it?" asked Rein-hardt. "Of course not. I was born in Maine. In Portland." But Yates started crying too. "Alright," he said. "You can do *The Quiet Man*. For a million and a half."[6]

It is purest Ford—telling A how he made up a story to fool B. And making up the story he is telling A at the moment, to fool *him*.

It is true, however, that Ford changed Maurice Walsh's locale to the county his own father came from. (His mother came from the Aran Isles—which explains the name of Ford's boat, the *Ara-ner*.) Maurice Walsh had to give up the local connections care-fully traced in his stories: "The scene was in my native Kerry. John Ford, who made the film, transferred the scene to Connemara."[7]

Everyone making *The Quiet Man* overdosed on Ireland. The principals lived in a castle, were drenched with Irish rain, and yearned toward the Irish whiskey Ford declared off limits for the duration of the shoot. After the cast gathered from different parts of the globe, Ford had to set his customary tone of discipline on the set. There would be no wandering off down picturesque lanes, no lolling in castles or glens. He told Andrew McLaglen, an assistant director, to have the whole cast on hand, made up and in costume, for the morning of the first day's filming.

McLaglen says it was understood by everybody that the Old Man could not mean to include his brother Frank, whose scenes came up later, and who had to spend an hour getting made up, since he would be wearing a wild prophet's beard. As everyone gathered, Ford made his entrance, sat and looked around, saw his troops all prepared, but one. "We'll begin with Frank." The crew dashed to get Frank up, slap on his beard, get his wardrobe adjusted. John did some makework shots with Frank, then got down to making *The Quiet Man*.[8]

When Ford first looked over his cast and crew in that spongy green air, he was gazing at the microcosmic community, the "clan," he always assembled on his sets. It has been said that

Ford played the Irish "squireen," creating feudal ties with his subordinates, lending them his patronage and protection in return for their obeisance. If that was the case, he should have had in the village of Cong, where they were shooting, a reality against which he could measure his own imitation of it.

Critics have admired the rich social layerings in the world of *The Quiet Man*. People of different strata seem to be brought in naturally—the barman and mailman and railway men, the Catholic pastor and his assistant, the Protestant minister and his visiting bishop, the men in the pub, the young revolutionaries who only dream and sing and drink, the visiting Englishman wrapped in his insularity, the petty squireen and his sycophantic workers, the meddlesome busybody and town bookmaker, the widow with her landed wealth, the marriageable young woman with dowry problems.

But in one important sense the community of "Innisfree" is less rounded and real than the cavalry post in *Fort Apache*. That had a band of strong women, who comfort their men and each other, serve as buffers against the tyranny of Colonel Thursday, and create ties that not even departure can break: "We do not say goodbye in the cavalry. To our next post, dear."

By contrast, the Irish village of "Innisfree" is entirely a man's world. Maureen O'Hara is stranded in her brother's home, serving him and his five workers, with no sisterhood, not even a weak one, to help or oppose her. Then, later, she is stranded alone in Wayne's cottage with no one to turn to but the demanding priest, who tells her to do her wifely duty by sleeping with her husband. The same is true of the isolated widow (Mildred Natwick) and the Protestant minister's wife (even more peripheral than her husband). Women as a group appear only once, when one of them offers Wayne "a good stick to beat the lovely lady with."

This failure in Frank Nugent's script does not represent the real Irish culture of the time, which had a matriarchal counterforce to patriarchy. But it does embody John Ford's world, as he had fashioned it around his camera over the years. The people who think Ford's crew reflected an Irish fiefdom have it backwards. The "Ireland" of *The Quiet Man* reflects John Ford's set, his own ideological world, in which women were usually peripheral. Ford tried to make an exception for Katharine Hepburn, but his *Mary of Scotland* was stiff, too distant from his normal scene. Maureen O'Hara got warm treatment, but who else? Shirley Temple was central only in the safe prepubescence of *Wee*

Willie Winkie. Once Shirley grew up, Ford treated her as rudely as he had Helen Hayes: "Now where did you go to school, Shirley? Did you graduate?"[9] In *The Quiet Man*, Maureen O'Hara is not part of a larger female presence, in the movie or in the village.

Ford's attitude toward women leads us directly to the part of this much-beloved film that has caused vague uneasiness when not outright disgust—the way Wayne drags O'Hara across the countryside to fling her back into her brother's custody. This looks dismayingly like the humiliation of women that Hawks made a feature of late Wayne films—all those scenes where he spanks an "uppity" woman and makes her his.

The omission of women as part of an interrelated world in *The Quiet Man* is the more surprising since Frank Nugent, who created the women's "chorus" of *Fort Apache*, was writing the script. Admittedly, the woman in Walsh's story was even more isolated—she is the *only* woman in the tale. But Ford made many changes to the original—of necessity, since Walsh's slim narrative had only four characters (one of them, Shawn's friend, very minor). Nugent introduced two women—the widow (barely mentioned by Walsh as Liam's motive for disposing of his sister) and the Protestant minister's wife. Why did he not make some social connection between them, as he did when he introduced a whole gallery of interconnected *men* who were not in the first story—the priest (Ward Bond), the minister (Arthur Shields), the matchmaker (Barry Fitzgerald), the squire's sycophant (Owen Glynn), the ancient Dan Tobin (Frank Ford), the IRA types in the pub, plus many minor figures?

Nugent clearly did not want to take away the vulnerability of the story's heroine, and he meant to insist on the separate identity symbolized by her dowry. The importance of the dowry was something that Nugent and Ford felt they had to explain. When Wayne says that love matters more than money, a thousand romantic movies had keyed audiences to agree with him. Many of Nugent's script changes were meant to create better understanding of the dowry's role in the Walsh tale. Walsh's hero understands the dowry system, since he grew up in Ireland and has been absent only a short time. By making Wayne someone who left the home country in his infancy, Nugent turns him into a surrogate for the audience, which also needs instruction in old marriage customs.

In the magazine story, there is only a cash dowry (two hundred pounds). In the movie, O'Hara's "treasure" includes furniture, china, pewter, her spinet, the silver bracelet her mother left her, fifty pounds in gold from her father, and thirty-odd "in notes and pounds I've earned these last fifteen years." All the years she was an outsider and servant in her brother's house, feeding him and his five fieldworkers, she dreamed "of having my own things about me . . . my own china and pewter shining about me." She tells Wayne he has no right to touch her: "Until I've got my dowry safe about me, I'm no wife, but the servant I've always been. . . . There's three hundred years of hopes and dreams in those things of mine." Wayne, angered that she thinks she is not really his wife, kicks down the door she locked between them, picks her up and throws her on the bed, which collapses. But then he goes outdoors to sleep in the bedroll he brought from America.

McLaglen's workmen show up the next morning with her furniture. But the struggle over it (added by Nugent) has given O'Hara a chance to explain what it means to her. It is a pledge of her separate dignity. In a world that treats women as property, having some property of her own makes a woman a disposer of commodities and not just a commodity herself. The place in society of the landholding widow (Mildred Natwick) indicates that.

Though he relented on her furniture, McLaglen has not given her the cash dowry he contracted for (Walsh's two hundred pounds had been lifted by inflation, intervening in the years when Ford tried to get his film made, to three hundred and fifty pounds). So O'Hara is still refusing to sleep with Wayne. In fact, carried away by his refusal to ask McLaglen for it even when they see him in the area's market (Castletown) being paid for his prize sheep, O'Hara raises her whip against Wayne, then uses it on the carriage horse he has just given her, driving off and leaving him stranded. Wayne walks the five miles home over hills and fields.

O'Hara, repenting her burst of anger, goes to the priest (Ward Bond), at his fishing spot, to tell him her troubles. She is embarrassed, and wants to tell him "in the Irish"—but the audience learns what she is saying when he does not understand the Gaelic words for "bedroll." She gives him that in English and he blows up at her. Catholic theology of the time said that a woman had to pay her "marriage debt" of sexual compliance (otherwise the husband would be tempted to fornication elsewhere). She is standing out for one kind of debt. He tells her she must pay another kind. (He tells her indirectly, preserving her modesty and the veil of Gaelic.)

O'Hara had come out of the house, the morning after the wedding, to harry Wayne out of his bedroll and into the house. She has heard the men coming with her furniture and did not want them to see his exclusion ("Don't be shaming me"). So she knows what the judgment of the community would be. With the priest's words instructing her, she goes home, prepares the meal like a dutiful wife, and offers Wayne a stick to beat her with—which he just throws into the fire. At last they consummate the marriage, and Wayne thinks all is settled.

But the next morning, when he rises and sings out happily, the marriage broker is at the door to tell him O'Hara has gone to the train station in Castletown and is leaving Innisfree. This is the weakest part of the story, in logic. She has no relatives anywhere, according to the story given us. She has no cash. It is hard to imagine where she would be going. But since she must pay the marriage debt if she stays with Wayne, and he will not exact her "treasury" debt, she will not stay with him. Nonetheless, the way she keeps looking around at the train station shows that she hopes he will come to get her.

Wayne rides his hunting horse to Castletown and comes down the train platform slamming train doors to great crashing chords. The bystanders cluster, buzz, and call the news to the pub. Where is he taking her—back home? Barry Fitzgerald takes a gun out to signal the route. He is humming fragments of a chug-chug tune, the second time we have heard it. The first time was when Wayne walked the five miles from Castletown.

Wayne walks her out onto the fields—now the music is chug-chugging merrily, retracing the five miles she forced *him* to walk the day before. When she loses a shoe, she tugs back to get it and flops on the ground to put it on. An approving woman breaks out of the pack to say, "Here's a good stick to beat the lovely lady with." Wayne says, "Thanks," but has no more intention of using it now than in the past. When O'Hara breaks free, for a moment, she tries to punch Wayne in the face (her third try in the movie). He ducks, as in the past, and boots her in the behind with the flat of his foot—in the direction of McLaglen's manor house.

Arrived there, Wayne asks one more time for the three hundred and fifty pounds. When McLaglen refuses, he spins O'Hara at McLaglen's feet and says she is returned: the contract is off when one side refuses its obligations. Shocked, O'Hara says,

"You would do this to me?" He says it is her system, not his. McLaglen pays up and Wayne starts toward the boiler. She instantly understands what he is doing and triumphantly opens the fire door for him to throw the money in. That done, she starts home, saying his dinner will be ready. With a coy smile, with flirts of her hair and her hips, she goes back off across the fields to the chug-chug tune of her dragging, now turned into a delicate little dance melody.

Wayne and Hawks—and Hawks's imitators—were guilty of movie after movie that humiliates women. This is definitely not one of them. O'Hara feels she has won because she has made Wayne take seriously her principle of getting what was her due. He accomplished this for her the only way he could. She knows he did it for her, despite his reluctance to use violence with anyone—even with McLaglen, and more especially with women. The comic offering of the stick to beat her offends some, who forget she offered him a stick herself, under the priest's censure, and he turned it down. When she happily collaborates with the burning of the three hundred and fifty pounds, she is proving it was not greed for money ("the purse") that motivated her, but vindication of her claim as an independent person. In the final scene of the film, Wayne is idly playing with a stick outside her cottage. This time she takes it and throws it away, whispers a suggestion for sex in the afternoon. It is a mini-replay of the dragging scene, with the initiative all hers. *She* throws away the stick. *She* crosses the rocks with him in tow.

Ford, who was not known for his love stories, boasted that *The Quiet Man* was a sexy film, and he is right. Wayne and O'Hara, good two years before in *Rio Grande*, are even better here. She glows when she looks at him, and he projects youthful ardor despite his calendar years. In making the hero a big man, not the featherweight fighter of the original, Nugent did not rely on the "worm turns" device of a bully being thrashed by a small man. Walsh's hero seems to avoid conflict because he is mismatched. For Wayne, from whom his audience would expect instant retaliation when provoked, Nugent invented a new twist: Wayne, called Sean Thornton in the movie, has killed a man in the boxing ring and renounced all fighting. That is another reason why he refuses to fight for money, even O'Hara's. He despises what he did "just for a purse."

Nonetheless, the whole village has been waiting for the eventual combat of the two large adversaries, and the audience's expectations are tickled by others' reactions—the priest who ducks and weaves with sympathetic motion as he watches, the minister (himself a bantamweight champion at school) betting with his bishop, the IRA types placing wagers in Barry Fitzgerald's book of odds. The fight begins with blows that get crashing chords like the slammed doors at the train platform, and it proceeds with ritual pacing and pausing. Of all Ford's brawling scenes, this is the only one I can view with entire comfort, since it is so clearly a kind of raucous ballet, its thunderously scored punches as harmless as the leaps of a pas de deux.

It is a tribute to McLaglen that he can hold up his end of the hilarious but strenuous battle sequence, at the age of sixty-six. The man who was comically unthreatening as the Irish sergeant in Ford's three cavalry films is a convincing scowler and bully, the "heavy" who is gulled by the conspirators of the village into giving his sister away in the hopes of getting the widow. (In the movie, Wayne and O'Hara are in love before the marriage—a key departure from Walsh's plot.) Good as Wayne and O'Hara are, *The Quiet Man* could not work without McLaglen's towering presence athwart their path to happiness.

McLaglen was a convincing fighter because he had been a professional boxer in the 1920s, who lasted six rounds with the deadly Jack Johnson. Ford, who liked the boxers and weightlifters of his thirties movies—George O'Brien, McLaglen, Ward Bond—thought they were so much brawn for which he had to supply the brains. McLaglen was a particular victim of this fantasy. After he fell out of Ford's graces by not dropping other commitments when Ford called, the director told a widely believed story that McLaglen only won the Oscar for *The Informer* because Ford got him drunk the night before the trial scene in order to make him appropriately disoriented. He had to be forced into the agony he was not an actor good enough to feign. Ford used similar tales about other actors. He said he had to get Woody Strode drunk to play *his* trial scene in *Sergeant Rutledge*.[10] Wayne, of course, was "the big sonofabitch" who could not act before *Red River*. Women actors could not cry unless Ford insulted them. He was the *primum mobile* of all effects on his set.

Actually, McLaglen was a shrewd and successful actor long before *The Informer*. He was stunning in Ford's own *Black Watch* (1929). He carried the Flagg-and-Quirt series of films spawned in the early thirties from *What Price Glory?* He knew exactly what the demands were on him as Gypo Nolan in *The Informer*. He predicted to his son, fourteen at the time, that the role would win him an Oscar.

Some are so little disposed to credit McLaglen's acting ability that they assume the Irish accent in the cavalry stories and *The Quiet Man* was his natural speech pattern, like Barry Fitzgerald's brogue. But McLaglen was not Irish. He never lived in Ireland. Born in London, educated in England, he was Scotch-English, the son of an Anglican clergyman who became a bishop in South Africa. Victor McLaglen was one of six brothers who became famous as "the Fighting Macks" when they all served in World War I. Victor had earlier served as a teenager in the Boer War. During World War I, he became a captain of Irish fusiliers, and served as the provost marshal of Baghdad during the postwar period of occupation—not a post that would be given to a dolt. After the war, he was a circus strongman. In a vaudeville act, he and one of his brothers posed, wearing white body stockings, as Greek statues in *tableaux vivants*. His acting career, begun in England, took off instantly in America with his 1926 roles in *Beau Geste* and *What Price Glory?* He played the bullfighter for Raoul Walsh in *Loves of Carmen* (1927). When he aged past the leading man category, he fell into obscure character roles until Ford, relenting, brought him back to repeat his ethnic sergeant part from *Wee Willie Winkie* in *Fort Apache*.

It is an odd thing that McLaglen was in fact what Wayne was only in fantasy—a patriot-soldier, military officer, athlete. McLaglen was such a good and enthusiastic horseman that he formed his own uniformed riding club for friends and children in the thirties. It was a time when other British actors were forming polo clubs and Ford himself created a yachting uniform for those who sailed with him in the *Araner*. (Pictures show Wayne wearing *this* uniform.) Actors George Brent and Gary Cooper also had riding clubs that wore uniforms. The fact that McLaglen, former captain of British troops, adopted a military-looking uniform for the club made the great California journalist Carey McWilliams accuse McLaglen, in a 1935 column, of fascist sympathies. But a survey of all mentions of McLaglen in the Los Angeles *Times* turned up nothing but social and charitable events attended by his troop.[11] McLaglen would later have nothing to do with the right-wing activities of Ward Bond or John Wayne. McWilliams's charges, still widely believed by film scholars, were unjustified.[12]

Ford kept the narrow and greedy nature of Walsh's squire,

played by McLaglen; but he leavened this, like everything else in the movie, with a sly subversive humor. Though the movie is sentimental, it is happy in forgiveness of sin, not devoid of sin. The characters are not idealized, but absolved. The squire is a bully and his helpers sycophants. The IRA is feckless and better at toasting liberty than fighting for it. The priest is another kind of bully, more benevolent than McLaglen, but not above venality (he is behind on the bookmaker's account). The Protestant minister has so little to do in town that we find him at home playing tiddlywinks by himself. Barry Fitzgerald is a lovable souse, but a compulsive one. The marriage customs are mocked even as they are observed. The trains run at odd hours because the railway personnel are too busy fighting and gossiping to do their work. O'Hara has a violent temper, and she is torn between superstition and defiance as she partly observes and partly tries to avoid the priest's directives, sleeping with Wayne but then running away from him.

Only two people keep their dignity throughout—Wayne is one, the puzzled outsider who has not succumbed yet to village habits and obstructive traditions. (O'Hara resists Wayne's idea of farming with a tractor since it is smelly and noisy.) The other dignified person, reversing Ford's treatment of him in movie after movie, is the village elder, "Dan Tobin," played by Frank Ford. We first see him kneeling behind Wayne at morning Mass on a weekday, when only three people have attended—Wayne (newly arrived), O'Hara, and Frank. From then on, Frank, in his dark cape and white beard, is at the races, at the wedding, shaking his head with approval of Wayne, disapproval of McLaglen, a chorus figure making silent and spoken comments. Even in his sickbed, he makes the young Catholic curate read him heroic Irish tales instead of the Bible; and when news of the showdown between Wayne and McLaglen reaches him, his eyes pop open and he is rejuvenated. This is the longest-running, most humane role John Ford ever gave to Frank—a fact that is emphasized in the filmed "stage calls" that bring people back on at the movie's end. Others take their "bows" in groups of two, three, or four. Only Frank gets a solo bow just before the climactic shot of Wayne and O'Hara together—he is waving his walking stick in triumph, a glorious farewell after years of inglorious bit parts.

Though he would appear in one more Ford film before his death (*The Sun Shines Bright*, 1953, again as a guzzling dotard), this is his proper departure. Ford had said, "We'll begin with

Frank" when they started shooting. In a profound sense he also ended with Frank, who not only gets up from his sickbed in the story but rose from a dead career for his final appearance as a wise man rather than a fool. Intoxicated in most of the bit parts his brother gave him, he is entirely sober in this movie, where everyone else seems to be downing the drink continually. Frank, who had himself directed *The Cry of Erin* as a young man, is allowed to share his brother's triumph this once. The Irish boys came home together.

If, as I suggested at the start, this fake Ireland of Ford's is as much his own repertory community as a picture of "the old country," where is Ford himself in the story? The boss of the community, with his sycophant saying "Mr. Danaher has the floor," like any lowly production assistant, is McLaglen. Can Ford, in the name of humane detachment and absolution, be making fun even of himself? We know he was capable of it. He would put a patent caricature of himself ("John Dodge") in *The Wings of Eagles* (1957), a movie that also starred Wayne and O'Hara. He even had another of his bully boys, Ward Bond, play the role with authoritarian growls.[13] *The Quiet Man* is a film of self-knowledge. McLaglen's "Danaher," along with Bond's "Dodge," may be as close to such self-knowledge as Ford ever lets us get while we are watching his product.

The movie has earned its cult status. It is far more complex than it looks on its sunny surface. Repeated viewing turns up nice overlooked touches and deepened relationships. Only rarely does it fall into slapstick (the horse that nods yes to Barry Fitzgerald's comment that it has good sense). The love of Wayne and O'Hara, thwarted, grows in intensity for every obstacle thrown in its way.

Maurice Walsh consoled himself for the loss of authentic detail from his own story with the reflection that "Barry Fitzgerald steals the show"—an authentic Irish triumph.[14] After all, Walsh's sister, a cloistered nun, was released from her convent to see the Irish premiere, "an unheard of concession in those days."[15] The village of Cong, where it was filmed, has become a tourist attraction, both for the Irish themselves and for visiting Americans. The movie is shown on television to celebrate St. Patrick's Day. It is the only great film Wayne ever made that was not a Western.

Yet this apparent exception to the Ford-Wayne run of Western movies is what Robert Ray calls a "disguised Western." What makes the Western so rich in potential drama is its necessary treatment of the clash between social systems. Ford had learned the implications of this genre from his earliest days in cinema, from his treatment of Harry Carey as the anarchistic loner surrendering to the advent of schoolmarm civilization. In his major silent film, *The Iron Horse* (1924), Ford celebrated technology's drive into the raw nature of the frontier. Yet his hero (George O'Brien) moved the train forward with "primitive" force more like that of his foes, the Indians, than that of railway engineers, financiers, and routine operatives. Wayne plays a similar role, as expediter of a military conquest that undoes his own affinity with Indians, in the cavalry movies.

Wayne in *The Quiet Man* is forced into the crease between historical epochs. The film's "Ireland" has absorbed and blunted the advances of modernity. The railway train that battered down "primitive" society in the American West has been dissolved in the emollients of Irish life. In the same way, Wayne's direct assaults on what he wants in this cumbrously traditional society are diverted, are expended in futile aggression (his impatient breaking of the marriage bed on the marriage night after he was excluded from it). He cannot by sheer American innocence and bluster win a bride for whom love is not enough without the treasured safeguards of her status. Imagine this as the story of a Western hero marrying a "squaw" who does not join his "superior" culture unquestioningly (like the masochistic female in Cecil DeMille's *Squaw Man* and all its imitators). Wayne has to "revert" to the social level of the tribe he is trying to join. Seen in this light, *The Quiet Man* is a far more interesting study of indigenous rights than Ford's "pro-Indian" *Cheyenne Autumn* (1964), a better treatment of a woman's independence than his "feminist" *Seven Women* (1966). "Ireland," for Ford, was a confection of the mind, so similar to "the West" as to be identical with it. Ford's "West" was always his mythical homeland.

THE FURY OF ETHAN

AFTER WAYNE PLAYED the driven avenger in *Red River*, some directors were quick to tap into the dark side of the actor's persona. He became a drunken and obsessive captain in *Wake of the Red Witch* (1948) and the disturbed Sergeant Stryker in *Sands of Iwo Jima*. But Ford did not call on this haunted face of Wayne, even when he had the perfect opening for it in Bellah's story for *Rio Grande*.

It was not until 1956, ten years after the filming of *Red River*, that Ford decided to fill Wayne's eyes with hate. He gave him his finest role, that of Ethan Edwards in *The Searchers*. In making this film, Ford had some of the same problems Hawks encountered in *Red River*. Once again, there was difficulty in ending the story. In both films' sources, the Wayne character dies—and the story *demands* that he die. Tom Dunson and Amos Edwards (the original name of Wayne's character in *The Searchers*) are one-dimensional figures of hate who must go.

Hawks and Ford, not wanting to kill off their star, labored to make him more complex and sympathetic, capable ultimately of some (though severely qualified) redemption. Each character undertakes a difficult task with iron determination, and is ready to knock down anybody who gets in his way. Each has a younger man resisting him, trying to make him relent when his ferocity becomes inhuman. That is what creates the problem with the plot. How can a person who is monstrously inflexible be made

251

to bend without killing him (the logical termination of such a story, as both original authors recognized)?

Despite the similarities given each director in his source, Ford was working with a far better story than Hawks. Instead of Borden Chase's sprawling magazine serial, Ford used Alan LeMay's spare and moving novel with the same title as the movie. Hawks had to prune Chase's episodic excrescences. Ford kept LeMay's entire plot. Ford even kept the novel's names for the characters, all but one. Amos became Ethan because the former name still had a faintly comic ring in 1956, thanks to the immense popularity of the radio and TV series *Amos 'n' Andy*.

LeMay's novel was an inversion of the traditional Indian captivity narrative. These tales of captivity were the second-oldest genre in European-American history—after the travel narratives of which they were an offshoot. Those who came and wondered at an alien culture were sometimes forced to see it "from the inside," as it were, when they were taken prisoner— Spanish explorers in Mexico (Cabeza de Vaca), English in Virginia (John Smith), French in Canada (Isaac Joques, a Jesuit missionary).

The New England Congregationalists perfected the captivity narrative as a tale of moral purification. They were building on the tradition of St. Augustine, who argued that Christians fallen into pagan hands were not soiled by action forced on them if they kept their intentions pure.[1] The Puritans considered the Indians devil-worshipers, so eating food they consecrated with their hunting rituals was eating food offered to idols (*Acts of the Apostles* 15:29)—what Mary Rowlandson, in the most famous captivity narrative, called the "black eucharist."[2] Puritans felt that those captured by Christian Indians, if they had been converted by the French Jesuits in Canada, were also in the hands of the devil, since Catholic Rome was the Antichrist of the Apocalypse.[3]

LeMay's novel shows us the other side of Indian captivity— not the captives' fate but that of those left behind after Indians have kidnapped their loved ones. After the failure of a first effort to regain a captive, should people keep on trying, or get on with their own lives? Will the captive, especially if young, be so integrated into the Indian world as to become incapable of leaving, or unwilling to? How can one be sure the captive is still alive to be sought for?

In *The Searchers* (the novel), an Indian named Scar raids a ranch, kills the husband and wife (raping the latter), and takes two daughters captive. The older sister (sixteen years old) is soon found, raped and dead. The younger (Debbie, age ten) disappears with Scar's men beyond a posse's resources to follow. But two men keep on searching for her. The dead man's brother, Amos Edwards, who was in love with his raped sister-in-law, monomaniacally seeks revenge from Scar. An orphan brought up in the family, eighteen-year-old Martin Pawley, seeks to recover a girl he thought of as a sister. As time goes on, Martin finds it impossible to leave Amos. He fears that the older man's hatred of Indians will make him kill Debbie, as one contaminated by her life with them. As the years pass and she is becoming an adolescent (if she is still alive), it is probable—indeed, close to certain—that she is having sexual congress with her captors, another reason for Amos to treat her as polluted. Besides, Martin thinks of Debbie as the heir to her father's farm, whose income Amos is using to finance his search, and which he seems intent on claiming as his own. The suspicion is confirmed in Martin's mind when, at a moment of danger, Amos produces a will, drawn up in the white community, that leaves his (Amos's) property to Martin in case of his death. Debbie is not considered.

So far, this is the plot as Ford filmed it, with few exceptions. Martin in the movie is made part-Indian, a reason for Ethan (as Amos is now called) to hate and distrust the young follower. Martin has a girlfriend who does not wait for him in the novel; in the movie she does. And Wayne's determination to kill Debbie is broken in the movie. In the novel, Amos has no time to make a decision in the matter. As he rides down the woman he thinks is Debbie, and is about to snatch her up, the woman whirls and fires a gun into his face, killing him. She is not Debbie after all. Amos's hatred, which blurred the distinction between Debbie and other "squaws," has undone him.

The novel's Debbie *has* grown into a seventeen-year-old betrothed member of Scar's household, and she does not want to leave. Martin knows the cavalry is about to raid her village, where she will be killed unless she leaves, so he kidnaps her. She suffers a breakdown in the stress of transition from one culture to another, and, as he nurses her back to health, they fall in love with each other. (He is not real kin, remember.) The LeMay story accepts the fact that Indian society is not the diabolic opposite of the white culture, but another culture, with its own humanity, which Debbie has experienced. The bigotry of Indian haters is condemned in the person of Amos, as it was in LeMay's other Western novel, *The Unforgiven* (made into a movie in 1960).

The moral center of LeMay's novel is Martin. Amos is just a force Martin must cope with in reaching his own goals. Like the ranch owner in Borden Chase's story for *Red River*, Amos is driven by a fierce desire for revenge. And, like Chase's Tom Dunson, he does not give up his quest for revenge until he is forced to by death.

Ford and Frank Nugent had to make the Amos character—now Ethan—more complex and sympathetic if he is to abandon his hatred and not be killed at the end. The LeMay character is just a drifter who comes back to his brother's ranch periodically to moon over his lost love. When Wayne comes back to his brother's ranch three years after the Civil War, he trails a rich history deftly sketched for us in asides and symbols. When Nugent first went to work for Ford, he received some advice that he followed in all later work for him: "Write out complete biographies of every character in the picture . . . take your character from his childhood and write all the salient events in his life leading up to the moment the picture finds him."[4] That advice was never put to better use than in the complex character of Ethan Edwards.

Wayne enters the movie wearing his military cloak and tells a former Confederate comrade (Ward Bond) that he still has his saber ("Don't believe in surrender"). He is not a person who changes, as his faithful but repressed love for his sister-in-law shows. When Bond tries to swear him in as a deputy to go after some rustlers, he says the oath would be no good. "Figure a man's only good for one oath at a time. I took one to the Confederate States of America. So did you, Sam." He is not only inflexible, but ruthless. A later reference makes it clear that the mint-condition gold he is carrying comes from an Army pay wagon (the Union is still his enemy). A medal he gives to Debbie is from Mexico, showing he has been a mercenary fighter there.

Others' reactions to this man of contradictions are registered in an opening that is the best narrative sequence Ford ever filmed. The screen is black at first, till a brightly lit hole opens in it and an all-black silhouette stands at what we see, in a moment, is a doorway. This is the wide-screen equivalent of irising in Ford's silent films. In *Straight Shooting*, a tight iris frames the face of the cattle boss when we first see him. The iris means that we are being drawn into his mind. Then the iris widens out to show a huge valley behind him covered with cattle—he was thinking of his empire. In *The Searchers*, the woman irised (Martha) is thinking of something we see as the camera moves up behind her, opening out our view beyond her. Still tiny in the landscape—it takes a search for our eyes to find him—a figure is riding slowly toward her. She has sensed his approach—he is her brother-in-law, whom she loves in a way she will never confess.

As Wayne, the figure in the landscape, draws nearer, the wife goes out on the porch, where her three children gather, and then her husband. Wayne comes hesitantly up to his brother, not offering his hand, not sure of his welcome. After a veiled look at Martha and a quick kiss on her forehead, he goes inside, where the first thing he does is swing little Debbie up into the air and hold her there, looking up at her. After he has given her his Mexican medal, he later takes the napkin out from under her chin when she is leaving the room.

When Martin Pawley comes riding up, late to dinner, we see him through the same doorway that "irised out" in the opening. He rides straight at the door, throws one leg forward over the horse's mane, and jumps to the ground at the doorsill—the same shot that showed Hoot Gibson, the young boy in *Straight Shooting*, riding to the door and leaping off his horse in a carefree dismount. Doors are charged symbols in Ford—the liminal dividers between home and danger, confinement and freedom, a female world of enclaves and a male world of expansion.

The interior geography of the Edwards home is as important a narrative instrument as the dimensions and recesses of Apache Wells were during the second stop in *Stagecoach*. There, shadows and sources of light reconfigured human relationships. In *The Searchers* there are three doors to the main room in the house: one onto the porch (the door through which we looked at Wayne riding toward us), a door to the attached storage room, and a door to the bedroom. When Martin Pawley is troubled by Wayne's treatment of him (as a "half-breed"), he goes outside to sit excluded. Before going to bed, Martin kisses Martha, and Wayne's expression reveals his jealousy of this adopted Indian's familiarity with Ethan's own beloved. (The movie must be seen in its wide-screen format to follow the choreography of all the people reacting inside the house's geography.)

When Wayne took off his coat, Martha had tenderly carried it into her bedroom to be brushed. The next morning, Ward Bond, the gruff sheriff, sees her through the bedroom door caressing the coat (as the daughter in *Straight Shooting* caressed the plate from her dead brother's place setting). Bond turns aside, revealing he knows of her love. When she brings the cloak out to Wayne, Bond stands ostentatiously looking away from them (toward us) as they face each other. Bond had earlier opened the outside door of the storage room to surprise Lucy, the teenage daughter, kissing her beau (Harry Carey, Jr.). In all directions, here, doors open up to intimacies or close them off.

On the night of his arrival, Wayne goes to sleep in the storage room, but first sits for a while on the porch. He sees, through the outer door, his brother lead Martha through the inner door and close it, doubly excluding the rejected lover. It is a silent but very telling *paraklausithyron* (the classical genre of a locked-out lover's plaint).

The posse Bond leads against putative cattle rustlers finds the cattle, killed but not carved up. That means the rustling was an Indian ploy to lure men away from the Edwards ranch. The others react emotionally and dash for home; but Wayne is not only inflexible and ruthless—he is controlled—in his passion. He knows horses need rest and grain; he takes off the saddle but his gaze across the horse's back tells us he feels more deeply than the hotheads who rode away from him.

We go directly, with no dissolve, from that gaze to an expressionistically red-hazed scene of the ranch about to be raided. Peter Stowell has shown that this kind of transition in a Ford movie takes us inside the mind of the character, much as an iris did in silent days.[5] This is not a flashback but a kind of flash-across to show what is happening *as Wayne imagines it.* We see the scene through the fiery colors of his hatred for what he knows Martha is suffering. Tag Gallagher has pointed out a similar change in lighting and style for the long flashback in *The Man Who Shot Liberty Valance,* where we are being made to see what happened through Jimmy Stewart's eyes.[6] There is a similar expressionist blur during Wayne's flashback to his boxing days in *The Quiet Man.*

When Wayne as Ethan reaches the burning ranch, we see him again through a doorway—he is framed looking into a storage house, as Martha had been framed looking out. But this time he is looking at her violated body, whose impact is registered only in his eyes. It is a look of tamped-down anger that will become more crazed after he finds Lucy's mutilated corpse. It reaches a climax when the camera tracks at breakneck speed up to his fierce expression when he sees, in captives reduced to lewd idiocy, the fate of Debbie.

The same "framing" effect is achieved when Martin's girl-friend, Laurie, reads her long letter from Martin. A flashback, introduced again without a dissolve, shows us what she is making of the letter. The offensively grotesque account in the letter of Marty's Indian "wife," foisted on him when he did not realize the consequences of a trade, is tinctured by Laurie's anger and resentment at hearing of such a "squaw." Peter Stowell makes a powerful case for the subjective nature of this flashback.[7]

Ethan's indomitability awes Marty, who is our surrogate for watching the man's hatred at work. It is clear that this man will *never* give up ("That'll be the day"). As he was still waging war against the Union three years after the war, he is waging war on the Indians, slaughtering buffalo they might eat, shooting an Indian's eyes to make him "wander between the winds forever."

The character is not harsh like Sergeant Stryker, out of concern for his men. Nor like Tom Dunson, out to take back his herd. Nor like the drunken captain in *Wake of the Red Witch*, feeling betrayed by his love. Ethan's anger outruns all rational cause. Loss of every sort has poured into it, fueled it—loss of Martha to his brother, loss in the war, loss of his place in the family to an Indian outsider, loss of his comrades (like Bond, who capitulated), then loss of three lives to Scar.

Loyalty, disappointed idealism, a starved love, a defeated cause—all these things drive him, but they do not explain him. This raging furnace of pent-in hatreds is not like the simple desire for revenge in LeMay's story. Here hatred is something bigger than its container, a fire tougher than the vessel that carries it, like the fury of Achilles. Achilles' fury (*mēnis*, a word usually used of divine wrath) outruns its occasion, the theft of his war prize by Agamemnon. When that offense is undone—when the seized girl is returned, untouched by Agamemnon, accompanied by rich retribution payments—nothing can slake the fury that is now self-fueling. Even Apollo is placated for a similar offense committed against his priest; but there is no price to Achilles' fury, no mechanism of placation for it. It is a law to itself. *It* wields *him*. As such, it is as fascinating as a force of nature, like the fire to which it is so frequently compared. He is possessed of it as other people are possessed by their "genius" or "muse" or "*daimon*."

In the end, of course, Achilles' wrath does burn itself out—but only after it has destroyed his best friend (Patroclus) along with that best friend's destroyer (Hector). With his anger still unslaked, Achilles continues inflicting indignities on Hector's corpse, killing it over and over, his rage insatiable—until Hector's father approaches him and makes him see the dehumanized object of his fury through the eyes of someone who loved him (just as Achilles loved Patroclus). Achilles recognizes himself in Priam, himself as his own fury's victim. He was punishing himself, and that is superfluous. His own death is fixed and was foreshadowed in *both* Patroclus' and Hector's slaughter. Only when he consents to his own death—*really*, not notionally—does Achilles' anger, too, expire.

What softens Wayne's anger? Not what should. When he at last confronts Scar, he is looking in a mirror, though he will not admit it. Scar, too, hates because his parents were killed. He is as clever as his tracker. He has outwitted Ethan for seven years, and meets him now only to show his control of the situation. Scar comes off as Ethan's equal in their edgy mutual insults. "You speak good English, for a Commanch." The response: "You speak good Commanch, for a white man." But this does not blunt Wayne's rage.

What else should slow Wayne's quest for blood? Debbie's condition. When he sees her in Scar's tepee, she is well cared for, beautiful, lucid—obviously not the object of the horrors that reduced other captives to a blithering inhuman blankness. Nugent's duty to write Debbie's biography would show that she had been treated well—better than an Indian girl would have been treated by Ethan or his like if captured by whites. But Ethan, of all people, is not permeable to such considerations.

Ethan tries to kill Debbie, but is stopped by Martin, who puts his body before hers as a shield. Courage is a thing Ethan does respect. When he thinks he will be killed himself, he makes out his will to Martin. This is not the prepared will "Amos" brought with him in the novel, to give to a white boy raised by Martha. It is a will made on the spot, given to a "half-breed" whose place in the Edwards family he resented. It is the first act of regard for another human being that Ethan has shown since the two of them began riding alone.

Martin refuses to accept the bequest. He has taken on some of Wayne's resolve. Yet he is not a typical follower in a Wayne movie. He does not, like a private subordinate to Sergeant Stryker, or a Monty Clift raised by Dunson, acquire the traits of his leader, though in softer and more human ways. If anything, the reverse is true. Wayne learns from him. He refused to recognize "little Debbie"—the girl he lifted into the air and gave a medal to, the one whose napkin he tenderly removed—in the "squaw" of Scar's tent. But he begins to see her through Martin's eyes. When Martin asks to go alone into the Indian camp by night, to save her before the Texas Rangers raid the village, Wayne does not oppose this (as he would have earlier, sure it would alert the camp and baffle his quest for Scar). Not only that, Wayne actually helps Martin descend (lowered off "John Ford Point" in Monument Valley) to the valley floor where the Indians are encamped.

Thus, even before the final scenes of attack, Wayne's character has been influenced by Marty, by a man he has come to respect despite his Indian blood. This is already a partial redemption. Not that his blood lust for Scar has weakened. It is true that Wayne does not now resent, as he surely would have before, the fact that Marty kills Scar. But Wayne goes into the tent after Scar's body and scalps it. When he comes out, his face has a post-orgasmic blurriness to it. We must be kept in suspense. Does that expression mean that his blood lust is up, ravening for more, or that the savagery has been sated? We do not learn this until Wayne lifts Debbie up over his head—the first thing he had done after his wary entry into her house in the opening sequence—and then cradles her: "Let's go home."

When Wayne carries Debbie up to the door of her new home (with his brother's neighbors, the Jorgensens), he is seen, again, framed in it. But this time he does not enter, as before, when Debbie was a child. Even then he was excluded from the inner door. Shut out, brooding on the porch. This time he does not linger at all. The door closes on him after he makes a gesture in homage to Harry Carey, then turns away.

People point out that this is "unrealistic." Would he not be welcomed in, thanked, asked for his story? Tag Gallagher worries the question in detail, in an unconscious parody of literal-mindedness:

> Why did Ethan not enter? Many explanations are plausible, from ones traditional to the western (distant horizons beckon; new duties call; the task is done; the hero belongs to the wilderness), to ones particular to *The Searchers* (Ethan is doomed to wander; happiness is for the simple; his new moral awareness excludes him from the older order). And there is the special explanation (as noted earlier) that the arm gesture Ethan makes was the signal gesture of Harry Carey, who often walked away at the end of pictures, and who greatly influenced Ford and Wayne— and, in fact, the house he walks away from here is Carey's

widow's (Olive Carey, playing Mrs. Jorgensen). Wayne's homage acknowledges debts and links Ethan to past Fordian heroes.

But, on the other hand, why—beyond the requirements of a happy ending—should Ethan *not* be left alone? Is he to live with fourteen-year-old Debbie? Surely she is better off with the Jorgensens. Is he to live with the Jorgensens? They are relative strangers. No, as in our world, people live separately, not in utopian communities. Ethan walks away for the most commonplace of reasons; that his walking away *seems* extraordinarily meaningful, that his arm gesture seems an admission of impotence, is perhaps because, in a moment, the hero disappears and only a lonely, aging man is left.[8]

This is a wonderful mishmash, replete with equally plausible suggestions. Wayne rides off at the end like Shane. He cannot live in a utopian society (is that what the Jorgensen home is?). He has "new duties." Or he is too old for new duties. At any rate, his reasons are "commonplace," not heroic. The Harry Carey gesture shows impotence (symbolic castration). That way lies muddledness. Gallagher's first premise is wrong—that narrative "plausibilities" are to be sought. The filming tells us we are in the realm of symbol.

The symmetry of the opening and ending is the most important element for understanding Wayne's place at the end. In the beginning, the black iris opened out as the camera tracked forward, revealing the world beyond the door's pitch-black outline. In the end, the camera tracks back, irising down to the door as a bright hole in a wide black border. As the other characters enter, they are turned to black silhouettes, absorbed into the darkness all around us. Wayne is left, stranded in his patch of color. He turns and walks off—not with his normal purposeful stride, but with stiff aimlessness, more like his stagger as he left Maureen O'Hara's tent in *Rio Grande*. He is not off to "new tasks." But is he just a commonplace "aging man"?

I do not know where Gallagher got the idea that Harry Carey often walked away at the end of his early John Ford pictures. He does not in the only two that are known to have survived. But he *did* walk away in an early Biograph (pre-Ford) film called *Olaf, an Atom* (1913), the story of a man who becomes a disheartened bum when his wife dies.[9] He overhears villains plotting to take away a young couple's property. He saves the husband, restores

him to the wife, and turns away from the happy home he wi
never have. It seems probable to me that Carey, working on
scripts with Ford, having to turn them out rapidly, used some
variant of this situation in a lost Western from their collaboration. But Ford takes his contrivance for pathos and elevates it to
tragedy. Wayne has been the carrier of his own demons too long
to relapse into the normal life of other humans. He may relent
on the matter of killing Debbie; but that does not erase an entire
life history that led to the monomania of his last seven years.
Achilles' fury could only be allayed by an acceptance of his death.
That, ultimately, is why Ethan cannot regain the society he tran-
scended by a blighting of all its softer elements. Aristotle said
that a man without a polis is either a god or beast, above or
below the compromised and accommodating world of interde-
pendent creatures. Ethan is both above and below that plane,
divine and bestial in the scale and ferocity of his willpower. His
end is not commonplace, but heroic; not patriotic but tragic. He
must be left outside. Achilles must die.

There is, in the very irising that frames the tale, a sense that
Wayne wanders in from an uncanny world but goes back to it.
Martha sensed his coming as a point of spiritual crisis. At the
end, as the other figures become silhouettes in the focused little
picture and are swallowed into a black box, we can sense the
camera eating its own objects. They step through the lens and
are put to rest for the story devices they are. The quick unreal
shutting of the door is like the closing of a camera lens. Wayne
is left outside, not taken off as an image inside the box. In his
distinct, brighter, more intense world, he is a suffering god we
can watch go by, without power to affect or assuage or save him.
He is the West, "our" West. The West that is no longer ours.

□ 21 □
FORD-WAYNE, INC.

AFTER FORD'S MASTERPIECES with Wayne—*The Quiet Man* and *The Searchers*—he made four more films with him, but only one was up to the standards of what went before: *The Man Who Shot Liberty Valance* (1962).

In the interval between *The Searchers* and *The Man Who Shot Liberty Valance,* his Wayne movies were *The Wings of Eagles* (1957) and *The Horse Soldiers* (1959). The former should have been a success. It was a project Ford had yearned to make for a long time, like *The Quiet Man.* It had the two stars of *The Quiet Man,* Wayne and O'Hara. It told the story of Ford's friend and hero, Frank "Spig" Wead, the naval flyer who was crippled by an accident in his home, became a screenwriter, and went back into the Navy in World War II as the promoter of "jeep" carriers—converted ships with landing decks, to fill the gap before real carriers could be built in sufficient numbers for the Pacific war. This mobilization of small craft in an emergency, before the large vessels showed up, resembles the use of patrol boats as offensive weapons in *They Were Expendable,* for which Wead wrote the screenplay.

Ford got away with "casting them old" when he put Wayne and O'Hara in *The Quiet Man.* But they needed to be even younger in *Wings,* made five years later, and they look older. Since *Wings* picks up Wead's story when he is at Annapolis, the stars have to play college kids in the first scenes, and their rushes of energy and hilarity are forced. Wayne is absurd as a fifty-year-old midshipman. Ford tries to cover this weakness in a riot of slapstick comedy of the sort he was not good at. We even get pie-throwing of the Mack Sennett variety. Presumably, all these hijinks are meant to contribute to the pathos when Wayne is paralyzed with a broken back, left alone after a split with his wife. O'Hara, stranded in her husband's active Navy days, is supposed to have become an alcoholic, but Ford cannot convincingly degrade his beautiful heroine. Ford's story is robbed of its bite when he hints at a squalor he does not have the nerve to display.

The role of the brave and devoted wife, who sees her husband through his time of physical trial, devolves upon Dan Dailey, playing a frisky subaltern who supports his superior with dreary cheerfulness, wearing down Wayne's despair and the audience's patience. Even the priceless vignette of Ward Bond as Ford buying Wead's scripts is not enough to save the story. The tearful farewell Wead bids to his ship is an echo of the sorrow over the demise of PT boats in *They Were Expendable*. In all his Navy films (except *Mister Roberts*, which was taken away from him when he loaded it up with slapstick touches), there is a reverential air toward the service that inhibits Ford. His sentimentality needs touches of skepticism, or hints of a harsher reality, for it to work.

The Horse Soldiers, made two years later (1959), is a better film, blessed with William Clothier's gorgeous photography; but it is a rambling combination of elements tied together by a strained grievance on Wayne's part, meant to give a touch of Ethan Edwards to Wayne's valor in conducting a suicidal Union cavalry mission deep into Southern territory. Wayne nags at the surgeon foisted on him (William Holden) because he feels that a surgeon killed his wife. An improbable love story with a Southern belle (poorly played by Constance Towers) does just as little to shape the story as does this phobia about doctors.

By this point, Ford was beginning to lose his concentration, and it showed in his work. Slipping in his own domain, he tried to insert himself into Wayne's *Alamo* project (1960), and his pride took a terrible blow when none of his footage was used. Ford needed Wayne, though, as he had learned when he made *Wagon Master* without him in 1950. That picture earned about a third of the money that its immediate predecessor and successor did —not because it was inferior to them but because they starred Wayne and *Wagon Master* did not. Ford had to face a dependency of the sort that troubled Fred Astaire in the late thirties: though he wanted to make musicals without Ginger Rogers, his take at the box office fell off precipitously whenever he did.

Thus, in the sixties, Ford had to use Wayne, two years after *The Alamo*, when he made another Western, *The Man Who Shot Liberty Valance*. But he gave him an astonishingly small role, compared with Jimmy Stewart's in the same film. At that time, Wayne was number four in box-office popularity, and Jimmy Stewart was not even in the top ten. Wayne's presence at the beginning and end of the film is an invisible one—he is inside a coffin that we never look into. In the major sequence of the film —a flashback narrated by Stewart, and seen through his eyes— Wayne loses the girl, despairs, and is saved from a drunken moment of self-destruction by his black sidekick (Woody Strode) while Stewart goes on to a brilliant political career, in Washington and England.

Wayne would not, at that stage of his career, have taken such a subordinate role for anyone but Ford, toward whom he was still dutifully loyal; but Ford, getting Wayne back on *his* set for the first time since *The Alamo*, showed no gratitude for this contribution. He tried to cancel the key speech where Wayne's character shows his nobility, renouncing the girl and urging Stewart to take credit for killing Valance. Only Stewart's intervention made Ford relent—though the speech is so important that Ford would probably have restored it after he had tortured Wayne over the matter.[1]

Ford also took the opportunity to renew his sardonic references to Wayne's lack of military service, contrasting his record with that of his new star, Woody Strode, who had played a military hero in *Sergeant Rutledge,* but had also been a real serviceman in World War II. Ford made the contrast between Wayne's short period on the USC bench and Strode's career as a star end at UCLA. The riding of Wayne rubbed his nerves so raw that he started a fight with Strode—which Ford had to end with hasty pleas to Strode not to hurt the older, weaker man because "We need him."[2]

Given all this tension on the set, it is surprising that *Valance* turned out so well. It is Ford's last great Western, and his last great film with Wayne. It is not a characteristic Ford Western. Filmed in the studio, not on one of Ford's favorite Western locations, it has a claustrophobic air, a sour and wistful note appropriate to Ford's declining fortunes. Part of this may come from the fact that the cynical James Warner Bellah worked on the script, though he did not supply the story—that came from Dorothy M. Johnson, who wrote other short tales made into movies (like *A Man Called Horse*).

In Johnson's tale, the Jimmy Stewart character ("Rance") is meaner and more selfish than in the film. An aristocrat who lost his money, he finds a masochistic delight in the humiliation he undergoes at the hands of a bullying gunman (Liberty Valance), upon whom he is planning his own revenge. This seems to be setting up a "little guy surprises bully" plot, as in the Walsh original for *The Quiet Man*. But then Johnson brings in a Cyrano character—the Wayne role in the movie.

This man helps Rance get his revenge, since the heroine has fallen in love with Rance, and the Cyrano wants only her happiness. To ensure her a better life, the Cyrano forces Rance into a political career he does not want. Only in time does Rance recognize his debt to the Cyrano and return to the West for his quiet funeral. Rance never reveals, in the story, what the Cyrano has done for him; and the heroine, oblivious to the sacrifice made for her, scatters prickly-pear blossoms on his casket out of mere pity.

From this material Bellah and Willis Goldbeck fashioned a far more complex screenplay. They change Stewart's character from a cynical and morose man to an idealist, a lawyer who comes west to spread civilization, to teach people about the Declaration of Independence. The screenwriters were drawing on Stewart's original Western image. Though he made a series of Anthony Mann Westerns as a dark and angry figure, he was still remembered as Thomas Jefferson Destry in *Destry Rides Again* (1939), a man who comes to town without a gun to tame lawlessness with sweet reason. In *Destry,* the Stewart figure gives up his idealistic opposition to the gun when his best friend is shot; but Marlene Dietrich saves him from himself by marching the town's women between the two bands of armed men, forcing pacifism back upon the pacifist. After Dietrich dies in this effort, we see Stewart as the unarmed sheriff peacefully strolling through his tamed village.

There are many visual links between Stewart's "Rance" in *Valance* and his part in *Destry*. The latter appeared in town carrying a lady's parasol and canary cage. He was mocked in the saloon by the town bully (Brian Donlevy) and was submitted to insult. In *Valance,* Stewart wears an apron in the saloon-restaurant and is mocked by Valance (Lee Marvin) as if he were a serving wench. His teaching in the classroom is seen as a feminine role, and Wayne spatters him by shooting a can of paint that is near him—just as Dietrich threw bottles at Stewart in *Destry*.

When Rance tries to go up against Valance in a gunfight, Tom (Wayne) saves him from himself, as Dietrich had saved Destry. Dietrich, who had been collaborating with the gangsters running the town, recognizes that her world is doomed and helps bring it down upon herself, making way for Destry's new reign of law. Wayne shoots Valance from an alley while Rance thinks he killed him in a fair fight. Wayne accepts the end of his gunfighter's era by violating his own code, to make way for a different society.

Hallie, the heroine in *Valance* (Vera Miles, the young lover "Laurie" in *The Searchers*), chooses the new order as well. She loves the danger and romance of Wayne, but feels that Stewart needs her more. She is maternal toward him and his civilization, which promises to replace death and the gun with law and life. But she has learned from Rance what Tom did for her, and the cactus rose she places on Tom's coffin shows that he was her deepest love. Stewart knows and accepts that, as he tells reporters the truth that is kept hidden in the Johnson short story.

It turns out that the heroine was wrong about Tom's not needing her. After his drunken suicide attempt (thwarted by his black helper, Strode), Tom goes into a decline that makes him die obscure and unrespected—the undertaker tries to steal his boots, to compensate for the pauper's burial he is conducting.

Peter Bogdanovich and others have linked the end of Valance with the final scenes of *Fort Apache*. An editor refuses to publish Stewart's confession that he is not really the man who shot Liberty Valance. He says, "When the legend becomes fact, print the legend." Critics compare that to Wayne's endorsement of the Custer myth in Fonda's Colonel Thursday ("Correct in every detail"). But the lie about Thursday was an endorsement of values the preceding story has discredited. It was an artistic betrayal.

The legend that Stewart killed Valance was an expression of a deeper truth. Destry tamed his town without a gun, though Dietrich had to help him do it. Rance really does bring an end to the reign of Valance, though he must depend on the intervention of Wayne. He comes preaching that those who live by the gun will perish by the gun, and by convincing Hallie, he makes

Wayne recognize the truth of that. After killing Valance, Wayne stopped wearing a gun (we are told by the sheriff at his funeral).

The gunman's demise is suggested by Wayne's own superannuated appearance in the film. Ford takes less care to pose his star, overweight and in declining health, in flattering ways. Some shots seem designed to emphasize his gut (a part of Ford's mean attitude toward Wayne). Ford made Wayne do without a double, who would have been more nimble in some scenes.[3]

Some have discovered an almost nihilistic darkness in this tale. Robert Ray, in a famous discussion of the film, says that the two versions of the shoot-out—a first one in which we do not see Wayne shoot from ambush, a second one in which we do—prove that Ford is destroying the assumption of the camera's reliability. This reading of the film neglects the fact that we see the whole flashback as it was experienced by the narrator, Rance. *He* did not see Wayne's intervention, so *we* do not. This accords with Ford's flashback technique in *The Quiet Man* and *The Searchers*, with his use of the subjective camera, part of his repertory of techniques from the days when we saw a scene blurred through Harry Carey's tears.

There is a deliberate artificiality in the whole flashback sequence. The studio set is undisguisedly fake. The lighting is darker than in the frame sequences. The snarls of Valance, the condescension of Wayne, the heroine's motherly solicitude, all are seen from Stewart's vantage point. He has set up this contrast by his expansive politician's way of dominating the conversation in the opening episode before the flashback. We see into Stewart's soul, into the cost *he* paid for success, the loss of Hallie's love to a dream she had to surrender but still cherishes. There is a delicacy here of unstated disappointments in the life of Hallie and Rance that is like the unstated emotions in the Edwards family as *The Searchers* opens.

The town of "Shinbone" has flourished since Rance brought law to it.[4] The countryside is fertile. But Hallie, so motherly toward Rance, has no children. His marriage is one that pays the cost of social change. No progress is made without costs, emotional as well as physical. Hallie's contained passion becomes a dead memory, symbolized in the cactus rose. Stewart has promised to show her real roses in the East, but that did not replace her first wilderness passion. Rance realizes that and must live with it, as we learn when he asks her who put the cactus rose plant on Tom's coffin, knowing that she did.

We all live with lies, with lost passions, friends left behind, potential selves that lie buried in what we become. Our own life is a burial place for our youth. The sad wisdom of going on, of making do—the quiet failures contained in any worldly success —all those things breathe through this wistful elegy.

Ford's next and last film with Wayne (with Lee Marvin again on hand) was *Donovan's Reef* (1963)—a movie that denies all the realities that *Valance* faced. It is Ford performing as a second-rate Hawks, making his Wayne a raucous boozer. It was not a suitable finale to the Ford-Wayne partnership.

But what a partnership it had been—thirteen films together, eight of them in the front rank of what either man had done. Only D. W. Griffith's many works with Lillian Gish can surpass it. (I exclude, of course, work by men like Chaplin and Keaton, who were *both* director and actor.) Hawks made five films with Cary Grant, four of them first-rate. Capra made two great films with Jimmy Stewart, and two with Gary Cooper. Hitchcock made four with Cary Grant. Von Sternberg's work with Dietrich (seven films) was repetitive but impressive. Cukor's eight films with Katharine Hepburn and Scorsese's seven with Robert De Niro set high standards. But despite these other combinations, the Ford-Wayne one remains stunning. Each drew on the best in the other. Only once, in *Red River,* was Wayne as good with another director as he proved in his best collaborations with Ford.

To put it in crass quantitative terms, over half of Ford's best work was done with Wayne.

WITH WAYNE:	WITHOUT WAYNE:
Stagecoach (1939)	*The Iron Horse* (1924)
The Long Voyage Home (1940)	*Black Watch* (1929)
Fort Apache (1948)	*The Informer* (1935)
Three Godfathers (1948)	*Young Mr. Lincoln* (1939)
She Wore a Yellow Ribbon (1949)	*The Grapes of Wrath* (1940)
Rio Grande (1950)	*How Green Was My Valley* (1941)
The Quiet Man (1952)	*My Darling Clementine* (1946)
The Searchers (1956)	*Wagon Master* (1950)
The Man Who Shot Liberty Valance (1962)	

Put another way: the *only* great films Ford made from 1950 on were his four made with Wayne. Wayne was carrying Ford by the end, where Ford had carried Wayne earlier on. If we look at Wayne's best films we see a match for the Ford list—over half of the top movies on Wayne's list of films were made with Ford.

WITH FORD:

Stagecoach (1939)
The Long Voyage Home (1940)
Fort Apache (1948)
Three Godfathers (1948)
She Wore a Yellow Ribbon (1949)
Rio Grande (1950)
The Quiet Man (1952)
The Searchers (1956)
The Man Who Shot Liberty Valance (1962)

WITHOUT FORD:

The Big Trail (1930)
The Shepherd of the Hills (1941)
Red River (1948)
True Grit (1969)
Big Jake (1971)
Rooster Cogburn (1975)
The Shootist (1976)

Another pattern is apparent. Over half the good movies Wayne made without Ford were made after Ford's effective demise, when, as we shall see, Wayne had entered a new stage of his legend (as eccentric survivor). At his peak, he was best when he made films for Ford. Why was this?

The Western form itself, presenting different styles of masculinity, makes it possible for a director to work with one type, playing variations on it. This is most obvious in B Westerns with a continuing hero—e.g., Bradbury's Monogram series with Wayne. At a higher level, there is the series of Westerns Anthony Mann made with Jimmy Stewart (five of them), or Budd Boetticher made with Randolph Scott (seven), or Sergio Leone with Clint Eastwood (three). These films used one aspect of the star involved in them—in Stewart's case, not his strongest one. Stewart was best as the naive idealist *(Philadelphia Story, Mr. Smith Goes to Washington)*, the wry idealist *(Destry Rides Again, Harvey)*, or the disappointed idealist *(It's a Wonderful Life, Vertigo)*. As a Western hero, he did not carry the menace of casual power —he was too spindly for that. The camera bulked him out, somewhat, though in person he looked like a breath would blow him over. Asked to wear a bathing suit with Katharine Hepburn in *The Philadelphia Story*, he refused to bare limbs thinner than hers, saying it would end his career. What Mann did with Stewart was drive a neurotic character toward a blowup, fueling his anger with tantrum energies. Randolph Scott's woodenness was used by Boetticher to express a stoic indifference to threat, and Leone turned Eastwood's taciturnity into misanthropy bordering on nihilism.

As opposed to these characters, Wayne was a warmer, more humane hero, without losing his air of unyielding control. Contrary to the general impression, he was not typecast in the Ford movies. Even in the tales most similar by reason of plot and setting, the cavalry stories, he was very different—down to the carriage of his body—as the subordinate chafing under a martinet superior *(Fort Apache)*, the sentimental old officer retiring from the service *(She Wore a Yellow Ribbon)*, and the careerist risking an illegal raid *(Rio Grande)*.

Of course the secret of great movies does not lie in just one artist. Wayne had the advantage, in his critical work with Ford, of the very sensitive writer, Frank Nugent, who saw how to bring nuance to the one-dimensional heroes contained in James Warner Bellah's stories, or in Maurice Walsh's "The Quiet Man." But when all such allowances are made, the greatest credit for Wayne's fine movies of the 1940s and 1950s must go to Ford, who resisted for some time the role of Western director.

He is the record-holding director, as far as Oscars go—six of them (four for commercial features, two for government-sponsored war films). None of these was awarded him for a Western. His commercial Oscars were for *The Informer, How Green Was My Valley, The Grapes of Wrath,* and *The Quiet Man.* Good as the first three were (and the fourth is a "disguised" Western), none quite equals *The Searchers,* the cavalry films, or *The Man Who Shot Liberty Valance.*

Ford had a great feeling for social dislocation, and that is what the Western film can deal with on many levels—communities in process of formation, threatened from without and within, dissolved by waves of new settlement, new technologies, new social articulations. The temporary but intense ties established at a cavalry outpost, the relations with previously displaced communities of Indians (in *The Searchers*), the coexistence of different historical eras in people who are not only contemporaries but intimates *(Liberty Valance)*—these bring out a pathos in Ford that was elsewhere weakened by a sentiment outrunning its object (as in the mooning over PT boats for *They*

Were Expendable or over "jeep" carriers in *The Wings of Eagles*). The Western was distanced enough from Ford, yet suffused enough with emotion, for him to succeed as he did not in his Navy films. The large drives of history, the costs paid by individuals, the frontier that erases itself in the very process of extending itself—those were his finest materials. He found in Wayne the combination of a man unconquerable yet paradoxically vulnerable—the powerful but moist-eyed Nathan Brittles, the rampaging yet ravaged Ethan Edwards, the fighting but pacifistic Sean Thornton, the conqueror of Liberty Valance who consumes himself. The range of characters has been unjustly dismissed, out of contempt for the Western or Wayne or both. But the real Ahab of our films is not the pallid Gregory Peck of John Huston's *Moby Dick*. It is, as rock critic Greil Marcus noted, Wayne's Ethan Edwards. In *The Searchers*, says Marcus, "Wayne changes from a man with whom we are comfortable into a walking Judgment Day ready to destroy the world to save it from itself."[5]

□ 22 □
RIO THIS AND RIO THAT

WHEN HOWARD HAWKS made his second film with Wayne, *Rio Bravo* (1959), it had been thirteen years since his first one, *Red River*. That earlier film, with its troubled release history, was Hawks's first effort at postwar independent production. He returned to independent production in 1955 to make the ambitious epic, *Land of the Pharaohs*, which was a bomb. He sought out Wayne, at the peak of the actor's commercial appeal, to make *Rio Bravo*, whose success made him rely on Wayne for four of his last six pictures—the only four that were box-office hits. Hawks in his artistic decline, like Ford, needed Wayne.

To a certain extent, Hawks tried to repeat the formula of *Red River* in *Rio Bravo*. As before, Wayne is at odds with his own followers (a town that will not enforce its laws against a powerful outlaw's gang). His grumpy sidekick is, once again, Walter Brennan (sinking further into self-parody as his gums recede behind a senescent grin). A pretty-boy gunman is on hand to help Wayne —instead of Montgomery Clift, we get Ricky Nelson, the pouty offspring of a chirpy TV team, Ozzie and Harriet. But Nelson is more Cherry Valance, in this plot, than Matthew Garth. And Hawks departs from the shape of *Red River* in important ways. Though he keeps to the two-generation plot he invented for Wayne, he moves the love interest back again from the younger to the older generation. It is not Ricky Nelson who wins the heroine. Angie Dickinson, early in her career, is smitten by Wayne, despite the quarter-of-a-century difference in their ages.

Hawks was still obsessively trying to turn pretty young things into stars, on the model of his one great discovery, Lauren Bacall. Late Hawks movies provide a "you-saw-her-here-first" parade of slender models and provocatively posed ingenues—Angie Dickinson in dance-hall tights, Elsa Martinelli and Michele Girardon in safari shorts, Michele Carey in cowgirl chic, Jennifer O'Neill undressed while unconscious, Sherry Lansing (before her producing days) in low-cut Mexican blouse.

Another great difference from *Red River* is that Wayne, in *Rio Bravo*, has no driving mission, as Tom Dunson had his cattle empire to build with fanatical determination. Wayne in *Rio Bravo* is a lawman who will not be frightened away from his post. He treats that post as just a job, not a crusade. Hawks in later interviews tried to give his *Rio Bravo* a political heft no one would suspect without his ex post facto gloss on the matter. He claimed that he and Wayne hated the "leftist" message of Fred Zinnemann's *High Noon*, a movie where a political message *was* suspected by some of its original audience.[1]

Gary Cooper, in *High Noon*, played a dedicated lawman. He will not run away from the outlaw who, just released from prison, has sworn to kill him. When Cooper calls for assistance from his town, the citizens are too frightened to stand up with him, Cooper must do the job all alone—except for his Quaker fiancée who violates her own principles to shoot an ambusher about to bring the sheriff down. Since the script was written by Carl Foreman, a leftist on the verge of being blacklisted, and McCarthyism was on everybody's mind in 1952, the cowering of the city under the threats of a bully was taken as a reference to McCarthy's "reign of terror." Wayne did not oppose (or, perhaps, get) that message. What he did not like was the disgusted way Cooper takes his badge off at the end and drops it in the street. The picture was intended to say that no office can be held without popular support—a profoundly democratic position. But Wayne misremembered the scene, saying that Cooper ground the star into the dirt with his heel. Wayne took this as a sign of disrespect for the law itself.[2] That is why he boasted, giving himself too much credit, that he drove Foreman out of the country. (Cooper, himself a right-wing supporter of the Alliance, was an unlikely person to indulge in left-wing gestures.)

Actually, the cowering populace is a regular device of the Western. Often, when a sheriff is too timorous to face up to a gang, the town calls in a hired gun to do its dirty work. Then the problem is: how to get rid of the mercenary. What makes *High Noon* different is that the sheriff, though frightened, does stay on and handle his problem. The moral dilemma that is expressly treated in *High Noon* is not the choice forced on the citizen, but that forced on the sheriff and his fiancée: Should he yield to her pleas for nonviolence? Should she stay with him if he does not yield? That, too, is a common motif of Westerns, ever since *The Virginian* of Owen Wister: how should the lone frontiersman accept the dubious blessings of progressive civilization. Wayne's *Angel and the Badman* (1947) had used that old moral dilemma, with Wayne taking the "leftist" nonviolent course, giving up his guns. (Only a bounty hunter, played by Harry Carey, protects Wayne from the consequences of his own pacificism.)

Commercial formulae were more important than ideology to screenwriters in the fifties. And that applied to "left-wing" writers as well as to others, as Murray Kempton has argued. *High Noon* was a straight remake of Cooper's identity-establishing Western, *The Virginian*—which was based on Wister's right-wing defense of the vigilantism of Johnson County, Wyoming. In *The Virginian*, the bad man challenges the hero to a duel on his wedding day. There is a countdown for the hero's decision ("by sundown"), and the heroine says she will not marry the hero if he stays to fight. But Cooper in both movies tells his bride that there are some things a man has got to do. The later dialogue echoes the earlier. In *The Virginian*, Cooper says: "I've got to stay. . . . You think I want to do this?" In *High Noon*: "I've got to stay. . . . You think I want this?"

By drawing on *The Virginian*, Foreman returned to a prime source of Western myth. Wister's novel, dedicated to his friend Theodore Roosevelt, made the West a crucible for separating "real men" from weaklings.

High Noon impressed critics who knew little about Westerns and did not recognize how its hoary themes were simply given stylish restatement. They even called this rearrangement of stereotypes an "anti-Western." These are the same kinds of critics who thought the truly original *Stagecoach* a "typical" Western. In any event, *High Noon*'s muddled message hardly calls for a search-and-destroy countermovie of the sort Hawks claimed he made in 1959. If the earlier movie were capable of doing political harm, that was presumably accomplished before Hawks made his "answer" seven years later.

Besides, what in *Rio Bravo* "refutes" *High Noon*? It is true that Wayne, in *Rio Bravo*, turns away help rather than begging for it—the townspeople seem too frightened to be effective, and Ricky Nelson, as the free-lance gunman, is not trustworthy enough. Since Nelson turned down a first request for help, Wayne says "You had your chance" when the boy volunteers later on.

Nonetheless, Nelson *does* rescue Wayne and join his little fortified band in the town's besieged jailhouse. If the movie were a counterexample to *High Noon*, Wayne should voluntarily do what Cooper is forced to do—stand up alone for the town against the town. Actually, Wayne is helped not only by Nelson but by his "sidekick" Walter Brennan, and by an old pal now become a drunk, a man rousable enough from degradation to redeem himself in the showdown (Dean Martin). This is hardly a case of one man showing a whole town how to act, as it should have been in order to "correct" the message of *High Noon*. In fact, the town *does* rally to Wayne in the end, making him accept the help he spurned.

Why did Hawks claim to be preaching Wayne's right-wing message in *Rio Bravo*? He was no reactionary, and no ideologue of any stripe. His politics, insofar as his movies had any, was a farcical anarchism. That is why he did his best work in screwball comedy—pioneering the form in *Twentieth Century* (1934) and giving it two of its canonical expressions in *Bringing Up Baby* (1938) and *His Girl Friday* (1940). He was still trying to flog life out of the genre's corpse in 1952 (*Monkey Business*, an embarrassing use of the long-in-the-tooth Ginger Rogers and retro-infantile Cary Grant) and 1953 *(Gentlemen Prefer Blondes)*.[3]

Despite a labored last "screwball" effort in 1964 *(Man's Favorite Sport)*, Hawks clearly needed a new formula to carry him —which he found in the schema of his last Wayne films. This was the formula, already tired when he took it up, of the "caper" movie, in which an improbable band uses its combined skills to overcome its obvious flaws, pulling off a crime turned by light comedy touches into a "caper." That is clearly the formula of *Rio Lobo* (1970) where Wayne goes after the gold that was stolen from Union troops during the war. Along the way, he picks up allies for his effort—an old coot (Jack Elam), a young pretty boy (Chris Mitchum), and a love interest (Jennifer O'Neill). The "caper" need not be a crime. It can be any feat that a disparate little band pulls off against long odds. That is the agenda of all the later Hawks films with Wayne. In *Hatari!* (1962) the task is to capture a live rhinoceros for a zoo. In *El Dorado* (1967), to prevent a scheme for monopolizing water rights. In *Rio Bravo*, to get a dangerous prisoner to trial.

The tone is what marks these as caper movies—the high-spirited cooperation in the small band. The light note takes away any grand purpose. While bad men and bystanders get killed, the happy little band survives. Hawks said that Ford was better at Westerns than he was, but that he (Hawks) was better at comedy. It is certainly true that Hawks's greatest work was in comedy. He was not normally up to epic themes or deep feeling—the one great exception being *Red River*. Even Hawks's two Bogart-Bacall films succeed because of their tongue-in-cheek quality. That is the great point of contrast between Hawks's high-spirited Marlowe in *The Big Sleep* and Huston's more cynical Sam Spade in *The Maltese Falcon*. Also, in Hawks, as befits comedy, Marlowe gets to "keep the girl."

For the late Wayne films, Hawks assembled roughly the same crew to bring off its caper in each movie. The sameness shows in the fact that the young pretty boy is usually given a geographical name (something normally reserved for women in Westerns)—Colorado (Ricky Nelson) in *Rio Bravo*, Mississippi (young James Caan) in *El Dorado*, Tuscarora (Chris Mitchum) in *Rio Lobo*. In *Hatari!* the young pretty boy is a German (Hardy Kruger), who can hardly be given a name from the American landscape. The place-name reverts, therefore, to the heroine, "Dallas" (Elsa Martinelli).[4]

Dean Martin's drunk sheriff was so well received in *Rio Bravo* that Hawks gave the same boozy routine to Robert Mitchum in *El Dorado*. In *Rio Lobo* Wayne is joined by a reforming Confederate sympathizer rather than a reforming drunk, and in *Hatari!* by a wounded American Indian who has somehow strayed into Africa (Bruce Cabot).

The old-coot slot is a stable one in the Hawks gangs. Arthur Hunnicutt and Jack Elam take over from Walter Brennan. In *Hatari!*, Red Buttons offers a comic variant—a young coot. Like Brennan in *Rio Bravo*, Buttons plays with explosives that facilitate the caper—Brennan with dynamite sticks that Wayne ignites in air with infallibly placed bullets, Buttons with a rocket that propels a net over monkeys perched in a tree.

An ugly note in the series is the way the woman who joins the gang must be initiated into the male company by a ritual humiliation—Angie Dickinson curtly rebuffed by Wayne and reduced to drunken babbling; Elsa Martinelli bounced around like a rubber ball in the back of the rhino-hunting truck and painted with dark stain for a farcical African "initiation"; Michele Carey wrestled down into a pile of hay (like Jane Russell in *The Outlaw*); Jennifer O'Neill stripped by men after she faints, and teased with tales of sleeping on skulls. They submit to this as the inevitable price to be paid for joining "the boys."

Some defenders of late Hawks say his films are "spoofs" of the normal Westerns—as if he were making *Destry Rides Again* or *Blazing Saddles*. This hardly fits with Hawks's own claim to be seriously countering *High Noon*. His films are not incoherent because he is taking apart some sacred form. A good test of this is *Hatari!*, a safari tale that gave him a perfect opportunity to mock the soap-opera plots of such safari tales as *Trader Horn* (1931), *Red Dust* (1932), or *Mogambo* (1953). Ford's *Mogambo* offered a large target, with its attempt to use Gable again in his *Red Dust* role two decades after the earlier film. But Hawks does not focus on weak aspects of the genre. He accepts them, giving us "cute" animal scenes, and male-female "hunting" to go with the animal quest. In *Hatari!*, baby elephants are made to "dance" by moving to Henry Mancini's calliope tunes. What is *that* a spoof of—*Fantasia*? The point of *Hatari!* insofar as it has one—amidst its vaudeville turns for Red Buttons, its cute monkeys, its pachyderm Fred Astaires—is the ancient and overworked one: the oblivious Great White Hunter is stalked by a spoiled little white girl.

Critics love to oppose popular verdicts and find unsuspected depths in unlikely movies. But the tendency is carried to perverse lengths when a Hawks expert like Robin Wood prefers *Rio Bravo* to *Red River*.[5] It is true that *Red River* is not "a Hawks movie" in any typical sense. *Rio Bravo* is closer to the authentic Hawks masterpieces—*Twentieth Century, Bringing Up Baby, His Girl Friday*. Hawks was not good at epic solemnity, as he proved with crashing finality when he made *Land of the Pharaohs*. In fact, *Red River* is a fluke, as I pointed out in Chapter 11. Hawks would have made a light Western, with layer on layer of double entendre, if he had completed *The Outlaw*. In trying to repeat that project in *Red River*, he stumbled on an aspect of the story that worked better, and reshaped it around Wayne's indomitability. A bit awed himself at what he had uncovered, Hawks wiped the smirk off his own face for once. But he never repeated the accomplishment. *Red River* is the great exception to his other important works.

The Wayne Hawks took up in 1959 was no longer the man

who, as he put it, "moved like a cat." Now Wayne was an institution, and Hawks used him in the most crass way, giving him a nubile young girl to humiliate, some hokey colleagues to shape up, and some snarly villains to be punched into submission or blown away. It was a formula good enough to bring in the trade, and other directors, who had no better ideas how to use Wayne in these years, repeated it.

Even Ford made a pseudo-Hawks film when he cast Wayne in the substanceless *Donovan's Reef*. Here is the pretty newcomer (Elizabeth Allen) to be humiliated—dumped in the water wearing her Bostonian business clothes, dragged from a jeep into the mud, finally spanked by Wayne as her initiation fee into a marriage where "I'll wear the pants." Here is the drunken pal to brawl and cooperate with—Lee Marvin confounding life and art in his patented lush of that era. Here is a caper for improbable associates to pull off—to deceive the Boston lady into thinking that the "half-breed" children on the island are Wayne's. If one must have secondhand Hawks, it is a shame to be receiving it from Ford.

Yet Wayne's own production company, Batjac, had no fresh ideas of its own. So it too turned out imitation Hawks "capers." In *McLintock!* (1963), made the year after *Donovan's Reef*, Wayne gets to spank Maureen O'Hara rather than Elizabeth Allen, and Patrick Wayne gets to spank Stefanie Powers—a two-generation plot becomes a two-spanking story. In *The War Wagon* (1967), the pretty-boy drunk who handles the explosives is twenty-seven-year-old Robert Walker, Jr. The old coot is a gray-bearded Keenan Wynn. In *The Cowboys* (1972), the improbable gang for pulling off the caper is a bunch of little boys. In *The Train Robbers* (1973), the double-cross common to other "caper" movies finally allows the woman (Ann-Margret) to humiliate the men for a change—she escapes with the loot.

But that was the exception. Most Wayne movies of the period reflected the views of his favorite writer, Jimmy Grant, who said: "All you gotta have in a John Wayne picture is a hoity-toity dame with big tits that Duke can throw over his knee and spank."[6] No wonder Wayne had so few fans among women. Those not repelled by his militarism must recoil from the blatant sexism of the films he made in the sixties and seventies—just the time when modern feminism was making its first important gains.

When he made *Red River*, Hawks created a whole new image

for Wayne—one that others used in creative ways. The unbalanced but commanding Tom Dunson became Sergeant Stryker and Ethan Edwards. The older man presiding over a younger generation's trials and love affairs became the Seventh Cavalry's Nathan Brittles or Kirby Yorke. But *Rio Bravo* and its spawn did not give Wayne a new beginning. It was a dead end—a fact disguised by the fact that it was a *lucrative* artistic failure.

The Hawks (and the pseudo-Hawks) films of the 1960s are as formulaic as Wayne's old Three Mesquiteers series. In those films, he always had "Tucson" and "Lullaby" to ride with him as he met up with a new girl in every episode. In later Hawks, where he rides with his old coot and his pretty boy, a nubile new girl of minimal talent always turns up. The production values are better in the 1960s, the dialogue snappier (and sexier), the villains more plausible (without ranking high on any probability scale). But the ideas are stale. While the sixties were changing American society in drastic ways, Wayne was unchanging—which was, no doubt, part of his appeal to an audience disoriented by change. People like to watch the old tales in a time of social chaos.

Why did Hawks make these sad late movies? Well, as Willie Sutton said, that is where the money was. Why did he try to claim he and Wayne were ideological buddies doing artistic battle with Carl Foreman and Fred Zinnemann? Hawks shared Ford's realization that Wayne was financially rewarding company to keep. Besides, maybe some of his magic would rub off on those trying to capitalize on his legend.

Part Seven

A THIRD COWBOY

Wayne had been a callow young cowboy until 1948, when he became a middle-aged figure of authority. During the 1960s he was in danger of becoming a figure of fun until his last identity emerged—the lone survivor of a past heroic time. The conscious anachronism.

It has been said that Wayne's later roles were a caricature of his earlier performances—as, say, John Barrymore's late type-casting as a faded lover and lush traduced earlier memories. But Wayne's personal idiosyncrasies were not the point of his best final movies. There was a *social* dimension to his aging, a sense that a period in *history* was slipping away, not just one man's natural powers. The anachronism was still impressive, though doomed.

□ 23 □

"I THOUGHT YOU WERE DEAD"

FOR A LONG TIME Wayne finessed the difficulties most aging actors encounter. From *Red River* on, his best roles often featured him as a man older than those he rides with or fights against—still tough, but hardly love's young dream. It looked as if he could play that role forever.

But as he reached his sixties (in the 1960s), he slowed on his feet and slumped in the saddle. After his lung cancer operation in 1964, when a rib and a lung were removed, exercise and dieting became harder for him. He grew paunchy and shorter of breath. He angrily destroyed the film of a photographer who caught him being given oxygen between takes on *The Sons of Katie Elder* (1965).[1] If Wayne could not play the aging but still powerful Western figure, what roles were open to him? His officer in *The Green Berets* was obviously past the raid-leading age.

Earlier experiments meant to break him out of the Western mold were not successful. He was miscast as a German sea captain in *The Sea Chase* (1955). As Genghis Khan in *The Conqueror* (1956), he looked like Warner Oland in his Charlie Chan makeup. Wayne wore a diplomat's high hat and knee breeches in John Huston's *The Barbarian and the Geisha* (1958). For Otto Preminger's naval soap opera, *In Harm's Way* (1965), a kind of floating *Peyton Place*, he had another rebellious son, as if he were a softened Sergeant Stryker.

By the sixties, then, he seemed on a decline that would produce nothing more memorable than his later stabs at being a city detective—a kind of Slightly Soiled Harry—in *McQ* (1974) and *Brannigan* (1975). His hard-core fans, of course, would go to see Wayne in anything—and some of his worst movies actually made good profits ($12 million worldwide for *The Conqueror*). But it seemed that the strong political symbol of the 1950s would fade into dim and not very dignified imitations of himself by the 1970s—until a fresh role in *True Grit* (1969) offered him a different character to play in the only three pictures of the 1970s that gave him new symbolic vitality—*Big Jake, Rooster Cogburn* (a sequel to *True Grit*), and *The Shootist*.

Wayne had leapfrogged the age problem in *Red River* (made in 1946) by playing a man close to his own years. In 1969, with *True Grit*, he faced the problem, playing an unabashedly fat and drunken man in his sixties. This was not a condition forced on him by the novel being adapted for the script. In Charles Portis's story, Rooster Cogburn is only fifty-one, and he lives for twenty-five years after the narrative's central incidents.

The novel, set in Arkansas by a literary celebrant of that region, is a first-person narrative written by a one-armed old maid who represents the narrow Calvinism of the Ozark hills. Brought up to hate the Republicans of Reconstruction, she has lived into the teens of this century. She finds herself divided over the subject of Al Smith, a Democrat but also a Catholic. Old Mattie (for Matilda) Ross cannot even abide fellow Calvinists who waver on the doctrine of Election. But she gives Smith the benefit of the doubt because he is not a Republican—and, after all, his party is led by that good Presbyterian Woodrow Wilson.

The force of the novel lies in the self-revelation of Mattie, whose Victorian language cannot hide her willingness to use dirty instruments (like Al Smith) to get her way. When, in 1878, her father was killed in Fort Smith, on the Oklahoma border, she went after the murderer, who had fled into the federal territories. She offered a special reward to the meanest federal marshal she could find—Reuben ("Rooster") Cogburn. Though she disapproves of Cogburn's drunkenness and irreligion (nothing is said of his ways with women), she wants his merciless bravery in pursuit of bounty. A grudging affection shows through her contained language. When she is bit in the hand by a rattler, Cogburn gets her to a doctor who saves her life (though she loses her arm). By the time she recovers, Cogburn is gone. Later she learns he is part of a Wild West show, and she goes to see him perform in Memphis. But he died several stops before Memphis.

She retrieves his body and buries it in her own family plot. The inscription says

REUBEN COGBURN

1835–1903

A Resolute Officer

of Parker's Court

The love story of this old maid's memories is never betrayed by a false note of sentiment or self-pity.

Since the movie is not narrated by Mattie, the consistent tone of the novel disappears. Her own language is pervasively theological and out of date, even when she is reporting the words of others. In the screenplay, the stilted talk sounds odd in the mouths of uneducated villains—though Cogburn can be presumed to be trying to clean up his language when talking to the little girl. Instead of seeing Cogburn through the eyes of Mattie, we see the spunky girl through the one flaring eye of "Rooster." The best bit of dialogue added to the tale is given to Wayne when he sees how the girl will not give up: "By God, she reminds me of *me.*"

The age of Mattie is a problem. We are deliberately confused about it in the book, where the narrator is looking back from Wilson's presidency to two earlier times—to Hayes's presidency for the principal part of the narrative, and to Theodore Roosevelt's first term for the time when Cogburn died. The erotic feeling of the pubescent younger Mattie is made evident only by its suppression in the narrative, up to the point where the old maid retrieves his body.

In the movie, Mattie develops a crush on the scoundrelly Cogburn, which he cannot reciprocate. Kim Darby was twenty-two when she made the film, and had just delivered her first child. Her little-girl clothes are thick enough, in all the first scenes where our impressions are formed, to hide her womanly form. Though one of the villains leers at her salaciously, and the Texas Ranger "La Beef" says he would have kissed her if she were not so obnoxious, we are to think of her as a female Huck Finn —prepubescent, but barely. Her crush on Cogburn is first displayed by a kind of hero worship, when she strides along behind him in a "manly" way. Only when she tries to arrange for his future burial (the movie's version of the way she returned for his body after a quarter of a century) does she betray her need for this grotesque challenge to all her religious beliefs. (The theological obsessions of Mattie are only hinted at in the film.)

The plot and dialogue of the novel are largely retained in the script. Some things are softened—Mattie does not lose her arm, and Rooster does not go off without saying goodbye. The girl's ordeal in a pit of snakes is less harrowing and long-drawn-out than it was in print. But some details are harsher in the film. The Texas Ranger played by Glen Campbell dies. Rooster himself, as played by Wayne, is made older, fatter, and drunker than in the original. Though he is still a veteran of Quantrill's murderous crew in the Civil War, he did not ride with them as a young boy —he must have been nearly fifty even then.

The unflattering aspects of Wayne's character drew the attention of critics when the movie first appeared. He is not the noble "bad man" of *Three Godfathers*. We see him trying to rob a dead man of his property. He is ready to shoot a man from ambush—a thing he did only as the confession of an historical era's end in *The Man Who Shot Liberty Valance*. It is clear that Rooster regularly shoots men without warning—without "calling them out" as the Ranger says in the film ("in the back," the book says more bluntly).[2] In earlier films, Wayne's drunkenness was presented as the result of disillusionment or deep loss—in *Red River, Wake of the Red Witch, Sands of Iwo Jima,* or *The Man Who Shot Liberty Valance.* Drink does not prevent him from doing his job. But in *True Grit* he drinks just because he is a drunkard, and his binge makes him take the searchers too near the enemy camp—a mistake for which the Ranger pays with his life.

What redeems the rogue, even in censorious Mattie's eyes, is Rooster's comic flamboyance. The girl's fascination is exactly that of Jim Hawkins with the theatrical villainy of Long John Silver. In fact, Wayne's one-eyed Rooster is a version of one-legged Long John, as played by scenery-chewers like Wallace Beery in the 1934 *Treasure Island* or Robert Newton in the 1950 version of Stevenson's tale. Close your eyes and listen to Wayne's deep gargling voice and its cadences—you'll swear it is Wallace Beery's voice, less perhaps because Wayne had Beery's Long John specifically in mind than because Beery had set the type for all such lovable grotesques. The Beery of the "Min and Bill" series of films is the prototype Wayne turned to as the most obvious part of his screen conditioning in the thirties. In that sense, his role was a literal throwback, almost an in-joke, most accessible to Wayne's contemporaries.

Wayne's performance was hardly as great as Vincent Canby claimed in the *New York Times* ("the richest performance of his long career").[3] Canby thought that Wayne was just delicately broadening his own mannerisms for new comic effect. But the mannerisms are not his—a thing that becomes obvious, in scenes of deeper feeling, when Wayne's own inflections show through the adopted Beeryisms. This was less a performance than an impression, and impressions are hard to sustain for the length of an entire movie.

Wayne won the Academy Award as Rooster Cogburn because of what many critics recognize as the putty-nose effect. Actors who put on disguises are supposed to be acting in profoundly different ways. Nor was the film, as some claimed, a comic "send-up" of Westerns in general, or of Wayne's Western heroes in particular. It was a basic *kind* of story, the "good bad man" tales Harry Carey invented for his Cheyenne Harry films, where he drinks and carouses with the bad guys before saving the girl. The main change here was in the age of the girl. She is made a child, to play Jackie Coogan to Wayne's Wallace Beery.

Though the merits of Wayne's performance and of the film itself have been overstated, *True Grit* did open a new career for Wayne. In a postimperial time of fuzzed ideological focus, Wayne was accepted as an impressive anachronism even by those whose political views were far from his. Only a year before *True Grit*, Wayne's *Green Berets* had shown what a dead end he had reached in pursuing the imperial certitudes of the Ford cavalry pictures. In the late forties and early fifties, Ford's message could be implicit in the making of political works of art. By the time of *The Green Berets*, the message had to be asserted, against the obvious resistance of national perceptions. The sixties had shattered confidence in the empire, even among those still trying to maintain the empire. *The Alamo*, made eight years before *The Green Berets*, had a certain reservoir of national assurance to draw on; but by 1969, the cocksureness of the past was seen as flawed, no matter how much people might yearn back toward it.

Wayne, with whom career opportunity scored higher than ideology, recognized that his success would now depend on becoming a living anachronism. He was still seen as larger than life; but he no longer posed a menace in the message he preached. At the very time when Eric Bentley had declared him the most dangerous man in America, the danger was draining away from him. The way to save his career was for him to recognize his own obsolescence. There was a two-edged irony in the tribute paid to Wayne in 1969 by the "hippie" and war protestor Abbie Hoffman: "Even cavemen felt a little admiration for the dinosaurs that were trying to gobble them up."[4] On the one hand, the dinosaur was big and strong; on the other, it was a disappearing species.

Wayne's later successes, in the midst of some clinkers and absurdities, came from his self-consciousness as a living monument. He would maintain his dignity, even while he accepted good-natured ridicule, because he was, after all, a *big* monument, to be treated with affectionate familiarity. Wayne became a regular on the television show *Laugh-In*, in its spectacularly successful first season (1968), where he walked through brick walls and was impervious to the comments of little men bustling around him.

It was hard to know where, in the legend, the reality left off and the laughter began. In real life Wayne performed a routine that might have been crafted for *Laugh-In*. When a naval ship was being launched in Bath, Maine, on September 25, 1975, it failed to go down its slip after the ceremonial champagne bottle had been cracked across its bow. Wayne, a guest of honor, stepped forward to give the ship a shove, and it slid away from him. Most people in attendance probably thought this was a rigged event, but the Secretary of Defense, attending while his wife wielded the champagne, assures me it was not.[5] Perhaps the mechanism just belatedly stirred while Wayne gave his push. But again and again, in these later years, there was a half-joking, half-awed sense that some figment of the public imagination had strolled into view, a tall tale made true, Paul Bunyan bantering with the irreverent.

Wayne's ability to play to these new perceptions of him got its supreme demonstration when he accepted a challenge, issued in 1973, to appear for baiting before the editors of the *Harvard Lampoon*. He showed up at "high noon" on January 15, 1974, riding the armored personnel carrier Harvard pranksters had borrowed from the Massachusetts National Guard. He handled the affair with the ease of a man impervious to insult. Asked where he got the "phony toupee," he answered: "It's not phony. It's real hair. Of course, it's not mine, but it's real." President

Nixon was known to give advice and plays to football coaches—did Wayne get help from him on his pictures? "No, they've all been successful." Did his horse recover from a hernia when Wayne dieted? "No, he died and we canned him, which is what you're eating at the Harvard Club."[6] The mockers' best shots recoiled upon themselves, as they ruefully admitted. Wayne by now was an icon impregnable in his own sense of the role assigned him. He was the fastest gun, even when words were flying instead of bullets.

Wayne saw the possibilities in the last reshaping of his image. He had tried to buy the rights to *True Grit* as a perfect vehicle for a new persona he could adopt. When the producer Hal Wallis got there first, Wayne even tried to buy it back—until Wallis told him he meant to star Wayne in it. There are touches in Wayne's own later productions that show he meant to play the colorful anachronism to the hilt. The best of these later films is *Big Jake* (1971), a neglected work. Critics are snobbish about its over-the-hill director, who was second-rate even in his prime—George Sherman. Wayne was sentimental about using Sherman, who had directed his Three Mesquiteers series at Republic, and whom he brought in as a producer for *The Comancheros* (1961). Wayne gave Sherman one of his last jobs as a director, and hoped for the best. But when he showed up on location (his arrival had been delayed by other business), he was shocked at the rushes. He had asked Dobe Carey how the old man was working out. Carey said, "He's doing O.K." Wayne, after looking at what was shot, took Carey aside and said, "I thought you said he was doing O.K.—he's doing shit." After that Wayne took over much of the directing. Carey says he strengthened the dialogue of scenes he was in, and rechoreographed the shoot-out at the end.[7]

The script, credited to Harry Julian Fink and R. M. Fink, draws heavily on earlier Wayne films, *Fort Apache, The Searchers*, and *The Man Who Shot Liberty Valance*. This "retrospective" aspect of the film is conscious and confessed, though less blatant than the actual clips from earlier Wayne films used to introduce his last movie, *The Shootist*. The aim of the echoes in *Big Jake* is to present Wayne as the remnant of some older order, brought back for a limited mission in "modern" times. People who hear his name (Jacob McCandles) say, respectfully, "I thought you were dead." The movie gives us a kind of resurrection, but only a partial one. Wayne uses a frontier ruthlessness to kill off an even older savagery—just his role in *Liberty Valance*.

The fact that Wayne's kind of heroism has been shoved aside in the new world is conveyed by the way Wayne enters the picture—nineteen minutes into the film, and only as a last resource when Maureen O'Hara, the empress of a huge Texas spread, decides that the United States Army and the Texas Rangers are not capable of the dirty work needed to rescue her grandson, kidnapped by sadistic killers. Wayne's entry has not been so delayed since he became a star—not since the wartime film *Reunion in France*. The long prologue begins as a documentary on the changes racing up to the year 1909. New inventions, including movies, are chronicled, and the film juggles black and white, sepia, and Technicolor sequences to show the dislocations and contrasts of a world subject to accelerating innovation. But the kidnapping gang is a social throwback, introduced as a group of misfits, displaced in geography as well as time, shuttling back and forth across the Mexican border to bring back the days O'Hara thought had disappeared.

The ranch O'Hara presides over has three generations living in peace, their lives sketched quickly in a hierarchical setting, with deferential servants, loyal ranch hands. Her grandson is taking a music lesson with his own private teacher. She scoffs at her foreman's fear of danger—though he tries to remind her that "It is just fifteen years ago that Himself, Mr. McCandles, hun—" A flash of warning in her face makes him freeze with the word uncompleted—her husband seems to have taken the law into his own hands and "hung" rustlers in the earlier, rawer days of the great ranch.

After the kidnapping, in which ten people at the ranch are killed and one of her three sons wounded—even then, when someone suggests calling her husband, O'Hara says, "I have no husband." Only after she accepts the unlikelihood of regaining her grandchild through official channels does she admit, reluctantly, that "It is, I think, going to be a very harsh and unpleasant kind of business and will, I think, require an extremely harsh and unpleasant kind of man to see to it." A quick cut, cued to her words, makes us gaze up the barrel of a rifle toward a wide eye sitting in a nest of wrinkles. Wayne's sighting eye looks like a fried egg with a blue yolk. He is aiming at vigilantes getting ready to lynch a sheepherder. He has moved farther west, where things are still more primitive. He lowers the rifle and says he has quit butting into other people's business. But then his dog growls at the beating of the shepherd's son. Wayne rides down to the lynching tree, buys the sheep, sends the shepherd to his own ranch, and says he will hunt down and kill each of the lynchers if they follow the man. We see why O'Hara wanted to bring up the children in a more law-abiding way.

Reached by courier, Wayne takes the train back to Texas, to the town named after him. In the prologue, people's worried glances out of a door frame, window, or porch as the raiders slowly come up from the landscape recalled the opening scene of *The Searchers*, the arrival of trouble at a secure homestead. But Wayne's arrival by train recalls the return of Jimmy Stewart to Shinbone in *Liberty Valance*. In both cases, a frontier town has succumbed to a modernism symbolized by the train itself. But McCandles is farther down the path of technological innovation. Wayne is met by a trusty friend-servant in a "velocipede," not by the surrey in which Andy Devine picked up Jimmy Stewart. The emphasis on modernity is increased by Wayne and O'Hara's two other sons, who come back home to hunt for the captured boy. (The third son, the boy's father, is still in bed recovering from his wound.) One of the returning sons has a rapid-fire handgun he pulls from a breakaway holster. The other rides a motorbike and uses a high-power telescope on his new rifle (his long vision contrasted with the weak eyes of an aging Wayne and of the Indian scout called back into service for this assignment). The Rangers try to pursue the villains in speedy new automobiles.

In *Liberty Valance*, Stewart returned to bury a symbol of harsher days. But in *Big Jake*, Wayne is called to *revive* a bit of the old savagery. O'Hara realizes that only Jake will have the unscrupulous determination needed to get her grandchild back —as only Ethan Edwards had the will to keep on the trail of Scar. The references to *The Searchers* include Wayne's use of Ethan's tag line, "That'll be the day." The scenarists went back to the Alan LeMay novel to use lines about what the hero wants to be called. "You can call me dad, you can call me father, you can call me a dirty sonofabitch, but if you . . ."

The reunion of Wayne and O'Hara over their endangered offspring recalls *Rio Grande*, and the clash of two powerful though affectionate personalities still works. O'Hara has a small part in the film, though she dominates the prologue before disappearing in the main body of the story. This division represents the two realms into which she has divided her life. She is the stable defender of the home, Jake is the adventurer, out and uncontained. Her face brightens as she sees him, though disagreements rise again when she decides to send *both* the sheriff and her husband on the quest. When she asks his advice after the fact, he says, "You made your decision. You live with it," and she flares up, "I thought you had changed, but you never will." But her face speaks her heart—fearful when her rebellious son defies his father, ruefully smiling when her fears are confirmed and Wayne knocks the son into the mud.

Yet these fighting partners think alike. Their affection, clear in their attitude toward each other when they meet, is spelled out in indirect ways throughout the film. Her son finds the mother's picture in Wayne's watch. Jake learns from a side comment that she insisted that his grandson bear his name. When the rebellious son (James) taunts his father for running off with other women, Wayne confidently says, "You never heard that at home." But the perfect symbol of this union in spirit is the way he nods at her assertion that the kidnappers must get what they are asking for. He has just looked into the casket to be carried into Mexico with a million dollars in it. By accident the casket is broken on the way and its contents are revealed—cut-up newspapers. The sons suspect that Wayne has stolen their mother's money. In fact, of course, she had refused to reward men who killed ten of her workers. We see in retrospect how complete was their mutual understanding in the earlier scene.

The breaking open of the casket is part of a neatly interwoven series of ordeals along the way to the kidnappers' lair. Another gang has followed Wayne, hoping to steal the million dollars before it can be given to the boy's captors. Outnumbered, Wayne's team disperses itself, to cope with the attackers on three different fronts, and the action cuts from one site to the others —Wayne in a barber shop, son James in the saloon, and a "staked-out" other son guarding the casket (while he in turn is guarded by Wayne's Indian friend and his nimbly aggressive dog). A stray bullet breaks the casket's lock in this showdown, dividing Jake's team against itself just when its divide-and-conquer strategy had overcome others.

Reunited after quarrels and explanations, Wayne's men go into the trap set for them by the kidnappers. Richard Boone here plays the best villain in any Wayne film—intense, but not overdone like Lee Marvin's gunman in *Liberty Valance*. He is a worthy adversary, as ruthless as Wayne, as ready to kill. The two have two fine scenes—one, when they meet in Wayne's camp, where each is pretending to be just a hired "errand boy" for his principal; and the other when they fence with words over the transfer of the casket. Boone voices a wearily weighted threat: "If anything happens at all, your fault, my fault, nobody's fault, the boy dies." A moment later, with a temporary shift of the advantage, Wayne whispers so that Boone's men cannot hear: "If anything happens, your fault, my fault, nobody's fault, I'm gonna blow your head off."

Earlier, Wayne's two sons had been shocked when Wayne ordered the Indian (Sam) to kill two gang members who might betray their position. But in the final showdown, the sons bring their skills and technology to Wayne's aid. All along he has confessed to his bad eyesight. In the darkness of the final scramble, it is the young eyes that are dependable. Even the grandson gets into the struggle when he has to shoot his first gun (Wayne's derringer). As at the end of *The Odyssey*, three generations fight together. The tale has other aspects of *The Odyssey*—the adventurer returned in a time of the house's need, the unspoken agreement between the homebody wife and the returned husband on what must be done. There is even a dog who dies, and a loyal servant (the Indian) whose help the husband needs.

Both the dog and the Indian die in the showdown. Wayne loses his wandering past, and when the rebellious son says, "Let's go home," one is made to understand that Wayne is no longer Tennyson's Ulysses, full of wanderlust, unable to settle down. When "Little Jake" scrambles over hay bales in the shoot-out and Wayne, doing his own stunt, throws his clumsy bulk over the same bales, the two lie together tending Wayne's wound. "I'm afraid," his grandson says. "So am I. But don't let *them* know it." He is confessing his own fear and mortality, before the boy who will carry his spirit forward—as Telemachus is fused with Odysseus in one renewed self. Wayne's era has passed. What was worth saving in it will appear now in the little boy we first saw at his piano lesson.

There are biographical resonances in this film that help give it its emotional richness. Sam, the Indian who used to hunt buffalo with Wayne but whose eyes are now fading, is played by Bruce Cabot, Wayne's best friend of the period, about whom he was deeply worried. Cabot, the bright-faced hero of *King Kong* (1933), the superspy in World War II, had succumbed to addictions combining alcohol and pills. Wayne, who had earlier cut off Dobe Carey for giving up alcohol—Wayne at that time thought it was unmanly not to drink—asked Dobe to help Bruce. Carey said Wayne was the only man he would listen to. But Wayne had tried and failed. He hoped Carey had some magic approach, discovered at Alcoholics Anonymous meetings, to penetrate the Cabot defenses.[8] Cabot died within a year of *Big Jake*.

A deeper nerve was touched in the resentment Wayne's rebellious son in the movie (played by his real son Patrick) expresses for the way he left his mother. Michael, Patrick's older brother, was producing *Big Jake*, and Wayne told his third wife, Pilar, that Michael always resented his abandonment of Josie, his first wife. Though Wayne brought Michael onto his production team, trying to heal the rift between them, he called his son "Khrushchev" behind his back because of his harsh bearing and unforgiving ways.[9] The supposed grandson, Ethan, of the story is actually Wayne's own son by Pilar, born twenty-eight years after his half-brother Michael. Though the family off-screen did not, finally, match that on-screen, the artistic vision was a profoundly felt one—as were Ford's films about the family life he could not bring himself to experience in reality. *True Grit* made this kind of vision possible—the vision of Wayne as an anachronism, releasing his hold on the world around him.

□ 24 □
"I WON'T BE WRONGED"

AT THE END OF *True Grit*, the girl tells Wayne he is too old and fat to be jumping his horse over fences. "Well," he says, sweeping his hat off, "come and see a fat old man sometime"—and whirls his horse about to jump it over the fence. A trick shot shows Wayne starting a jump before a quick cut puts his double over the fence. Then we go back to a freeze-frame of Wayne starting the jump, hat waved in the air. The film-makers could not risk letting Wayne fall on the jump. But that stirring end—the picture of Wayne seeming to defy age and weight and ridicule—helped win the actor his Oscar. It also meant that some kind of reprise of the Rooster Cogburn role was inevitable, unless Wayne's health should forbid.

The surprising thing is that it took six years to make the sequel, *Rooster Cogburn* (1975). There was not much time left— the next year's movie would be Wayne's last *(The Shootist)*. The delay was partly caused by the problem of creating a script. The obvious thing to do was pick up the story of Mattie Ross at a later age. Kim Darby could then play someone close to her actual age (she was twenty-eight by 1975). But her sexuality could not be ignored in such a story. She was still too young to be romantically involved with the aged Rooster Cogburn. Would Wayne be a grandfather type blessing her union with some younger man? The comparison of the sequel with the original would probably be embarrassing, since the new show would not have Portis's fine novel as its basis.

The solution was to give Rooster a postsexual "client," as *Grit* had given him a presexual one. Katharine Hepburn was persuaded to repeat her role from *The African Queen,* but at a later stage of life. Hepburn was born in 1907, just five months after Wayne. In *The African Queen* (1951), she had played a spinster missionary teaching children in Africa. While trying to avenge her brother, she falls in love with Humphrey Bogart (who was fifty-two to her forty-four). By 1975, Hepburn was (like Wayne) sixty-eight. There could be no sexual affair between them.

The comparison of Portis's *True Grit* with C. S. Forester's novel *The African Queen* had a surface plausibility. In both a puritanical female seeks revenge for a slain relative (father in the first case, brother in the second), using a drunken reprobate as her instrument. By the end the unlikely duo has developed a deep bond of respect, each for the other. The scenarist for *Rooster Cogburn,* Martin Julien, increases the similarities by putting Wayne and Hepburn on a raft carrying explosives down dangerous cataracts—as Bogart and Hepburn had shot the rapids in a steamboat carrying explosives.

Good as the idea may have sounded—*True Grit* takes to the water!—Julien turned it into a talkative movie where every point in the dialogue is underlined and drained of subtlety. Wayne stands around expressing wonder at Hepburn's toughness, and she tartly punctures his boasts. Anything said gets repeated:

—We in the West treasure a woman with backbone almost as much as a spirited horse.
—Almost as much?
—Almost as much. Not quite. But almost.

Wayne lets his Wallace Beery impression slip away even earlier and oftener than in *True Grit.* The film is redeemed only by Hepburn's delicate playing over and around the script's crudities. When Wayne, rubbing her sore back, says the horse must have left her backside the sorest thing about her, she laughs with a dry combustibility, impishness breaking through the spinsterhood. "Well, we can't do anything about that, can we?" Her wobbly, incandescent face is a marvel when she hears Wayne, for the first time, defend her Bible ways to another man. In touch after touch she shows that her artistry had increased since *The African Queen.* Though the 1951 movie, with script by James Agee and direction by John Huston, is far better than *Cogburn*, whenever she is asked to do the same thing in the later movie she does it better—glowing, for instance, with exhilaration after shooting the rapids. In the former movie, she fans her flushed cheeks in an obvious gesture. In the later, she is so dizzied with joy that she looks about her as if not recognizing the world: "I didn't know—my God!" Only when she bursts into laughter do we realize that pleasure, not fear, has disoriented her.

Though *Cogburn* is not a great movie, it proved important for the Wayne legend: it continued and confirmed his status as a beloved anachronism, the important third image in his gallery of different hero types. The pairing with his contemporary, Katharine Hepburn, a legend herself, was equally important. Hepburn had been imperious for John Ford in *Mary of Scotland*, a free spirit for Howard Hawks in *Bringing Up Baby*, kittenish for George Cukor in a galaxy of feminine poses. In *African Queen* she played an old maid whose righteousness melts when she is placed in a boat's narrow confines with Bogart. In *Cogburn*, she is an old maid beyond sexual awakening, but she acquires new vitality as she recognizes Wayne's equally fierce willpower.

So Wayne and Hepburn are *both* anachronisms. That was not the case in either of the source novels. In *True Grit*, Mattie is a voice from the future looking back a third of the century to the world that was disappearing all around her youth. In *The African Queen*, Rose and Charlie on their boat are the English spirit that will overcome the Germans in World War I.[1] But in *Cogburn*, both figures are in process of replacement by the "modern" West. Cogburn's badge has been removed by a judge interested in proper legal procedures. Cogburn is then called back into service only because he knows the territory a posse must penetrate (but he rides off without the posse). When Hepburn's mission school is burnt around her aged father, she does not stay with her Indian charges, as she first claimed she would, but gives up on that vanished world and seeks only one thing, revenge for the murdered father, before dying herself. Both people mean to live their last days with fiery resolve.

Though John Wayne seemed immortal to his fans, even in 1976 there was an air of death over the whole project of his last film, *The Shootist*. It concerns a gunfighter who knows he is dying of cancer, and those working with Wayne felt that might well be his own situation—though he denied it, even to himself.

He had boasted, ten years earlier, that "I licked the Big C," as if cancer were a thing you could shoot down like a cattle rustler. (Actually, he "licked it" by letting doctors remove half a lung.) By the mid-1970s (his late sixties) he fatigued easily, constantly needed oxygen between scenes, and was plagued with gout, flu, and allergies. There were unspoken fears that he could not finish the film, despite director Don Siegel's effort to pace him, not keeping him on the set for extended periods. When, despite Wayne's gallant effort, and with the finish line not far off, the star had to surrender and enter a hospital (for flu and severe earache), his absence was extended—first one week, then two. Shooting had to continue, around Wayne's lines, then with a double. Siegel worked on the assumption that the film would be completed without Wayne's further participation. When Wayne did return, he was furious that the crew had assumed he could not pull through.[2] Siegel offered to resign, but it was not his fault, as Wayne had to realize, that the studio took unavoidable precautions.

It is surprising, given his unwillingness to discuss his own body's breakdown, that Wayne accepted the role of J. B. Books in *The Shootist*. It is a grim tale, full of violence described with a clinical ferocity. Admittedly, Wayne had Siegel, who was working on the script, mute the details of the colon and prostate cancer that is killing Books, though the cushion he carries to sit on (in the movie, as in the book) would alert the knowledgeable. More important, the character of Books is changed, as is the gunfighter's relation to the boy he meets (played by Ron Howard). Wayne's character becomes the very definition of death with dignity. His past is seen in a series of clips from earlier Wayne films. His present is expressed in a spoken code that Wayne fans have been glad to accept as the actor's own creed. "I won't be wronged. I won't be insulted, and I won't be laid a hand on. I don't do these things to other people, and I require the same from them." That is changed only slightly from the words in the novel; but there the code is that of a killer, whose life is taken up by the young boy (Gillom) he meets.

In the movie, Ron Howard as Gillom does a voice-over/narrative while the clips from Wayne's past are running. Gillom is made to say: "He wasn't an outlaw. In fact, for a while he was a lawman" (clips show the younger Wayne wearing a badge). That is far from the character of Books in Glendon Swarthout's novel. He is a man who enjoys killing. It gives him a *frisson* nothing else can equal. We do not know that (yet) in the book's opening scene, where Books shoots in the stomach a man who is trying to rob him, then offers to shoot him in the head if the man does not want to suffer more. Actually, Books wants the pleasure of killing him on the spot. That offer is omitted from the movie, where Wayne just shoots the man in the stomach.

Books in the novel is friendless, was never a lawman, has never communicated with the parents and siblings he left, and entertains a hedonist vision of the way he will celebrate if he learns that his problem is not cancer:

> I will go to a parlor house and have them top up a bathtub with French champagne and I will strip and dive into it with a bare-assed blonde and a redhead and an octoroon and the four of us will get completely presoginated and laugh and let long bubbly farts at hell and baptize each other in the name of the Trick, the Prick, and the Piper-Heidsieck.[3]

That is not the tone struck by a solemn and elegiac Wayne.

Swarthout's character has come to Carson City, Nevada, in 1901 to consult a doctor who treated him, years ago, for a gun-shot wound. Though the "modernity" of Carson City is empha-sized, to show that Books is a throwback to more primitive ways, the bustling city had to be built on the back lot for the movie, since Wayne's health would not let him work at locations too high for his breathing. Wayne takes a room in a boarding house run by a widow (Lauren Bacall) whose son is sullen and resent-ful. In the movie, Wayne helps tame Gillom for his mother's sake. When the movie's Gillom secretly sells Books's horse and pockets the money, it is to help his mother (her other boarders have moved away because of the scandalous Books's presence). In the novel, he is stealing for himself. In fact, when the novel's Books leaves five hundred dollars behind for the widow, Gillom steals *that.*

Rather than die in agony of his cancer, Books plans to make himself a target for any enemies or aspiring hotheads who might have heard of his disease. Gillom helps set up a showdown in a barroom. After Books has killed the three men challenging him, he is shot in the back by the barkeeper. Not yet dead, he asks Gillom to shoot him in the head—what he offered the robber in the novel's opening scene. Gillom does it, and experiences the same pleasurable *frisson* that drove Books to his life of killing.

In the movie, by contrast, Gillom kills the bartender, then, as the dying Wayne approves with his eyes, he throws away the gun for good.

In Siegel's script, when one of Wayne's assailants has been wounded and is trying to get through the barroom door, Wayne was supposed to shoot him in the back. But he refused. "It's unthinkable for my image."[4] The original Books had no problem shooting people in the back. In fact, he deliberately shoots one spread-eagled man in the rectum, as a personal revenge for the site of his own cancer—the bullet travels up the man's spine, "destroying the central nervous system."[5]

The joy that Books takes in killing calls for a lingering and specific description of each bit of damage his bullets do:

> It penetrated the temporal bone above and forward of the ear, exposed the brain, passed through the brain, carrying with it segments of shell, and exited through the right orbit, or eye socket, taking off the ethmoid plate and the bridge of the nose. On the tile floor under what remained of Jay Cobb's face lay an eyeball and the brain matter which housed the accumulated knowledge of his twenty years, a greyish, adhesive slop of girls and kings and arithmetic and cows and prayer and mountains but primarily of how to fire a revolver accurately and hate himself and deliver milk and cream and butter.[6]

In Swarthout's text, violence just breeds violence, and Books's taste for killing is passed on to Gillom. Nothing good comes from the death of four "bad men" along with Books—whose only desire in the barroom shoot-out was to commit suicide in a spectacular way. In the movie, Wayne's death must be given social utility. Not only is Gillom redeemed by seeing the sad end of a gunfighter, but Wayne deliberately rids the town of its worst characters—all described for him as undesirable by the town's sheriff (beautifully played by Harry Morgan). The sheriff even lets one bad man out of jail so Books can shoot him. (When the young firebrand boasts what he will do to Books, Morgan nods his head patronizingly and says, "Just don't wet your pants.")

If Wayne must go down, he will benevolently take down with him the evil remnants of a world he inhabited and is losing. This is the function he was given in *The Man Who Shot Liberty Valance*, where Wayne accepted the obsolescence of the world he was killing in Lee Marvin. The gun that brought law to the West is surrendered in a final act of immolation that destroys a cognate lawlessness. The myth of the beneficent gun is perpetuated in this third stage of Wayne's heroic image. Even the censorious widow played by Lauren Bacall has love in her eyes for J. B. Books, who takes his last walk away from her house. Wayne fans, who are often gun fanciers, flock to buy his memorabilia, never guessing at the dark truth buried under this last movie, the crazier and more accurate picture of the gunman created in Swarthout's novel. The ideal of the American individual as a walking and armed arbiter of justice is as alive in the militia movement of the 1990s as in the Green Beret camps of the 1960s. Most Americans are not what Wayne was in his movies—a kindly killer—and even to dream of being such an avenger is a dangerous game for the mind to play.

□ Conclusion □
AMERICAN ADAM

WHY WAS WAYNE the Number One Movie Star, even as late as 1995? He embodies the American myth. The archetypal American is a displaced person—arrived from a rejected past, breaking into a glorious future, on the move, fearless himself, feared by others, a killer but cleansing the world of things that "need killing," loving but not bound down by love, rootless but carrying the Center in himself, a gyroscopic direction-setter, a traveling norm.

Other cultures begin with a fixed and social hearth, a temple, a holy city. American life begins when that enclosure is escaped. One becomes American by going out. We are a people of departures, not arrival. To reach one place is simply to catch sight of a new Beyond. Our basic myth is that of the frontier. Our hero is the frontiersman. To become urban is to break the spirit of man. Freedom is out on the plains, under endless sky. A pent-in American ceases to be American. In his 1844 lecture on "The Young American," Emerson said that Americans need the boundless West in order to become themselves.

> The nervous [strong-nerved] rocky West is intruding a new and continental element into the national mind, and we shall yet have an American genius [ethos]. . . . Whatever events in progress shall go to disgust men with cities, and infuse into them the passion for country life, and country pleasures, will render a service to the whole face of this

302

continent, and will further the most poetic of all the occu-
pations of real life, the bringing out by art [of] the native
but hidden graces of the landscape. . . . We must regard
the land as a commanding and increasing power on the
citizen, the sanative and Americanizing influence, which
promises to disclose new virtues for ages to come. . . .[1]

The "young American" Emerson imagined out on the horizon
had the easy gait and long stride of John Wayne.

When, half a century after Emerson's lecture, Frederick
Jackson Turner gave an even more influential address announcing that the frontier was closed, that America had run out of
"free land," there was a crisis of identity in the country. Without
frontiers, we were a place without freedom. If, as Emerson said,
"the land is the appointed remedy for whatever is false and fan-
tastic in our culture," then we were left with no cure for our
falsehood.[2] We would become all City, after being all Frontier.

The city in the American imagination has played roughly the
role of hell in Christian theology. America will cease to be virtuous, Thomas Jefferson said, when its citizens "get piled upon one
another in large cities as in Europe and we are as corrupt as
Europeans."[3] When François Marbois inquired after the state of
Virginia, Jefferson noted proudly, "We have no townships, only
villages or hamlets."[4] This anti-city note sounds throughout our
history. "A really human life is impossible in our cities," said
Henry Demarest Lloyd in 1894 (one year after Turner's address).[5]

Why this fear and hatred of cities in America? Of course,
people have hated cities in the past. Not many satirists can top
Juvenal on the dangers of chaotic living in ancient Rome. The
pastoral genre is built on the contrast between natural life in the
country and the perversion of nature's rhythms in clogged and
disease-ridden towns. But the Rome from which Juvenal fled
had begun in a glow of romantic myth. The gods guided Romu-
lus and Remus to its foundation around an altar. Ovid, in his
clever way, even reversed the commonplaces by saying that
Rome was a good city when it started because it was that para-
doxical thing, "a rustic city."[6] The cities of antiquity arose by
divine favor. Poseidon built the walls of Troy and Delos, Apollo
those of Thebes and Megara. Babylon's and Mecca's original
sites were created by the gods before they made anything else.
Nineveh's plan was traced by the stars. Jerusalem was built
on the central rock of the earth.[7]

Ancient cities had not only a sacred center—a temple, an *arx*, a hearth fire, an acropolis—but sacred precincts, a magic circuit of places protecting them. In fact, François de Polignac has made a strong case that all eighth-century Greek cities except Athens were founded from the periphery inward, tracing first the sacred enclosure with guardian sanctuaries.[8] Constantine's Christian executors, and St. Ambrose's, created a similar circle of churches around Rome and Milan. The heroes' tombs of ancient cities have parallels in the holy tombs of Italy: St. Peter's in Rome, St. Mark's in Venice, Ambrose's own tomb in Milan. And where whole bodies could not be claimed for burial at sacred sites, major relics were: St. John the Baptist's for instance, in Florence. Western culture felt this holiness of the city until the Enlightenment. Medieval Paris was the city of Our Lady and medieval London the city of St. Paul. The city, that is, was central not only to the lives of citizens, but to the order of the cosmos itself. It was the place where heaven touched earth, where traffic with the gods was possible, where cult processions went up to the sacred place, as the psalms of ascent urged people to do.

There is no more defining note to our history than the total absence of a sacred city in our myths. We never had a central cultic place. Remnants of such a tradition exist only in names like "St. Francis" (San Francisco) or "The Angels" (Los Angeles) in Mexican territory we conquered. Our attitude toward the city is just one consequence of the greatest political innovation in our system: the separation of church and state. Even the religion to be kept separate from the state was anti-cultic. Religious sects in America have typically avoided building large, ornate churches. Congregationalist and Quaker meeting houses—not cathedrals, not shrines—have been our most authentic style. Even Episcopalians in Virginia resisted giving glebe money to religious ministers. When St. Patrick's was built in New York, it was considered the foreign indulgence of Irish immigrants. True, St. John's and the so-called National Cathedral in Washington were raised, but lackadaisically, over many decades, on the fringes of American interest. Our attitude is best expressed in Henry Adams's treatment of his friends' work when H. H. Richardson and Oliver La Farge were creating Trinity Church in Boston's Copley Square. He thought the whole exercise irrelevant to American culture and wrote the novel *Esther* to prove it. For most Americans, a church was not a structure but a body of believers, and this was so wherever they met—in a town hall, a revivalist tent, or out West in a commandeered saloon. The church as a building was not sacred of itself.[9]

In fact, even the body of believers mattered less than the individual soul's lonely encounter with God. American individualism found its supreme New England expression in the practice of going off on your own to be saved, and then, after that entirely lonely experience, coming back to produce evidence for your salvation as the only credential that would allow you to join the congregation.[10] You could, furthermore, save only yourself. Before the "halfway covenant," children could not be considered saved just because their parents were. And New England purists denounced the halfway covenant as a terrible falling off from original purity.[11]

Just as one had to go off alone to be saved, Americans have always felt that reality will be encountered and spiritual growth will occur when we go out from society's constrictions toward cleansing solitude, toward nature—toward Walden: "I go and come with a strange liberty in Nature, a part of herself. . . . I have, as it were, my own sun and moon and stars."[12] America's religious art runs from the Hudson River painters, through Ansel Adams's treatment of Yosemite, to John Ford's celebration of Monument Valley. The great urge of the American imagination is to light out for the territory.

Israel's psalmists might sing of ascent to the city. Our literature portrays the arrival in town as a dismaying fall from innocence. The classic instance is Theodore Dreiser's *Sister Carrie*, where the heroine's train trip to Chicago results in her being progressively stripped of her family, her friends, her known world, exposing her to physical disorientation, spiritual loneliness, and the first attention of the seducer who will derail her life. Chicago, when Carrie entered it, was not an ancient holy city that had grown corrupt in time. The first generation of that city's novelists—Henry Blake Fuller, Robert Herrick, Frank Norris, Dreiser himself—presented its founding energies as decidedly unholy.[13] The place was a whirlpool of wheat, a cesspool of hog intestines, a soulless cash market. Chicago, Fuller wrote, was "the only great city in the world to which all its citizens have come for the avowed purpose only of making money."[14] He was exaggerating perhaps, but he and others obviously felt the lack of any social bond that was holier than the cash nexus.

Asked why he attacked the city so often in his novels, Herrick said he was trying to "raise this dirt pile to some dignity," though his critics thought he was not elevating the dirt but lowering people into it. Subsequent treatments of the place by James T. Farrell, or Richard Wright, or Saul Bellow have not done much to dignify it either. Indeed, Chicago became the archetypal city of American literature because it is the midway place, the quick-growth metropolis, the truly native product. Cities on the East Coast still had some European airs, but Chicago was our very own, a place of risk identified with catastrophes: the Chicago fire, the Haymarket bombing, the Pullman strike, the stockyard stench, the Capone mob, the Daley machine.[15]

Our cities are always sizzling in the American imagination and ready to boil over. The most destructive fire in American history was not the Chicago fire, which killed about three hundred people, but the nearly simultaneous fire in Peshtigo, Wisconsin, which wiped out a whole county and killed 1,500 people.[16] But who remembers Peshtigo? That was not an urban fire, and catastrophes are supposed to happen in cities. If they do not, then they do not count.

The relation of country to city was brilliantly traced in F. W. Murnau's *Sunrise,* the film he made at the Fox Studios, where it so impressed John Ford that he called it "the greatest picture that has been produced."[17] In that 1927 movie, the city woman comes out into the country and corrupts a Jeffersonian yeoman played by George O'Brien. At night, the two sit down on an idyllic bankside and start talking about the city, and over this peaceful scene, up in the clouds, you suddenly see flashes of city lights, traffic, trolleys, moving things, jazz musicians, dancers. The woman is so excited, she stands up and starts dancing with the people in the clouds. O'Brien tries to pull her down but he cannot, so he lifts her up physically to the level of the visionary dancers. The next morning, of course, they leave for the city.

That scene is the birth of film noir, the bringing together of German expressionism and pulp fiction to create the "naked city" through which criminals run—black sedans washing the mean streets with bullets in New York or Chicago. Woody Allen acknowledged the power of those images when he began his movie *Manhattan* with a voice-over: "God, I love New York. It's a city in black and white with Gershwin music playing." Then, attempting to go deeper, the speaker says, "No, no. I love New York. It's beautiful women; it's street-smart men. No, no, that won't do." He tries a third time. "I adore New York. For me it is a metaphor for civilization in decline." That is the American dogma reasserting itself.

Serious literature in America has almost always treated the city as a trap and a delusion—as, in the title of one play, *Dead End*. True, there have been journalistic celebrators of the city—Jimmy Breslin's New York, H. L. Mencken's Baltimore, Studs Terkel's Chicago. But when literary form is imposed on such jauntiness, we get tales of plucky people overcoming the pitfalls of the city—O. Henry stories, Neil Simon plays, Damon Runyon tales of gangsters shooting marshmallow bullets, Ring Lardner stories of athletes on the town, and any number of films: *A Tree Grows in Brooklyn, My Sister Eileen*, Busby Berkeley's *42nd Street*. Ruby Keeler and King Kong dance on the skyline. Gene Kelly and Gwen Verdon dance in the ballpark. Much of the more hopeful literature of the city is the tale of creative enclaves in a hostile environment—Greenwich Village, the ethnic Bronx. But the push is still outward. People try to write in the Village; but if they succeed, they move upstate. The real "Miracle on 34th Street" is that Santa finds for Natalie Wood a perfect home in the suburbs; Mr. Blandings labors on Madison Avenue in order to build his dream house in Connecticut.

It is true that both blacks and whites celebrated Harlem in its brief Renaissance, and some African-Americans maintained a lifelong optimism about the city (Romare Bearden, for instance, or James Van Der Zee). But the hope the cities offered to black migrants from the South was soon blighted for novelists like Richard Wright or James Baldwin. Jacob Lawrence painted the process in his Migration series, which conducts southern migrants into northern labor camps, tenements, and white-terrorist riots. The view of the city as unhealthy and cramped is expressed in the funeral picture (Number 55), to which Lawrence appends this caption: "The Negro being suddenly moved [from] out of doors and cramped into urban life, contracted a great deal of tuberculosis. Because of this the death rate was very high."[18] That recalls the photos of Jacob Riis and Lewis Hine.

We have only one truly urban art (*pace* Norman Mailer, who thinks that graffiti are urban art). The great art of the cities is jazz. And for many people even that is associated with the danger of the night. Hart Crane, beginning his poetic sequence "The Bridge," mingled the Brooklyn Bridge's spires at first with the stars, as if giving it a Nineveh holiness. But it quickly becomes an unholy city. Not only are subways demonic, gaping to devour people like the jaws of hell in medieval art, but even comparatively innocent things like revolving doors turn sinister:

> Avoid the glass doors gyring at your right
> Where, boxed alone a second, eyes take fright
> —Quite unprepared, rush naked back to light.

The real point to Crane's epic of the Brooklyn Bridge is that it is not going to stay in Brooklyn. The bridge tramps off across the continent, moving on its girder stilts, seeking to catch up with the twentieth century. At times it drifts down the Mississippi, at times it hunts buffalo. It finds God lavish in Colorado but passing sly. So even the Brooklyn Bridge has to get out of Brooklyn.

Walk through any large gallery of American art, and you will be surprised at how little space is devoted to city life. Mountains, forests, rivers, glades, villages, farms—plenty of those, but few tenements or factories. When a city is treated in our art, it is often unpeopled. In architectural photography, or in Lyonel Feininger's crisscrossing girders of light and steel, the forms are pure. When people are shown, they are often anonymous: the blur of marchers in a Childe Hassam parade; the fleshy overlap of Reginald Marsh's whores sluicing along the street; the eerie highlighting of Edward Hopper's patron in a diner, creating an atmosphere more desolate than the darkness around. Even when people are shown, they are often escaping the city within the city —Eakins's scullers at rest on their oars in Philadelphia's Schuylkill, or George Bellows's snowballers in Central Park.

In all these artistic indictments of the city, few denounce the farm. To curse a farm is like desecrating the flag. The note is so rare that it comes as a relief when Eugene O'Neill sounds it, as Anna Christie remembers her sojourn with Swedish relatives in Minnesota: "Men on the farm ordering me, beating me. One of them, the youngest son, starting me when I was sixteen." Blame prostitution on the farm? That is supposed to be blamed on the city. When Greta Garbo, in her first talking role, recited those words of Anna's in 1930, her Swedish accent was not the only foreign thing about her. Any American girl would have known what you ought to say about the farm, about Jefferson's rustic virtues. To attack farmers is like cutting off aid from them, which is very hard to do even when the "farmers" are agribusiness magnates. It is very easy, though, to cut off aid to cities. They are sinful in any event.

Nor have *big* cities been the sole targets of these attacks. Dashiell Hammett found Chandler's mean streets in the small towns of upstate New York *(The Glass Key)* or of upstate California *(Red Harvest)*. In the burg of that last novel, The Continental Op says, "There's no use taking anyone to court here, no matter what you have on them. They own the courts." Even small towns in Western movies, those repositories of American lore, are often in thrall to gambling interests, or huge ranching interests, or railroad interests. Everything, of course, except farm interests. The sod busters are the ones who have to be rescued from the other factions. In *Shane*, Van Heflin needs a golden knight to ride in and rescue his endangered stake.

To breathe free on the land, the *real* American must shake off the weight of institutions—not only of laws and government, but of schools and libraries. Emerson said that the wisdom of America would not be found by tending the gathered maxims of the past. The American hero must *get out*. Out of the capital cities: "Leave government to clerks and desks." Out of the sickly company of bookworms: "Not out of those on whom systems of education have exhausted their cultures comes the helpful giant to destroy the old or to build the new." Out from the intimidating mass of dead knowledge: "I had better never see a book than to be warped by its attractions clean out of my orbit, and made a satellite instead of a system."[19] Out from the company of the great, to rub shoulders with nature's noblemen:

> I ask not for the great. The remote, the romantic; what is doing in Italy or Arabia; what is Greek art, or Provençal minstrelsy; I embrace the common, I explore and sit at the feet of the familiar, the low. Give me insight into today, and you may have the antique and future worlds. What would we really know the meaning of? The meal in the firkin; the milk in the pan; the ballad in the street; the news of the boat; the glance of the eyes; the form and gait of the body —show me the ultimate reason for these matters.[20]

Emerson's hero is innocent, like Wayne, of bookish ways—which just strengthens the "form and gait of the body." Emerson thinks even of thinking as frontiersmanship: "So much only of life as I know by experience, so much of the wilderness have I vanquished and planted, or so far have I extended my being, my dominion."[21]

Modern intellectuals are puzzled by the popularity of John Wayne. But their forebears created the cultural assumptions on which that popularity is based. He is the unwitting heir to the long tradition of anti-intellectualism created precisely by American intellectuals. It was George Bancroft, who had gone to Germany to get a doctorate in philosophy, who said that Andrew Jackson's greatness was the result of a blessed obliviousness about such things:

> Behold, then, the unlettered man of the West, the nursling of the wilds, the farmer of the Hermitage, little versed in books, unconnected by science with the tradition of the past, raised by the will of the people to the highest honor. . . .[22]

Jefferson had earlier warned against sending Americans to Europe for their education, a disastrous choice that would "admit the hollow, unmeaning manners of Europe to be preferable to the simplicity and sincerity of our country."[23] The native wisdom of our fields can only lose by exposure to European artificialities: "State a moral case to a ploughman and a professor. The farmer will decide it as well, and often better than the latter, because he has not been led astray by artificial rules."[24]

According to Jefferson, American exceptionalism was to be maintained by closeness to the native soil:

> Cast your eyes over America: who are the men of most learning, of most eloquence, most beloved by their countrymen, and most trusted and promoted by them? They are those who have been educated among them, and whose manners, morals, and habits, are perfectly homogeneous with those of the country . . . [so] the consequences of foreign education are alarming to me as an American.[25]

The American homogeneity will be destroyed by too great an influx of people not formed by the native soil:

> They will bring with them the principles of the governments they leave. . . . In proportion to their numbers, they will share with us the legislation [of this country]. They will infuse into it their spirit, warp and bias its direction, and render it a heterogeneous, incoherent, distracted mass.[26]

This sense of American separateness, of exemption from the sins and follies of the past, is perfectly conveyed in Kenyon Coxe's triptych painted for the Wisconsin State Capitol at the time of the Panama Canal's opening. The Canal is presented as a wedding of the Pacific and the Atlantic, presided over by America's tutelary goddess, Columbia. Seated above the isthmus in the pose of Pheidias' Zeus, she raises a scepter to ward off undue influence from the East (Europe), while opening her hand and spreading rays of light to the West, where "natives" on their virgin land or South Sea islands receive her bounty. She raises a barrier between civilization and nature, corruption and purity. To the West there are no cities in this triptych, just what Melville called "that unfallen western world, which to the eyes of the old trappers and hunters revived the glories of those primeval times when Adam walked majestic as a god."[27]

John Wayne is the most obvious recent embodiment of that American Adam—untrammeled, unspoiled, free to roam, breathing a larger air than the cramped men behind desks, the pygmy clerks and technicians. He is the avatar of the hero in that genre that best combines all these mythic ideas about American exceptionalism—contact with nature, distrust of government, dignity achieved by performance, skepticism toward the claims of experts. The yearning back toward such ideals of freedom reemerges in the oddest places. When Jim Morrison of the rock group The Doors sang of freedom, he asked, "What have they done to the Earth? . . . Tied her in fences and dragged her down."[28] In Westerns, the Easterner is a dude, comically encumbered with useless knowledge, ignorant of the basics, too crippled with theory to act. In him, the instincts that lead to Wayne's easy responses have been blunted, have atrophied in the stale air of commerce or technology, in the conditioning to life on a smaller scale than the open range.

The Western popularized the sophisticates' claims for American exceptionalism by putting them in vivid visual form—the frontier was a landscape with freely moving men and horses. The equality of opportunity was symbolized by "nature's noblemen." This ability to put so much of the American myth into such visual immediacy made the Western what Jean-Luc Godard called "the most cinematographic genre in cinema."[29] The appeal of the Western has been long-lived. The first narrative film of any complexity was a Western, *The Great Train Robbery* of 1903.[30] The early cowboy actor, Broncho Billy Anderson, made nearly four hundred silent Western films between 1903 and 1920. Over four thousand Western movies have been made in the sound era.[31] For most of the years between 1926 and 1967, Westerns made up a quarter of all movies being made, more than any other genre over this long span.[32] In 1925 alone, there were 227 Westerns put on film. There was a drop in production with the coming of sound (down to sixty-five made in 1933); but the fewer being made were larger-budget efforts from the mid-thirties on. In the 1950s, there was a falling off of movie production, mainly because the B Western gave way to an extraordinary number of Western series on television (forty-eight of them were running in 1959).[33]

The demise of the Western has often been predicted over the decades, but something always seems to revive it. In the 1960s, there was a surge of nihilistic Westerns by Sergio Leone and Sam Peckinpah. The form is plastic to many reshapings. Though the Western is considered "old-fashioned," it has been used to explore sensitive "new" issues—the evils of war (*Soldier Blue*, 1970), the plight of black Americans (*Buck and the Preacher*, 1972), ecology (*Dances with Wolves*, 1990), feminism (*Unforgiven*, 1992).

Though there has been a drastic reduction in the production of Westerns, most of the numbers are accounted for by the disappearance of product aimed at a juvenile market—the matinee features of Gene Autry, Roy Rogers, and others—and the reduction of Westerns on television. Ambitious large-budget movies have been steadily produced. In fact, in all of movie history up to 1989, only one Western had won the Academy Award for Best Picture—*Cimarron* (1931). Since 1989, two Westerns, *Dances with Wolves* and *Unforgiven*, have won—and the 1995 winner *(Braveheart)* used many formulae of the Western on a different frontier. In 1985, moreover, *Silverado* deserved an Award.

The fact that so many Westerns were aimed at children has led many people to dismiss the whole genre as juvenile. But the kiddy market was boxed off almost entirely from the "adult" Westerns. Only one real star crossed the boundary dividing the two—Wayne, when he moved up from the B series to *Stagecoach* and what followed.[34] And once he made the shift, he hardly ever resorted to the clichés of the formula Western. After *Stagecoach*, he rarely walks down the street to a conventional shoot-out—as Gary Cooper did in *High Noon*.[35] He is not a "quick-draw artist"—in fact, he usually prefers a rifle to a revolver. He does not play the lone ranger who comes to a place, solves its problems, and rides off—as Alan Ladd did in *Shane* or Clint Eastwood in *Pale Rider*. Wayne was not invincible. Wayne's movie character died in nine movies, and four of those were Westerns *(The Alamo, The Man Who Shot Liberty Valance, The Cowboys, The Shootist)*. The man who "never dies" in Westerns is Clint Eastwood.

It is true that Wayne became what Richard Widmark calls him, "the ideal Western hero." When, in 1988, British critics chose the best ten Westerns of all time, Wayne was in four of them, the ones ranked 2, 3, 5, and 7. No other leading man appeared more than once on the list.[36] If Wayne became archetypal, it was not by playing typical cowboys in typical cowboy movies. He made an impact when he carried his Manifest Destiny assurance into compromising situations—into the clash of cultures in *The Searchers*, the trauma of economic change in *Red River*, the demands of empire in Ford's cavalry trilogy, the pathos of social displacement in *The Man Who Shot Liberty Valance*. Westerns, like science fiction or horror movies, push a fixed moral system out into alien space where its assumptions no longer apply; but the Western does better in a "realistic" setting, making the challenge more intimate to us.

The Western can deal with the largest themes in American history—beginning with the "original sin" of our country, the seizing of land from its original owners. It deals with the waves of emigration west—trappers, miners, herders, ranchers, farmers. It tracks the racing, overlapping new technologies—the stagecoach, the Conestoga wagon, the telegraph, the cavalry, the railroads, barbed wire, successively improved firearms, new breeds of horse. It explores the relations of people with the land, of the individual with the community, of vigilante law to settled courts. It is entirely a story of change, since the disappearance of the frontier is the necessary corollary of pushing the frontier on. These themes may be exhausted in our culture, though the continuing popularity of Wayne seems to suggest that the need for this hero will call up again the kinds of story where he operated best, and the problems native to the form have certainly not disappeared.

Is Wayne the most dangerous man of Eric Bentley, or the American Adam of Melville? He is both. He is the former *because* he is the latter. He reflects our society back upon itself, which is the source of his appeal, and of his danger. It is a mixed and terrifying image, full of the unresolved contradictions in our own ideal country. We may have no literal frontier left; but neither do we have a cult city, a temple, a holy center to our society. Our meaning lies still in motion, or so we seem to think—in the independent individual, the need for space as an arena of freedom. Do we really believe that we have escaped the myth of the frontier, the mystique of the gun, the resistance to institutions?

That'll be the day.

NOTES

KEY TO BRIEF CITATIONS

BYU   Howard Hawks Papers at Brigham Young University

Davis   Ronald L. Davis, *John Ford: Hollywood's Old Master* (University of Oklahoma Press, 1995)

Gallagher   Tag Gallagher, *John Ford: The Man and His Films* (University of California Press, 1986)

Heroes   Harry Carey, Jr., *Company of Heroes: My Life as an Actor in the John Ford Stock Company* (The Scarecrow Press, 1994)

Lilly   John Ford Papers at Lilly Library, Indiana University in Bloomington

My Kingdom Draft of John Wayne's interrupted autobiography "as told to" Maurice Zolotow, *My Kingdom for a Horse.* When this project was suspended, Zolotow used his Wayne interviews to complete his own biography of Wayne. The draft autobiography is in the Zolotow papers at the University of Texas, Austin.

Pappy   Dan Ford, *Pappy: The Life of John Ford* (Prentice-Hall, 1979)

Roberts and Randy Roberts and James S. Olson, *John Wayne, American* (The Free Press, 1995)
Olson

Shooting Star Maurice Zolotow, *Shooting Star* (Simon & Schuster, 1974)

Zolotow   Maurice Zolotow Papers at the University of Texas, Austin; includes Zolotow's ghost-written materials for Wayne and interviews with and about Wayne

Prologue. THE MOST DANGEROUS MAN

1. Louis Harris & Associates polls.

2. The Quigley poll of film distributors has been the accepted measure of box-office moneymakers since 1931. The top stars for the first fifty years of the poll were Wayne, Eastwood, and Gary Cooper. Eastwood was in the top ten nineteen times (the top four fourteen times). Cooper was in the top ten eighteen times (the top four seven times). See *International Motion Picture Almanac* 1992 (Quigley Publications), pp. 50–51. Distributors' rating of stars was important because it affected contracts for the stars and the distribution prices of their pictures. See Tino Balio, *Grand Design: Hollywood as a Modern Business Enterprise, 1930–1939* (Charles Scribner's Sons, 1993), p. 145.

3. John Wayne, *Playboy* Interview, May, 1971, reprinted in Judith M. Riggin, *John Wayne: A Bio-Bibliography* (Greenwood Press, 1992), p. 40. Charles John Kieskalt, *The Official John Wayne Reference Book* (Citadel Press, 1993), p. 176.

4. Eric Bentley, "The Political Theatre of John Wayne." Bentley (and his editors) thought enough of this essay to publish it in three places—*Performance* (December, 1971), *Film Society Review* (March-May, 1972), and *Theatre of War* (Viking Press, 1972).

5. Dale Russakoff, "He Knew What He Wanted," Washington *Post*, December 8, 1994, p. A28. Gingrich told the reporter, "I went over and over [to Wayne movies] and saw *The Sands of Iwo Jima* four times in one day." Ron Kovic, *Born on the Fourth of July* (McGraw-Hill, 1976), p. 98. See also pp. 43, 72 for Kovic's fascination with Wayne.

6. "Nixon Press Statement," New York *Times*, August 4, 1970. Nixon, who had just seen *Chisum*, said that it represented the coming of law into American society.

7. Reagan became an independent agent in Hollywood in order to make Westerns after "John Wayne, saber in hand, rode right into the number one box-office spot." Reagan, *Where's the Rest of Me?* (Hawthorn Books, 1965), p. 233.

8. Claudia Dreifus, article on General John Shalikashvili, New York *Times Sunday Magazine*, May 21, 1995: "I must have gone to all kinds of movies. But I remember most the John Wayne movies"—each of which Shalikashvili watched "at least twice" to improve his English.

9. Oriana Fallaci, *Intervista con la storia* (Rizzoli, 1974), p. 29. Kissinger was still at it in 1995, when he wrote "Superstars Strive for Approbation, Heroes Walk Alone" in the New York *Times Book Review*, July 16, 1995, p. 7. A right-wing leader in Italy was "radicalized" when Communist demonstrators prevented him from getting to a Wayne movie—see New York *Times Sunday Magazine*, April 21, 1996, p. 43, on Gianfranco Fini.

10. Joan Didion, "John Wayne, A Love Song," in *Slouching Towards Bethlehem* (Touchstone, 1968), p. 41.

11. G. Edward White makes the point that Westerns are a national myth, not a sectional one, in *The Eastern Establishment and the Western Experience* (Yale University Press, 1968), p. 1.

12. One way to overcome this was to equate his war films with Westerns. In *Sands of Iwo Jima,* Wayne's rallying call as Sergeant Stryker of the infantry is "Saddle up!" In *Green Berets,* the Special Forces camp is called, on a timber sign with rough lettering, "Dodge City."

13. Author's interview with Richard Widmark, January, 1995.

14. Didion, op. cit., p. 31.

15. Joseph McBride, *Hawks on Hawks* (University of California Press, 1982), p. 116. Wayne's consciousness of his own screen presence comes out in his draft of an autobiography: "When you look at an actor's eyes, you've got to feel the cock-a-doodle strength coming at you" (*My Kingdom* I, Chapter 5, p. 11).

16. Reagan, op. cit., pp. 112, 121–22.

17. Author's interview with Harry Carey, Jr., October, 1994. McBride, op. cit., pp. 114–16.

18. Roger Ebert interview with Wayne, Los Angeles *Times,* October 8, 1968.

19. Author's interview with Andrew McLaglen, January, 1995.

20. Author's interview with Richard Widmark, January, 1995.

21. McBride, op. cit., p. 114.

22. Ibid., p. 118.

23. Dan Ford interview with Olive Carey (Lilly).

24. Author's interview with Joanne Dru, Barbara Ford's best friend, January, 1995. Chuck Roberson, who doubled Wayne in later years, said that one effect he had to imitate was the way "he puts his palm on the top of the horse, making him even taller" (in the saddle). Zolotow interview with Roberson, Zolotow, Box 12, Folder 6.

25. Katharine Hepburn, *Me* (Alfred A. Knopf, 1991), p. 259.

26. Author's interview with Harry Carey, Jr., and Marilyn Fix Carey, November, 1994.

27. Author's interview with Richard Widmark, January, 1995.

28. George Plimpton, "Shootout at Rio Lobo," 1970s television cassette viewed at the Library of Congress. The Wayne walk as a guarantor of masculinity is the basis of jokes in shows like *La Cage aux Folles*— jokes that became reversible when director William Wyler is quoted saying that Wayne "walked like a fairy" (Lawrence Suid, *Guts and Glory,* Addison Wesley Publishing Co., 1978, p. 107).

29. John Ford, "The Colter Craven Story," Episode of *Wagon Train* TV series, 1960, New York Museum of Television and Radio.

30. Didion, op. cit., p. 30.

31. McBride, op. cit., p. 120.

32. Plimpton, op. cit.

33. Dan Ford interview with Wayne (Lilly).

34. For Griffith and Ruth St. Denis, see Agnes De Mille, *Martha: The Life and Times of Martha Graham* (Random House, 1991), p. 52. For Graham teaching actors like Richard Boone to be pantherlike, see Don McDonagh, *Martha Graham* (Praeger, 1973), pp. 194–98.

35. Gene Fowler, *Good Night, Sweet Prince* (Blakiston Company, 1944), p. 194.

36. The greatest master of bodily moves was, of course, Chaplin— "a goddam *ballay* dancer," as W. C. Fields complained.

37. Virginia Wright Wexman, "Kinesics and Film Acting: Humphrey Bogart in *The Maltese Falcon* and *The Big Sleep*," in *The Journal of Popular Film and Television* 7:1 (1978), pp. 42–55.

38. *Graham Greene on Film*, edited by John Russell Taylor (Simon and Schuster, 1972), p. 221.

39. David Thomson, *A Biographical Dictionary of Film*, Third Edition (Alfred A. Knopf, 1994), p. 416: "Perhaps because he leaped and tumbled so naturally, it was scarcely noticed that all Lancaster's movements were beautiful."

40. Laura Mulvey, "Visual Pleasure and Narrative Cinema," *Screen* 1975, contained in Mulvey, *Visual and Other Pleasures* (Indiana University Press, 1989), pp. 14–26. Mulvey made women in film the victims of a double voyeurism, that of the camera looking at the man looking at the woman. She argued (p. 20) that "the male figure cannot bear the burden of sexual objectification"—which is shifted entirely onto women.

41. Michel Mourlet, article in *Cahiers du Cinéma* 107 (May 1960), translated by David Wilson in *Cahiers du Cinéma II: The 1960s* (Routledge & Kegan Paul, 1986), quoted in Colin McArthur, "The Real Presence," and Richard Dyer, *Stars* (British Film Institute, 1990), p. 148, and Leon Hunt, "What Are Big Boys Made Of," *You Tarzan: Masculinity, Movies and Men*, edited by Pat Kirkham and Janet Thumin (St. Martin's Press, 1993), p. 68.

42. Hunt, op. cit., p. 74, and Gore Vidal in *The New Yorker*, October 2, 1995. Heston, of course, denies the story in his autobiography, *In the Arena* (Simon & Schuster, 1995), p. 187.

43. See, from a vast literature, Graham McCann, *Rebel Males: Clift, Brando and Dean* (Hamish Hamilton, 1991).

44. For Stewart, see Dennis Bingham, "James Stewart: Your Average Bisexual," in *Acting Male* (Rutgers University Press, 1994, pp. 21–96), which makes Harvey the Rabbit a closeted gay partner. Fonda has been discussed as part of the jointly androgynous imagery of Henry, Peter, and Jane Fonda, building on Richard Dyer's influential discussion in *Stars*, op. cit., pp. 72–98.

45. Peter Brown writes of the Roman Empire: "It was never enough to be male: a man had to strive to remain 'virile.' He had to learn to exclude from his character and from the poise and temper of his body all telltale traces of softness. . . ." *The Body and Society* (Columbia University Press, 1988), p. 11. See also pp. 19, 28–19.

46. Cicero says the worst orator pitches about as if trying to stand in a tilting skiff (*Brutus* 59.216). For training with wrestlers in the palaestra, see *De Oratore* 3.22. The manly stamping of one's foot (*supplosio pedis*) was a strong point of emphasis (*Brutus* 38.141, *De Oratore* 3.59). Cicero liked to quote Demosthenes' saying that the first requisite in oratory is "action, action, and more action" (*Brutus* 38.142, *Orator* 17.56, *De Oratore* 3.56).

47. Lucian, *The Teacher of Rhetoric* 12. See Maud W. Gleason,

Making Men: Sophists and Self-Presentation in Ancient Rome (Princeton University Press, 1995).

48. For these citizen-revenge movies, see Susan Jeffords, *Hard Bodies: Hollywood Masculinity in the Reagan Era* (Rutgers University Press, 1994). For the connection of such films (especially those of John Milius) with the end (and the betrayal) of empire, see James William Gibson, *Warrior Dreams: Paramilitary Culture in Post-Vietnam America* (Hill and Wang, 1994).

49. Stephen Neale argued that all Westerns are implicitly homo-erotic in *Genre* (British Film Institute, 1980), p. 59, and some work was done on Anthony Mann's and Howard Hawks's films (rarely John Ford's—though we shall see that his own actors found some gay themes there). The Stallone-Schwarzenegger films (pecs against tanks) are partly a throwback to Steve Reeves "classical" epics and Victor Mature Bible stories—films where, as Groucho Marx put it, the man's chest is bigger than the woman's. For Dirty Harry's phallic firearms, see Peter Lehman, "Penis-Size Jokes and Their Relation to Hollywood's Unconscious," in *Running Scared* (Temple University Press, 1993), pp. 105–9.

Chapter 1. MAN FROM NOWHERE

1. For the Iowan migration to California, see Carey McWilliams, *Southern California Country: An Island on the Land* (Dell, Sloan & Pierce, 1946), pp. 162–64. Also Josephine Kingsbury Jacobs, "Sunkist Advertising—The Iowa Campaign," in *Los Angeles: Biography of a City*, edited by John and Laree Caughey (University of California Press, 1976), pp. 136–38.

2. For Winterset rumors of Wayne's secret visit, author's interview with David Trask, August, 1994.

3. Author's interview with David Trask of the Chamber of Commerce, who heard the tale from Michael Wayne.

4. *Simpsonian Monthly*, October, 1901, p. 13; December, pp. 11–13.

5. Indianola *Record*, October 3, 1901. I am grateful to Joseph W. Walt, the Simpson College historian, for this reference. The game the paper is reporting was played by Simpson against the Des Moines high school team (*Simpsonian Monthly*, October, 1901, p. 13).

6. The year-end summary, saying the mandatory good things about the small team, reported that Morrison provided "especially strong interference, and could also cover the ball for good gains" when substituting from the bench (*Simpsonian Monthly*, December, 1902, p. 10).

7. Information on the enrollment in the Simpson College of Liberal Arts from Joseph W. Walt. Though Clyde Morrison is sometimes called a college graduate, Professor Walt tells me there is no record of his graduating after the two years he spent there. For the 1901 football roster of sixteen players, see the 1901–1902 yearbook *(Zenith)*, p. 108.

8. Roberts and Olson, p. 33: "Clyde had been a talented athlete at

Simpson College, playing tackle on the football team and winning All-State honors." Clyde played halfback. The authors assign him his son's position at USC.

9. Author's interview with David Trask, August, 1994.

10. *Shooting Star,* p. 5.

11. Author's interview with David Trask, August, 1994.

12. For tourism at the birthplace, author's interview with Jan Pergoli, director of the house, August, 1994. The number has no doubt increased since then. Winterset is now a tourist attraction because of the novel and movie set there, *The Bridges of Madison County.* Some of the many now making a pilgrimage to the bridges will stop at the well-marked Wayne site.

13. *The Madisonian,* November 14, 1907, p. 3.

14. Roberts and Olson are very good at tracing the Morrisons' erratic moves about Iowa (pp. 18–20).

15. "Clyde L. Morrison Drugs and Jewelry" advertised paint, paintbrushes, and wallpaper most weeks of 1911 in the Earlham *Advocate.* The football legend pursues Clyde to the town, where he is supposed to have coached the Earlham Academy team, though newspaper accounts of the school's games do not mention him. In fact, the only use of his name (outside the ads) that I could find in the spottily preserved newspaper is this: "Mr. and Mrs. Clyde Morrison visited Monday and Tuesday in Des Moines" (September 28, 1911).

16. *My Kingdom* I, Chapter 1, page 7.

17. Ibid.

18. Letter to Glen A. Settle, author of *Lancaster Celebrates a Century: 1884–1984* (City of Love Press, 1984), in the local history files of the Lancaster Public Library.

19. E. Coswell Perry and Carroll W. Parcher, *Glendale Area History,* Second Edition (Xanadu Gardens, 1981), p. 30, in Lancaster Public Library.

20. Glendale High School yearbooks, 1922–1925.

21. Roberts and Olson, pp. 40–41.

22. For Arbuckle, see Glendale *Evening News,* June 14, 1918, and July 30, 1919 (*Classic Images* Number 93, p. 60). For Fairbanks, Glendale *Evening News,* August 11, 1922.

23. For Helen Holmes at Kalem, see the article on her director-husband, "James Holmes's Own Story," *Photoplay,* February, 1916. Wayne's comments on her are in *My Kingdom* I, Chapter 1, p. 10. For Kalem's time in Glendale (1910–1917), see Joni L. Atkinson, "The Silent Era Comes to Glendale," in *Glendale Today,* August, 1992 (Glendale Public Library).

24. See Glendale *Evening News,* August 26, 1913, March 28, 1918, June 9, 1923, February 18, 1926.

25. *My Kingdom* I, Notes, Folder 2, p. 23.

26. Ibid., I, Chapter 2, p. 9.

27. Author's interview with Richard Widmark, January, 1995.

28. Aristotle, *Politics,* 1253a6–7.

29. *Stylus* (Glendale High School Yearbook) 1925, p. 46.

30. Wayne remembered the speech but placed it in the wrong play *(Henry IV)*. See *My Kingdom* I, Chapter 2, p. 2.

31. *My Kingdom* I, Chapter 2, p. 2. *Stylus* 1924, pp. 47, 50.

32. *Stylus* 1924, p. 75.

33. *Stylus* 1924, p. 202; 1925, p. 98.

34. *Stylus* 1925, p. 125.

35. *Stylus* 1924, p. 137; 1924, p. 59.

36. Some alumni remembered Wayne's injury as to his leg *(Trojan Daily,* October 20, 1978).

37. USC, *Pigskin Review,* September, 1925, p. 6.

38. *My Kingdom* I, Chapter 2, p. 3.

39. *Trojan Daily,* October 10, 1978: "Insiders had said that Morrison might have attained All-America status had not the injury thrown a damper on his career."

40. Los Angeles is full of stories inflated from some contact with an actor. Mix, the highest paid movie star of his day, a superb athlete and trick rider, with an entourage of his own, hardly needed a failed college tackle to keep him in shape. If he made some vague invitation to Wayne, it is a measure of the latter's naïveté to think it meant anything.

41. Zolotow (*Shooting Star,* pp. 30–32) found this resentment in Glendale at Wayne's disregard for his past—though he notes that Wayne did go back once, for the high school graduation of his stepsister, Nancy Buck. (Clyde had married Nancy's mother after his divorce from Molly.) That was in 1939. See Wayne clip file in Glendale Public Library.

Chapter 2. RAOUL WALSH

1. Kevin Brownlow, *The War, the West, and the Wilderness* (Alfred A. Knopf, 1979), pp. 100–102. Walsh played the *young* Villa himself. Though Walsh did not play as loose with the facts about his own life as Ford did, his autobiography has some ludicrous whoppers (like his tale of kidnapping John Barrymore's corpse to take it partying). Nonetheless, the Griffith, Mexican, and other adventures are independently verifiable.

2. Author's interview with Harry Carey, Jr., August, 1995.

3. Ibid.

4. Brownlow, op. cit., p. 197.

5. Author's interview with Harry Carey, Jr., November, 1994.

6. Dan Ford interview with George O'Brien (Lilly), transcript pages 31–32.

7. Walsh filmed the outdoor location scenes with himself on horseback as the Cisco Kid, scenes that remained in the film. But a car accident on the way back to Los Angeles cost him his eye, and Warner Baxter had to be hastily substituted—creating a role he would play several times, then pass on to Cesar Romero, Duncan Renaldo, and Gilbert Roland. If Walsh had finished the picture, he might have contin-

ued his acting career (he always liked to perform). The lost eye settled that.

8. Walsh's efforts might have succeeded had not studio politics led to his brother's replacement in *Ben-Hur* by Ramon Novarro. (Ford, on the other hand, took his older brother, Frank, who had been a genuine star of silent films, and repeatedly cast him as a drunken fool.)

9. The film was so popular in its silent version that five sequels were made in sound—*The Cock-eyed World* (1929), *Women of All Nations* (1931), *Hot Pepper* (1933), *No More Women* (1934), *Under Pressure* (1935).

10. Ford remade Walsh's movie, not very well, in 1952.

11. Hal Evarts, Jr., *Skunk Ranch to Hollywood: The West of Author Hal Evarts* (Capra Press, 1989), pp. 144–62. Evarts, who had done nature writing in the West, was useful to Walsh in getting Park Service help and permissions at various locales.

12. Arthur Edeson had worked with Walsh on *The Thief of Bagdad* and his first "talky" Western, *In Old Arizona*. While Edeson was filming the 70mm version of *The Big Trail*, Lucien Andriot made a 35mm version.

13. Ford idolized Lincoln. In *The Iron Horse* he has the actor George O'Brien as a youth meet Lincoln and get his blessing on the national benefits of western expansion.

14. Robert Parrish, who would become a well-known film editor and director, was only fourteen in 1929, but he was taken along with *The Big Trail*'s crew since his little sister was playing the heroine's sister. He gives an account of the sexual hanky-panky on the shoot. Parrish, *Growing Up in Hollywood* (Harcourt Brace Jovanovich, 1976), pp. 63–71.

15. Raoul Walsh, *Each Man in His Time: The Life Story of a Director* (Farrar, Straus and Giroux, 1974), p. 243.

16. But there is a sophisticated layering of sound effects behind the speakers, suggesting the vast range of noises on the big screen— cattle, dogs, children, the sounds of a community going about its multiple businesses. This was a technology already developed by the radio, where it created unseen ambiences.

17. A 1930 takeover of Fox by AT&T and the Chase National Bank did not check the downward plunge of the company. "Fox's earnings fell from $10 million in 1930 to minus $4 million in 1931.... Fox Films lost nearly $11.5 million in 1931 and 1932, which pushed it to the brink" (Tino Balio, *Grand Design: Hollywood as a Modern Business Enterprise, 1930–1939*, Charles Scribner's Sons, 1993, pp. 15–17).

Chapter 3. YEARS WITH YAK

1. Tino Balio, *Grand Design: Hollywood as a Modern Business Enterprise, 1930–1939* (Charles Scribner's Sons, 1993), pp. 13–16.

2. The movies were a college farce (*Girls Demand Excitement*) and a gangsters-in-society melodrama *(Three Girls Lost)*. Wayne used to say in later life that the first was "the worst motion picture in the history of motion pictures" (*My Kingdom* I, Chapter 4, p. 4).

3. Sam Goldwyn had made Ford sign an agreement not to drink while making *Arrowsmith*, but frustration with Helen Hayes, who did not submit to his bullying, helped send him to the bottle. When the studio tried to reach him, he was on Catalina Island drinking. When he did come in, he was incoherent. (The studio got four signed statements of eyewitnesses to prove this latter point to Fox.) His own studio gave Ford the choice of announcing his resignation or being fired "for unsatisfactory service." This firing has not been noticed in the Ford literature because he understandably did not keep a record of it in his own papers (now at the Lilly Library). The correspondence is in the Fox files at UCLA, December through May, 1931–1932. While renegotiating with Fox, Ford made *Air Mail* for Universal (1932).

4. Balio, op. cit., pp. 29, 100.

5. Ibid., p. 103.

6. *Shooting Star*, pp. 94–95.

7. Balio, op. cit., p. 28.

8. Jon Tuska, *The Vanishing Legion: A History of Mascot Pictures, 1927–1935* (McFarland & Company, 1982), pp. 8–23. An appreciation of Levine by one who worked closely with him is Yakima Canutt, *Stunt Man* (Walker and Company, 1979), pp. 84–88.

9. The three serials (none a Western) were:

> *The Shadow of the Eagle*, about sabotaging an airline company.
> *The Hurricane Express*, which has Wayne chasing trains with planes (a lot of process shots). Tully Marshall, who had been effective as Wayne's earthy sidekick in *The Big Trail*, mugs impressively.
> *The Three Musketeers*. Buddies in a foreign legion uncover a traitor among the colonial occupiers. Though stock desert footage was used, Levine filmed on location in Yuma, Arizona, where Wayne had begun the ordeal of making *The Big Trail*.

10. While he was at Warner's Wayne did some bit work in the lot's modest A productions. In *The Life of Jimmy Dolan*, a Douglas Fairbanks, Jr., fight film, he is a boxer full of bluster in the locker room who stammers more nervously as each battered fighter returns from his ordeal. In *Baby Face*, a Barbara Stanwyck social-consciousness film, Wayne is billed sixth in a large cast, and one wonders why he is that high, given his brief appearance. But most of his scenes were cut, a victim of the Hays office. The risqué story tells how Stanwyck literally

sleeps her way to the top of a company—the camera climbs the office façade as she moves up, office by office, floor by floor. Wayne is a naive clerk, at the bottom of the ladder, whom she uses to get started. Her tactics were clearly too obvious for the censors. See Richard Maltby, " 'Baby Face,' or How Joe Breen Made Barbara Stanwyck Atone for Causing the Wall Street Crash," in *The Studio System*, edited by Janet Staiger (Rutgers University Press, 1995), pp. 251–78. Dealing with Wayne's role, the studio assured Hays that "The affair with the office boy is cut in such a manner that he has no affair with her" (p. 272).

11. Stout made sixteen Monogram films with Wayne (in three years):

> *Riders of Destiny* (1933)
> *Sagebrush Trail* (1933)
> *The Lucky Texan* (1934)
> *West of the Divide* (1934)
> *Blue Steel* (1934)
> *The Man from Utah* (1934)
> *Randy Rides Alone* (1934)
> *The Star Packer* (1934)
> *The Trail Beyond* (1934)
> *The Lawless Frontier* (1934)
> *'Neath the Arizona Skies* (1934)
> *Texas Terror* (1935)
> *Rainbow Valley* (1935)
> *The Desert Trail* (1935)
> *The Dawn Rider* (1935)
> *Paradise Canyon* (1935)

12. Author's interview with Harry Carey, Jr., January, 1995.

13. John Wayne, Notes for *My Kingdom* (Zolotow Folder 2), p. 25.

14. "Yakima" was often taken for an Indian name. His character was *called* Yak when he played an Indian in *The Star Packer* (1934) and the Apache woman in Ford's *Stagecoach* is called "Yakima" as an in-joke.

15. Canutt, op. cit., pp. 62–66.

16. Yet Maynard was a wizard. In *The Red Raiders* (1927) he rides after a comrade who has been shot and is hanging down from his saddle. Maynard, lying backward on his own horse at full gallop, reaches down and pulls the man back onto his saddle—a feat of sheer strength as well as riding skill.

17. See *Sagebrush Trail* (1933). The horse bucks, amazed at this unexpected arrival. For a description of Yak's use of this mount in rodeo shows, see Canutt, op. cit., p. 70.

18. In his autobiography, Canutt says this took place in *'Neath the Arizona Skies* (p. 92). It is in *The Lucky Texan* (1933).

19. Vladimir Nabokov, *Lolita* (G. P. Putnam's Sons, 1980), p. 30.

20. Later Wayne would adopt the movie convention of galloping with a straight-up posture as, for example, William S. Hart did so spec-

tacularly in *Tumbleweeds*. This is contrived. The crouch of jockeys lowers the center of gravity, cuts wind resistance, and gives better control of the horse. But the straight-up posture gives an "image" of mastery, and Canutt sometimes used it for that purpose. In Ford's cavalry pictures, later on, Wayne kept the straight posture of parade formations even when galloping.

21. Charlton Heston, *In the Arena* (Simon & Schuster, 1995), p. 247.

22. Canutt, op. cit., pp. 27–66.

23. Wayne and Yak worked together for other directors—for Raoul Walsh *(Dark Command)* in 1940, for Howard Hawks *(Rio Lobo)* in 1970. Yak created the train-stopped-by-trees stunt in the latter film.

24. For the confidence Yak inspired in stuntmen who worked for him, see the oral history interview with Jack Williams, who drove a chariot for him in *The Fall of the Roman Empire*. The chariots were specially designed, the sequences arranged, the drivers all trained by Canutt. (Kenneth Hoff interview with Williams, May 5, 1970, Arizona Historical Society.) For Yak's intransigence with producers where safety was concerned, see his account of the difficulty in getting MGM to lay the proper surface for *Ben-Hur*'s chariot race (op. cit., pp. 9–12).

25. For the Wyler quote, see Lawrence Suid, *Guts and Glory* (Addison Wesley Publishing Co., 1978), p. 107.

26. Author's interview with Dean Smith (stuntman in eight Wayne films), August, 1994.

27. "The Economic Imperative," in *Kings of the B's*, edited by Todd McCarthy and Charles Flynn (E. P. Dutton & Co., 1975).

28. Wayne's six Universal films are:

The Sea Spoilers (1936)
Conflict (1936)
California Straight Ahead (1937)
I Cover the War (1937)
Idol of the Crowds (1937)
Adventure's End (1937)

29. Richard Maurice Hurst, *Republic Studios: Between Poverty Row and the Majors* (The Scarecrow Press, 1979), pp. 129–35. Wayne did these eight films:

Pals of the Saddle (1938)
Overland Stage Raiders (1938)
Santa Fe Stampede (1938)
Red River Range (1938)
The Night Riders (1939)
Three Texas Steers (1939)
Wyoming Outlaw (1939)
New Frontier (1939)

In later Three Mesquiteers films, the role of Tucson (Crash Corrigan's role in Wayne's time) was taken by Bob Steele, Wayne's Glendale friend.

Chapter 4. SADIST

1. *Shooting Star,* p. 44.
2. *Pappy,* p. 40.
3. Davis, p. 257. *Heroes,* pp. 25, 256.
4. Ford called Harry Carey, Jr., "Melwood" because he knew it irked him. He also called Richard Widmark "Duke," since he knew that Widmark disliked Wayne. Author's interviews with Widmark and Carey, January, 1995.
5. *Heroes,* p. 120.
6. Dan Ford interview with Wayne (Lilly). McLaglen, who had boxed Jack Johnson, was hardly going to be intimidated by a movie wrestler.
7. Peter Bogdanovich, "The Duke's Gone West," *New York,* June 25, 1979, p. 69.
8. Dan Ford interview with Wayne (Lilly). Wayne half-admits his movie with Walsh might explain this period in the doghouse, then loyally retracts the suspicion.
9. Author's interview with Andrew McLaglen, January, 1995, on the eleven-year "banishment" of Victor McLaglen for accepting better-paying roles with other directors when Ford wanted to use him. Ford regularly punished those who showed their independence—Harry Carey, Yakima Canutt, Ben Johnson, George O'Brien (who said or did something on his Asian trip that kept Ford from using him for seventeen years).
10. John Ford, BBC interview, 1969 (private collection of Harry Carey, Jr.).
11. *Pappy,* pp. 47–51.
12. Annapolis had objections to the filming of a feature movie on campus (Memorandum of C. P. Snyder, November 14, 1929), but the Navy Department authorized the studio to make "movietone [newsreel] scenes . . . for incorporation in the photography" (Memorandum of C. F. Hughes, February 15, 1929). Naval Academy Archives.
13. Letter from Charles F. Boren, September 4, 1929 (Lilly).
14. The Ford-Wayne-Bond circle later claimed that James McGuinness wrote the movie while at Annapolis. But the Annapolis archives show that a script had to be submitted beforehand for approval, and Academy reports on it were sent to the Navy Department. Ford's subject—the Army-Navy football game—was a delicate one when he was filming in June of 1929, since the football series had been suspended. Navy had accepted the new intercollegiate rules of competition and Army had not. Negotiations were under way to renew the rivalry, and there was fear that Ford's film would upset the result. See Annapolis *Evening Capital,* June 12, 1929, p. 1. In surveys taken after officers viewed the completed film, Ford was criticized for making the rivalry too fierce. I am grateful to Professor David P. Peeler at the Academy history department for making these and other archival materials available to me.

15. Musicians were regularly kept on silent movie sets, to establish moods for the actors during their scenes. Ford had used such musicians, as a picture from his silent days shows. He kept Borzage as an adaptation of that custom. Nothing made Ford's sets more distinctive than this musical "cheerleading" that took place, off and on, all day. (For a reminiscence of the set musicians' importance, see Chaplin's *Limelight*.)

16. John Agar, who grew up going to a dude ranch during his summers, was a good rider when Ford hired him for *Fort Apache*. But Ford insisted he show up early in the morning to undergo horse training from Pennick.

17. Dan Ford interview with George O'Brien (Lilly).

18. Author's interview with Denver Pyle, January, 1995.

19. Davis, p. 166.

20. Author's interview with Denver Pyle (in Pyle's office), January, 1995.

21. Tino Balio, *Grand Design: Hollywood as a Modern Business Enterprise, 1930–1939* (Charles Scribner's Sons, 1993), p. 145.

22. Dan Ford interview with Olive Carey (Lilly).

23. Ford letter to Captain Elias Zacharias, USN (Lilly).

24. *Heroes*, p. 81.

25. Author's interview with John Agar, January, 1995.

26. Ford had already used O'Hara in his stage production of *What Price?*—and reviewers rightly said she was miscast. Reviews in Harry Carey, Jr., papers (BYU).

27. *Heroes*, pp. 188–89.

28. Author's interview with Harry Carey, Jr., October, 1994.

29. Ibid.

30. *Heroes*, p. 23.

31. Ibid., p. 25.

32. Patrick McGilligan, *Cagney as Auteur* (A. S. Barnes and Company, 1975), p. 72. Cagney called Ford "truly a nasty man" in his authorized biography: Doug Warren, *Cagney* (St. Martin's Press, 1983), p. 181. Henry Fonda told Charlton Heston that Ford was a great director, but "he was also a cruel son of a bitch." Heston, *In the Arena* (Simon & Schuster, 1995), p. 465. Robert Montgomery criticized Ford, on the set, for insulting Wayne before other actors.

33. Author's interview with Richard Widmark, January, 1995.

34. Kenneth Barrow, *Helen Hayes, First Lady of the Theatre* (Doubleday, 1985), p. 103.

35. *Heroes*, p. 47.

36. James D'Arc interview with Patrick Ford, April 25, 1979: "My conversations with him, as his only son—that I know of—was 'Yessir,' until one day I said, 'No sir,' and then I was no longer around. . . . In fact, our family life was pretty much like that of a shipmaster and his crew, or a wagonmaster and his people. He gave the orders, and we carried them out."

37. Barbara tried to join her father's masculine troupe by marrying

Ken Curtis, the actor in his films and singer at his parties; but that did not work out. After her breakup with Curtis, Ford and his chauffeur had to break into Barbara's apartment to rescue her from an alcoholic coma. Author's interview with the chauffeur, Bob Stevens, January, 1995.

38. Davis, p. 103.

Chapter 5. ARTIST

1. *Shooting Star,* pp. 141–42; Davis, p. 87.

2. Nolan, though still comparatively fresh to pictures, was not really young—thirty-seven, and the Kid is supposed to be just out of his teens, if that. (Wayne, of course, was already thirty-two.)

3. Edward Buscombe, *Stagecoach* (British Film Institute, 1992), pp. 17–19.

4. Davis, p. 87.

5. Roberts and Olson, p. 161.

6. Will Wright, *Sixguns and Society: A Structural Study of the Western* (University of California Press, 1975), pp. 59–61.

7. Nichols made more of the "Wanted" poster that first introduces the Kid and his image (Ford wanted to save that for the first glimpse of Wayne himself). The script, in response to the censor's objections, makes it clear in the concluding dialogue that the Kid was framed and is no longer a wanted man. Ford scraps that, too. He knows the audience is not (or should not be) interested in the Kid's revenge, which is a plot *excuse,* not a plot *concern.*

8. Trivial uses of the same plot device, with shallow engagement of characters and a happy ending all around, give us a TV show like *The Love Boat* or an old radio show like *Grand Central Station.* Tales of pioneer voyages have some resemblance to the ship-of-fools genre— e.g., Ford's own *The Iron Horse* and *Wagon Master.* But those trips go on so long that they set up stable social relations that will last when the pioneers reach their goal.

9. Ford's claim to the Maupassant source is in Peter Bogdanovich, *John Ford* (University of California Press, 1968), p. 69.

10. *Collier's,* April 10, 1937, pp. 18–19, 68–69. The other characters are very sketchy—a cattleman who insults the whore, a whiskey salesman who dies of a heart attack, a gambler who suspects that the whore may be his daughter. Two die during the short ride, and all the attention is directed to "Malpais Bill" and the whore. She sees him at the end "high and square in the muddy sunlight, coming toward her with his smile."

11. Gallagher, p. 162. Robert Warshow, "Movie Chronicle: The Western" (1954), in *The Immediate Experience* (Atheneum, 1971), p. 149.

12. Other 1939–1940 Westerns not affected by *Stagecoach*'s release were DeMille's *Union Pacific,* Lloyd Bacon's *The Oklahoma Kid,* Allan Dwan's *Frontier Marshal,* Michael Curtiz's *Santa Fe Trail* and *Virginia*

City, King Vidor's *Northwest Passage*, Fritz Lang's *The Return of Frank James*, William Wyler's *The Westerner*. For 1939 and 1940 as the peak period of the classical sound Western, not its point of origin, see André Bazin, "The Evolution of the Western," introduction to S.-L. Rieupeyrout's *Le western ou le cinéma americain par excellence* (1953), translated by Hugh Gray, in *What Is Cinema?* Vol. 2 (University of California Press, 1971), p. 49.

13. Many of the "town-taming" stories imitated William S. Hart's *Hell's Hinges* (1916). A good example is Harry Carey's *Satan Town* (1926).

14. Bazin, op. cit., p. 149:

> *Stagecoach* (1939) is the ideal example of the maturity of a style brought to classic perfection. John Ford struck the ideal balance between social myth, psychological truth, and the traditional western *mise en scène*. None of these elements dominated any other. *Stagecoach* is like a wheel so perfectly made that it remains in equilibrium on its axis in any position.

Chapter 6. RHYTHMED MOTION

1. Patrick McDonnell, Karen O'Connell, and Georgia Riley de Havenon, *Krazy Kat: The Comic Art of George Herriman* (Harry N. Abrams, 1986), pp. 68–76.

2. Carlo Gaberscek, *Il West di John Ford* (*Arti Graphiche Friulane*, 1994), pp. 29–32. This useful book draws on Gaberscek's earlier articles devoted to Western film locales. It is superior to the treatment of Monument Valley in David Rothel's *An Ambush of Ghosts: A Personal Guide to Favorite Western Film Locations* (Empire Publishing, Inc., 1990), pp. 132–47, though Rothel's book is beautifully illustrated.

3. Reports to Walter Wanger Productions, October 28, 1930 (five single-spaced pages in Lilly).

4. Goulding's own account is put on record in Samuel Moon, *Harry Goulding, Monument Valley Trader* (University of Oklahoma Press, 1992), pp. 144–48. In an interview given in 1978, Goulding denied there had been any earlier filming at the Valley for movies, something he had to know was false from his admitted dealings with the Wetherills. See Todd McCarthy, "John Ford and Monument Valley," *American Film*, May, 1978, pp. 10–16.

5. Ford also portrayed himself as first giving work to unemployed Navahos, who live on the reservation containing the Valley. But the Wanger documents show there was an established procedure for dealing with the Indians' agents through a New Deal bureaucracy. (Social Security was hard to explain to them, so it was not withheld.) See the Wanger reports of October 28, 1930.

6. I take the timings from Peter Stowell's useful chart in *John Ford* (Twayne Publishing, 1986), pp. 126–27.

7. Nichols, *Stagecoach*, Final Shooting Script (Lilly). I turn the chart around, since Ford makes his horses run left on the screen. I also substitute type-names for the character names Nichols used. Copies of the Nichols script are at Lilly, UCLA, and the Wisconsin Film Archives. I compared them all and there are no differences. This is the text (used without the place charts for the interior of the coach) contained in *Twenty Best Film Plays*, edited by John Gassner and Dudley Nichols (Crown Publishers, 1943). Ford made many departures from this script in filming, and the order of some sequences was altered in the editing.

8. Edward Buscombe, *Stagecoach* (British Film Institute, 1992), p. 9. The "star" entry is a commonplace of early film. Ken Maynard swings open a door and poses for implied applause in *The Red Raiders* (1927). William S. Hart, with his stage training, also contrived to make his first appearances dramatic. For other examples of the device, see Andrew Britton, "Stars and Genre," in *Stardom*, edited by Christine Sledkill (Routledge, 1991), pp. 199–200. For Garbo's "entrances" see Charles Affron, *Star Acting* (E. P. Dutton, 1979), p. 95.

9. Ford improves on the Nichols script by getting rid of the crippled horse, which stood beside the Kid as the scene was written.

10. Wayne wears the "placket front" shirt he made a trademark. Vaguely military, as if it were a breast plate, the shirt has two rows of buttons widening toward Wayne's shoulders, emphasizing their breadth.

11. Bob Stevens, who worked for Ford as chef and chauffeur, did not recognize Wayne the first time he came in through the Fords' kitchen. "He was not wearing his hairpiece and he was shorter than I am." Stevens is exactly six feet four. (Author's interview with Stevens, January, 1995.) Wayne is no taller than Randolph Scott in the non-Westerns they made together. The impression of size he gave depended on factors other than sheer height.

12. James D'Arc, the film curator at Brigham Young University who is completing a book on movies made in Utah, points out to me that Wayne and Trevor are never shown on-screen against a real shot of Monument Valley. It is doubtful that they worked in the valley. The Monument Valley shots were something to take back to California, where the chase scenes were made.

13. Wayne even retains his *spurs* as he climbs into the coach— though they would be clumsy and dangerous in the space between others' feet.

14. Using a breakaway set, showing only one seat at a time, Ford once forgets the arrangement of the phantom other seat and has the banker address the doctor while looking to his left (it should be to his right).

15. Buscombe, op. cit., pp. 68–69. Charlton Heston, *In the Arena* (Simon & Schuster, 1995), pp. 183, 247.

16. The studio sent Yak over to handle one difficult horse team in *Young Mr. Lincoln*. Ford's response was "What are you doing here, Yak?"

Canutt did animal photographs for Ford's *Mogambo,* but in a separate unit reporting only to the studio, having no contact with Ford. Canutt, *Stunt Man* (Walker and Company, 1979), pp. 114, 148–61.

Chapter 7. INNER SPACES

1. Roberts and Olson, p. 161.
2. Edward Buscombe, *Stagecoach* (British Film Institute, 1992), pp. 21–22.
3. Peter Bogdanovich, *This Is Orson Welles* (HarperCollins, 1992), pp. 77–78.

Chapter 8. WAR YEARS

1. After two of her films proved major flops, distributors took out an ad in *Variety* asking Paramount not to send them any more of her product. Paramount responded by buying out her contract, paying her $250,000 *not* to make any more films for them.
2. Maria Riva, *Marlene Dietrich* (Bloomsburg, 1992), pp. 488–89.
3. Tay Garnett with Fredda Dudley Balling, *Light Your Torches and Pull Up Your Tights* (Arlington House, 1973), pp. 244–45.
4. Dietrich did not deliver the line in 1922, but she watched night after night as the superstar, Elizabeth Bergner, delivered it. Bergner was her idol at the time.
5. OWI misgivings about *Pittsburgh* are quoted in Clayton E. Koppes and Gregory D. Black, "What to Show the World: The Office of War Information and Hollywood, 1942–1957," in *The Studio System,* edited by Janet Staiger (Rutgers University Press, 1995), pp. 285–88, 295–96.
6. Andrew McLaglen claimed that the Dietrich affair was the effective end of Wayne's first marriage. Author's interview with Andrew McLaglen, January, 1995.
7. Pilar Wayne, with Alex Thorleifson, *John Wayne: My Life with the Duke* (McGraw-Hill, 1987), pp. 39–40.
8. Riva, op. cit., p. 501.
9. Ibid., p. 502.
10. Mary Ford to John Ford, June 1, 1943 (Lilly).
11. Von Sternberg said he found Dietrich playing a bit part in a revue where she had one line. Actually, she was the star of the show, with a solid stage career behind her and several movies that made American producers ask about her. Von Sternberg had the advantage of being on the scene in Berlin. Steven Bach, *Marlene Dietrich: Life and Legend* (William Morrow, 1992), pp. 96–97, 115. An earlier stage show had already made Marlene "*the* girl in Berlin" (p. 85).
12. Josef von Sternberg, *Fun in a Chinese Laundry* (Macmillan, 1965), p. 254.
13. Roberts and Olson consulted Wayne's draft records and found

the studio sought repeated deferments, even after Wayne was classified 1-A (draft eligible) in May of 1944 (pp. 212–13, 666).

14. Author's interview with Marilyn Fix Carey, November, 1994.

15. Quoted in Ray Merlock, "Gene Autry and the Coming of Civilization," in *Shooting Stars*, edited by Archie P. McDonald (Indiana University Press, 1987), pp. 102–3.

16. Letter of Patrick Ford to John Ford, February 4, 1944 (Lilly).

17. Dan Ford's interview with Olive Carey, p. 15 (Lilly).

18. Mary Ford to John Ford, June 1, 1943 (Lilly).

19. John Ford to John Wayne, July 9, 1943 (Lilly).

20. *Pappy*, p. 182.

21. John Wayne to John Ford, August 1, 1943 (Lilly).

22. Pilar Wayne, op. cit., p. 43.

23. *Pappy*, p. 182.

24. Roberts and Olson, p. 3.

25. The four war films that appeared during actual hostilities were *Flying Tigers* (1942), *Reunion in France* (1942), *The Fighting Seabees* (1944), and *Back to Bataan* (1945). *They Were Expendable* appeared after the war was over, though it was shot during its final days. (In *Reunion in France*, Wayne does not actually wear a military uniform, but only because he is a downed RAF pilot in disguise.)

26. Ford created a myth that he did not want to make *Expendable* but was forced to by his naval superiors. But a letter to his wife shows that, as early as July 19, 1943 (Lilly), he was enthusiastic about Wead's script, and opposing MGM efforts to rewrite it. The Fox records at UCLA show how vehemently Zanuck opposed Ford's making the film for MGM (Zanuck to G. Wasson, October 4, 1944, with response of October 11). A rear admiral overcame these objections, telling Fox that Ford was given leave to make the movie (A. S. Merrill to Zanuck, October 14, 1944).

27. Lindsay Anderson's interview with Robert Montgomery, in Anderson, *About John Ford* (Plexus, 1981), p. 226.

28. Ibid., p. 228.

29. Ford not only accepts but wildly exaggerates the propaganda for the PT boats that was created to boost morale early in the war. For the sorry actual record of the PT boats, see Nigel Hamilton, *J.F.K.: Reckless Youth* (Random House, 1992), pp. 503–6. The book *They Were Expendable*, by W. L. White (Harcourt Brace and Company, 1942), was comparatively sober in its claims, emphasizing the role of the boats in carrying MacArthur out of danger, not false hits of enemy ships sunk by the plywood vessels.

30. Ford's generosity in this act has been exaggerated by authors who do not realize that Senator Truman's investigations of war waste had made it unwise to the point of impossibility for producers and directors to draw Hollywood money while in the service. An early focus of Truman's committee was the suspicion that Hollywood was profiteering from training films made for the military. Since Darryl Zanuck was on the Research Council of the Academy of Motion Picture Arts

and Sciences, which channeled the training projects to various studios, he was a particular target of the investigation. For his own testimony on the Research Council, see David Culbert, *Film and Propaganda in History* (Greenwood Press, 1990), Vol. II, Part 1, pp. 294–369. For the testimony of others about Zanuck, see pp. 111–15, 140–47, 231–42, 283. The resulting publicity from Zanuck's own double dipping—into military pay *and* his studio salary—forced Zanuck to resign from the Army. It no doubt galled Zanuck when Ford used the Navy to break his contract in making *Expendable,* and then finessed the double-dipping problem by using his salary from the movie to prolong his own happy military experience at the Field Farm.

31. Author's interview with Harry Carey, Jr., September, 1995.

32. Author's interview with James Warner Bellah's son, January, 1995.

Chapter 9. HARRY CAREY

1. Lang, who won the Academy Award in 1933 (for *A Farewell to Arms*) had the assistance of Technicolor expert W. Howard Greene for this, his first color film.

2. See, for instance, Kenneth Hufford's interview with Wayne in the Arizona Historical Society oral history project. Hufford asked if he had admired men like William S. Hart or Tom Mix. Wayne answered, "I think Harry Carey gave something, some quality that we like to think of in men of the west that, maybe, those other fellows didn't have. Mix was pretty showy."

3. Bryan S. Sterling and Frances W. Sterling, *Will Rogers in Hollywood* (Crown Publishers, 1984), p. 149.

4. There is a full set of clippings on Carey's early theater work in the Robinson Locke Collection at the Richard Rodgers branch of the New York Public Library in Lincoln Center. Locke Series 2, Vol. 13, pp. 71–154. Patrick Loughney of the film department at the Library of Congress was good enough to retrieve for me the copyright copy of *Montana,* which Carey's son thought lost. The play is based, like Owen Wister's *The Virginian,* on the famous vigilante range war of "Stuart's Stranglers." Carey ("Jim") enters dramatically on his horse, ending an impromptu race with the heroine. A misunderstanding parts the lovers (she thinks he killed her father), but a noble squaw informs on her "half-breed" lover to straighten out the plot. Dobe Carey says his father's characteristic cadences are already traceable in the dialogue.

5. *The Master Cracksman* and *McVeagh of the South Seas* (both 1914).

6. All quotations from Olive Golden Carey come from Dan Ford's interview with her (Lilly).

7. Author's interview with Harry Carey, Jr., October, 1994.

8. *Heroes,* p. 3.

9. Davis, p. 218.

10. Gallagher, p. 260.

11. Olive Golden letter to John Ford, September 7, 1944. Ford to Golden, September 18, 1944. Dan Ford interview with Olive Golden (Lilly).

12. Author's interview with Richard Widmark, January, 1995.

13. G. K. Chesterton, *Charles Dickens*, 1906: "We understand a devout occultism, an evil occultism, a tragic occultism, but a farcical occultism is beyond us. Yet a farcical occultism is the very essence of *The Midsummer Night's Dream.*" *The Collected Works of G. K. Chesterton*, Vol. 15 (Ignatius Press, 1989), p. 50.

14. *Heroes*, pp. 39–46.

15. "The Man's Story," Ford typescript (Lilly).

Chapter 10. HOWARD HAWKS

1. The revised shooting schedule for *Red River* shows that it was filmed in Arizona from August 26 through October 16, and in a Hollywood studio from October 21 through November 13 in 1946. Ford filmed *Fort Apache* a year later, in August and September of 1947. *Red River*'s release was delayed by Hawks's inability to pay unions in Arizona and labs in California. It was also held up by charges of plagiarism brought by Howard Hughes. Hawks papers, BYU.

2. Davis, p. 224.

3. *"Red River* was my first Western." Hawks interview for American Film Institute, April 23, 1976 (BYU).

4. There is an early glimpse of "Fen," the woman Wayne loses fourteen years before the main action begins; but the love story is given to Montgomery Clift and Joanne Dru.

5. Win Sharplis, Jr., interview with Howard Hawks, July 27, 1977, Part 2, p. 3 (BYU).

6. Hawks deposition against the Hughes plagiarism injunction, August 17, 1948 (Wisconsin Historical Society Ms. 99AN, Record Group II, Box No. 49).

7. Charles Higham, *Howard Hughes: The Secret Life* (G. P. Putnam's Sons, 1993), pp. 96–97.

8. Hawks's test-shootings script in Hawks papers (BYU MSS. 1404, Box 15, Folder 12).

9, For Hawks's use of "pretty boys" in his films, see Gerald Mast, *Howard Hawks, Storyteller* (Oxford University Press, 1982), pp. 301–2, 380 n. 7.

10. *The River Is Red* is the shooting-tests title of the movie (Note 8 above). Apart from the test scripts, there are four draft scripts for *Red River* in the Hawks papers (MSS. 1404). I distinguish them this way:

SCRIPT 1 (Box 11, Folder 1) has "the river is red" in the dialogue (p. 2) and description of the bracelet as *Groot's*, not Dunson's.

SCRIPT 2 (Box 10, Folder 15), still has the bracelet as Groot's. This is the script submitted to the censor, as one can tell by comparing it with the Breen office letter of August 26, 1946 (Box 10, Folder 13).

SCRIPT 3 (Box 11, Folder 2) is the scrambled working script used on the set, with Hawks's alterations and "script girl" shorthand dictated by him.

SCRIPT 4 (Box 10, Folder 16) is a partial dialogue-continuity of the film as shot.

Gerald Mast fancifully derives the movie's title from the biblical crossing of the Red Sea (op. cit., p. 336), hesitantly endorsed by Roberts and Olson (p. 302). Script 1 proves that Hawks had *bloody* currents in mind, or a contested place of human suffering.

11. *Saturday Evening Post*, December 7, 1946, p. 160. The naval background of Chase's Dunson is probably what made Wayne refer, over the years, to *Red River* as a landbound *Mutiny on the Bounty*. Wayne would have read the original story when accepting the role, since the script was still being worked on. The final movie has no real similarity to the story of Captain Bligh, with whom Mr. Christian has no father-son relationship.

12. *Saturday Evening Post*, January 11, 1947, p. 32.

13. *Red River*, Script 2, p. 29.

14. Ibid., p. 49.

15. Ibid., p. 120.

16. Ibid., p. 117.

17. Ibid., p. 42.

18. Ibid., p. 117.

19. *Saturday Evening Post*, December 7, 1946, p. 148.

20. Mast, op. cit., p. 301. Chase's comments are in *Film Comment* 6 (Winter 1970–71), pp. 40–42. Hawks's comments on Ireland, and on Chase, are in Joseph McBride, *Hawks on Hawks* (University of California Press, 1982), pp. 119–21.

21. *Red River*, Script 2, p. 111.

22. Author's interview with Joanne Dru, January, 1995. Actually, Dru had just been in the hapless 1946 filming of the popular stage play *Abie's Irish Rose*, but that had not appeared when she started filming with Hawks.

23. Ibid.

Chapter 11. THE NEW WAYNE

1. Gerald Mast, *Howard Hawks, Storyteller* (Oxford University Press, 1982), p. 329.

2. Mary Ford to John Ford, July, 1943 (Lilly).

3. Wayne was living with the Fixes to hide his affair, not only because of the studio and its "morals clause," but because his draft

deferment premised that he was still home with his wife taking care of four children.

4. Author's interview with Fix's daughter, Marilyn Carey, November, 1944. A number of Fix's screenplays are in the Brigham Young University film archives.

5. Only in *The Spoilers* did Wayne choose the "bad girl" Dietrich—and that choice was in a stacked situation, because the "good girl" turned out to be an ally of the crooks. In *Seven Sinners,* Dietrich did not *let* Wayne choose her. In *Pittsburgh,* she was herself "the good girl."

6. Hawks's correspondence and his deposition in the Hughes suit are at the Wisconsin Historical Society, MS. 99AN, Record Group II, Box 49, Series 2A.

7. Chase's story had a Groot Nadine who cooked on the cattle drive. But he was not Dunson's friend from the past. How Walter Brennan becomes the cook on the drive is overexplained in the movie—unnecessarily. This is a remnant of the early story not fully purged from the new one.

8. *Red River,* Script 2, p. 74.

9. Ibid., pp. 36–37.

10. Ibid., p. 153.

11. Ibid., p. 157.

12. Ibid., p. 43.

13. *Heroes,* pp. 2–3. Hawks also told Wayne to get rid of a bad habit he had fallen into, of making a "charming" grimace, head ducked, eyes looking up, forehead wrinkled. That would always be part of Wayne's repertoire, but it had become too frequent and obvious before Hawks told him to cut back on its use. Author's interview with Joanne Dru, January, 1995.

14. Joseph McBride, *Hawks on Hawks* (University of California Press, 1982), p. 116.

15. Wayne told this to Zolotow, who misunderstood which scene was at issue (*Shooting Star,* p. 234).

16. American Film Institute interview with Hawks, April 23, 1976, p. 20 (BYU, MS 1404, Box 1, Folder 13).

17. Script 1, pp. 11–12.

18. Script 2, p. 135.

19. Ibid., p. 143.

20. Ibid., p. 157.

21. Ibid., p. 163.

22. In Script 2 (p. 15), Dunson responds to Matt's complaint about the brand by saying "I'll add a little m—that should make you happy," and Matt responds: "A *little* happy."

23. Michael Goodwin and Naomi Wise, "An Interview with Howard Hawks," *Take One,* July–August 1971, p. 21.

24. Clift's real scene of defiance had occurred earlier, and he was effective in it. When Dunson says he is going to hang a drover, Matt says with quiet anguish and finality: "No."

25. McBride, op. cit., p. 123.

26. Barney Hoskins, *Montgomery Clift: Beautiful Loser* (Grove Weidenfeld, 1991), p. 34 (also p. 143). Clift's inept fighting is most evident in the brawl for *From Here to Eternity* (1953).

27. Mast, op. cit., p. 329.

Chapter 12. AUTHORITY FIGURE

1. Elizabeth Drew, *Showdown* (Simon & Schuster, 1996), p. 35.

2. Lawrence H. Suid, *Guts and Glory: Great American War Movies* (Addison Wesley Publishing Co., 1978), p. 100.

3. Ron Kovic, *Born on the Fourth of July* (McGraw-Hill, 1976), p. 43.

4. Parker Bishop Albee, Jr., and Keller Cushing Freeman, *Shadow of Suribachi: Raising the Flags on Iwo Jima*, p. 139.

5. Ibid., p. 40.

6. It is interesting that the two most popular photographs from World War II celebrate victory rather than battle—the other being Eisenstadt's picture of the sailor kissing a stranger in Times Square on V-E Day.

7. Albee and Freeman, op. cit., pp. 62–65.

8. Ibid., pp. 35–37.

9. The National Sculpture Society questioned de Weldon's artistic competence. See Karal Ann Marling and John Wetenhall, *Iwo Jima: Monuments, Memories, and the American Hero* (Harvard University Press, 1991), pp. 154–55.

10. Ibid., pp. 175–77. Miller's script was written on the assumption that Pima Indians would cooperate with the film's production. The producers planned to use Hayes's own reservation as a shooting site. But the tribal authorities did not want a picture that would confirm the unjust stereotype of "the drunken Indian." So Hayes's disintegration had to be blamed on those who forced celebrity upon him. NBC, producing the show, was less fearful of Marine than of Indian reaction.

11. Suid, op. cit., pp. 104–5. This movie, like *Sands*, was made on Marine property (Fort Pendleton), so the Marines were exonerated and society at large was blamed. The NBC story had blamed *Sands of Iwo Jima* for Hayes's troubles. On the set of *The Outsider*, director Delbert Mann asked the real Marines on the base why they had enlisted, and half of them gave Wayne movies (principally *Sands*) as their reason.

12. Ibid., pp. 128–42. A cast of de Weldon's monument, along with the original flag, was on display at the Washington premiere of the movie.

13. The existence of a second, smaller flag is alluded to in the movie. One Marine has been carrying a flag in his blouse, intending to raise it on a Japanese island. When he pulls it out for use on Suribachi, he is told it is too small for the huge mountain height. He puts it back, saying he will raise it somewhere else.

14. Suid, op. cit., pp. 97–98.

15. For 1949 as "the pivotal year for the postwar combat film," see Thomas Doherty, *Projections of War: Hollywood, American Culture, and World War II* (Columbia University Press, 1993), p. 272.

16. The Republic octopus used in *Wake* made another appearance, prized by connoisseurs of the great bad films of Ed Wood. In *Bride of the Monster* (1956), a drug-ravaged Bela Lugosi is hugged to death by it. The tentacles had lost their coiling apparatus, so Lugosi had to wrap them around him as he succumbs to them.

17. Gallagher, pp. 101, 173, 177.

Chapter 13. CUSTER AND COLD WAR

1. *Pappy*, pp. 78–79.

2. For producers' uneasiness about the politics of *The Grapes of Wrath*, see Davis, pp. 112–13.

3. Richard Fine, *Hollywood and the Profession of Authorship* (UMI Research Press, 1985), p. 145. Fine goes on to say (p. 146) that "the quality of Nichols's work with Ford, like Raphaelson's with Lubitsch, indicates that writers *could* collaborate effectively if they were paired with a sympathetic partner and then left alone by the front office." This exaggerates the degree to which Zanuck left Ford alone. Zanuck dictated the new ending of *The Grapes of Wrath*, and regularly "corrected" Ford after looking at rushes.

4. Murray Kempton, *Part of Our Time: Some Monuments and Ruins of the Thirties* (Dell Publishing Co., 1967), p. 194.

5. Dudley Nichols file, UCLA.

6. Philip Dunne, *Take Two* (McGraw-Hill, 1980), pp. 188–220.

7. Clifford regretted the Truman hysteria he helped ignite. See his *Counsel to the President* (Random House, 1981), pp. 175–84. He says that Truman "yielded to pressure from [J. Edgar] Hoover and [Attorney General Tom] Clark," with the result that he "abhorred his own [security] program." Clifford had told Carl Bernstein the same thing in 1978 (Bernstein, *Loyalties*, Simon & Schuster, 1989, pp. 197–200).

8. Richard Dunlop, *Donovan: America's Master Spy* (Rand McNally & Company, 1982), p. 421. *Pappy*, p. 208.

9. *Pappy*, p. 208.

10. Anthony Cave Brown, *The Last Hero: Bill Donovan* (Times Books, 1982), p. 171.

11. Robin Winks, *Cloak and Dagger: Scholars in the Secret War* (William Morrow and Company, 1987), p. 115.

12. Ibid.

13. Evan Thomas, *The Very Best Men: Four Who Dared: The Early Years of the CIA* (Simon & Schuster, 1995), p. 15.

14. Ibid., p. 16.

15. For Ford's limousine flags, author's interview with Richard Widmark, January, 1995. For his yacht flags, Roberts and Olson, p. 493.

16. Michael Sherry, *In the Shadow of War: The United States Since the 1930s* (Yale University Press, 1995).

17. Arthur M. Schlesinger, Jr., Introduction to De Voto's *The Year of Decision, 1846,* American Heritage Library edition (Houghton Mifflin, 1984). At a time when the America First movement seemed to be riding high, De Voto's first volume stoutly defended President Polk's expansionist policies for making America a force on the world scene.

18. The same process had occurred in earlier periods that aspired to empire. In the mid-century expansionist euphoria that De Voto celebrated, the histories of conquest by Parkman (for North America) and Prescott (for South America) were at the peak of their reputation and influence.

19. Catton connected the Manifest Destiny imperative of the Mexican War with America's destiny as it was tested and confirmed in the Civil War.

20. Author's interview with Dan Ford, January, 1995.

21. Author's interview with James Bellah, Jr., January, 1995. Bellah, like Ford, would embroider his experiences before the unsuspecting, as when he told Dan Ford that he grew up on cavalry posts (*Pappy*, p. 214).

22. Interview with James Warner Bellah, *Saturday Evening Post,* June 8, 1946, p. 4.

23. Author's interview with James Warner Bellah, Jr., January, 1995.

24. Thomas, op. cit., pp. 55, 69, 89, 140.

25. Ibid., pp. 91, 125.

26. Bellah, "Massacre," *Saturday Evening Post,* February 22, 1947, p. 143.

27. Ibid.

28. Ibid., p. 41.

29. Bellah, "War Party," *Saturday Evening Post,* June 19, 1948, p. 109.

30. "Massacre," p. 19.

31. Frank S. Nugent, review of *Wee Willie Winkie,* New York *Times,* July 24, 1937. The movie is better than the original story, whose baby-talking young hero is far less palatable than La Temple.

32. Thomas, op. cit., p. 89.

33. Ibid., p. 179.

34. Ibid., pp. 69, 140.

35. For Ford's anger at McLaglen for not sacrificing better-paid roles to work with him, author's interview with Andrew McLaglen, January, 1995.

36. Author's interview with John Agar, January, 1995.

37. Richard Dyer, *Stars* (British Film Institute, 1990), p. 166.

38. George Turner, "Dust and Danger at *Fort Apache,*" *American Cinematographer,* June, 1966, pp. 106–10.

39. Richard Slotkin, *The Fatal Environment* (Atheneum, 1985), p. 436.

40. Bellah, "Massacre," p. 142.

41. Wayne's speech on the cavalry is expanded from Bellah's earlier description. But it gives a more hopeful twist to Bellah's world-weary stoicism:

> The column moved out with the mists of the morning still cold, moved out in a long breath of saddle soap on still-stiffened leather, rough wool, not yet sweat-damp, and the thin brown of gun oil. Dog-faced cavalry, the like of which has passed from the knowledge of the world.

Chapter 14. WASHINGTON AND SHERIDAN

1. James Warner Bellah, "War Party," *Saturday Evening Post*, June 19, 1948, p. 23.

2. For Sheridan's accusations of a "conspiracy" to defraud the Indians, see Paul Andrew Hutton, *Phil Sheridan and His Army* (University of Nebraska Press, 1985), p. 98.

3. "Ranald Slidell Mackenzie," *Dictionary of American Biography*.

4. Hutton, op. cit., p. 185.

5. Ibid., pp. 222, 412–13.

6. Ibid., p. 225.

7. James Warner Bellah, "Mission with No Record," *Saturday Evening Post*, September 27, 1947, p. 30.

8. Ibid., p. 31.

9. Ibid., pp. 140, 142.

10. Ibid., p. 142.

11. Ibid.

12. Ibid., pp. 131, 138.

13. Ibid., p. 31.

14. Letter of Joseph Breen to Republic Pictures on the *Rio Bravo* (later *Rio Grande*) script, May 12, 1950 (Lilly).

Chapter 15. FORT HOLLYWOOD

1. Roberts and Olson, p. 336.

2. Walton Bean, *California: An Interpretive History* (McGraw-Hill, 1968), pp. 234–38.

3. Greg Mitchell, *The Campaign of the Century: Upton Sinclair's Race for Governor of California* (Random House, 1992), pp. 369–72.

4. Larry Ceplair and Steven Englund, *The Inquisition in Hollywood* (Doubleday, 1980), p. 150.

5. Victor Navasky, *Naming Names* (Penguin, 1991), p. 80.

6. Wood's daughter is the source for his feelings of rejection over *Goodbye, Mr. Chips*. Ceplair and Englund, op. cit., p. 80.

7. Navasky, op. cit., p. 980.

8. Murray Kempton, *Part of Our Time: Some Monuments and Ruins of the Thirties* (Dell Publishing Company, 1967), p. 204.

9. Ronald Reagan, President of the Screen Actors Guild to Guild member Gale Sondergaard, reprinted in Walter Goodman, *The Committee* (Farrar, Straus and Giroux, 1968), p. 300.

10. Wayne, *Playboy* Interview, May, 1971, reprinted in Judith M. Riggin, *John Wayne: A Bio-Bibliography* (Greenwood Press, 1992), p. 59.

11. Ibid., p. 59: "I did tell him [Foreman] that I thought he'd hurt Gary Cooper's reputation a great deal. Foreman said, 'Well, what if I went to England?' I said, 'Well, that's your business.' He said, 'Well, that's where I'm going.' And he did."

12. Wayne, *Playboy* Interview, p. 57.

13. Ibid., p. 58.

14. Roberts and Olson, p. 340. It is true that McGuinness, an Irish drinking pal of Ford's, lost his production job at MGM in 1949, probably because of personality clashes. That he was not blacklisted is shown by his work, the very next year, on the screenplay for *Rio Grande*. If he had not died in 1950, his career would undoubtedly have continued with no interruption of the sort blacklisted authors faced.

15. Wayne, *Playboy* Interview, p. 57.

16. Navasky, op. cit., pp. 371–72.

17. *Jet Pilot* gave Wayne his one opportunity to work with the "discoverer" of his old flame Marlene Dietrich. But von Sternberg was so submissive, and Hughes so insistent and interfering, that there was nothing for Wayne to learn from him. The man who made Dietrich mysterious and shadowy with veils had to use his camera to ogle Janet Leigh in the crassest, most juvenile way.

18. Andrew McLaglen, the principal director of the *Gunsmoke* series, hints that Arness had the grace to know his limits. After his stiff performance in *Big Jim McLain*, he turned down Wayne's offer of a role in *The Alamo*. Author's interview with Andrew McLaglen, January, 1995.

19. Roberts and Olson, p. 378.

20. Evan Thomas, *The Very Best Men: Four Who Dared: The Early Years of the CIA* (Simon & Schuster, 1995), p. 50.

21. Author's interview with Andrew McLaglen, assistant director for *Blood Alley*, January, 1995.

22. Garry Wills, *Nixon Agonistes* (Houghton Mifflin, 1970), p. 253.

23. Author's interview with Harry Carey, Jr., November, 1994.

24. Patrick Ford, Script for *The Alamo* (BYU).

25. Frank Thompson, *Alamo Movies* (Wordware Publishing, 1991), p. 59.

Chapter 16. *ALAMO:* LEGEND

1. Ronnie Dugger, *The Politician: The Life and Times of Lyndon Johnson* (W. W. Norton & Company, 1982), p. 33.

2. Ford was in the Méliès production *The Immortal Alamo*, made

shortly after Gaston Méliès shifted his production center to San Antonio. The film was made at Hot Wells, using the ruins of Mission San José as part of the Alamo. Frank Thompson, *Alamo Movies* (Wordware Publishing, 1991), p. 30.

3. For Bradbury's *Davy Crockett at the Fall of the Alamo*, see Thompson, ibid., pp. 31–35, and the cassette made by Thompson containing the film, *Alamo Classics* (Old Mill Books, 1993).

4. Dugger, op. cit., p. 34.

5. Stephen L. Hardin, *Texian Iliad: A Military History of the Texas Revolution, 1835–1836* (University of Texas Press, 1994), pp. 110–11.

6. Houston had also told Colonel Fannin to blow up the fort he held. "War must not depend upon forts; the woods, and ravines suit us best." See James Atkins Shackford, *David Crockett: The Man and the Legend* (Bison Books reprint of 1956 edition, 1994), pp. 224–25.

7. Hardin, op. cit., pp. 110–11. Houston had a military furlough through the whole month of February and resumed command on March 4, just two days before the Alamo fell. See John Hoyt Williams, *Sam Houston* (Simon & Schuster, 1993), pp. 132–42.

8. Ibid., p. 111.

9. Ibid., p. 131.

10. José Enrique de la Peña, *With Santa Anna in Texas: A Personal Narrative of the Revolution*, translated by Carmen Perry (Texas A&M University Press, 1975), pp. 26–28.

11. Paul D. Lack, *The Texas Revolutionary Experience: A Political and Social History, 1835–1836* (Texas A&M University Press, 1992), pp. 7–8, 17–18.

12. On the racism of the leaders of the Texas revolution, see Lack, ibid., pp. 14 (Austin), 94 (Travis), 160 (Houston). Fear of their own slaves, and of Mexicans' alliance with them, helped panic the Anglo-Texans into the 1836 flight of a whole region called "The Runaway Scrape" (p. 243).

13. Juan N. Seguin, *A Revolution Remembered: The Memoirs and Selected Correspondence*, edited by Jesús F. de la Teja (State House Press, 1991), pp. 118–19. Of his service to the Texas revolution, he wrote: "My services paid by persecutions, exiled and deprived of my privileges as a Texas citizen, I was in this country a being out of the pale of society."

14. John H. Jenkins and Kenneth Kesselus, *Edward Burleson: Texas Frontier Leader* (Jenkins Publishing Company, 1990), pp. 57, 93. Though Burleson was in charge of the forces attacking Cos, legend says that a man named Milam started the assault by saying "Who will go with old Ben Milam into San Antonio?" That was another legend dear to Lyndon Johnson. When he recommended support for the French at Dien Bien Phu, he asked, "Would you tell me who will go in with old Ben Milam?" (Dugger, op. cit., p. 32).

15. De la Peña, op. cit., pp. 9–10, 18–19, 24, 36, 42–43.

16. Ibid., pp. 47–49.

17. Raymond W. Thorp, *Bowie Knife* (University of New Mexico Press, 1948).

18. Hardin, op. cit., p. 120.

19. Archie P. McDonald, *Travis* (Jenkins Publishing Company, 1976), p. 152.

20. On the *lack* of suicidal spirit at the Alamo, see Hardin, op. cit., pp. 111, 129, 130. He concludes: "Far from being bent on self-sacrifice, Travis and the garrison remained in the fort because they were convinced that they could hold it until reinforcements arrived."

21. Paul Andrew Hutton, Introduction to *A Narrative of the Life of David Crockett, by Himself* (University of Nebraska Press, 1987), pp. xxvii–xxx.

22. Shackford, op. cit., p. 216.

23. Ibid., pp. 217–21. The myth that Crockett would sacrifice himself for Houston, a Jackson ally, runs up against the fact that Crockett claimed (stretching things, as usual) to have led a mutiny against Jackson in the Creek War (Hutton, op. cit., pp. xi–xii, 93–95).

24. De la Peña, op. cit., p. 53.

25. Bill Groneman, *Defense of a Legend: Crockett and the de la Peña Diary*. For a convincing refutation of Groneman, see James E. Crisp, "The Little Book That Wasn't There: The Myth and Mystery of the de la Peña Diary" (*Southwestern Historical Quarterly*, October, 1994), pp. 261–96.

26. Dan Kilgore, *How Did Davy Die?* (Texas A&M University Press, 1978). The copies of this I read in the research section (not the open stacks) of the San Antonio Public Library had an obscenity scrawled in the margin.

Chapter 17. *ALAMO:* ORDEAL

1. For Wayne's interest in Panama as a site, see Donald Clark and Christopher Anderson, *John Wayne's "The Alamo"* (Midwest Publishing, 1994), p. 11. For Mexico, see pp. 18–20.

2. Ibid., pp. 21–22.

3. Wayne's film used a "San Antonio" with a street that had buildings on only one side and a church "plaza" open on three sides. Shahan later put up buildings on the other side of the street, to serve as the all-purpose western town where shoot-outs occur. Dozens of Western films and TV shows have been made there, including John Ford's *Two Rode Together*, made with Widmark (but not Wayne) the year after *The Alamo* shooting stopped.

4. Clark and Anderson, op. cit., pp. 18–20.

5. Ibid., p. 72.

6. The company did its own odd service to preservation by accidentally burning down the oldest building at Fort Clark, where Wayne's Batjac production team was staying. The post headquarters, built in 1857, was reduced to a shell. Neither Ford nor Wayne realized that this fort was the base for the raid into Mexico that formed the plot of *Rio Grande*. Instead, they sought some spurious tie to Robert E. Lee's service in the Mexican War.

7. Susan Prendergast Schoelwer, with Tom Glaser, *Alamo Images* (Southern Methodist University Press, 1985), p. 22. This book, the catalogue of a 1985–1986 exhibit at SMU, is the best record on the appearance of the Alamo over the years. It includes previously unpublished prints, plans, and paintings.

8. Ibid., pp. 47–51.

9. The church's importance is also emphasized by the fact that Ybarra built it to exact scale, though the rest of the mission was reduced to three-quarters its known size. (So much for boasts of original-plan authenticity.)

10. During the 1836 siege, three guns faced out the *back* of the church, the most exposed area at that time. They rested at the top of a dirt ramp heaped up along the church's nave. See Stephen L. Hardin, *Texian Iliad: A Military History of the Texas Revolution, 1835–1836* (University of Texas Press, 1994), pp. 112–13.

11. Holly Beachley Brear, *Inherit the Alamo: Myth and Ritual at an American Shrine* (University of Texas Press, 1995), p. 109.

12. Ibid., pp. 81, 164.

13. Ibid., pp. 21–22, 123–25.

14. Ibid., p. 127.

15. San Antonio *Light*, October 25, 1992, p. J-9. The Marine reservists left Gonzales at 3 P.M. on foot, reaching the Alamo at 4:45 A.M. See original story, San Antonio *News*, October 24, 1960, p. 12-A.

16. Smith took one bone-rattling fall when he was playing a Mexican assailant shot from his saddle. Lyons had a harness that plucked him off the horse, going at full gallop. Author's interview with Dean Smith, August, 1994.

17. Frank Thompson, *Alamo Movies* (Wordware Publishing, 1991), p. 77.

18. This and other quotes and information in the chapter from the author's interview with Widmark, January, 1995. Wayne, by calling Widmark the "laughing son-of-a-bitch," made fun of Widmark's first role as Tommy Udo in *Kiss of Death* (1947).

19. Roberts and Olson, p. 462.

20. Clark and Anderson, op. cit., p. 45. By the end of filming, Harvey had been made an honorary deputy sheriff in seven Texas counties (ibid., p. 71).

21. Author's interview with Denver Pyle, January, 1995.

22. Clark and Anderson, op. cit., pp. 78–86.

23. Maurice Zolotow, interview with William Clothier, January, 1973. Zolotow Papers, University of Texas, Austin.

24. Author's interview with Denver Pyle, January, 1995.

25. Ibid.

26. Author's interview with Marilyn Carey, October, 1994.

27. Brian Huberman, in the documentary appended to the 1992 laser disk edition of *The Alamo* (MGM/UA), identifies a scene as Ford's by connecting Pyle's story with the red pompoms stuck up above one unit's helmets. But these latter are obviously a part of the helmet's

original design, and Pyle is precise about *flat* cloth medallions being stapled to cloth hats. The Batjac records dutifully note three scenes "made with his involvement"—i.e., when he was kibitzing (Clark and Anderson, op. cit., p. 82). None of these is a second-unit scene with extras, the only ones where Ford was in charge.

28. Widmark, despite his dislike of Wayne, said he handled the large action scenes of *The Alamo* well. "He would have made a great second-unit director." Wayne's weakness, he thought, was in the love scenes—"Ford's weak point, too." But he said nothing about the scenes where Bowie, Travis, and Crockett do their little dances of defiance and reluctant collaboration.

Chapter 18. GREEN BERETS

1. John Wayne, letter to President Lyndon Johnson, December 28, 1965. Document 109 in *Film and Propaganda in America: A Documentary History, Volume IV: 1945 and After,* edited by Lawrence H. Suid (Greenwood Press), 1991, p. 390.

2. Roberts and Olson, pp. 538–39.

3. *Film and Propaganda,* p. 408.

4. Robin Moore, *The Green Berets* (Crown Publishers, 1965), pp. 121–22.

5. Ibid., pp. 41–42.

6. Ibid., p. 119.

7. Ibid., p. 175.

8. Ibid., p. 113.

9. Ibid., p. 125.

10. Ibid., p. 136.

11. Ibid., p. 292.

12. John Wayne, letter to Bill Moyers, February 18, 1966, *Film and Propaganda,* pp. 395–96.

13. See the group portrait of these reporters by William Prochnan, *Once Upon a Distant War* (Times Books, 1995).

14. Moore, op. cit., pp. 149–50.

15. John Wayne, letter to Senator Richard Russell et al., April 15, 1966, *Film and Propaganda,* pp. 399–400.

16. *Film and Propaganda,* p. 396. The book was short on comic moments, but the movie kept the dedication of a latrine to a dead man and the comparison of posts in Vietnam to forts in the "old West" (Moore, op. cit., pp. 87, 17).

Chapter 19. "IRELAND"

1. Lindsay Anderson, *About John Ford* (Plexus, 1981), p. 9.

2. Gallagher, p. 358.

3. Steve Matheson, *Maurice Walsh, Storyteller* (Brandon Book Publishing, Ireland, 1985), p. 91.

4. Maurice Walsh, "The Quiet Man," *Saturday Evening Post*, February 11, 1933, p. 83. Walsh changed the name of his two male characters when he reprinted his story in a collection called *Green Rushes* (1935). Liam O'Grady became Will Danaher, the name Ford keeps. Shawn Kelvin became Paddy Bawn Enright, a name that fell by the way. Matheson, op. cit., p. 73.

5. Roberts and Olson, p. 358.

6. Anderson, op. cit., pp. 28–29.

7. Matheson, op. cit., p. 91.

8. Author's interview with Andrew McLaglen, January, 1995.

9. Roberts and Olson, p. 292.

10. Gallagher, p. 374.

11. Even headlines that suggest a possible political animus turn out to be misleading. When McLaglen, attended by his Light Horse Brigade, put his handprints in the cement at Grauman's Chinese Theatre, two eggs were lobbed at him by a heckler—who turned out to be a movie extra who claimed McLaglen broke his nose in a filmed fight scene. Dan Ford repeated the claim that McLaglen was pro-fascist in the book on his grandfather; but he has changed his mind since getting to know some of the living members of the "Light Horse"—including his mother-in-law. Author's interview with Dan Ford, January, 1995.

12. Carey McWilliams, "Hollywood Plays with Fascism," *The Nation*, May 29, 1935, pp. 623–24. McWilliams was especially fearful of Gary Cooper's "Hollywood Hussars," because William Randolph Hearst is supposed to have given them some money. (Cooper had acted with Marion Davies—always a way to Hearst's favor.) McWilliams was not impressed by the patronage of Reverend George G. Fox, of the Society of Jesus, and Rabbi Isadore Isaacson of Temple of Israel. The latter, especially, seems an odd sponsor of a fascist group—odd that a rabbi would join and even odder that they would want him. The true measure of the group's menace is that its uniforms were designed by the actor Montagu Love, who had been a newspaper illustrator in London before he took up acting.

13. The "Dodge" of the film, pretentiously embroidering his past, says he acted as a youth in Joyce's *Ulysses*—he played Robert E. Lee (opposing *Ulysses* Grant).

14. Matheson, op. cit., p. 91.

15. Ibid.

Chapter 20. THE FURY OF ETHAN

1. St. Augustine, *The City of God* 1.12–28. Augustine says that Christians deprived of the sacraments, of Christian burial, are still in God's care. He counsels sexually abused women against suicide.

2. For a good discussion of Mary Rowlandson's *The Sovereignty and Goodness of God . . . a Narrative of the Captivity and Restoration* (1682), see Richard Slotkin, *Regeneration Through Violence: The Mythology of the American Frontier, 1600–1860* (Wesleyan University Press, 1973), pp. 95–112.

3. See John Demos's tale of the captive young woman who voluntarily weds an Indian in a Catholic ritual, to the horror of her relations when they hear of it: *The Unredeemed Captive: A Family Story from Early America* (Vintage Books, 1995).

4. Gallagher, p. 247.

5. Peter Stowell, *John Ford* (Twayne Publishers, 1986), pp. 139–40.

6. Gallagher, pp. 408–9.

7. Stowell, op. cit., pp. 139–40.

8. Gallagher, p. 338.

9. I am grateful to Charles Silver for pointing out this film in the archives of the Museum of Modern Art and noting the similarity of its end to that of *The Searchers*. The film, from Carey's period at Biograph, was not directed by Griffith, though he may have overseen the project. Tony O'Sullivan is credited with the direction.

Chapter 21. FORD-WAYNE, INC.

1. Dan Ford interview with Wayne (Lilly).

2. Woody Strode, with Sam Young, *Goal Dust* (Madison Books, 1990), p. 211.

3. Ibid., p. 212.

4. The comic name, not contained in Johnson's story, recalls the town in Destry—"Bottleneck."

5. Greil Marcus, *The Dustbin of History* (Harvard University Press, 1995), p. 212.

Chapter 22. RIO THIS AND RIO THAT

1. Joseph McBride, *Hawks on Hawks* (University of California Press, 1982), p. 130.

2. Wayne, *Playboy* Interview, May, 1971: "It's the most un-American thing I've ever seen in my whole life. The last thing in the picture is ol' Coop putting the United States marshal's badge under his foot and stepping on it" (reprinted in Judith M. Riggin, *John Wayne: A Bio-Bibliography*, Greenwood Press, 1992, p. 59). Actually, a marshal removing his badge occurs in Wayne's own *Stagecoach*, when the marshal lets the Ringo Kid escape and takes off his badge before inviting the doctor to have a drink with him. Throwing the badge away can be a right-wing gesture as easily as a left-wing one, as when Clint Eastwood, in *Dirty Harry* (1971), throws the badge in the river out of disgust at the "coddling" of criminals.

3. The genius of *His Girl Friday* was not that Hawks changed the gender of Hildy Johnson, but that he changed a wisecracking crime story into a screwball comedy. As the anarchic John Barrymore drags along the resisting-then-yielding Carole Lombard in Hawks's *Twentieth Century* (1934), so Cary Grant drags along the resisting-yielding Rosalind Russell. This is a gender switch from the more common formula of an anarchic Katharine Hepburn dragging along Cary Grant in *Bringing Up Baby*. In other seminal screwball comedies Barbara Stanwyck hauls males from their stuffy retreats into "real life" (Fonda in *The Lady Eve*, Cooper in *Ball of Fire*), or the flighty Claudette Colbert takes Gable for the famous bus ride in *It Happened One Night*. The formula can use two members of the same gender. In *Gentlemen Prefer Blondes*, it is the anarchic Marilyn Monroe who precipitates Jane Russell into screwy mishaps—a formula already developed in the play *My Sister Eileen* and its various screen adaptations.

4. The naming of women for locales may originally have been a way to indicate that they were prostitutes—"the woman to see in Laramie," or "the woman from [a brothel in] Laramie." But that can hardly be the reason for calling the virginal Shirley Temple "Philadelphia" in *Fort Apache*. It became a convention to have women called Reno or Dallas or Pittsburgh or Colorado or Nevada.

5. For Robin Wood's comparison of *Rio Bravo* and *Red River,* see Gerald Mast, *Howard Hawks, Storyteller* (Oxford University Press, 1982).

6. Frank Capra, *The Name Above the Title* (Macmillan, 1971), pp. 489–90.

Chapter 23. "I Thought You Were Dead"

1. Roberts and Olson, p. 518.

2. "You will shoot him in the back?" the ranger asks, and Cogburn replies: "It will give them to know our intentions are serious." Charles Portis, *True Grit* (Simon and Schuster, 1968), p. 132.

3. Roberts and Olson, p. 572.

4. Ibid., p. 5.

5. Author's interview with Donald Rumsfeld, October, 1995, on the launching of the USS *Oliver Hazard Perry.* Rumsfeld's claim that this was not a "stunt" is confirmed if one reflects that the dock (Bath Iron Works) would not advertise any mechanical inadequacies before the Secretary of Defense.

6. Roberts and Olson, p. 617.

7. Author's interview with Harry Carey, Jr., November, 1994.

8. Ibid.

9. Pilar Wayne, with Alex Thorleifson, *John Wayne: My Life with the Duke* (McGraw-Hill, 1987), pp. 139–40.

Chapter 24. "I WON'T BE WRONGED"

1. The tone of Forester's novel is entirely different from the movie's. In the novel, the thirty-three-year-old spinster is sensually awakened, and the cowardly little "Charlie" becomes brave and resourceful, because she prods and finally admires him. The fulfillment of their lives in the weeks before they die is described with an erotic frankness foreign to mainstream American films even in 1975. The two never do blow up the German ship they have worked so hard to destroy. In the movie, they blow it up and swim merrily off to a British victory. Their sexual affair is condoned in a glow of patriotism. They even get married on the German ship before the torpedoes float into it. They swim together as newlyweds. Agee made fun of endings like that when other people were writing them.

2. Don Siegel, *A Siegel Film* (Faber and Faber, 1993), p. 31.

3. Glendon Swarthout, *The Shootist* (Doubleday & Company, 1975), p. 18.

4. Siegel, op. cit., p. 32.

5. Swarthout, op. cit., p. 84.

6. Ibid., pp. 176–77.

Conclusion. AMERICAN ADAM

1. Ralph Waldo Emerson, "The Young American" (1844), in *Essays and Lectures* (The Library of America, 1983), pp. 216–17.

2. Ibid., p. 214.

3. Jefferson to Madison, December 20, 1787 (*Papers*, edited by Julian Boyd et al., Vol. 12, 1955), p. 422.

4. Jefferson, *Notes on the State of Virginia*, Query XII (The Library of America, 1984), p. 233.

5. Henry Demarest Lloyd, *Wealth and Commonwealth* (Harper and Brothers, 1894), p. 499.

6. Ovid, *Ars Amatoria* 3.113: "Simplicitas rudis ante fuit, nunc aurea Roma est."

7. Stephen Scully, *Homer and the Sacred City* (Cornell University Press, 1990), pp. 25, 52–53, 141–44.

8. François de Polignac, *La naissance de la cité grecque: Cultes, espace et société* (Paris, 1984), pp. 44–92.

9. The exception is the Mormons' temple, fetched (like Jerusalem's) from heaven.

10. Edmund Morgan, *The Puritan Dilemma: The Story of John Winthrop* (Little, Brown and Company, 1958), pp. 78–80.

11. Perry Miller, *The New England Mind: From Colony to Province* (Belknap Press of Harvard University, 1953), pp. 234–36.

12. Henry David Thoreau, *Walden, or Life in the Woods* (The Library of America, 1985), pp. 425–26.

13. For the Chicago novelists, see Garry Wills, "Chicago Under-

ground" and "Sons and Daughters of Chicago," *New York Review of Books*, October 21, 1993, and June 9, 1994.

14. Henry B. Fuller, quoted in Carla Cappetti, *Writing Chicago* (Columbia University Press, 1993), p. 11.

15. See Carl Smith, *Urban Disorder and the Shape of Relief: The Great Chicago Fire, the Haymarket Riot, and the Model Town of Pullman* (University of Chicago Press, 1995).

16. Ibid., p. 282.

17. Gallagher, pp. 49–50.

18. Elizabeth Hutton Turner (editor), *Jacob Lawrence: The Migration Series* (The Rappahannock Press, 1993), number 55.

19. Ralph Waldo Emerson, "The American Scholar" (1837), in *Essays and Lectures*, pp. 67, 62, 57.

20. Ibid., pp. 68–69.

21. Ibid., p. 60.

22. Bancroft quotation from Richard Hofstadter, *Anti-Intellectualism in America* (Vintage Books, 1963), p. 159.

23. Thomas Jefferson, Letter to Walker Maury, August 19, 1785 (*Papers* 8.409).

24. Thomas Jefferson, Letter to Peter Carr, August 10, 1787 (*Papers* 12.15).

25. Thomas Jefferson, Letter to John Bannister, Jr., October 15, 1785 (*Papers* 8.637).

26. Thomas Jefferson, *Notes on the State of Virginia*, Query VIII (The Library of America, 1984), p. 211. Franklin, too, feared an influx of Germans into Pennsylvania, which would make it impossible to preserve the native language "and even our government will become precarious." Benjamin Franklin, Letter to Peter Callinson, May 9, 1753 (*Papers*, edited by Leonard Labaree and Whitfield Bell, Jr., Yale University Press, Volume 4, 1961, p. 485).

27. Herman Melville, *Moby-Dick*, Chapter 42 (The Library of America, 1983), p. 996.

28. Jim Morrison, "The End." In "Break on Through," Morrison loved a woman for "the country in your eyes." He also wrote of the need "to escape sin and the mire of cities." See James Riordan and Jerry Prochnicky, *Break on Through: The Life and Death of Jim Morrison* (William Morrow and Company, 1991), p. 26.

29. Jean Narboni and Tom Milne, *Godard on Godard* (Viking Press, 1972), p. 117.

30. Though Edwin S. Porter's *The Great Train Robbery* was not the first film to tell a story, it was the first to weave together three strands of narrative. See Charles Musser, *The Emergence of Cinema* (University of California Press, 1994), pp. 352–55.

31. Les Adams and Buck Rainey, *Shoot-Em-Ups* (Arlington House, 1978), p. 15, and Buck Rainey, *The Shoot-Em-Ups Ride Again* (The World of Yesterday, 1990).

32. Edward Buscombe (editor), *The BFI Companion to the Western* (Da Capo Press, 1988), p. 35.

33. Ibid., pp. 426–28.

34. Randolph Scott made a partial move in the opposite direction when he went from major non-Western roles to his low-budget films with Budd Boetticher. But even those "oaters" were adult films, not made for the kids.

35. There is an aborted shoot-out in *Tall in the Saddle,* where Wayne sees that his opponent is too drunk to draw. Even in *Stagecoach,* Wayne does not do a quick draw from a standing position, as in the classic shoot-out's resolution, but throws himself on the ground where he can steady his rifle.

36. *BFI Companion,* p. 427. Wayne's films were *The Searchers* (2 on the list), *Stagecoach* (3), *Red River* (5), and *Rio Bravo* (tied for 7). Clint Eastwood was on the list once, for *The Outlaw—Josey Wales* (tied for 7), and Gary Cooper once, for *High Noon* (1).

INDEX OF WAYNE FILMS CONSIDERED

(italics for those given greater attention)

INDEX